MW00913757

THE WORLD ALMANAC ALMANAC FOR KIDS 2004

WORLD ALMANAC BOOKS
A Division of World Almanac Education Group, Inc.
A WRC Media Company

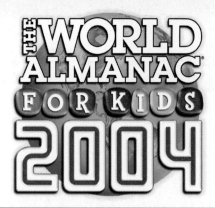

THE WORLD ALMANAC FOR KIDS 2004

EDITOR: Kevin Seabrooke

CURRICULUM CONSULTANT:
Susan Ohanian, Senior Fellow, Vermont Society for the Study of Education

CONTRIBUTORS: Sean Alfano, Elizabeth Barden,
Joseph Gustaitis, Raymond Hill, Matthew Kiernan,
Rachael Mason, Catherine McHugh, Randi Metsch-Ampel,
Carol Moran, Donna Mulder, Eileen O'Reilly, Kerria Seabrooke
Consultant: Lee T. Shapiro, Ph.D. (Astronomy)

KID CONTRIBUTORS: Casey Acosta, Andrew Barral, John Bodi,
Ashley Bruggeman, Harry Larson, Elana Metsch-Ampel, Kelly Moran,
Christin Mulder, Maya Master Park, Kristyn Romaine, Alexis Shine

Thanks to all the kids who wrote to us with their great ideas!

DESIGN: Bill SMITH STUDIO
Creative Director: Brian Kobberger **Project Director:** Sandra E. Will
Design: Brock Waldron, Scott Palmer, Colleen A. Sweet
Photo Research: Christie Silver **Production:** James Liebman

WORLD ALMANAC BOOKS

Vice President–
Sales and Marketing
James R. Keenley

**Editorial
Director**
William McGeveran Jr.

Managing
Editor
Lori P. Wiesenfeld

Desktop Production Manager: Elizabeth J. Lazzara
Editorial Staff: Erik C. Gopel, Christopher Larson, Associate Editors;
Lloyd Sabin, Desktop Publishing Associate

WORLD ALMANAC EDUCATION GROUP
Chief Executive Officer, WRC Media Inc.: Martin E. Kenney Jr.
President: Robert Jackson
Publisher: Ken Park
Director–Purchasing and Production/Photo Research: Edward A. Thomas
Director of Indexing Services: Marjorie B. Bank; **Index Editor:** Walter Kronenberg
Marketing Coordinator: Sarah De Vos

The World Almanac For Kids 2004
Copyright © 2003 by World Almanac Education Group, Inc.
The World Almanac and The World Almanac For Kids are registered trademarks of World Almanac Education Group, Inc.
ISBN (softcover): 088687-902-7
ISBN (hardcover): 088687-903-5
Printed in the United States of America
The softcover and hardcover editions are distributed to the trade in the United States by St. Martin's Press.
WORLD ALMANAC® BOOKS
An Imprint of World Almanac Education Group, Inc.
512 Seventh Avenue
New York, NY 10018
E-Mail: Waforkids@waegroup.com

Web site: http://www.worldalmanacforkids.com

The addresses and content of Web sites referred to in this book are subject to change.
Although The World Almanac For Kids carefully reviews these sites, we cannot take responsibility for their content.

CONTENTS

Science
192-200

Space
201-211

Sports
212-227

Transportation
228-232

Travel
233-236

FACES & PLACES

MUSIC MAKERS

Complic8ed Canadian

Canadian rocker Avril Lavigne made it big with her Grammy-nominated CD Let Go, featuring the hit singles "Complicated," "I'm With You," and "Sk8er Boi."

Go 'n Solo

'N Sync member Justin Timberlake went solo at the end of 2002 with his CD Justified. Justin planned to tour with Christina Aguilera in the summer of 2003.

M!ssundaztood

Pink poses for the camera after winning the award for Best Female Video at the 2002 MTV Video Music Awards.

AT THE MOVIES

More Potter Magic

Dobby the House-Elf, a computer-generated character from the hit film Harry Potter and the Chamber of Secrets.

Dig It!

Shia LaBeouf (Stanley Yelnats) and Khleo Thomas (Zero), from the film Holes, based on the award-winning book by Louis Sachar.

X2

X2: X-Men United stars, from left to right, Alan Cumming (Nightcrawler), Rebecca Romijn-Stamos (Mystique), and Hugh Jackman (Wolverine).

Bend It Like Beckham

Parminder Nagra (right) stars as Jess, a young girl fighting the traditions of her strict Indian family to play football (soccer). Here Jess teams with Jules Paxton (Keira Knightley).

TV TERRIFIC

Steve's the One On Top

Everyone's favorite wildlife expert Steve Irwin—star of The Crocodile Hunter—gets down and dirty at the Australia Zoo with "Agro," a 14-foot-long, 1,300-pound saltwater crocodile.

Takin' Over Everything

Nick Cannon, star of TV's The Nick Cannon Show (and the film Drumline), might "take over" Hollywood in real life!

Come On and Zoom!

Zoom, the Emmy-nominated series that is "by kids, for kids," is science, games, jokes—and fun.

SPORTS STARS

Nearly 10 Miles of Rushing

Emmitt Smith broke Walter Payton's all-time rushing record in October 2002, on his way to a career total of 17,162 yards by year's end.

Shaq and Yao

Yao Ming and Shaquille O'Neal met on the court for the first time, January 17, 2003. The 7-foot-5-inch Yao was a number-one draft pick and a former MVP in the Chinese Basketball Association.

Taking On the Boys

Annika Sorenstam, one of the hottest golfers around, has won more than 40 women's tournaments. Annika took on the men at the Colonial PGA tournament in May 2003. She's the first woman since 1945 to play in a PGA tournament.

CHAMPS

Angels in the Series

The Anaheim Angels defeated the San Francisco Giants to win their first-ever World Series. Shown here are (left to right) Angels manager Mike Scioscia, World Series MVP Troy Glaus, and Scott Spiezio.

Peerless Paula

British running sensation Paula Radcliffe smashed her own world record by nearly two minutes (1:53). The picture tells the rest of the story.

Serena Slam!

After winning the French Open, Wimbledon, and the U.S Open in 2002, Serena Williams went on to win her fourth Grand Slam title in a row—the Australian Open—in January 2003.

Kwan Still Queen

By winning the U.S. and World Championships in 2003, Michelle Kwan proved she was still the queen of the ice. That made seven world and five U.S. titles!

19

IN THE NEWS

Remembering *Columbia*

Pictured here are the seven astronauts—including the first from Israel—who lost their lives when the Shuttle Columbia burned up during its reentry into Earth's atmosphere, on February 1, 2003. (See page 208.)

Dancing Despite Disease

At ballet class in Hong Kong, kids wear masks to protect them from a contagious disease—severe acute respiratory syndrome (SARS)—that threatened many people in East Asia and elsewhere.

Book Five Arrives!

Waiting would-be wizards around the world were finally rewarded on June 21, 2003, when British writer J. K. Rowling's Harry Potter and the Order of the Phoenix hit bookstores everywhere.

New Design For WTC

The selected design for the rebuilding of the World Trade Center site includes a memorial to September 11. The planned 1,776-foot tower would be the world's tallest.

IRAQ WAR

▲ Iraqi kids look over the toppled statue of former Iraqi president Saddam Hussein on April 12, 2003. Statues of the former dictator were destroyed by U.S. and British troops and angry Iraqis, as the power of the old regime faded.

◄ A U.S. Marine dashes over foothills and trenches under skies filled with the dark smoke of oil fires, during fighting in Zubayr, Iraq.

Huge crowds of Shi'a Muslims gather at the shrine of Imam Hussein in Karbala. Under Saddam Hussein's rule, the Shi'a had been forbidden to make their annual pilgrimage there. ▶

U.S. Defense Secretary Donald Rumsfeld, seen here with General Tommy Franks, addresses troops at Central Command Forward headquarters in Qatar, in late April. ▶

◀ Wounded Army Private Jessica Lynch, 19, shown in a television image. She was rescued by U.S. troops in early April, in a nighttime raid on a hospital in Baghdad.

In February, students in Madrid carry posters calling for "peace" and opposing war in Iraq, then in the planning stages. There was widespread opposition to the war in Spain and many other countries. ▶

Animals

How many legs do insects have?
page 25

ANIMAL FACTS

▶ **LONGEST MIGRATION FLIGHT.** Arctic terns are long-distance specialists.They eat on the wing, diving into the ocean for shrimp and plankton. Each year, they follow the warmer weather from the Arctic to the Antarctic, and back—a round-trip of about 22,000 miles!

▶ **LONGEST MIGRATION SWIM.** Gray whales make the world's second-longest migration, more than 12,000 miles round-trip. Each winter they swim from their cold water feeding grounds off the Alaskan coast down to the coast of Mexico for breeding, heading north again in the spring.

▶ **MOST MUSCULAR NOSE.** An elephant's trunk has 40,000 muscles. It's strong enough to pull up small trees and delicate enough to pick up a piece of straw. It can also suck up about 1.5 gallons of water at a time—to spray into its mouth or over its body.

▶ **FROG FREEZE.** Several species of frog—like the wood frog and the gray tree frog— hibernate over the winter by letting their bodies freeze. Breathing stops and so does the heart. The frogs, like other cold-blooded animals, can survive because their bodies produce glycerol, a substance similar to what's used in antifreeze for cars. The glycerol keeps ice from forming inside the frog's cells, which would damage them. The frogs can still absorb what little oxygen they need through the skin.

▶ **DIVING DEEP.** Elephant seals feed on squid that live deep in the ocean. To hunt them, the seals often dive to depths of more than 3,000 feet. Swimming in total darkness, they can stay down for an hour on one breath. In 2002, a female elephant seal known as C-699 dove to 5,351 feet—more than a mile! Sperm whales are the only mammals thought to dive deeper. They've been tracked by sonar to only about 4,000 feet—but fish that live 10,000 feet down have been found in their stomachs.

WHAT ARE GROUPS OF ANIMALS CALLED?

Here are some, often odd names for animal groups.

BEARS: *sleuth* of bears	**KITTENS**: *kindle* or *kendle* of kittens
CATTLE: *drove* of cattle	**LEOPARDS**: *leap* of leopards
CROCODILES: *bask* of crocodiles	**LIONS**: *pride* of lions
CROWS: *murder* of crows	**MULES**: *span* of mules
ELKS: *gang* of elks	**NIGHTINGALES**: *watch* of nightingales
FISH: *school* of fish	**OWLS**: *parliament* of owls
FOXES: *skulk* of foxes	**PEACOCKS**: *muster* of peacocks
GEESE: *flock* or *gaggle* of geese	**SHARKS**: *shiver* of sharks
GNATS: *cloud* of gnats	**RAVENS**: *unkindness* of ravens
HAWKS: *cast* of hawks	**WHALES**: *pod* of whales

IT'S A BUG'S WORLD

Humans may be the smartest creatures on the planet, but they're greatly outnumbered! About half of all known living species are members of the class Insecta. If you could put all life on Earth on a scale all at once, insects would make up about 80% of the weight.

Insects are Arthropods (see page 31). Other Arthropods include crabs, spiders, lobsters, and scorpions.

You wouldn't mistake a crab for an insect, but many people think spiders are. To some people they're all just "bugs." One way to tell the difference is that spiders have 2 body segments and 8 legs, while insects have 3 body segments and 6 legs. Spiders are in their own class (Arachnida).

All About... ANTS

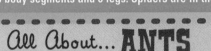

There are about 9,500 known species of ant, but myrmecologists (scientists who study ants) think that's not even half the total number of ant species. Ants have been around for about 100 million years, and can be found in almost every land environment. They are social insects that live together in large groups, or colonies. Most make their homes in underground tunnels and chambers, but some ants are different. Carpenter ants carve tunnels in wood (but don't eat it). In the South American rain forest, many ants live in trees. And Army ants don't build at all. They travel in big groups looking for food.

Ants communicate by touching each other with their antennae. They show other ants where food is by making a path with a chemical (called a pheromone) that leaves a scent for the other ants to follow. Each ant has a specific job. The **queen** lays eggs to populate the colony. **Workers** collect food, feed members of the colony, and enlarge the nest. **Soldiers** are large workers that defend the colony and sometimes attack ants who are strangers. All these hard-working ants are female. **Males** have wings to fly to another colony, where they mate with a queen and die soon afterwards.

INSECT ARCHITECTS

Many animals build nests or burrows to provide a safe place to raise their young. But few can compare with the "cities" of these social insects:

TERMITES in Australia and Africa are the champion builders of the animal world. They use soil and saliva to make towers that reach up to 20 feet tall (below left). Australia's "magnetic termites" build north-facing wedges to regulate the nest's exposure to the Sun.

BALD-FACED HORNETS build rounded nests out of paper-like material made from chewed wood fibers mixed with saliva (above right). The nest has egg chambers inside and can be up to three feet long. The entrance is a hole at the bottom. By the end of summer, there may be as many as 400 workers in a nest.

HONEYBEES live in hives. Inside the hive is a comb with six-sided hollow cells made from beeswax. The wax comes from glands on the abdomen of the worker bees. In some combs the bees store honey; in others, the queen lays eggs that are nursed by workers.

IN THE WORLD

WORLD'S LARGEST ANIMALS

MARINE MAMMAL: blue whale (110 feet long, 209 tons)

LAND MAMMAL: African bush elephant (13 feet high, 8 tons)

TALLEST MAMMAL: giraffe (19 feet tall, 2 tons)

REPTILE: saltwater crocodile (16 feet long, 1,150 pounds)

SNAKE: Heaviest: anaconda (27 feet, 9 inches long, 500 pounds)
Longest: reticulated python (26–32 feet long)

FISH: whale shark (41¼ feet long, 15 tons)

BIRD: ostrich (9 feet tall, 345 pounds)

INSECT: stick insect (15 inches long)

WORLD'S FASTEST ANIMALS

MARINE MAMMAL: blue whale (30 miles per hour)

LAND MAMMAL: cheetah (70 miles per hour)

FISH: sailfish (68 miles per hour)

BIRD: peregrine falcon (100–200 miles per hour)

INSECT: dragonfly (36 miles per hour)

WORLD'S SMALLEST ANIMALS

MAMMAL: bumblebee bat (1.1 to 1.3 inches)

FISH: dwarf goby (length 0.3 inches)

BIRD: male bee hummingbird (2.2 inches)

SNAKES: thread snake and brahminy blind snake (4.25 inches)

LIZARD: Jaragua lizard (0.63 inches)

INSECT: fairy fly (0.01 inches)

FROG: Brazilian frog (0.33 inches)

HOW FAST DO ANIMALS RUN?

Some animals can run as fast as a car. But a snail needs more than 30 hours just to go one mile. If you look at this table, you will see how fast some land animals can go.

	MILES PER HOUR
Cheetah	65
Antelope	60
Lion	50
Elk	45
Zebra	40
Rabbit	35
Reindeer	32
Cat	30
Elephant	25
Wild turkey	15
Squirrel	12
Snail	0.03

How Long Do Animals Live?

Most animals do not live as long as human beings do. A monkey that is 14 years old is thought to be old. A person who is 14 is still considered young. The average life span of a human today is 65 to 70 years. The average life spans of some animals are shown here.

Galapagos tortoise	200+ years
Box turtle	100 years
Blue whale	80 years
Gray whale	70 years
Alligator	50 years
Humpback whale	50 years
Bald eagle	40 years
African elephant	35 years
Bottlenose dolphin	30 years
Grizzly bear	25 years
Horse	20 years
Polar bear	20 years
Black bear	18 years
Tiger	16 years
Lion	15 years
Cow	15 years
Tarantula	15 years
Monkey (rhesus)	15 years
Sheep (domestic)	12 years
Cat (domestic)	12 years
Dog (domestic)	12 years
Sea lion	12 years
Giraffe	10 years
Pig	10 years
Squirrel	10 years
Goat	8 years
Kangaroo	7 years
Goldfish	7 years
Rabbit (domestic)	5 years
Mouse	3 years
Adult housefly	3-4 weeks
Adult mosquito	3-4 weeks

KITS, CUBS, AND OTHER ANIMAL BABIES

ANIMAL	MALE	FEMALE	YOUNG
alligator	bull	cow	hatchling
bear	boar	sow	cub
cheetah	male	female	cub
duck	drake	duck	duckling
ferret	hob	jill	kit
fox	reynard	vixen	kit, cub, pup
giraffe, whale, hippopotamus	bull	cow	calf
gorilla	male	female	infant
hawk	tiercel	hen	eyas
horse	stallion	mare	foal, filly (female), colt (male)
opossum	jack	jill	joey
tiger	tiger	tigress	cub

ENDANGERED SPECIES

When an animal species begins to die out, the animal is said to be endangered or threatened. Throughout the world today, 1,932 species of animals are endangered or threatened, according to the World Wildlife Fund (WWF).

SOME ENDANGERED ANIMALS

CALIFORNIA CONDOR—North America's largest bird. There are about 60 of them now living in the wild. About half of them live in Arizona

GIANT PANDA—China's most loveable animal. As few as 1,000 of these creatures remain in the mountains of southwest China.

LEATHERBACK SEA TURTLE—the largest living turtle in the world. These turtles are facing extinction. Habitat destruction, fishing nets , and the harvesting of its eggs are the biggest threats to their survival.

WHOOPING CRANE—"Operation Migration" has been leading these endangered birds with ultra-light airplanes from Wisconsin to Florida since 2001. In April 2003, 15 whooping cranes (14 from 2002 and 1 from 2001) flew back north on their own for the summer.

HOW DO ANIMALS AND PLANTS BECOME ENDANGERED?

CHANGES IN CLIMATE. Animals are endangered when the climate changes in a major way. For example, if an area becomes very hot and dry and a river dries up, the fish and other plant and animal life in the river will die.

HABITAT DESTRUCTION. Sometimes people destroy habitats where animals live. For example, wetlands, home to many types of waterfowl, fish, and insects live, might be drained for new houses or a mall. The animals would have to find a new home or else die out.

OVER-HUNTING. Bison or buffalo once ranged over the entire Great Plains, but they were hunted almost to extinction in the 19th century. Since then, they have been protected by laws, and their numbers are increasing.

HABITATS: *Where Animals Live*

This table lists some large habitats and some animals that live in them.

HABITAT	SOME ANIMALS THAT LIVE THERE
DESERTS (hot, dry regions)	camels, bobcats, coyotes, kangaroos, mice, Gila monsters, scorpions, rattlesnakes
TROPICAL FORESTS (warm, humid climate)	orangutans, gibbons, leopards, tamandua anteaters, tapirs, iguanas, parrots, tarantulas
GRASSLANDS (flat, open lands)	African elephants, kangaroos, Indian rhinoceroses, giraffes, zebras, prairie dogs, ostriches, tigers
MOUNTAINS (highlands)	yaks, snow leopards, vicunas, bighorn sheep, chinchillas, pikas, eagles, mountain goats
POLAR REGIONS (cold climate)	polar bears, musk oxen, caribou, ermines, arctic foxes, walruses, penguins, Siberian huskies
OCEANS (sea water)	whales, dolphins, seals, manatees, octopuses, stingrays, coral, starfish, lobsters, many kinds of fish

All About... SHARKS

Sharks are among the oldest animals on Earth; they have ruled the seas for over 400 million years. The two largest kinds of fish are sharks, and both are threatened species. At more than 40 feet long (about the size of a bus!), **whale sharks** are the biggest fish of all. They are actually harmless to humans. With their huge mouths, they swim along slowly near the surface, filtering tiny plankton out of the water. The **basking shark** also eats plankton and grows to about 33 feet long.

▲ Whale shark

These slow moving fish are easy targets for harpoon fishermen. These sharks can also get tangled in commercial fishing nets.

▲ Silky shark

When most people picture a shark, they think of the streamlined "mackerel" sharks—like the **great white** (which are actually pretty rare)—or "requiem" sharks like the **silky shark**. But many sharks don't look the way you might imagine. Sharks live in many different parts of the ocean and have developed specialized shapes, teeth, fins, and coloration to fit their habitats. The 350+ species are divided into eight orders. The common names of these types of sharks are: angelsharks, sawsharks, dogfish and cookiecutter sharks, ground sharks, mackerel sharks, carpet sharks, horn sharks, and frilled and cow sharks. About half of all sharks only grow to around 40 inches long. One of the smallest kinds is the seven-inch pygmy spiny shark.

▲ Horn shark

Unlike a tuna or salmon, sharks have no bones. A shark's skeleton is made up of a tough, flexible material called **cartilage**. Sharks can see, hear, smell, taste, and feel. They also have a sixth sense. Through tiny pores in their heads, they can pick up electrical impulses that every animal emits. This ability, combined with strength and razor-sharp teeth, makes them excellent hunters.

However, sharks have a big enemy of their own: humans. People kill 30 to 70 million sharks each year. The great white may be the top predator of the sea, but its fins, jaws, and teeth are valuable in international markets. Many other types of sharks are also killed for their fins. Shark fin soup is a big favorite in parts of Asia, and it can sell for up to $90 a bowl in Hong Kong. Shark meat is growing in popularity in the U.S. Other parts are used to make health and beauty aids. Some people also hunt sharks for sport. Because sharks reproduce slowly, these killings are a serious problem, and the future of the shark is threatened in many parts of the world.

WHO AM I?

was born in London on April 3, 1934. From the time I was a little girl, I dreamed of living with wild animals in Africa. In 960, I went to Gombe National Park, in what is now Tanzania, study chimpanzees in their natural habitat. I spent nearly ten ears there and wrote a bestselling book, *In the Shadow of Man*, bout my experiences. Do you know who I am?

Answer: Jane Goodall

LIFE ON EARTH

This time line shows how life developed on Earth and when land plants developed. The earliest animals are at the top of the chart. The most recent are at the bottom of the chart.

	YEARS AGO		ANIMAL LIFE ON EARTH
PRECAMBRIAN	4.5 BILLION		Formation of the Earth. No signs of life.
	2.5 BILLION		First evidence of life in the form of bacteria and algae. All life is in water.
PALEOZOIC	570–500 MILLION		Animals with shells (called trilobites) and some mollusks. Some fossils begin to form.
	500–430 MILLION		Jawless fish appear, oldest known animals with backbones (vertebrates).
	430–395 MILLION		Many coral reefs, jawed fishes, and scorpion-like animals. First land plants.
	395–345 MILLION		Many fishes. Earliest known insect. Amphibians (animals living in water and on land) appear.
	345–280 MILLION		Large insects appear. Amphibians increase in numbers. First trees appear.
	280–225 MILLION		Reptiles and modern insects appear. Trilobites, many corals, and fishes become extinct.
MESOZOIC	225–195 MILLION		Dinosaurs and turtles appear. Many reptiles and insects develop further. Mammals appear.
	195–135 MILLION		Many giant dinosaurs. Reptiles increase in number. First birds and crab-like animals appear.
	135–65 MILLION		Dinosaurs develop further and then become extinct. Flowering plants begin to appear.
CENOZOIC	65–2.5 MILLION		Modern-day land and sea animals begin to develop, including such mammals as rhinoceroses, whales, cats, dogs, apes, seals.
	2.5 MILLION–10,000		Earliest humans appear. Mastodon, mammoths, and other huge animals become extinct.
	10,000–PRESENT		Modern human beings and animals.

Animal Kingdom

The world has so many animals that scientists looked for a way to organize them into groups. A Swedish scientist named Carolus Linnaeus (1707–1778) worked out a system for classifying both animals and plants. We still use it today.

The animal kingdom is separated into two large groups—animals with backbones, called **vertebrates**, and animals without backbones, called **invertebrates**.

These large groups are divided into smaller groups called phyla. And phyla are divided into even smaller groups called **classes**. The animals in each group are classified together when their bodies are similar in certain ways.

VERTEBRATES:
Animals With Backbones

FISH	Swordfish, tuna, salmon, trout, halibut
AMPHIBIANS	Frogs, toads, mud puppies
REPTILES	Turtles, alligators, crocodiles, lizards
BIRDS	Sparrows, owls, turkeys, hawks
MAMMALS	Kangaroos, opossums, dogs, cats, bears, seals, rats, squirrels, rabbits, chipmunks, porcupines, horses, pigs, cows, deer, bats, whales, dolphins, monkeys, apes, humans

INVERTEBRATES:
Animals Without Backbones

PROTOZOA	The simplest form of animals
COELENTERATES	Jellyfish, hydra, sea anemones, coral
MOLLUSKS	Clams, snails, squid, oysters
ANNELIDS	Earthworms
ARTHROPODS	
Crustaceans:	Lobsters, crayfish
Centipedes and Millipedes	
Arachnids:	Spiders, scorpions
Insects:	Butterflies, grasshoppers, bees, termites, cockroaches
ECHINODERMS	Starfish, sea urchins, sea cucumbers

Homework Help

How can you remember the animal classifications from most general to most specific? Try this sentence:

King **P**hilip **C**ame **O**ver **F**rom **G**reat **S**pain.
K = Kingdom; **P** = Phylum; **C** = Class; **O** = Order; **F** = Family; **G** = Genus; **S** = Species.

All About... DOGS

We know that dogs are human's best friend—they love us and we love them. However, we're not so sure where they came from. Many scientists think they came from wolves 15,000 years ago. Although wolves are wild and dogs are tame, they're still a lot alike. Both wag their tails when happy and put their tails between their legs when scared. They also growl when angry, mark their territory, and want to be part of a "pack," or community. Other scientists think today's nearly 400 breeds of pet dogs came from wild dogs.

▲ *African wild dogs*

No matter who their ancestors were, dogs have a "leg up" on their wilder cousins when it comes to reading humans' signals. In one experiment, conducted with chimpanzees, dogs, and wolves, food was hidden under one of two containers. The dogs did much better than the other animals because they watched the human experimenter, who pointed to, looked at, or tapped the container with food.

▲ *Wensleydale sheepdogs*

Dogs make great pets, but some are specially trained to do more than keep us company. "Working dogs" guide blind people, help police sniff out bombs or drugs, herd sheep and cattle, lift the spirits of sick people, locate stranded travelers, and even act in movies or on TV!

The FBI uses working dogs because they're good at finding things using their keen senses. A dog's sense of hearing is 44 times more powerful than ours, and dogs can sometimes pick up a scent up to half a mile away, even if it's underground or underwater!

The FBI dogs are trained by Special FBI agents, or "handlers," to know what to search for. Handlers teach the dog how to find specific things in all different places like trees, woods, suitcases, or cars.

PETS AT THE TOP

TOP TEN DOG BREEDS

Here are the ten most popular U.S. dog breeds with the numbers of dogs registered by the American Kennel Club in 2002:

#	Breed	Number	#	Breed	Number
1	Labrador retriever	154,616	6	Yorkshire terrier	37,277
2	Golden retriever	56,124	7	Boxer	34,340
3	German shepherd	46,963	8	Poodle	33,917
4	Beagle	44,610	9	Chihuahua	28,466
5	Dachshund	42,571	10	Shih Tzu	28,294

MOST POPULAR PETS

Here are the ten most popular pets in the U.S. today:

1. Cats
2. Dogs
3. Parakeets
4. Small animals, such as rabbits, cavies, gerbils, and hamsters
5. Fish
6. Reptiles
7. Finches
8. Cockatiels
9. Canaries
10. Parrots

TOP TEN PET NAMES

Here's what veterinarians told the American Society for the Prevention of Cruelty to Animals (ASPCA), when asked to list the ten most popular names for pets:

1. Max
2. Maggie
3. Buddy
4. Bailey
5. Jake
6. Sam
7. Molly
8. Nicky
9. Coco
10. Sadie

EAGLE MAZE

START

FINISH

ANSWERS ON PAGES 314-317. FOR MORE PUZZLES GO TO WWW.WORLDALMANACFORKIDS.COM

Art

What kind of art is "chewed paper"?

page 36

THROUGH ARTISTS' EYES

Artists look at the world in a new way. Their work can be funny or sad, beautiful or disturbing, real-looking or strange.

► Throughout history, artists have painted pictures of nature (called **landscapes**), pictures of people (called **portraits**), and pictures of flowers in vases, food, and other objects (known as **still lifes**).

► Today many artists create pictures that do not look like anything in the real world. These are examples of **abstract art,** or modern art.

► **Photography**, too, may be a form of art. Photos record both the commonplace and the exotic, and help us look at events in new ways.

► **Sculpture** is a three-dimensional form made from clay, stone, metal, or other material. Many sculptures stand freely so that you can walk around them. Some are mobiles that hang from the ceiling. Sculptures can be large, like the Statue of Liberty, or small. Some are real-looking. Others have no form you can recognize.

·· All About... Painting on the Wall ··

If you drew on the walls when you were a little kid, you probably got into trouble. But did you know you were following a tradition thousands of years old? Humans have drawn and painted on walls for at least 17,000 years! **Prehistoric people** used earth pigments and animal fat to paint animal scenes on walls of their **caves.** The most famous of these cave paintings today were discovered in 1940 in a cave near Lascaux in France.

Frescoes are another type of wall painting. They are made by painting on fresh, wet plaster. The most famous fresco in history was done by Michelangelo when Pope Julius II gave him the job of repainting the ceiling of the Sistine Chapel with scenes from the Bible. It took years for him to finish this masterpiece (1508-1512), which he painted lying on his back on a scaffold. You can still see this work of art today if you travel to Rome and visit the Vatican.

You don't need to be famous to paint on walls. You could join a community group that paints murals (with permission) on walls or the sides of buildings. Some murals are aimed mainly at brightening a neighborhood. Others are done to remember special people or events. Murals are a kind of art that is for the people and by the people.

◄ Peace Wall *mural in Philadelphia*

All About... Cubism

The Cubist movement in painting was developed by Pablo Picasso of Spain and Georges Braque of France beginning around 1907. The main idea behind Cubism is that objects are shown from different points of view all at the same time. To accomplish this, Cubist artists splintered people and objects into shapes like cubes and cones. They were not true to life, but they showed a new way of looking at reality.

At first the artists used subdued colors and simple shapes. After 1912, they used brighter colors, more decorative shapes, stenciling, and collage. Some even began to use pieces of cut-up newspaper in their paintings.

Three Musicians, ▶
Pablo Picasso

SOME FAMOUS WORKS OF ART

PAINTING	ARTIST	WHEN PAINTED	WHERE IT IS
American Gothic	Grant Wood	1930	Art Institute of Chicago
Guernica	Pablo Picasso	1937	Reina Sofía Museum, Madrid, Spain
Lavender Mist	Jackson Pollock	1950	National Gallery of Art, Washington, DC
Mona Lisa	Leonardo da Vinci	1503-1506	Louvre Museum, Paris, France
The Persistence of Memory	Salvador Dalí	1931	Museum of Modern Art, New York
The Scream	Edvard Munch	1893	National Gallery, Oslo, Norway
The Starry Night	Vincent van Gogh	1889	Museum of Modern Art, New York
George Washington	Gilbert Stuart	1795	Metropolitan Museum of Art, New York

DID YOU KNOW? **WATTS TOWERS:** *The fanciful Watts Towers in Los Angeles—including one 99 feet tall—were all built by one man! For over 30 years (1921-1954), Simon Rodia worked on them in his spare time. He used steel, stone, and cement for the main structures. Into the wet cement, he pressed china, glass, seashells, bottlecaps, and other items into patterns called mosaics. In 1990, his towers were named as a national landmark.*

MAKE A PAPIER-MACHE MASK!

The art of making decorative objects from paper and glue is called papier-mache, which means "chewed paper" in French. The French used this technique in the 1500s to make dolls' heads. Much earlier, around 200 BC, the Chinese used this technique to make warrior helmets, which they coated with lacquer for strength. Today, papier-mache is used to make objects such as masks, dolls, tables, chairs, vases, puppets, and piñatas. It's easy and fun. Find out for yourself by making your own papier-mache mask.

WHAT YOU'LL NEED: Glue, newspaper, water, balloon, brush, paints, tissue paper, scissors, black marker (soft point), ribbon or elastic, tape, a piece of heavy cardboard, stapler

1: Blow up the balloon to about the size of your head and use the marker to draw a mask outline on the balloon. Tape the balloon to the cardboard. Mix one part water and two parts glue in a bowl. Tear (don't cut) the newspaper into strips about the size of your fingers.

Be sure to put lots of newspaper under your project so you don't make a big mess!

2: Dip a strip of newspaper into the glue mix. Get it good and wet, then place it on the balloon inside the outline of your mask. Don't cover up the eyes or the nose. Keep applying strips until your outline is filled in. When you are done you should have three to five layers over the entire mask. Smooth out any bubbles or wrinkles with your fingers.

Don't worry if you don't follow your outline exactly—you can always trim the mask with scissors after it has dried. You can build up areas and details using pieces of cardboard or tissue paper soaked in glue.

3: Let the mask dry for at least a day. When it's all dry, snip a small hole in the balloon right next to the knot and let the air out. The mask will pull away from the balloon and you can trim off any rough edges. Now you can paint and decorate the mask. (Be sure to leave a quarter of an inch on each side to staple the elastic or ribbon, so you can wear the mask when you're done.) Any kind of water-based paint will work.

You can add feathers, beads, macaroni, beans, yarn, sequins, string, fabric, marbles, aluminum foil, or buttons. The possibilities are endless!

ON THE JOB
Artist

Most kids like to draw or paint. But what is it like to be an artist as your job? *The World Almanac for Kids* talked to Robert Longo, an artist who lives in Brooklyn and whose studio is in Manhattan. He draws, paints, and sculpts. His artworks can be found in many museums and art galleries.

▲ December, *by Robert Longo*

Q: You liked drawing as a kid?
Yes. I could always draw. I drew comic book and TV cartoon characters. I drew sports figures. I drew airplanes and cars. I entertained my friends with my drawings.

Q: Did you study art in college?
Yes. But it wasn't the first thing I did. When I finally did come to art, I knew I had found what I wanted to do. In a short time I went from being just about the worst student in class to being the best. I am very lucky. I found a job doing something I love doing.

Q: How do you pick what to paint?
I do series of works—a lot of paintings or drawings or sculpture on one basic theme or idea. I've done series on Flags, Cars, Ocean waves, Nuclear bombs ... I try to find a subject that connects in some way to me personally, but also links up with what's going on in our world today. Sometimes it's my kids who provide the ideas. My oldest son told me that one day when he went to play basketball, another kid had a gun. I was very upset about this and I couldn't stop thinking about it. This made me do a series of very big drawings of guns.

Q: Is there any advice you would give to a kid about becoming an artist?
You should look at as many different kinds of art as possible. You can learn a lot by copying and tracing—comic books and photographs for example. Art is like everything else; if you want to be good at it you have to practice, practice, practice. It has its tricks too: how to proportion a human figure, for example, or how to draw a perfect circle. When I was younger I worked as an apprentice for an established artist. I mixed paints and cleaned floors. I learned a lot.

Birthdays

January

◄ January 14

1 Paul Revere, *patriot*, 1735
2 Princess Stephanie of Monaco, 1965
3 J.R.R. Tolkien, *writer*, 1892
4 Dave Foley, *actor*, 1963
5 Warrick Dunn, *football player*, 1975
6 Joan of Arc, *warrior, saint*, 1412
7 Nicolas Cage, *actor*, 1964
8 Elvis Presley, *singer*, 1935
9 A.J. McLean, *singer*, 1978
10 George Foreman, *boxer*, 1949
11 John MacDonald, *Canada's 1st prime minister*, 1815
12 Jack London, *author*, 1876
13 Orlando Bloom, *actor*, 1977
14 Shannon Lucid, *astronaut*, 1943
15 Rev. Martin Luther King Jr., *civil rights leader*, 1929
16 Aaliyah, *singer*, 1979
17 Muhammad Ali, *boxer*, 1942
18 Kevin Costner, *actor*, 1955
19 James Watt, *inventor*, 1736
20 Edwin "Buzz" Aldrin, *astronaut*, 1930
21 Hakeem Olajuwon, *basketball player*, 1963
22 Diane Lane, *actress*, 1965
23 Edouard Manet, *painter*, 1832
24 Mary Lou Retton, *gymnast*, 1968
25 Alicia Keys, *singer*, 1981
26 Vince Carter, *basketball player*, 1977
27 Lewis Carroll, *author*, 1832
28 Elijah Wood, *actor*, 1981
29 Oprah Winfrey, *TV personality*, 1954
30 Dick Cheney, U.S. *vice president*, 1941
31 Justin Timberlake, *singer*, 1981

February

1 Langston Hughes, *poet*, 1901
2 Garth Brooks, *singer*, 1962
3 Nathan Lane, *actor*, 1956
4 Rosa Parks, *civil rights activist*, 1913
5 Hank Aaron, *baseball player*, 1934
6 Babe Ruth, *baseball player*, 1895
7 Ashton Kutcher, *actor*, 1978
8 Seth Green, *actor*, 1974
9 David Gallagher, *actor*, 1985
10 Laura Dern, *actress*, 1967
11 Jennifer Aniston, *actress*, 1969
12 Arsenio Hall, *actor/host*, 1955
13 Chuck Yeager, *pilot*, 1923
14 Drew Bledsoe, *football player*, 1972
15 Matt Groening, *cartoonist*, 1954
16 Jerome Bettis, *football player*, 1972
17 Michael Jordan, *basketball player*, 1963
18 John Travolta, *actor*, 1955
19 Jeff Daniels, *actor*, 1955
20 Brian Littrell, *singer*, 1975
21 Jennifer Love Hewitt, *actress*, 1979
22 Steve Irwin, *wildlife expert*, 1960
23 Dakota Fanning, *actress*, 1994
24 Jeff Garcia, *football player*, 1970
25 Sean Astin, *actor*, 1971
26 Johnny Cash, *musician*, 1932
27 Ariel Sharon, *Israeli prime minister*, 1928
28 Gilbert Gottfried, *actor*, 1955
29 Alex Rocco, *actor*, 1936

◄ February 22

Who shares your birthday?

March

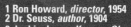

March 12 ►

1 Ron Howard, *director*, 1954
2 Dr. Seuss, *author*, 1904
3 Jackie Joyner-Kersee, *Olympic champion*, 1962
4 Patricia Heaton, *actress*, 1959
5 Niki Taylor, *model*, 1975
6 Shaquille O'Neal, *basketball player*, 1972
7 Laura Prepon, *actress*, 1974
8 Freddie Prinze Jr., *actor*, 1976
9 Bow Wow, *rapper*, 1987
10 Shannon Miller, *Olympic gymnast*, 1987
11 Sam Donaldson, *TV journalist*, 1934
12 Amelia Earhart, *pilot*, 1905
13 William H. Macy, *actor*, 1950
14 Billy Crystal, *actor/comedian*, 1947
15 Sean Biggerstaff, *actor*, 1983
16 Jerry Lewis, *actor/comedian*, 1926
17 Mia Hamm, *soccer player*, 1972
18 Queen Latifah, *rapper/actress*, 1970
19 Wyatt Earp, *lawman*, 1848
20 Mr. (Fred) Rogers, *TV host*, 1928
21 Rosie O'Donnell, *TV personality*, 1962
22 Reese Witherspoon, *actress*, 1976
23 Jason Kidd, *basketball player*, 1973
24 Harry Houdini, *magician*, 1874
25 Sheryl Swoopes, *basketball player*, 1971
26 Martin Short, *actor/comedian*, 1950
27 Mariah Carey, *singer*, 1970
28 Reba McEntire, *singer, actress*, 1955
29 Jennifer Capriati, *tennis player*, 1976
30 Norah Jones, *musician*, 1979
31 Ewan McGregor, *actor*, 1971

April

1 Ali MacGraw, *actress*, 1938
2 Emmylou Harris, *singer*, 1947
3 Amanda Bynes, *actress*, 1986
4 Maya Angelou, *poet*, 1928
5 Colin Powell, *secretary of state*, 1937
6 John Ratzenberger, *actor*, 1947
7 Jackie Chan, *actor*, 1954
8 Kirsten Storms, *actress*, 1984
9 Dennis Quaid, *actor*, 1954
10 Mandy Moore, *singer*, 1984
11 Meshach Taylor, *actor*, 1947
12 Claire Danes, *actress*, 1979
13 Jane Leeves, *actress*, 1963
14 Sarah Michelle Gellar, *actress*, 1977
15 Emma Watson, *actress*, 1990
16 Wilbur Wright, *aviation pioneer*, 1867
17 Sean Bean, *actor*, 1959
18 Melissa Joan Hart, *actress*, 1976
19 Kate Hudson, *actress*, 1979
20 Joey Lawrence, *actor*, 1976
21 John Muir, *naturalist*, 1838
22 Jack Nicholson, *actor*, 1936
23 William Shakespeare, *playwright*, 1564
24 Kelly Clarkson, *singer*, 1982
25 Renee Zellweger, *actress*, 1969
26 Natrone Means, *football player*, 1972
27 Coretta Scott King, *activist*, 1927
28 Jessica Alba, *actress*, 1981
29 Andre Agassi, *tennis player*, 1970
30 Kirsten Dunst, *actress*, 1982

▲ April 16

May

▲ May 12

1 Tim McGraw, *musician*, 1967
2 The Rock, *wrestler*, 1972
3 James Brown, *singer*, 1933
4 Lance Bass, *singer*, 1979
5 Tammy Wynette, *singer*, 1942
6 Tony Blair, *British prime minister*, 1953
7 Johannes Brahms, *composer*, 1833
8 Enrique Iglesias, *singer*, 1975
9 Billy Joel, *songwriter*, 1949
10 Kenan Thompson, *actor*, 1978
11 Salvador Dali, *painter*, 1904
12 Tony Hawk, *skateboarder*, 1968
13 Stevie Wonder, *singer*, 1950
14 Cate Blanchett, *actress*, 1969
15 Emmitt Smith, *football player*, 1969
16 Janet Jackson, *singer*, 1966
17 Jordan Knight, *singer*, 1971
18 Spencer Breslin, *actor*, 1992
19 Malcolm X, *black nationalist, civil rights activist*, 1925
20 Cher, *singer/actress*, 1946
21 Fairuza Balk, *actress*, 1974
22 Sir Arthur Conan Doyle, *author*, 1859
23 Drew Carey, *actor/comedian*, 1958
24 Billy Gilman, *singer*, 1988
25 Mike Myers, *actor*, 1963
26 Dr. Sally Ride, *astronaut*, 1951
27 Wild Bill Hickok, *frontiersman*, 1837
28 Jim Thorpe, *Olympic champion*, 1888
29 Bob Hope, *actor*, 1903
30 Wynonna Judd, *singer*, 1964
31 Clint Eastwood, *actor*, 1930

June

1 Marilyn Monroe, *actress*, 1926
2 Dana Carvey, *comedian*, 1955
3 Lalaine (Varaga-Paras), *actress*, 1987
4 Angelina Jolie, *actress*, 1975
5 Mark Wahlberg, *actor*, 1971
6 Anson Carter, *hockey player*, 1974
7 Allen Iverson, *basketball player*, 1975
8 Frank Lloyd Wright, *architect*, 1867
9 Natalie Portman, *actress*, 1981
10 Maurice Sendak, *author/illustrator*, 1928
11 Joshua Jackson, *actor*, 1978
12 Anne Frank, *diary writer*, 1929
13 Ashley and Mary-Kate Olsen, *actresses*, 1986
14 Steffi Graf, *tennis player*, 1969
15 Courteney Cox-Arquette, *actress*, 1964
16 Yasmine Bleeth, *actress*, 1968
17 Venus Williams, *tennis player*, 1980
18 Paul McCartney, *musician*, 1942
19 Paula Abdul, *singer*, 1963
20 John Goodman, *actor*, 1952
21 Prince William of Great Britain, 1982
22 Carson Daly, *TV personality*, 1973
23 Kurt Warner, *football player*, 1971
24 George Pataki, *N.Y. governor*, 1945
25 Dikembe Mutumbo, *basketball player*, 1966
26 Derek Jeter, *baseball player*, 1974
27 Tobey Maguire, *actor*, 1975
28 John Cusack, *actor*, 1966
29 Theo Fleury, *hockey player*, 1968
30 Mitch Richmond, *basketball player*, 1965

◄ June 21

July

July 6 ▶

1 Jarome Iginla, *hockey player*, 1977
2 Richard Petty, *auto racer*, 1937
3 Tom Cruise, *actor*, 1962
4 Louis "Satchmo" Armstrong, *jazz musician*, 1900
5 P. T. Barnum, *circus founder*, 1810
6 George W. Bush, *43rd president*, 1946
7 Michelle Kwan, *figure skater*, 1980
8 Kevin Bacon, *actor*, 1958
9 Tom Hanks, *actor*, 1956
10 Jessica Simpson, *singer*, 1980
11 Jeff Corwin, *wildlife expert*, 1967
12 Bill Cosby, *comedian*, 1937
13 Harrison Ford, *actor*, 1942
14 Robin Ventura, *baseball player*, 1967
15 Rembrandt, *artist*, 1606
16 Orville Redenbacher, *popcorn maker*, 1907
17 David Hasselhoff, *actor*, 1952
18 Vin Diesel, *actor*, 1967
19 Edgar Degas, *artist*, 1834
20 Sir Edmund Hillary, *Everest climber*, 1919
21 Robin Williams, *actor/comedian*, 1952
22 David Spade, *actor*, 1965
23 Daniel Radcliffe, *actor*, 1989
24 Jennifer Lopez, *actress/singer*, 1970
25 Matt LeBlanc, *actor*, 1967
26 Sandra Bullock, *actress*, 1964
27 Alex Rodriguez, *baseball player*, 1975
28 Beatrix Potter, *author*, 1866
29 Martina McBride, *singer*, 1966
30 Lisa Kudrow, *actress*, 1963
31 J. K. Rowling, *author*, 1966

August

1 Ashley Angel, *singer*, 1981
2 Edward Furlong, *actor*, 1977
3 Tom Brady, *football player*, 1977
4 Jeff Gordon, *auto racer*, 1971
5 Neil Armstrong, *astronaut*, 1930
6 Lucille Ball, *actress/comedian*, 1911
7 Charlize Theron, *actress*, 1975
8 Joshua "JC" Chasez, *singer*, 1976
9 Chamiqua Holdsclaw, *basketball player*, 1977
10 Antonio Banderas, *actor*, 1960
11 Hulk Hogan, *wrestler*, 1953
12 Pete Sampras, *tennis player*, 1971
13 Fidel Castro, *president of Cuba*, 1927
14 Steve Martin, *actor/comedian*, 1945
15 Napoleon Bonaparte, *French emperor*, 1769
16 Vanessa Carlton, *singer*, 1980
17 Jorge Posada, *baseball player*, 1971
18 Meriwether Lewis, *explorer*, 1774
19 Lil' Romeo, *rapper*, 1989
20 Todd Helton, *baseball player*, 1973
21 Kenny Rogers, *singer/actor*, 1938
22 Howie Dorough, *singer*, 1973
23 Kobe Bryant, *basketball player*, 1978
24 Rupert Grint, *actor*, 1988
25 Kel Mitchell, *actor/comedian*, 1978
26 Tom Ridge, *homeland security secretary*, 1945
27 Alexa Vega, *actress*, 1988
28 Shania Twain, *musician*, 1965
29 Michael Jackson, *singer*, 1958
30 Andy Roddick, *tennis player*, 1982
31 Hideo Nomo, *baseball player*, 1968

◀ **August 5**

September

1 Tim Duncan, *basketball player*, 1966
2 Keanu Reeves, *actor*, 1964
3 Charlie Sheen, *actor*, 1965
4 Beyoncé Knowles, *musician*, 1981
5 Jesse James, *outlaw*, 1847
6 Jane Curtin, *actress*, 1947
7 Briana Scurry, *soccer player*, 1971
8 Pink, *singer*, 1979
9 Adam Sandler, *actor*, 1966
10 Randy Johnson, *baseball player*, 1963
11 Harry Connick Jr., *musician/actor*, 1967
12 Yao Ming, *basketball player*, 1980
13 Roald Dahl, *author*, 1916
14 Adam Lamberg, *actor*, 1984
15 Prince Harry of Great Britain, 1984
16 Alexis Bledel, *actress*, 1982
17 John Ritter, *actor*, 1948
18 Lance Armstrong, *cyclist*, 1971
19 Trisha Yearwood, *singer*, 1964
20 Guy Lafleur, *hockey player*, 1951
21 Faith Hill, *singer*, 1967
22 Tom Felton, *actor*, 1987
23 Bruce Springsteen, *musician*, 1949
24 Eddie George, *football player*, 1973
25 Will Smith, *actor*, 1968
26 Serena Williams, *tennis player*, 1981
27 Avril Lavigne, *singer*, 1984
28 Hilary Duff, *actress*, 1987
29 Bryant Gumbel, *TV personality*, 1948
30 Lacy Chabert, *actress*, 1982

September 27

October

1 Richard Harris, *actor*, 1932
2 Sting, *musician*, 1951
3 Gwen Stephani, *singer*, 1969
4 Alicia SIlverstone, *actress*, 1976
5 Bernie Mac, *actor/comedian*, 1958
6 Jack De Sena, *actor*, 1987
7 Vladimir Putin, *Russian president*, 1952
8 Matt Damon, *actor*, 1970
9 Annika Sorenstam, *golfer*, 1970
10 Brett Favre, *football player*, 1969
11 Eleanor Roosevelt, *first lady*, 1884
12 Marion Jones, *Olympic champion*, 1975
13 Ashanti (Douglas), *singer*, 1980
14 Natalie Maines, *singer*, 1974
15 Emeril Lagasse, *TV chef*, 1959
16 Kordell Stewart, *football player*, 1972
17 Nick Cannon, *actor/comedian*, 1980
18 Peter Boyle, *actor*, 1935
19 Omar Gooding, *actor/host*, 1976
20 Viggo Mortensen, *actor*, 1958
21 Jeremy Miller, *actor*, 1976
22 Jonathan Lipnicki, *actor*, 1990
23 Al Leiter, *baseball player*, 1965
24 Monica, *singer*, 1980
25 Pablo Picasso, *painter*, 1881
26 Hillary Rodham Clinton, *U.S. senator*, 1947
27 Kelly Osbourne, *TV personality*, 1984
28 Julia Roberts, *actress*, 1967
29 Richard Dreyfuss, *actor*, 1947
30 Diego Maradonna, *soccer player*, 1960
31 Dan Rather, *TV news anchor*, 1931

◄ *October 11*

November

November 14

1 Stephen Crane, *author*, 1871
2 Daniel Boone, *frontiersman*, 1734
3 Roseanne, *actress*, 1952
4 Laura Bush, *first lady*, 1946
5 Javy Lopez, *baseball player*, 1970
6 James A. Naismith, *basketball inventor*, 1861
7 Marie Curie, *scientist*, 1867
8 Courtney Thorne-Smith, *actress*, 1968
9 Nick Lachey, *singer*, 1973
10 Sinbad, *actor/comedian*, 1956
11 Leonardo DiCaprio, *actor*, 1974
12 Sammy Sosa, *baseball player*, 1968
13 Whoopi Goldberg, *actress*, 1949
14 Condoleezza Rice, *national security advisor*, 1954
15 Zena Grey, *actress*, 1988
16 Trevor Penick, *singer*, 1979
17 Danny DeVito, *actor*, 1944
18 Christina Vidal, *actress*, 1981
19 Gail Devers, *Olympic champion*, 1966
20 Ming-Na Wen, *actress*, 1967
21 Ken Griffey Jr., *baseball player*, 1969
22 Billie Jean King, *tennis player*, 1943
23 Billy the Kid, *outlaw*, 1859
24 Scott Joplin, *composer*, 1868
25 Jenna and Barbara Bush, *President Bush's daughters*, 1981
26 Charles Schulz, *cartoonist*, 1922
27 Anders Celsius, *scientist*, 1701
28 Scarlett Pomers, *actress*, 1988
29 Mariano Rivera, *baseball player*, 1969
30 Ben Stiller, *actor*, 1965

December

1 Woody Allen, *actor/director*, 1935
2 Britney Spears, *singer*, 1981
3 Brendan Fraser, *actor*, 1967
4 Orlando Brown, *actor*, 1987
5 Frankie Muniz, *actor*, 1985
6 Tom Hulce, *actor*, 1953
7 Aaron Carter, *singer*, 1987
8 Teresa Weatherspoon, *basketball player*, 1965
9 Clarence Birdseye, *frozen food pioneer*, 1886
10 Raven Symone, *actress*, 1985
11 Teri Garr, *actress*, 1949
12 Frank Sinatra, *singer/actor*, 1915
13 Jamie Foxx, *comedian*, 1967
14 Craig Biggio, *baseball player*, 1965
15 Mo Vaughn, *baseball player*, 1967
16 Ludwig van Beethoven, *composer*, 1770
17 Bill Pullman, *actor*, 1954
18 Steven Spielberg, *film producer*, 1947
19 William Parry, *Arctic explorer*, 1790
20 Rich Gannon, *football player*, 1965
21 Jane Kaczmarek, *actress*, 1955
22 Lady Bird Johnson, *first lady*, 1912
23 Scott Gomez, *hockey player*, 1979
24 Ricky Martin, *singer*, 1971
25 Clara Barton, *American Red Cross founder*, 1821
26 Susan Butcher, *sled dog racer*, 1954
27 Louis Pasteur, *scientist*, 1822
28 Denzel Washington, *actor*, 1954
29 Mary Tyler Moore, *actress*, 1936
30 Tiger Woods, *golfer*, 1975
31 Henri Matisse, *painter*, 1869

▼ *December 30*

Books

Who are Violet, Klaus, and baby Sunny? page 47

HARRY

After four fun-filled books—and two hit movies—nearly everyone knows Harry. Harry Potter, that is. He's the talented young wizard-in-training at Hogwarts School of Witchcraft and Wizardry. We first met him when he was almost 11, in *Harry Potter and the Sorcerer's Stone*. Then came *Harry Potter and the Chamber of Secrets*, followed by *Harry Potter and the Prisoner of Azkaban*. All three were published in the U.S. in 1999. *Harry Potter and the Goblet of Fire* came out a year later.

He's learned a lot of spells and potions, and made both friends and enemies in his adventures. J.K. Rowling plans to write a total of seven books about Harry—one for each of his years at Hogwarts. *Harry Potter and the Order of the Phoenix*, the fifth book in the series, was a long time in coming. And at nearly 900 pages, it's the longest one yet! It was due to be on sale June 21, 2003.

◀ *J.K. Rowling*

Are You a Muggle or a Magician?

MATCH THE CHARM WITH ITS NAME:

1. Tickling Charm   a. *Tarantallegra*
2. Dancing Charm   b. *Wingardium Leviosa*
3. Charm Ending   c. *Rictusenpra*
4. Levitation Charm   d. *Finite Incantatem*

PICK THE ANSWER:

5. What was thought to be the most severely haunted house in England?
a) Castle of Doom   b) The House of Screams   c) The Shrieking Shack   d) Monster Manor

6. Who is known as the Grand Sorcerer, Chief Warlock, and Supreme Mugwump?
a) Cyril Nevermore   b) Angus Everbore   c) Nigel Grumblemore   d) Albus Dumbledore

7. Who is the Keeper of the Keys and Grounds at Hogwarts?
a) Hagrid   b) Harvey   c) Harry   d) Fred

8. Who opened the Chamber of Secrets 50 years ago?
a) Tim Joke   b) Terry Limerick   c) Tom Tankengine   d) Tom Riddle

9. Who works at the Misuse of Muggle Artifacts Office at the Ministry of Magic?
a) Mrs. Sneezy   b) Mr. Weasley   c) Mr. Cheesy   d) Ms. Beasley

10. What do You-Know-Who's supporters call themselves?
a) The A-Team   b) The Doom Eaters   c) The Death Eaters   d) The Egg Beaters

HOW MANY DID YOU GET RIGHT?

0-3, *a muggle you'll be;* **4-6,** *you know some tricks;* **7-9,** *you did just fine;* **10,** *off to Hogwarts with you then!*

ANSWERS ON PAGES 314-317. FOR MORE PUZZLES GO TO WWW.WORLDALMANACFORKIDS.COM

Book Awards, 2002-2003

Caldecott Medal
For the artist of the best children's picture book
2003 WINNER: Eric Rohmann for *My Friend Rabbit*

Newbery Medal
For the author of the best children's book
2003 WINNER: Avi for *Crispin: The Cross of Lead*

Coretta Scott King Award
For artists and authors whose works encourage expression of the African-American experience
2003 WINNERS: Author Award: *Bronx Masquerade*, by Nikki Grimes **Illustrator Award:** *Talkin' About Bessie: The Story of Aviator Elizabeth Coleman*, illustrated by E.B. Lewis

BEST NEW BOOKS OF THE YEAR

Among those chosen in 2003 by the American Library Association

Crispin: The Cross of Lead, by Avi (ages 9-12)—Known only as "Asta's son," a 13-year-old boy and his mother are poor peasants living in England in the 1300s. After his mother dies, he finds out that his real name is Crispin. Accused of a murder he did not commit, he runs away, taking only his mother's lead cross.

Hoot, by Carl Hiaasen (ages 9-12)—Roy is the new kid in school and has a hard time making friends. To make matters worse, the school bully is making his life miserable. But the real adventure begins when Roy finds himself in the middle of a mystery, surrounding some miniature owls that are being threatened by a construction company.

My Friend Rabbit, by Eric Rohmann (ages 4-8)—This is an adventure story of two friends, Rabbit and Mouse. When Rabbit launches his airplane with Mouse as the pilot and the plane gets stuck in a tree, Rabbit has to find a way to get it down. Great illustrations.

Noah's Ark, by Jerry Pinkney (ages 5-8)—This Bible story tells how Noah and his family built the ark, gathered provisions, and brought the animals on board to save life on Earth during the great flood. Pencil-and-watercolor pictures also help tell the story.

Pictures of Hollis Woods, by Patricia Reilly Giff (ages 9-12)—Twelve-year-old Hollis Woods has lived in many foster homes, and keeps running away. When she is sent to live with Josie, an elderly artist, they quickly hit it off. But Hollis worries as Josie gets more and more forgetful, and the girl longs to live with the Regans, her previous foster family.

Talkin' About Bessie: The Story of Aviator Elizabeth Coleman, by Nikki Grimes; illustrated by E.B. Lewis (ages 5-9)—Elizabeth "Bessie" Coleman lived in a world that was always telling her what she could and couldn't do. But these troubles did not stop her. At the age of 11, she vowed to become the first African-American female pilot. This is the story of how she overcame poverty and discrimination to make her dream come true.

BOOKS TO ENJOY

FICTION Fiction books come out of the writer's imagination. Some stories are set in a world of fantasy. Others seem very real.

A Corner of the Universe, by Ann M. Martin (ages 9-12). Twelve-year-old Hattie Owen is enjoying a quiet summer at home when she learns a family secret. Her Uncle Adam was sent away years ago because of "mental problems." Now Uncle Adam's "school"—an institution for the mentally disabled—is closing, and Hattie's family must deal with a childlike young man whose existence they've denied for years.

Eloise Takes a Bawth, by Kay Thompson with Mart Crowley, illustrated by Hilary Knight (ages 5-8). In this tale Eloise takes a soaking that sends water roaring through the pipes of Manhattan's Plaza Hotel and makes a "splawsh" at the Venetian Masked Ball.

Hondo & Fabian, by Peter McCarty (ages 5-8). Hondo the dog and Fabian the cat live in the same house but lead very different lives. Hondo and his puppy friend Fred head for the beach for a day of adventure, while Fabian stays home to play with the baby. Read this beautifully illustrated book to find out who has more fun, and who causes the most trouble.

Saffy's Angel, by Hilary McKay (ages 9-12). In this story of an eccentric but delightful British family, Saffy's discovery of her true identity leads to an unlikely friendship, a secret trip to Siena, and a new appreciation for the family that raised her.

The Same Stuff as Stars, by Katherine Paterson (ages 10-12). In this novel set in rural Vermont, 11-year-old Angel looks out for her younger brother after their mother leaves them with their great-grandmother. Angel's friendship with a mysterious "star man," and the way she handles even the toughest challenge, convinces readers she will come out on top in any situation.

The Spider and the Fly, by Mary Howitt; illustrated by Tony DiTerlizzi (ages 5-8). This age-old poem is illustrated with black-and-white drawings inspired by horror movies of the 1920s and 1930s. It begins, "'Will you walk into my parlor?' said the Spider to the Fly…"

Surviving the Applewhites, by Stephanie S. Tolan (ages 9-12). Thirteen-year-old trouble-maker Jake Semple has gotten kicked out of school—again. He is sent to a home school run by the Applewhites, an outrageous, artistic family. While starring in a production of *The Sound of Music* being produced by the Applewhite family, Jake learns how special he really is.

SOME POPULAR SERIES

Anne of Green Gables,
   by L. M. Montgomery
Baby-Sitters Club, by Ann M. Martin
Boxcar Mysteries,
   by Gertrude Chandler Warner
Eloise, by Kay Thompson
Encyclopedia Brown, by Donald J. Sobol
The Fudge Books, by Judy Blume

Hardy Boys, by Franklin W. Dixon
I Spy, from Scholastic
Little House Books,
   by Laura Ingalls Wilder
The Mad Scientists' Club,
   by Bertrand R. Brinley
Nancy Drew, by Carolyn Keene
Tarzan, by Edgar Rice Burroughs

POETRY
Poems use language in new and imaginative ways, sometimes in rhyme.

Falling Up, by Shel Silverstein (grades 3-6). This collection of more than 150 poems highlights gross, scary, absurd, and comical things. The drawings add a lot to the words, and the book's clever design makes it hard to put down.

Pieces: A Year in Poems & Quilts, by Anna Grossnickle Hines (all ages). Each of these 20 poems about nature is illustrated with a beautiful miniature quilt that the author created.

A Poke in the I, by Paul B. Janeczko, editor (ages 9-12). In "concrete" poems words are arranged into a shape that reflects the poem's meaning. This collection of 30 concrete poems may just inspire readers to write a few of their own!

Winter Eyes, by Douglas Florian (ages 4-8). Here is a collection of 28 simple and humorous poems that express a child's view of winter. They are accompanied by watercolor and pencil illustrations

NonFICTION
These books prove facts can be fascinating.

Action Jackson, by Jan Greenberg and Sandra Jordan, illustrated by Robert Andrew Parker (ages 4-8). We are there on a late spring morning when abstract artist Jackson Pollock begins work on the painting that becomes known as *Number 1, 1950* (also known as *Lavender Mist*). In this unique picture book the authors discuss the creative process of this great artist. Parker's atmospheric watercolors complement the story and honor the spirit of Pollock.

Confucius: The Golden Rule, by Russell Freedman (ages 9-12). Freedman digs deep into Chinese history, blending its culture and language into a complete and thoughtful biography of the philosopher Confucius.

Rap a Tap Tap, by Leo and Diane Dillon (ages 4-8). This book of verse and colorful illustrations tells the story of the legendary African-American tap dancer Bill "Bojangles" Robinson. Each line of poetry is followed by "Rap a tap tap—think of that!"

Six Days in October: The Stock Market Crash of 1929, by Karen Blumenthal (ages 9-12). Wall Street Journal reporter Karen Blumenthal describes the events surrounding the 1929 stock market crash. There are gripping accounts of the power struggles between Wall Street and Washington, and poignant stories from those who lost their life savings.

REFERENCE
Many reference materials are stored on CD-ROMs and are also available on the Internet.

Almanac: A one-volume book of facts and statistics.

Atlas: A collection of maps.

Dictionary: A book of words in alphabetical order. It gives meanings and spellings and shows how words are pronounced.

Encyclopedia: A place to go for information on almost any subject.

For more on children's books, go to:

WEB SITE *http://www.ala.org/booklist/v99/002.html*

ON THE JOB

Writer

Those books on your bookshelf and in the library didn't just happen—people wrote them. What's it like to be one of those people? To find out, *The World Almanac for Kids* talked to author Claudia Mills, who has written more than 30 books for children. They include *Standing Up to Mr. O* (about a 7th-grader who thinks it's wrong to dissect animals for biology class) and *Losers, Inc.* (the main character keeps a journal called "LIFE ISN'T FAIR: A PROOF"). Claudia lives in Colorado, where she also teaches philosophy in a college.

◄ *Claudia Mills*

Q: Did you always want to be a writer?
I wrote stories and plays when I was young. My mother, who was a teacher, encouraged me, and so did my teachers. In fifth grade I wrote a play that my teacher let me put on for the class.

Q: Who were some of the authors you read as a child?
Maud Hart Lovelace—she wrote the Betsy-Tacy books. And Frances Hodgson Burnett, who wrote *The Secret Garden*.

Q: How do you start a book?
I start with a character with a problem. I think of events that will highlight the problem and lead to a resolution. A lot happens before I reach the end of a story.

Q: Do you have a fixed time to work?
I get up early and write from five until seven in the morning. I try to do a page a day. My handwriting is small, so one page on my pad is actually about two pages printed.

Q: What's hardest about being a writer?
Criticism is hard. But it's important so I can make my writing better. Another hard thing is waiting. The book I'm working on now, in 2003, kids won't be reading until 2006.

Q: Do you have any advice for kids who want to become writers?
I would just say, try to write as much as you can. Stories and plays are good, but any kind of writing will help: journals, letters, e-mails, anything. And it's very important to read a lot if you want to become a writer.

You Be the Author

You can be an author too. Why not give it a try?

For example, you could write reviews of some movies you have seen or books you have read. If you write a review of *The World Almanac for Kids*, send it to review@worldalmanacforkids.com.

Or make up a story of your own. Or write a collection of poems.

You can design a nice cover for your book, with a picture you paste on to it, or maybe a drawing.

Don't forget to give it a title, and put your name on the front! Then you can share it with classmates and friends.

All About... LEMONY SNICKET

Did you ever hear of the mysterious Lemony Snicket and his series of "unfortunate events" involving the Baudelaire children? His real name is Daniel Handler, and he's a rock musician with an odd sense of humor. In *Book the First: The Bad Beginning*, readers are warned, "If you are interested in stories with happy endings, you would be better off reading some other book. In this book there is no happy ending, there is no happy beginning, and very few happy things in the middle." Violet, Klaus, and baby Sunny become orphans in the first book. They soon fall into the clutches of Count Olaf, a treacherous and evil man who, in many ridiculous disguises, chases the children through *The Reptile Room, The Wide Window, The Miserable Mill, The Austere Academy, The Ersatz Elevator, The Vile Village, The Hostile Hospital,* and *The Carnivorous Carnival.* Along with the gloom and doom come some pretty good laughs. In all, 13 books are planned for the series—a most unfortunate number!

Daniel Handler, a.k.a. Lemony Snicket ▶

I was born in Missouri in 1835 and grew up on the Mississippi River. In fact I became a riverboat pilot for a few years before becoming a reporter. I visited many places around the world and wrote humorous stories about my travels for the newspapers. But I am not known for writing newspaper articles or for lecturing abroad as much as for the books I wrote about boyhood adventures along the Mississippi River. I am not even known by my real name. Do you know who I am?

Answer: Mark Twain (real name, Samuel Clemens)

Buildings

TALLEST BUILDINGS IN THE WORLD

What was the world's tallest structure for 4,000 years?
•••
page 49

Here are the world's tallest buildings, with the year each was completed. Heights listed here don't include antennas or other outside structures.

PETRONAS TOWERS 1 & 2, Kuala Lumpur, Malaysia (1998) **Height:** each building is 88 stories, 1,483 feet ▶

SEARS TOWER, Chicago, Illinois (1974) **Height:** 110 stories, 1,450 feet

JIN MAO BUILDING, Shanghai, China (1998) **Height:** 88 stories, 1,381 feet

TWO INTERNATIONAL FINANCE CENTRE*, Hong Kong, China (2003) **Height:** 88 stories, 1,352 feet

CITIC PLAZA, Guangzhou, China (1997) **Height:** 80 stories, 1,283 feet

SHUN HING SQUARE, Shenzhen, China (1996) **Height:** 69 stories, 1,260 feet   *Scheduled to be completed in 2003.

World's Tallest When Built

The New York World Building, NY. Built 1890. Height: 309 feet. Torn down 1955.
• Home of the **New York World** newspaper, which started **The World Almanac** in 1868.

Metropolitan Life Insurance Tower, NY. Built 1909. Height: 700 feet.

Woolworth Building, NY. Built 1913. Height: 792 feet.

Chrysler Building, NY. Built 1930. Height: 1,046 feet.

Empire State Building, NY. Built 1931. Height: 1,250 feet.

World Trade Center Towers 1 & 2, NY. Built 1973. Height: 1,368 feet and 1,362 feet. Destroyed in September 2001.

Two Tall Facts

The world's **tallest free-standing structure** is the 1,815-foot **CN Tower** in Toronto, Canada. It is not exactly a *building* since it does not have stories. "Free-standing" means it supports its own weight and is not attached to anything. Brave visitors can walk across the glass floor at the 1,122-foot level!

The **tallest structure** is the **KVLY-TV tower** in Fargo, North Dakota. It's 2,063 feet tall (including the 113-foot antenna) and made of steel. The tower is anchored and supported by more than 7.5 miles of steel wires.

◀ *CN Tower*

A SHORT History of TALL Buildings

For over 4,000 years, the world's tallest structure was the 480-foot-tall Great Pyramid at Giza. Next to top the list was the cathedral spire in Cologne, Germany (513 ft., built in 1880), then the Washington Monument in Washington, D.C. (555 ft., 1884). These buildings all had thick stone walls, with not much space inside.

The biggest challenge to building tall was gravity. Whether made of mud, stone, brick, timber, or concrete, most buildings had load-bearing walls. This meant that the walls had to support their own weight, the roof, the floors, and everything in the building. The higher the walls, the thicker they needed to be, and too many windows would weaken the building.

By the 1880s, three **key factors in the evolution of tall buildings** were in place:

▶ A NEED FOR SPACE Crowded cities had less space for building, and land got expensive. To create more space, buildings had to go up instead of out.

▶ BETTER STEEL PRODUCTION Mass-producing steel made more of it available for construction. Long beams could be connected to make **columns**. These were braced with horizontal beams called **girders**. The columns and girders formed a strong three-dimensional grid called a **superstructure**. This type of building was lighter than a similar one made of stone or brick and its weight was directed down the columns, which were supported by a solid **foundation**.

▶ THE ELEVATOR Too many stairs! The first elevator, powered by steam, was installed in a New York store in 1857. Electric elevators came along in 1880.

The first American "skyscraper" was built in Chicago in 1885. Though it was only 10 stories and 138 feet tall, the **Home Insurance Building** ▶ was the first tall building to have a metal superstructure and many windows.

As buildings got taller, a new problem sprang up—**wind**. Too much movement could damage buildings or make the people inside uncomfortable. Some tall buildings, like New York's Citicorp Center, actually have a counter-weight near the top. A computer controls a 400-ton weight, moving it back and forth to lessen the building's sway.

In California and Japan, **earthquakes** are a big problem and special techniques are needed to make tall buildings safer from quakes.

Chicago ▶

Did You KNOW?

THE ORIGINAL PLANS were to tear down the Eiffel Tower (986 ft.) after 20 years! Built for the Paris World's Fair in 1889, it held the "world's tallest" title until 1930. Its iron superstructure, like a skyscraper without a covering, had many critics. But it proved so popular that it is still standing today.

It's Not All About... Tall!

When it comes to buildings, the tall ones grab people's attention. But many other buildings are interesting and fun to look at. Here are a few really cool buildings.

Burj al Arab Hotel, Dubai, United Arab Emirates

If you think the unusual design of this luxury hotel looks like a ship under full sail—you're right. British architect Tom Wills-Wright started with the idea of a dhow (an ancient Arab sailing vessel) and transformed it into this modern image. Built in 1999, the Burj al Arab (meaning "Tower of the Arabs") sits on an artificial island just off shore in the Persian Gulf.

La Grand Arche de la Défense, Paris, France

The missing middle makes this 360-foot-tall cube hard to forget. Finished in 1989, this government office building was designed as a modern version of the city's famous military memorial, L'Arc de Triomphe. You could fit another famous Paris landmark, the Cathedral of Notre Dame (198.5 ft.), underneath the arch!

The Guggenheim Museum, Bilbao, Spain

People from all over visit this building by the architect Frank O. Gehry—maybe as much to see the outside as for the art that's inside! Completed in 1997, it's made of steel, glass, and titanium, in a design that was inspired by fish and boats. This wild, curvy wonder is a good example of the power of imagination.

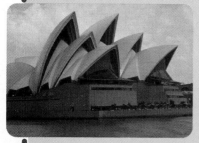

Sydney Opera House, Sydney, Australia

Though it looks like a giant sea creature rising out of Sydney Harbor, architect Joern Utzon had the sections of an orange in mind when he designed this building. Finished in 1973, the shells were made of over 2,000 concrete sections held together by 217 *miles* of steel cable. The roof cover—bolted on in 4,240 sections—is covered with 1.5 million ceramic tiles.

El Temple de La Sagrada Familia, Barcelona, Spain

Antonio Gaudí was another architect with no shortage of imagination—and the "Temple of the Holy Family" cathedral he designed proves it. Work began in 1883, and it is still in progress. This very detailed project has so many carvings and towers yet to be built, that it may be many years before it's ever finished!

Computers

C omputers perform tasks by using programs called **software**. **Programs** tell the computer what to do when the user enters certain information or commands. This is called **input**.

Where can you find the world's fastest computer? page 56

The computer then processes the information and gives the user the results **(output)**. The computer can also save, or store, the information.

The machines that make up a computer system are kinds of **hardware**. The largest and most powerful computers are called **mainframes**. Most people are more familiar with personal computers (PCs). These can be used at a desk **(desktops)**, carried around **(laptops)**, worn on your belt **(wearable computers)**, or even held in your hand **(palm computers)**.

SOFTWARE

KINDS OF SOFTWARE When you write on a computer you use a type of software called a word processing program. This program can be selected by using the **keyboard** or a **mouse**.

Other common types of software include programs for doing math, keeping records, playing games, and creating pictures.

ENTERING DATA In a word processing program, you can input your words by typing on the **keyboard**. The backspace and delete keys are like erasers. You can also press special **function keys** or click on certain symbols **(icons)** to center or underline words, move words around, check spelling, print out a page, and do other tasks.

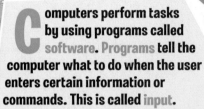

HARDWARE

INSIDE THE COMPUTER The instructions from the program you use are carried out inside the computer by the **central processing unit**, or **CPU**. The CPU is the computer's brain.

GETTING THE RESULTS The **monitor** and **printer** are the most commonly used output devices in a computer system. When you type a story, the words show up on a **monitor,** which is like a TV screen. Your story can be printed on paper by using a **printer**.

If you print out a story, you can mail it to a friend. But if you both have **modems**, it can get from your computer to your friend's computer. A **modem** allows information from a computer to travel over telephone or cable lines.

STORAGE KEEPING DATA TO USE IT LATER

A computer also stores information. You can save your work and return to it at your convenience. It is important to save often.

FLOPPY DISK

Information can be saved on a **"floppy" disk** that goes into a slot in the computer called a **disk drive**. If you use a disk to save your story, you can use the disk on another computer and your story will be there to work on. Disks today are usually stiff. Older computers used larger disks that were light and easy to bend, so people began calling them floppy disks.

ZIP DISK

Zip® disks hold much more information than floppy disks. They are used in special Zip drives. A **Jaz® disk** holds a gigabyte of information, 10 times as much as a Zip disk.

HARD DISK

Most computers have a **hard drive**. The hard drive contains a **hard disk** that is not removed. It holds much more information than zip or floppy disks. It stores your software and information you have entered into the computer.

CD-ROMs

Many computers have a CD-ROM drive. This allows you to play special disks called **CD-ROMs**, similar to music CDs. A CD-ROM can hold a huge amount of information, including pictures and sound. Almanacs, games, encyclopedias, and many other types of information and entertainment are on CD-ROMs. Newer computers can often write information to CDs ("burn CDs"), as well as read pre-recorded CDs.

DVDs

Digital Versatile Disks look like CD-ROMs, but hold about eight times more information on a single side. DVDs are currently used to store movies, encyclopedias, and other products with lots of data.

Monitor

CPU

Printer

Keyboard

CD-ROM

Modem

Zip Drive

Mouse

Floppy Disk

COMPUTER TALK

artificial intelligence or AI The ability of computers and robots to imitate human intelligence by learning and making decisions.

bit The smallest unit of data.

browser A program to help get around the Internet.

bug or glitch An error in a program or in the computer.

byte An amount of data equal to 8 bits.

chip A small piece of silicon holding the circuits used to store and process information.

cookie Some websites store information, like your passwords and other preferences, on your computer's hard drive. When you go back to that site later, your browser sends the information (the "cookie") to the website.

database A large collection of information organized so that it can be retrieved and used in different ways.

desktop publishing The use of computers to design and produce magazines, newspapers, and books.

download To transfer information from a host computer to a personal computer, often through a modem.

encryption The process of encoding (changing into a code) information, especially passwords, or financial or personal information, to prevent other people from reading it.

gig or gigabyte (GB) An amount of information equal to 1,024 megabytes.

hacker A computer expert who likes to look at the code of operating systems and other programs to see how they work. Some hackers tamper with other people's information and programs illegally.

html The abbreviation for HyperText Markup Language, a computer language used to make web pages.

Internet A worldwide system of linked computer networks.

K Stands for *kilo*, or "thousands," in Greek. Used to represent bytes of data or memory.

megabyte (MB) An amount of information equal to 1,048,516 bytes.

network A group of computers linked together so that they can share information.

portal A website that serves as a gateway to the Internet.

RAM or random access memory The memory your computer uses to open programs and store your work until you save it to the hard drive or a disk. The information in RAM disappears when the computer is turned off.

ROM or read only memory ROM contains permanent instructions for the computer and cannot be changed. The information in ROM remains after the computer is turned off.

spam Electronic junk mail.

thread A series of messages and replies that relate to a specific topic.

virus A program that damages other programs and data. It gets into a computer through telephone lines or shared disks.

SMILEYS

Smileys, or **emoticons**, are letters and symbols that look like faces when turned sideways. They tell things about yourself in messages you send. Here are a few with what they mean.

(:+(	Scared	:-o	Alarmed!	:-k	Biting lip
(:-(	Very sad or frowning	:-]	Shocked	:-o	Frightened; Uh-oh
(:-<	Frowning	:-----}	Liar; Pinocchio	<*:-)	Magician
(:-#	Wearing braces	:-[	Vampire	@>+-+--	Rose

Homework Help

RESEARCH ON THE INTERNET

The first step in doing any research is to decide on a topic. If you have a choice, pick a topic that's not too big so you can focus on it better. A report on "American Presidents" would be pretty tough. Better to pick just one—say, for example, President George Walker Bush.

Using Library Resources

Your school or public library is a great place to start. It probably has a list (catalog) of its books and periodicals (newspapers and magazines) available from computers at the library, or even from home over the Internet through your library's web site. You can search using **keywords** (words that describe your subject) in three basic ways: by **author**, by **title**, or by **subject**.

For example, doing a subject search for "George Walker Bush" will generate a list of books and articles about him, along with their locations in the library.

Your library may also subscribe to on-line reference databases that companies like The World Almanac create especially for reference. These are accessible over the Internet and could contain almanacs, encyclopedias, other reference books, or collections of articles. You can access these databases from the library, and maybe even from home from your library's web site.

When you write your report, don't copy directly from books, articles, or the Internet—that's **plagiarism**. Keep track of all your **sources**—the books, articles, and websites you use—and list them in a **bibliography**. (Ask your teacher how exactly to list them.)

Why shouldn't I just search the Internet?

The library's list may look just like other information available on the Internet. But these sources usually have been checked by experts. This is not true of all the information on the Internet. It's cool that almost anyone can put information on the Internet, but that also means that not all the information is trustworthy.

When can I use the Internet?

The Internet is still a great way to look things up. You can find addresses or recipes, listen to music, or find things to do. You can look up information on hobbies or musical instruments, or read a magazine or newspaper online.

Using a Search Engine

The best way to find web sites is to use a search engine. Here are some helpful ones:

Yahooligans (www.yahooligans.com)
Kidsclick (www.kidsclick.org)
Lycos Zone (lycoszone.lycos.com)
Ask Jeeves Kids (www.ajkids.com)

Start by typing one or two search terms—words that describe your topic. The search engine scans the Internet and gives you a list of sites that contain them. The results appear in a certain order, or **rank**. Search engines use different ways of measuring which web sites are likely to be the most helpful. One way is by counting how many times your search terms appear on each site. The site that's listed first may not have what you want. Explore as many of the sites as possible.

You might have to narrow your search by using more keywords. Or try using **directories** to help find what you need.

New GADGETS

Today's electronic devices not only do many different things; they are often small enough to hold in your hand or carry in your pocket. Here are some of the coolest gadgets around.

❶ CELL PHONE CAMERAS Now when you call your friends or family on your cell phone you can also show them how you look. You can already send and receive e-mail, play games, and surf the Internet on a cell phone. Now you can take and send pictures, too. Some models even record 10-15 seconds of video. Oh, yeah, and you can still make plain old phone calls!

❷ A REAL POCKET PC The Eightythree, by Tiqit Computers, may look like a PDA (personal digital assistant), but you can do much more with it than e-mail, surf the Web, or organize addresses. It's a real PC, just like the desktop models you may have at home or school. The Eightythree has a 300-MHz processor, 256 MB of RAM, and a 10 GB hard drive—and it's only 5.9 inches long, 4 inches wide, and 1.1 inches thick! You can type on its "thumb" keyboard or use a special pen to write on the screen.

❸ PEN TEXT SCANNER Also called Digi Pens, these don't have ink, but are great for taking notes from textbooks. Just roll the pen over the print, then download it to your computer. The information is saved and you've got notes. You do still have to *study* the notes.

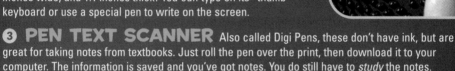

COMPUTER GAMES

Harry Potter and the Chamber of Secrets *Electronic Arts, for Windows*—Now, you can be Harry Potter, second-year student at Hogwarts. Will you be a Quidditch star, too? Not only will you interact with over 20 unforgettable characters from J.K. Rowling's magical world, you'll see things that weren't in the books or the movies.

Backyard Baseball 2003 *Atari, Inc., for Windows and Mac*—Can you put together a winning team? Choose your lineup from 30 real Major League players or 30 different "Backyard Kids." There are 12 different fields to play on. You can manage, have batting practice, or play a whole season and track all the players' stats.

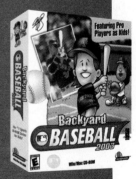

SpongeBob SquarePants Operation Krabby Patty *THQ, Inc., for Windows*—Head on down to Bikini Bottom! Cruise through "Boating School 101," where you drive your speedboat through a maze. Flip into "Invasion of the Patty Snatchers," where you are a fry cook, too. Take a wild guess what you do in "Hide N' Go Jellyfishing."

Ultimate Ride Coaster: Disney Edition *Disney Interactive for Windows*—Create your own Disney theme park. Choose from five kinds of track—hanging, flying, steel, wooden, or standing—to design the awesome coasters, complete with loop-de-loops, dips, and huge vertical drops. Build in Frontierland, Main Street, Toontown, or Tomorrowland.

DID YOU KNOW?

THE EARTH SIMULATOR is the world's fastest computer. Completed in 2002 by the Tokyo-based NEC Corp., this supercomputer studies the Earth's weather and geology. It performs 35.86 trillion calculations per second—that's more computations per second than there are stars in our galaxy. It's more than four and a half times faster than the next-fastest machine, and as fast as the top 5 U.S. supercomputers combined.

This machine, in Yokohama, Japan, is so huge it's housed in a building the size of an aircraft hangar. The building has almost 1,900 miles of computer cable roped together under its floors. That's enough to stretch from New York to Las Vegas! Thirty-five million cubic feet of air pass through the building every 10 seconds to keep the big machine from overheating.

Japanese scientists use the $350 million computer to create a "virtual Earth" that enables them to track global sea temperatures, rainfall, and movement of the Earth's crust and predict possible natural disasters and important climate and geological trends over the next few centuries. The Earth Simulator can already predict the likely path of a typhoon or a volcanic eruption. Earthquakes are still hard to predict, but maps of previous quakes and their damage are a big help in figuring out which buildings, dams, or bridges might need to be made stronger.

COMPUTER CROSSWORD

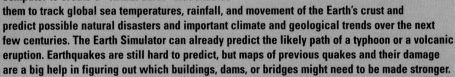

Across

1. Putting information in code so it can be secret.
4. An error in a program.
6. Information or commands given to a computer.
8. Permanent instructions for a computer.
10. Digi_____, for taking notes from textbooks.
11. Computer language used to make web pages.
12. Electronic junk mail.

Down

2. The brain of the computer.
3. A number of computers linked together.
4. A program to help you find your way around the Internet.
5. Equals 1,024 MB (megabytes).
6. Symbol on the screen you can click on to perform commands.
7. A website that acts as a gateway to the Internet.
9. A piece of silicon that stores information.

ANSWERS ON PAGES 314-317. FOR MORE PUZZLES GO TO
WWW.WORLDALMANACFORKIDS.COM

Dinosaurs

Who is Sue?
• •
page 59

Dinosaurs last roamed the Earth some 65 million years ago. So how do we know so much about them?

Fossils: Clues to Ancient Life

A fossil

PALEONTOLOGISTS are scientists who use fossils to study the past. **Fossils** are the remains of long-dead animals (like dinosaurs) or plants. Most fossils are formed from the hard parts of an animal's body, such as bones, shells, or teeth. Some fossils are **imprints**, like the outline of a leaf, or dinosaur footprints. Most fossils are found in **sedimentary rocks**, which form from the mud or sand (sediment) at the bottom of oceans, rivers, and lakes. Fossils have also been found in ice and tar. Insects that lived millions of years ago are sometimes found preserved in amber (hardened tree sap).

EARLY DISCOVERIES

▶ In 1824 British geologist William Buckland recognized some fossils as part of a giant extinct reptile. He named this first dinosaur **Megalosaurus,** from the Greek words *megalos* ("big") and *sauros* ("lizard").

▶ In 1842 Sir Richard Owen used the Greek words *deinos* ("terrible") and *sauros* to coin the term dinosaur.

▶ The partial skeleton of a **Hadrosaurus** was found in New Jersey in 1858. This was the first major dinosaur discovery in North America. The remains were made into a full dinosaur skeleton, the first ever displayed, at the Philadelphia Academy of Natural Sciences.

▶ Discovered in Germany in 1861, the **Archaeopteryx** is one of the most famous fossils in history. It had bones, teeth, and a skull like a dinosaur's. But it also had feathers and could fly.

RECENT FINDS

TOOTHY ROCKER **Masiakasaurus knopfleri** ("vicious lizard Knopfler") was the name given to this 6-foot meat eater in 2001. It had four rows of long teeth sticking almost straight out the front of its mouth—that's the "vicious lizard"part of the name. The other part comes from singer Mark Knopfler, from the music group Dire Straits. Fossil hunters said his music brought them luck.

GLIDING DINOSAUR In January 2003 scientists in China announced the discovery of **Microraptor gui** (named for Chinese paleontologist Gu Zhiwei), the first four-winged dinosaur ever found. This tiny relative of *T. rex* had a feather-covered body the size of a pigeon's, but was 30 inches long from head to tail. Scientists ithink it lived in trees.

▲ *Microraptor gui*

CELEBRITIES of th

APATOSAURUS

Deceptive lizard
Plant-eating
Length: 70+ feet
Period: Jurassic
Found in: Western U.S.

VELOCIRAPTOR

Speedy thief
Meat-eating
Length: 6 feet
Period: Cretaceous
Found in: Asia

HADROSAURUS

Big lizard
Plant-eating • Length: 30 feet
Period: Cretaceous
Found in: Asia, Europe, North and South America

WHEN DID DINOSAURS LIVE?

Dinosaurs roamed the Earth during the Mesozoic Era, which is divided into three periods:

TRIASSIC PERIOD, from 225 to 195 million years ago

► **Pangea**, Earth's one big continent, began to break up in this period.

► The earliest known mammals, such as the tiny, rat-like Morganucodon, began to appear.

► Evergreen plants were the most common vegetation.

► The earliest known dinosaur, **Eoraptor**, or "dawn thief," was a meat-eater only about 40 inches long. Herrersaurus, also a meat-eater, was about 10 feet long.

► Large marine reptiles, like long-necked **plesiosaurs** and dolphin-like **ichthyosaurs**, ruled the sea.

JURASSIC PERIOD, from 195 to 135 million years ago

► Flowering plants appeared.

► Plant-eating **sauropods**, like **Apatosaurus** and **Brachiosaurus**, were the biggest land creatures ever! These dinosaurs were eaten by meat-eaters like **Allosaurus** and **Megalosaurus**.

► **Archaeopteryx** was born—the earliest link between dinosaurs and birds.

► Flying reptiles called **pterosaurs**, close relatives of the dinosaur, dominated the sky.

CRETACEOUS PERIOD, from 135 to 65 million years ago

► The climate was warm, with no polar ice caps.

► Meat-eating **theropods** like **Tyrannosaurus Rex** and **Giganotosaurus** walked on two legs.

► All dinosaurs and other reptiles such as **ichthyosaurs** and **pterosaurs** became extinct by the end of this period. It may have been because a huge asteroid or comet hit the Earth. This would have filled the atmosphere with dust and debris, blocking most of the sun's light and heat. As a result many plants and animals would die out.

DINOSAUR WORLD

TYRANNOSAURUS REX ("T-REX")

King of the tyrant lizards
Meat-eating • **Length:** 40 feet
Period: Cretaceous
Found in: Western U.S., Canada, Asia

TRICERATOPS

Three-horned face • **Plant-eating**
Length: 30 feet • **Period:** Cretaceous
Found in: North America

STEGOSAURUS

Plated lizard • **Plant-eating**
• **Length:** 30 feet • **Period:** Jurassic
• **Found in:** North America

SOME GREAT DINOSAUR EXHIBITS

Academy of Natural Sciences (Philadelphia)—If you want to check out the largest predator ever discovered, this is the place. ▶
The oldest science institution in the U.S. has a new dinosaur hall, and *Giganotosaurus* is the star. Take an online tour at:
http://www.acnatsci.org/museum/dinohall

American Museum of Natural History (New York City)—This museum has the biggest collection of dinosaur fossils in the world, with more than 100 on display in its dinosaur hall. For more information, see: http://www.amnh.org/exhibitions/permanent/fossils

The Field Museum of Natural History (Chicago)—There are lots of reconstructed skeletons here, but the big attraction is "Sue" the *T. rex*. Named after Sue Hendrickson, who discovered her in South Dakota, "Sue" is the biggest, best preserved, and most complete *T. rex* skeleton ever found. She has more than 200 of her original bones. If you can't go see Sue in person, check out her online exhibit at: http://www.fieldmuseum.org/sue

National Museum of Natural History (Washington, D.C.)—The first thing you'll see is the 87-foot-long *Diplodocus longus*. Don't miss those fearsome two-legged predators, *Allosaurus*, and *T. rex*. You might also want to check out the working lab, to see how scientists study fossils. Go to http://www.nmnh.si.edu/paleo/dino for more information.

Energy

What are the three basic fossil fuels? page 62

The term energy comes from energeia, the Greek word for "work." Energy is defined as the capacity to do work.

Energy cannot be created or destroyed, but it can change form. Heat, light, and electricity are forms of energy. Other forms include **mechanical, chemical,** and **nuclear** energy. You can feel heat and see light, but most energy, like electricity, is invisible. We only see the result—like the lighting of a bulb.

All of the forms of energy we use come from the energy stored in natural resources. Sunlight, water, wind, petroleum, coal, and natural gas are natural resources. From these resources, we get heat, electricity, and mechanical power to run machines.

It STARTS WITH THE SUN

All of our energy traces its source to the Sun. Inside the Sun, hydrogen atoms join together and become helium. This process releases energy that radiates into space in the form of waves. These waves give us heat and light. Energy from the sun is stored in plants and animals that we eat. Long before humans existed, trees and other plants absorbed the Sun's energy. Animals ate plants and smaller animals. After the plants and animals died, they got buried deeper and deeper underground. After millions of years, they turned into coal and petroleum—fossil fuels.

Plants absorb energy from the Sun (solar energy) and convert it to chemical energy for storage.

Animals eat plants and gain the stored chemical energy.

Food gives the body energy.

People eat plants and meat.

Who Produces and Uses the MOST ENERGY?

The United States produces about 18% of the world's energy—more than any other country—and it also uses 25%. The table below on the left lists the world's top-ten energy-producers and the percent of the world's production that each nation was responsible for in 2000. The table on the right lists the world's top energy-users and the percent of the world's energy that each nation consumed.

TOP ENERGY PRODUCERS		TOP ENERGY CONSUMERS	
United States	18%	United States	25%
Russia	11%	China	9%
China	9%	Russia	7%
Saudi Arabia	5%	Japan	5%
Canada	5%	Germany	4%
Great Britain	3%	Canada	3%
Iran	3%	India	3%
Norway	3%	France	3%
India	2%	Great Britain	2%
Mexico	2%	Brazil	2%

WHERE DOES OUR ENERGY COME FROM?

In 2001, most of the energy used in the United States came from fossil fuels (39% from petroleum, 24% from natural gas, and 23% from coal). The rest came mostly from hydropower (water power), nuclear energy, and renewable resources such as geothermal, solar, and wind energy, and from burning materials such as wood and animal waste.

Petroleum 39.4%

Natural Gas 24.0%

Coal 22.6%

Nuclear power 8.3%

Hydro-power 2.5%

Other 3.4%

Homework Help

The different forms of energy fall into two main categories, and it helps to try and picture each one:

Kinetic Energy is the energy of objects in motion. Water in a river, electricity in a wire, and a sled going down a hill are good examples.

Potential energy is the energy of objects that are not moving—but could move. If you stretch a rubber band and hold it, it has potential energy. Let it go and its potential energy changes to kinetic energy with a snap! Natural gas, coal, and food are other examples of potential energy.

SOURCES OF ENERGY

FOSSIL FUELS

Fuels are called "fossil" because they were formed from ancient plants and animals. The three basic fossil fuels are **coal, oil,** and **natural gas.** Most of the energy we use today comes from these sources. **Coal** is mined, either at the surface or deep underground. Pumpjacks pump **oil,** or petroleum, from wells drilled in the ground. **Natural gas,** which is made up mostly of a gas called methane, also comes from wells. Natural gas is a clean-burning fuel, and it has been used more and more. Oil and coal bring a greater risk of air pollution.

All fossil fuels have one problem: they are gradually getting used up. There are special problems about oil, because industrial countries must often import lots of it and can become greatly dependent on other countries for their supply.

▼ *A pumpjack*

NUCLEAR ENERGY

A nuclear power plant

Nuclear power is created by releasing energy stored in the nucleus of an atom. This process is nuclear **fission,** which is also called "splitting" an atom. Fission takes place in a **reactor,** which allows the nuclear reaction to be controlled. Nuclear power plants release almost no air pollution. Many countries today use nuclear energy.

Nuclear power does cause some safety concerns. In 1979 a nuclear accident at Three Mile Island in Pennsylvania led to the release of some radiation. A much worse accident at Chernobyl in Ukraine in 1986 led to the deaths of thousands of people.

WATER POWER

Water power is energy that comes from the force of falling or fast-flowing water. It was put to use early in human history. **Water wheels,** turned by rivers or streams, were common in the Middle Ages. They were used for tasks like grinding grain and sawing lumber.

Today water power comes from waterfalls or from specially built dams. As water flows from a higher to a lower level, it runs a turbine—a device that turns an electric generator. This is called **hydroelectric power** (hydro = water). Today, over half of the world's hydroelectric power is produced in five countries: Brazil, Russia, Canada, China, and the United States.

Hoover Dam, on the Colorado River between Arizona and Nevada

A row of wind turbines

WIND ENERGY

People have used the wind's energy for a long time. **Windmills** were popular in Europe during the Middle Ages. Later, windmills became common on U.S. farms. Today, huge high-tech windmills with propeller-like blades are grouped together in **"wind farms."** Dozens of wind turbines are spaced well apart (so they don't block each other's wind). Even on big wind farms, the windmills usually take up less than 1% of the ground space. The rest of the land can still be used for farming or for grazing animals.

Wind power is a rapidly growing technology that doesn't pollute or get used up like fossil fuels. In 2002, there was four times as much electricity generated by wind as there had been in 1996. Unfortunately, the generators only work if the wind blows.

GEOTHERMAL ENERGY

Geothermal energy comes from the heat deep inside the Earth. About 30 miles below the surface is a layer called the **mantle.** This is the source of the gas and lava that erupts from volcanoes. Hot springs and geysers, with temperatures as high as 700 degrees, are also heated by the mantle. Because it's so hot, the mantle holds great promise as an energy source, especially in areas where the hot water is close to the surface. Iceland, which has many active volcanoes and hot springs, uses lots of geothermal energy. About 85% of homes there are heated this way.

BIOMASS ENERGY

Burning wood and straw (materials known as **biomass**) is probably the oldest way of producing energy. It's an old idea, but it still has value. Researchers are growing crops to use as fuel. Biomass fuels can be burned, like coal, in a power plant. They can also be used to make **ethanol,** which is similar to gasoline. Most ethanol comes from corn, which can make it expensive. But researchers are experimenting with other crops, like "switchgrass" and alfalfa.

Recently, a biomass power plant was opened in Burlington, Vermont. It turns wood chips, solid waste, and switchgrass into a substance similar to natural gas.

SOLAR POWER

Energy directly from sunlight is a promising new technology. Vast amounts of this energy fall upon the Earth every day—and it is not running out. Energy from the sun is expected to run for some 5 billion years. Solar energy is also friendly to the environment. One drawback is space. To get enough light, the surfaces that gather solar energy need to be spread out a lot. Also, the energy can't be gathered when the sun isn't shining.

A solar cell is usually made of silicon, a **semiconductor.** That means it can change sunlight into electricity. The cost of solar cells has been dropping in recent years. Large plants using solar-cell systems have been built in several countries, including Japan, Saudi Arabia, the United States, and Germany.

◄ *A solar power plant*

63

All About... SOLAR CARS

Solar cars don't have gas tanks. Instead, they have panels of solar cells—small wafer-like units that change light into electrical energy. They won't replace gas-powered cars anytime soon, but designing and testing them is a good way to develop the technology for this renewable resource. The big challenge is to design a battery that can store enough energy to keep the car running when the sun isn't shining. Engineers test their latest designs by racing them. There are two major competitions:

The World Solar Challenge in Australia runs 1,800 miles, from Darwin to Adelaide. First held in 1987, it is the oldest solar race. In 2001, a Dutch team won, setting a record of 32 hours, 39 minutes, with an average speed of 57 miles per hour—all without a single gallon of gas.

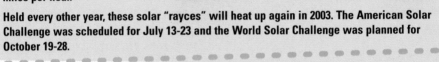

The 2,300-mile American Solar Challenge, which follows historic Route 66 (see page 233) from Chicago to Southern California, is the longest race. In 2001, the University of Michigan's M-Pulse (seen here), which finished third in Australia, won the American race, averaging 40 miles per hour.

Held every other year, these solar "rayces" will heat up again in 2003. The American Solar Challenge was scheduled for July 13-23 and the World Solar Challenge was planned for October 19-28.

POWER MATCHUP

Can you match these items with the form of energy that runs them? You should be able to find at least one item for each energy source listed. If you're really good, you'll find things that can run on more than one form of energy.

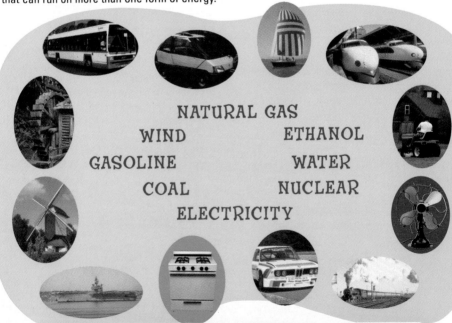

NATURAL GAS
WIND   ETHANOL
GASOLINE   WATER
COAL   NUCLEAR
ELECTRICITY

Environment

What is an "alien species"?
•••
page 68

SHARING THE EARTH

We share the planet with trees, flowers, insects, fish, whales, dogs, and many other plants and animals. Each species (type) of animal or plant has its place on Earth, and each one is dependent on many others. Plants give off oxygen that animals need to breathe. Animals pollinate plants and spread their seeds. Animals eat plants and are in turn eaten by larger animals. When plants and animals die, they become part of the soil in which new plants take root and grow.

PEOPLE AND THE ENVIRONMENT

In prehistoric times, people killed animals for food and built fires to cook food and keep themselves warm. They cut down trees for fuel, and their fires released pollution into the air. But there were so few people that their activities had little impact on the environment.

In modern times, the world's population has been growing very fast. In 1850 there were around a billion people in the world. By 2003 there were about 6.3 billion. By 2050, according to United Nations estimates, there will be 8.9 billion. Their activities have a big impact on the environment.

People are becoming more aware that human activities can seriously damage the planet and the animals and plants on it. Sometimes this damage can be reversed or slowed down. But it is often permanent. On the following pages you'll learn about the damage, and about some things that can be done to help clean up and protect our planet.

Did You Know?

Every April 22, the world celebrates Earth Day to help make people aware of environment problems and ways they can help. One way for kids to help is the **Earth Day Groceries Project**, a cool Internet project your school or class can do. It's easy. Have your teacher borrow paper bags from a local grocery store. Each kid decorates a bag with pictures and messages about helping the environment. Then the bags go back to the store, where they will be used for shoppers' groceries on Earth Day.

WEB SITE For more information, go to http://www.earthdaybags.org

You can learn more about the environment at:
WEB SITE http://www.nwf.org/kids

HOME SWEET BIOME

A "biome" is a large natural area that is the home to a certain type of plant. The animals, climate, soil, and even the amount of water in the region also help distinguish a biome. There are more than 30 kinds of biomes in the world. But the following types cover most of Earth's surface.

FORESTS

Forests cover about one-third of Earth's land surface. Pines, hemlocks, firs, and spruces grow in the cool **evergreen** forests farthest from the equator. These trees are called **conifers** because they produce cones.

Temperate forests have warm, rainy summers and cold, snowy winters. Here **deciduous trees** (which lose their leaves in the fall and grow new ones in the spring) join the evergreens. Temperate forests are home to maple, oak, beech, and poplar trees, and to wildflowers and shrubs. These forests are found in eastern United States, southeastern Canada, northern Europe and Asia, and southern Australia.

Still closer to the equator are the **tropical rain forests,** home to the greatest variety of plants on Earth. About 60 to 100 inches of rain fall each year. Tropical trees stay green all year. They grow close together, shading the ground. There are several layers of trees. The top, **emergent layer** has trees that can reach 200 feet in height. The **canopy,** which gets lots of sun, comes next, followed by the **understory.** The **forest floor,** covered with roots, gets little sun. Many plants cannot grow there.

Tropical rain forests are found mainly in Central America, South America, Asia, and Africa. They once covered more than 8 million square miles. Today, because of destruction by humans, fewer than 3.4 million square miles remain. More than half the plant and animal species in the world live there. Foods such as bananas and pineapples first grew there. Woods such as mahogany and teak also come from rain forests. Many kinds of plants there are used to make medicines.

When rain forests are burned, carbon dioxide is released into the air. This adds to the **greenhouse effect** (see page 73). As forests are destroyed, the precious soil is easily washed away by the heavy rains.

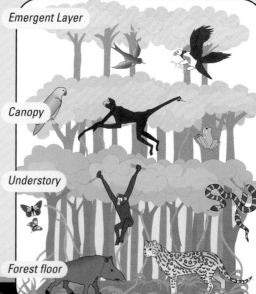

Emergent Layer

Canopy

Understory

Forest floor

A rain forest

TUNDRA AND ALPINE REGION

In the northernmost regions of North America, Europe, and Asia surrounding the Arctic Ocean are plains called the **tundra.** The temperature rarely rises above 45 degrees Fahrenheit, and it is too cold for trees to grow there. Most tundra plants are mosses and lichens that hug the ground for warmth. A few wildflowers and small shrubs also grow where the soil thaws for about two months of the year. This kind of climate and plant life also exists in the **alpine** region, on top of the world's highest mountains (such as the Himalayas, Alps, Andes, and Rockies), where small flowers also grow.

WHAT IS THE TREE LINE? On mountains in the north (such as the Rockies) and in the far south (such as the Andes), there is an altitude above which trees will not grow. This is the **tree line** or **timberline.** Above the tree line, you can see low shrubs and small plants.

DESERTS

The driest areas of the world are the **deserts.** They can be hot or cold, but they also contain an amazing number of plants. Cactuses and sagebrush are native to dry regions of North and South America. The deserts of Africa and Asia contain plants called euporbias. Dates have grown in the deserts of the Middle East and North Africa for thousands of years. In the southwestern United States and northern Mexico, there are many types of cactuses, including prickly pear, barrel, and saguaro.

▲ *Arizona desert*

GRASSLANDS

▲ *Grassland in Alberta, Canada*

Areas that are too dry to have green forests, but not dry enough to be deserts, are called **grasslands.** The most common plants found there are grasses. Cooler grasslands are found in the Great Plains of the United States and Canada, in the steppes of Europe and Asia, and in the pampas of Argentina. The drier grasslands are used for grazing cattle and sheep. In the **prairies,** where there is a little more rain, wheat, rye, oats, and barley are grown. The warmer grasslands, called **savannas,** are found in central and ssouthern Africa, Venezuela, southern Brazil, and Australia. Most savannas have moist summers and cool, dry winters.

OCEANS

▶ *Coral reef*

Covering two-thirds of the earth, the **ocean** is by far the largest biome. Within the ocean are smaller biomes that include **coastal areas, tidal zones,** and **coral reefs.** Found in relatively shallow warm waters, the reefs are called the "rainforests of the ocean." Australia's Great Barrier Reef is the largest in the world. It is home to thousands of species of plant and animal life.

WHAT IS BIODIVERSITY?

Our planet, Earth, is shared by millions of species of living things. The wide variety of life on Earth, as shown by the many species, is called "biodiversity" (bio means "life" and diversity means "variety"). Human beings of all colors, races, and nationalities make up just one species, *Homo sapiens* .

SPECIES, SPECIES EVERYWHERE

Here is just a sampling of how diverse life on Earth is. The numbers are only estimates, and more species are being discovered all the time!

MAMMALS (9,000 species)
  rodents: 1,700 species
  bats: 1,000 species

BIRDS (9,000 species)
  perching birds: 5,200-5,500 species
  penguins: 17 species
  ostrich: 1 species

REPTILES (8,000 species)
  snakes: 2,900 species
  lizards: 4,500 species

AMPHIBIANS (5,000 species)
  frogs & toads: 4,500 species
  newts & salamanders: 470 species

FISH (24,500 species)
  bony fish: 23,000 species
  skates & rays: 450 species
  sharks: 350 species

ARTHROPODS (1.1 million species)
  crustaceans: 44,000 species
  insects: 750,000 species
  spiders: 35,000 species

PLANTS (260,000 species)
  flowering plants: 250,000 species
  evergreens: 550 species

Fascinating Facts

—Bats are the only mammals that can fly—not just glide.
—There are 30,000 species of edible plants, but just 20 of those provide 90% of the world's food.
—One out of every 3 insects in the world is a beetle.
—The ostrich is the world's biggest bird, reaching a height of 9 feet and weighing over 300 pounds.
—All species of penguins live in the southern hemisphere.
—There are two mammals that lay eggs, Australia's platypus and the Echidna, found in both Australia and New Guinea. All other mammals bear live young.

Some Threats to Biodiversity

When a species becomes extinct, it reduces the variety of life on Earth. But humans have been able to save some endangered animals and are working to save more. Factors that can help make a species endangered are: **pollution** of the air, water, and land; **habitat destruction,** like the clearing of rain forests for wood, farmland, and cattle ranges; and **over-harvesting** of animals, especially fish. **Alien species** are also a problem. These are plants or animals that have been moved by humans into areas where they are not naturally found. They may have no natural enemies. They can push out existing species and become a nuisance. Red fire ants and Africanized bees are alien species in the U.S.

Wildlife Biologist

What is it like to spend your days watching and learning about animals in the wild? *The World Almanac for Kids* asked Sharon Fuller. She is part of a team of researchers sponsored by the Wildlife Research Institute who study eagles and other birds of prey—raptors—in Montana. Sharon, 26, has a bachelor of science degree in wildlife biology.

Q: What exactly are you trying to find out? We're trying to learn about the migration habits of golden eagles and other raptors. Some of these birds spend spring and summer in Northern Alaska, then go as far south as Mexico in winter to find better hunting. We want to learn the routes they take and how they disperse. The golden eagles face a number of dangers—electrocution from power lines, poisoning—and their population is declining; we're studying these "mortality factors."

Q: Do you do anything besides watch them? We use a lure to draw the eagles in. If they go for the lure, a 7-foot bow net springs open and traps them. We put hoods on the birds to calm them and Velcro their legs together, to protect us from the talons. We weigh the birds and measure them and put on vinyl wing markers so they can be recognized. Then we release them.

Q: Have you worked with other animals? Yes. I've worked with numerous songbird species, spotted owls, bats, small mammals such as chipmunks, as well as reptiles and amphibians.

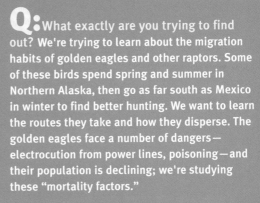

Q: Did you have pets growing up? Oh yes. I had lizards, guinea pigs, rabbits, a turtle, hermit crabs, and cats.

Q: Do you have any advice for kids who might be interested in this kind of work? Get involved with your local Audubon Society chapter. Also, you may find a local animal study project you can volunteer time for.

WHERE GARBAGE GOES

Most of the things around you will be thrown away someday. Skates, clothes, the toaster, furniture—they can break or wear out, or you may get tired of them. Where will they go when they are thrown out? What kinds of waste will they create?

LOOK AT WHAT iS NOW iN U.S. LANDFILLS

Metal
8%

Plastic
24%

Food and
Yard Waste
11%

Rubber
and Leather
6%

Other
Trash
21%

Paper
30%

What Happens to Things We Throw Away?

LANDFILLS
Most of our trash goes to places called landfills. A **landfill** (or dump) is a low area of land that is filled with garbage. Most modern landfills are lined with a layer of plastic or clay to try to keep dangerous liquids from seeping into the soil and ground water supply.

THE PROBLEM WITH LANDFILLS
More than half of the states in this country are running out of places to dump their garbage. Because of the unhealthful materials many contain, landfills do not make good neighbors, and people don't want to live near them. Many landfills are located in poor neighborhoods. But where can cities dispose of their waste? How can hazardous waste — material that can poison air, land, and water — be disposed of in a safe way?

INCINERATORS
One way to get rid of trash is to burn it. Trash is burned in a furnace-like device called an **incinerator.** Because incinerators can get rid of almost all of the bulk of the trash, some communities would rather use incinerators than landfills.

THE PROBLEM WITH INCINERATORS
Leftover ash and smoke from burning trash may contain harmful chemicals, called **pollutants**, and make it hard for some people to breathe. They can harm plants, animals, and people.

Did You KNOW?

A growing problem for the U.S. is "e-trash," short for electronic trash. It's just what you might think—old or broken computers, video games, radios, TVs, cell phones, and other stuff. More than 4.6 million tons of these products went into U.S. landfills in 2000. Over 90% of this trash ends up in landfills because it is hard or dangerous to recycle. Many people are worried that toxic substances like lead, cadmium, and mercury that are used in these items will get into the soil, water, and air.

REDUCE, REUSE, RECYCLE

You can help reduce waste by reusing containers, batteries, and paper. You can also recycle newspaper, glass, and plastics to provide materials for making other products. Below are some of the things you can do.

	TO REDUCE WASTE	TO RECYCLE
PAPER	Use both sides of the paper. Use cloth towels instead of paper towels.	Recycle newspapers, magazines, comic books, and junk mail.
PLASTIC	Wash food containers and store leftovers in them. Reuse plastic bags.	Return soda bottles to the store. Recycle other plastics.
GLASS	Keep bottles and jars to store other things.	Recycle glass bottles and jars.
CLOTHES	Give clothes to younger relatives or friends. Donate clothes to thrift shops.	Cut unwearable clothing into rags to use instead of paper towels.
METAL	Keep leftovers in storage containers instead of wrapping them in foil. Use glass or stainless steel pans instead of disposable pans.	Recycle aluminum cans and foil trays. Return wire hangers to the dry cleaner.
FOOD/ YARD WASTE	Cut the amount of food you throw out. Try saving leftovers for snacks or meals later on.	Make a compost heap using food scraps, leaves, grass clippings, and the like.
BATTERIES	Use rechargeable batteries for toys and games, radios, tape players, and flashlights.	Find out about your town's rules for recycling or disposing of batteries.

What is made from RECYCLED MATERIALS?

► *From* **RECYCLED PAPER** we get newspapers, cereal boxes, wrapping paper, cardboard containers, and insulation.

► *From* **RECYCLED PLASTIC** we get soda bottles, tables, benches, bicycle racks, cameras, backpacks, carpeting, shoes, and clothes.

► *From* **RECYCLED STEEL** we get steel cans, cars, bicycles, nails, and refrigerators.

► *From* **RECYCLED GLASS** we get glass jars and tiles.

► *From* **RECYCLED RUBBER** we get bulletin boards, floor tiles, playground equipment, and speed bumps.

The air surrounding the Earth is made up of different gases: about 78% nitrogen, 21% oxygen, and 1% carbon dioxide, water vapor, and other gases. All human beings and animals need air to survive. Plants also need air. Plants use sunlight and the carbon dioxide in air to make food, and then give off oxygen.

Humans breathe more than 3,000 gallons of air a day. Because air is so basic to life, it is important to keep it clean. Air pollution causes health problems and may bring about acid rain, smog, global warming, and a breakdown of the ozone layer.

What is Acid Rain?

Acid rain is a kind of air pollution caused by chemicals in the air. Eventually these can make rain, snow, or fog more acidic than normal. The main sources of these chemicals are exhaust from cars, trucks, and buses, waste incinerators, factories, and some electric power plants, especially those that burn fossil fuels, such as coal. When these chemicals mix with moisture and other particles, they create sulfuric acid and nitric acid. The wind often carries these acids many miles before they fall to the ground in rain, snow, and fog, or even as dry particles.

Acid rain can harm people, animals, and plants. It is especially harmful to lakes. Thousands of lakes in Canada, Finland, Norway, and Sweden have been declared "dead." Not even algae can live in them. Birds and other species that depend on the lakes for food are also affected. Acid rain can also affect crops and trees. Buildings, statues, and cars can be damaged as it eats away metal, stone, and paint.

What is Smog?

The brownish haze seen mostly in the summer and especially around big cities is **smog**. The main ingredient in smog is ozone. When ozone is high up in the atmosphere, it helps protect us from the Sun's stronger rays. But near the ground, ozone forms smog when sunlight and heat interact with oxygen and particles produced by the burning of fossil fuels. Smog makes it hard for some people to breathe, especially those with asthma. "Ozone Alerts" are not just for Los Angeles (famous for its smog). Many cities in the U.S. issue them through newspapers, TV, and radio stations to let people know when the air can be unhealthy for outdoor activities. For more information visit http://www.epa.gov/airnow/aqikids

What is the Ozone Layer?

Our atmosphere is made up of different layers. One layer, between 6 and 30 miles above the Earth, is made up of ozone gas. This **ozone layer** protects us from the Sun's harshest rays, called **ultraviolet** or UV **rays**. These rays can cause sunburn and skin cancer.

When refrigerators, air conditioners, and similar items are thrown away, gases from them (called **chlorofluorocarbons**, or CFCs) rise into the air and destroy some of the ozone in this layer. Most countries no longer produce CFCs, but the gas can stay in the atmosphere for years—destroying ozone and adding to the greenhouse effect.

Each August, a **hole in the ozone layer** forms over Antarctica (it usually closes by December). Since it was discovered in the 1980s, it has doubled to about the size of North America. It sometimes extends over southern Chile and Argentina. On some days, people in Punta Arenas, Chile (the world's southernmost city), may limit their sun exposure to no more than 20 minutes between noon and 3 P.M. Other days, they don't go out at all!

BREATHE

What is Global Warming? The average surface temperature on Earth was 58°F in 2000. That's about 1°F higher than it was 100 years ago. Since accurate record-keeping began in 1880, the hottest year in history was 1998. The second hottest year was 2002, and the third was 2001. The nine hottest years have all been since 1990. This gradual rise is called **global warming**. On that much, scientists agree. Where they can't agree is on the cause. Some think it is part of a natural cycle of warming and cooling. But most scientists believe that increased gases in the air play a big role.

The **greenhouse effect** is a natural process, needed for life to exist on Earth. Certain gases in the atmosphere act like the glass walls of a greenhouse: they let the rays of the Sun pass through to the Earth's surface but hold in some of the heat that radiates from the Sun-warmed Earth. These naturally occurring greenhouse gases are water vapor, carbon dioxide, methane, nitrous oxide, and ozone. Without these gases, Earth's average temperature would be 60°F colder and we couldn't live here.

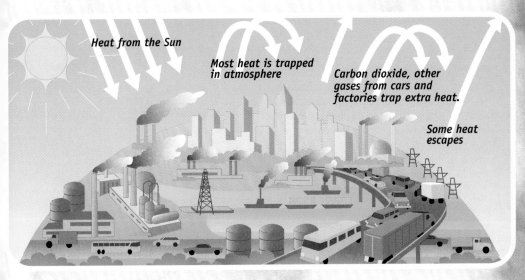

Heat from the Sun

Most heat is trapped in atmosphere

Carbon dioxide, other gases from cars and factories trap extra heat.

Some heat escapes

Human activity is putting more of these gases into the air. As cities have grown in size and population, people have needed more and more electricity, cars, and manufactured things of all kinds. As industries have grown, more greenhouse gases have been produced by the burning of fossil fuels such as oil, coal, and natural gas. The increases in these gases make greenhouse "glass" thicker, causing more heat to be trapped than in the past.

It doesn't seem like much, but a slight warming could cause changes in the climate of many regions. If the climate changed enough, the plants and animals that normally live there could no longer survive. Many scientists think average temperatures could rise as much as 6°F over the next 100 years. This warming could cause a lot of ice near the North and South Poles to melt, making more water go into the oceans. Many areas along the coasts would be flooded.

WATER, WATER EVERYWHERE

Earth is the water planet. More than two-thirds of its surface is covered with water, and every living thing on it needs water to live. Water is not only part of our life (cooking, cleaning, bathing), it's about 75% of our brains and 60% of our whole bodies! Humans can survive for about a month without food, but only for about a week without water. People also use water to cool machines in factories, to produce power, and to irrigate farmland.

HOW MUCH IS THERE TO DRINK? Seawater makes up 97% of the world's water. Another 2% of the water is frozen in ice caps, icebergs, glaciers, and sea ice. Half of the 1% left is too far underground to be reached. That leaves only 0.5% of freshwater for all the people, plants, and animals on Earth. This supply is renewable only by rainfall.

WHERE DOES DRINKING WATER COME FROM? Most smaller cities and towns get their freshwater from groundwater—melted snow and rain that seeps deep into the ground and is drawn out from wells. Larger cities usually rely on lakes or reservoirs for their water. Some areas of the world with little fresh water are turning to a process called desalinization (removing salt from seawater) as a solution. But this process is slow and expensive.

THE HYDROLOGICAL CYCLE: WATER'S ENDLESS JOURNEY
Water is special. It's the only thing on Earth that exists naturally in all three physical states: solid (ice), liquid, and gas (water vapor). It never boils naturally (except around volcanoes), but it evaporates (turns into a gas) easily into the air. These unique properties send water on a **cycle** of repeating events.

clouds
rain
evaporation
snow
ocean

HOW DOES WATER GET INTO THE AIR? Sunlight causes surface water in oceans, lakes, swamps, and rivers to turn into water vapor. This is called **evaporation**. Plant photosynthesis releases water vapor into the air. Animals also release a little bit when they breathe. This is **transpiration**.

HOW DOES WATER COME OUT OF THE AIR? Warm air holds more water vapor than cold air. As the air rises into the atmosphere, it cools and the water vapor **condenses**—changes back into a tiny water droplets. These form clouds. As the drops get bigger, gravity pulls them down as **precipitation** (rain, snow, sleet, fog, and dew are all types of precipitation).

WHERE DOES THE WATER GO? Depending on where the precipitation lands, it can:
1. evaporate back into the atmosphere; **2.** run off into streams and rivers; **3.** be absorbed by plants; **4.** soak down into the soil as ground water; **5.** fall as snow on a glacier and be trapped as ice for thousands of years.

WHY WE NEED WETLANDS

Wetlands are—you guessed it—**wet lands**. They are wet (covered with water, or with water at or near the surface) at least part of every year. Bogs, swamps, and marshes are all kinds of wetlands.

Wetlands have at least three important functions:

▶ **storing water.** They absorb water like giant sponges and hold it in, releasing it slowly. During floods an acre of wetland can hold in 1.5 million gallons of water.

▶ **cleaning up water.** They slow water flow down and let harmful sediments drop to the bottom. Plant roots and tiny organisms remove human and animal waste.

▶ **providing habitats.** They are home to huge numbers of plants, fish, and wildlife. More than one-third of all threatened and endangered species in the U.S. live only in wetlands.

There are about 100 million acres of wetlands left in the lower 48 states, less than half of what there were in 1600. Wetlands are lost when people drain and fill them in for farmland, dam them up to form ponds and lakes, or pave and build up surrounding areas.

◀ *Wetlands, Everglades National Park*

WATER WOES

Pollution Polluted water can't be used for drinking, swimming, watering crops, or provide a habitat for plants and animals. Major sources of water pollutants are sewage, chemicals from factories, fertilizers and weed killers, and landfills that leak. In general, anything that anyone dumps on the ground finds its way into the water cycle. The United Nations declared 2003 as the **"Year of Freshwater"** to remind people how important it is to protect precious freshwater.

Overuse Using water faster than nature can pass it through the hydrological cycle can create other problems. When more water is taken out of lakes and reservoirs (for drinking, bathing, and other uses) than is put back in, the water levels begin to drop. Combined with lower than normal rainfall, this can be devastating. In some cases, lakes become salty or dry up completely.

THE DREADED DRIPPING FAUCET: Just one faucet, dripping very slowly (once a minute), can waste 38 gallons a year. Multiply that by several million houses and apartments, and you see a lot of water going down the drain!

Games & Toys

What happens in Wildwood, New Jersey, every June?
•••
page 78

BOARD GAMES

Most board games are part luck and part skill. Have you tried the ones below?

MONOPOLY® is a real estate trading game for two or more players, who move their pieces around by the throw of the dice. The object is to get "rich" and force your opponents into bankruptcy. You do it by trading or buying properties, building houses or hotels on them, and hoping your opponents will land on them and have to pay big rents. Landing on a hotel on Boardwalk costs $2,000.

Monopoly was first sold by Parker Brothers in the 1930s. Charles P. Darrow is known as its inventor, but he actually got the idea from two earlier games, the Landlord Game, invented in 1904 by Elizabeth Magie Phillips, and a game about Atlantic City created by Charles Todd.

DID YOU KNOW? *The game Monopoly is produced in 26 languages, including Arabic, Croatian, Czech, Icelandic, Italian, Portuguese, and Russian. Boardwalk and Park Place are known in England as Mayfair and Park Lane, in France as Rue de la Paix and Champs Elysees, and in Germany as Schlossallee and Parkstrasse.*

SCRABBLE is a crossword game in which two, three, or four players use letter tiles to form words on a board. Each letter has a point value depending on how commonly it is used. And certain squares on the board give double or triple the points for a letter or whole word. A good vocabulary is important, and it also helps to be a good speller.

Alfred M. Butts, an unemployed architect, tried unsuccessfully in the 1930s to market his game first as "Lexiko," then "It," then "Criss-Cross Words." In 1947, he and a friend made some changes to the game and renamed it "Scrabble." The rest is H-I-S-T-O-R-Y!

DID YOU KNOW? *Since 1991, the School Scrabble Program has been hosting state and regional tournaments for kids in grades 5-8. The program's first national tournament was held in Boston in April 2003.*

BACKGAMMON is a game for two players. Each has 15 pieces to move around the board. There are four sections of triangles or points. The first player to move all the pieces off the board is the winner. There is skill in deciding which pieces to move, but the luck of the dice decides how far they can go.

Backgammon was played in ancient Egypt, Greece, and Rome. It is thought to be one of the oldest games, possibly first played in Sumeria (now southern Iraq) as early as 3000 B.C.

DID YOU KNOW? *Modern dice, with opposite sides that add to seven, are the same design as the "tesserae" the Romans carved out of bone, ivory, and wood.*

A TIME-LINE OF VIDEO GAMES

1961—*Spacewar!*, played on an early microcomputer, is the first fully interactive video game.

1974—Atari's *Pong*, one of the first home video games, has "paddles" to hit a white dot back and forth on-screen.

1980—*Pac-Man*, *Space Invaders*, and *Asteroids* (first to let high scorers enter initials) invade arcades.

1985—Russian programmer Alex Pajitnov develops *Tetris* for play on a PC.

1986—Nintendo Entertainment System comes to the U.S. *Super Mario Bros.* is a huge hit!

1987—*Legend of Zelda* game released.

1989—Nintendo's hand-held video game system, Game Boy, debuts. *Adventures of Link* game released.

1990—The Sega Genesis system comes out.

1991—Sega's *Sonic the Hedgehog* makes his debut.

1996—Nintendo 64 is released.

1998—Game Boy Color and *Pokémon* hit the U.S.

2000—Sony's Playstation 2 arrives.

2001—Microsoft's XBOX and Nintendo's GameCube hit the shelves. *Luigi's Mansion* and *Super Smash Bros. Melee* make a big splash.

For more information about computer games, see page 55.

Homework Help: LUCKY 7: UNDERSTANDING PROBABILITY

Probability can be a fun subject, and it may be a little more fun and easier to learn about if you think of it in terms of the dice you use to play games with.

A single die has six different faces, numbered **1** though **6**. Each has an equal chance of coming up. So the chance, or **probability**, of rolling any one of the numbers with one die is one in six. We write this as a ratio or fraction: 1/6.

There were six possible **outcomes**, and of these, one was "favorable"—that is, was the one you wanted or were talking about.

What if you roll two dice? There are 36 possible outcomes, because each die can come out one of six ways; 6 x 6 = 36. The lowest possible outcome would be 2 (a **1** on each die). The highest possible outcome would be 12 (a **6** on each die).

With two dice, some totals are more likely to come up than others because there are more possible outcomes that add up to those totals. Pretend that the dice are red and blue. The the only way to roll a total of 2 ("snake eyes") is for the red die to come up as a **1** and the blue die to come up as a **1**. So the probability of shaking 2 is 1 in 36 (1/36). But there are two ways to shake a 3. The red die could have a **1** and the blue die could have a **2**, or the red die could be a **2** and the blue die could be a **1**. So the probability shaking a 3 is 2 in 36 (2/36, which equals 1/18).

The table below shows the chances of shaking each total with the two dice.

2	*1 in 36*
3	*2 in 36*
4	*3 in 36*
5	*4 in 36*
6	*5 in 36*
7	*6 in 36*
8	*5 in 36*
9	*4 in 36*
10	*3 in 36*
11	*2 in 36*
12	*1 in 36*

The total that has the most possible outcomes is 7. The red die can be any of the numbers from **1** to **6**, and the blue die can be the number that makes seven when added to the number on the red die (**1** and **6**, **2** and **5**, **3** and **4**, **4** and **3**, **5** and **2**, **6** and **1**). Since there are six possible combinations to total 7, the chances of rolling a 7 are 6 in 36 (6/36, which equals 1/6, or one out of six).

Playground games, also called street or sidewalk games, have been around as long as people have. Games like jump rope, tag, and hide and seek are so old that nobody knows when they were first played. Evidence of some games played far in the past, like hopscotch, jacks, and marbles, has been discovered by archaeologists (scientists who study ancient human life). Other playground games like stickball, kickball, and street hockey are offshoots of organized sports like baseball and ice hockey.

Even the most basic games have many different versions and many names—more than we could list here. Rules can be different from country to country, city to city, and even from one neighborhood to the next. And two bored kids can always add new rules to an old game, or invent a new one on the spot!

Here are three of the oldest and most widely played playground games. They've been around for thousands of years, and are still going strong.

HOPSCOTCH

Hopscotch has been around at least since Roman times and may have been spread throughout the Empire by soldiers. The game is played on squares (usually 8 in the U.S.) or circles drawn with chalk or scratched in dirt, with a marker (a rock works well). Players hop through the game on one leg—sometimes two—until the course is completed. The rules and diagrams for hopscotch are different around the world. It's also known as "rayuela" (Argentina), "marelles" (France), "Templehupfen" (Germany), "ekaria dukaria" (India), "hinkelbaan" (The Netherlands), and "pico" (Vietnam).

DID YOU KNOW? *The "scotch" in hopscotch has nothing to do with Scotland. It comes from the Middle English word* scocchen *(to cut), and refers to the diagram cut or scratched in the dirt.*

MARBLES

Baked clay marbles dating back to 3000 B.C. have been found in prehistoric caves. Roman and Egyptian marbles were made of bone, clay, stone, polished nuts, and—of course—marble. The first mass-produced toys in the U.S. were clay marbles made in 1884. This made them cheap enough for many children to afford them—a penny a handful. In 1902, a machine that made glass marbles was patented, and soon factories were making millions of the marbles we know today. There are many ways to play marbles, but the basic goal is usually to knock marbles out of a circle using a larger marble called a "taw" that a player flicks with the thumb.

DID YOU KNOW? *The National Marbles Tournament is held every June in Wildwood, New Jersey, for kids age 15 and younger. Check out http://www.nationalmarblestournament.org for more information.*

JACKS

As played in the U.S., the game of jacks involves tossing a ball, picking up a number of six-pointed "jacks," then catching the ball (either before or after it bounces)—all with the same hand. Also called jackstones, the game is believed to have come from Asia, where the knuckle bones of sheep or other animals were used. Ancient Greeks played knuckle bones, and so did the Romans. Kids around the world often use stones (beans, or any other small objects, will also work). The metal (later plastic) six-pointed jacks have been made since the beginning of the 19th century. There are many variations of the game of jacks, with names like "Eggs in Basket," "Toad in the Hole," and "Pigs in the Pen."

TOP SELLING TOYS OF 2002

(ranked by sales in dollars, not including video games)

1. *LeapPad Books* by LeapFrog
2. *LeapPad* by LeapFrog
3. *Bratz* by MGA Entertainment
4. *Hot Wheels Basic Cars* by Mattel
5. *Trivial Pursuit 20th Edition* by Hasbro Games
6. *Spider-Man Dual Web Blaster* by Toy Biz
7. *Star Wars Episode II* by Hasbro
8. *My 1st LeapPad* by LeapFrog
9. *Rapunzel Barbie* by Mattel
10. *Yu-Gi-Oh! Collector Tin* by Konami

CLASSIC TOYS . . . STILL GOING STRONG

You may be surprised to find out how long some popular toys have been around.

In 1902, Rose Michtom made stuffed bears to sell in a store she ran with her husband in Brooklyn. She named them after President Teddy (Theodore) Roosevelt, and started a big trend. Stieff (1903) and Gund (1906) are the oldest **TEDDY BEAR** makers in business today.

Edwin Binney and C. Harold Smith made their first box of **CRAYOLA CRAYONS** in 1903. There were 8 colors—compared to 120 today. The Crayola factory in Easton, Pennsylvania, now turns out nearly 3 billion crayons each year (12 million per day!).

Plastic **LEGO** bricks were invented in Denmark by Ole Kirk Christiansen in 1949. The company, whose name comes from the Danish words "LEg GOdt" (play well) has since made more than 206 billion of them! Imagine if you had to clean up that many in your room.

▲ *Racing legend Richard Petty*

In 2003, the Hot Wheels Hall of Fame opened in Los Angeles to celebrate the 35th anniversary of **HOT WHEELS** brand cars. Emphasizing speed and racetrack building made this brand the hottest selling toy car ever.

DID YOU KNOW? *The first diecast metal toy car was a replica of the Ford Model T, made by the Dowst Brothers Co. (later Tootsie Toys) of Chicago in 1910.*

One of the most popular toys in history, the **BARBIE DOLL** was "born" in 1959. Created by Mattel, Inc., founders Ruth and Elliot Handler, the doll was named after their daughter Barbie. Ken, named after their son, came out in 1961.

PLAY-DOH started out as a wallpaper cleaner! It was first sold as a toy in 1956 at a department store in Washington, D.C. It only came in off-white. Red, yellow, and blue were added in 1957. The original formula is still a secret!

Made of polyurethane foam, the first **NERF** ball hit the scene (and didn't break any lamps!) in 1969. This indoor/outdoor ball sold 4 million in its first year. In 1972, the king of all Nerf toys—the Nerf football—was introduced.

More Classic Toys

Lionel Trains	1901
Erector Set	1913
Tinker Toys	1914
Lincoln Logs	1916
Tonka Trucks	1947
Silly Putty	1950
Matchbox cars	1952
Mr. Potato Head	1952
Etch-A-Sketch	1960
Easy-Bake Oven	1963
G.I. Joe	1963

Geography

Who led the "Corps of Discovery" 200 years ago
•••
page 86

AMAZING GEOGRAPHY FACTS

DEEP WATER: The deepest dent in the Earth's surface is the **Marianas Trench** in the Pacific Ocean. The water there is about 35,800 feet, or almost seven miles, deep.

PLENTY OF POLES: The Earth actually has three North Poles. First, there is the **geographic** pole, which marks the exact top of the Earth (90° north latitude). Second is the **magnetic** North Pole. It's the one a compass points to. It represents the northernmost point of the magnetic forces inside the Earth. Finally, there is the **geomagnetic** pole. It marks the ends of the geomagnetic force field that surrounds the Earth. As for the South Pole, you could say there are four of them. But one is just for taking pictures! It's a striped barbershop pole, a few hundred yards away from the geographic pole, with a mirrored ball on top surrounded by flags of the Antarctic Treaty nations.

TRULY GREAT LAKES: The Great Lakes—Huron, Ontario, Michigan, Erie, and Superior— are the largest system of fresh surface water in the world. They hold about 5,500 cubic miles of water. (Think about it: a cubic mile is 1 mile high, 1 mile wide, and 1 mile deep!) That's almost one-fifth of all of the fresh water on the planet. Lake Superior got its name for a very good reason—it holds more than 2,900 cubic miles of water, or enough for all the water from the other Great Lakes combined, plus three times the volume of Lake Erie.

 ## Homework Help

Here's an easy way to remember the names of the Great Lakes. Just remember one word: HOMES.
H = Huron, O = Ontario, M = Michigan, E = Erie, S = Superior

TALLEST, LONGEST, HIGHEST, DEEPEST

Longest River: Nile, in Egypt and Sudan (4,160 miles)

Highest Waterfall: Angel Falls, in Venezuela (3,212 feet)

Tallest Mountain: Mount Everest, in Tibet and Nepal (29,035 feet)

Deepest Lake: Lake Baykal, in Asia (5,315 feet)

Biggest Lake: Caspian Sea, in Europe and Asia (143,244 square miles)

Biggest Desert: The Sahara, in Africa (3,500,000 square miles)

Biggest Island: Greenland, in the Atlantic Ocean (840,000 square miles)

Deepest Cave: Lamprechtsofen-Vogelschacht, in Salzburg, Austria (5,354 feet deep)

THE SEVEN CONTINENTS AND FOUR OCEANS

ASIA
Area: 12,000,000 square miles
2003 population: 3,817,000,000
Highest pt.: Mt. Everest (Nepal/Tibet) 29,035 ft.
Lowest pt.: Dead Sea (Israel/Jordan) −1,348 ft.

PACIFIC OCEAN
64,186,300 square miles
12,925 feet avg. depth

AUSTRALIA
Area: 3,200,000 square miles
2003 population: 32,000,000
Highest pt.: Mt. Kosciusko 7,310 ft.
Lowest pt.: Lake Eyre −52 ft.

INDIAN OCEAN
28,350,500 square miles
12,598 feet avg. depth

EUROPE
Area: 8,800,000 square miles
2003 population: 729,000,000
Highest pt.: Mt. Elbrus (Russia) 18,510 ft.
Lowest pt.: Caspian Sea −92 ft.

ATLANTIC OCEAN
33,420,000 square miles
11,370 feet avg. depth

AFRICA
Area: 11,500,000 square miles
2003 population: 856,000,000
Highest pt.: Mt. Kilimanjaro (Tanzania) 19,340 ft.
Lowest pt.: Lake Assal (Djibouti) −512 ft.

5,105,700 square miles
3,407 feet avg. depth

NORTH AMERICA
Area: 8,300,000 square miles
2003 population: 505,000,000
Highest pt.: Mt. McKinley (AK) 20,320 ft.
Lowest pt.: Death Valley (CA) −282 ft.

PACIFIC OCEAN
64,186,300 square miles
12,925 feet avg. depth

SOUTH AMERICA
Area: 6,800,000 square miles
2003 population: 364,000,000
Highest pt.: Mt. Aconcagua (Arg.) 22,834 ft.
Lowest pt.: Valdes Peninsula (Arg.) −131 ft.

ANTARCTICA
Area: 5,400,000 square miles
2003 population: no permanent residents
Highest pt.: Vinson Massif 16,864 ft.
Lowest pt.: Bently Subglacial Trench −8,327 ft.

N E S W

LOOKING AT OUR WORLD

THINKING GLOBAL

A **globe** is a small model of Earth. Like Earth, it is shaped like a ball or sphere. Earth isn't exactly a sphere because it gets flat at the top and bottom and bulges a little in the middle. This shape is called an oblate spheroid.

Because Earth is round, most flat maps that are centered on the equator do not show the shapes of the land masses exactly right. The shapes at the top and bottom usually look too big. For example, the island of Greenland, which is next to North America, may look bigger than Australia, though it is really much smaller.

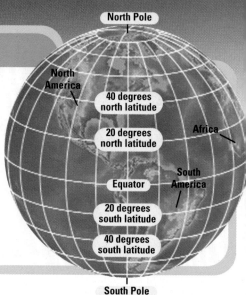

North Pole

North America

40 degrees north latitude

20 degrees north latitude

Africa

South America

Equator

20 degrees south latitude

40 degrees south latitude

South Pole

LATITUDE and LONGITUDE

Imaginary lines that run east and west around Earth, parallel to the equator, are called **parallels**. They tell you the **latitude** of a place, or how far it is from the equator. The equator is at 0 degrees latitude. As you go farther north or south, the latitude increases. The North Pole is at 90 degrees **north latitude**. The South Pole is at 90 degrees **south latitude**.

Imaginary lines that run north and south around the globe, from one pole to the other, are called **meridians**. They tell you the degree of **longitude**, or how far east or west a place is from an imaginary line called the **Greenwich meridian** or **prime meridian** (0 degrees). That line runs through the city of Greenwich in England.

Which Hemispheres Do You Live In?

Draw an imaginary line around the middle of Earth. This is the **equator**. It splits Earth into two halves called **hemispheres**. The part north of the equator, including North America, is the **northern hemisphere**. The part south of the equator is the **southern hemisphere**.

You can also divide Earth into east and west. North and South America are in the **western hemisphere**. Africa, Asia, and most of Europe are in the **eastern hemisphere**.

DID YOU KNOW? In February 2000, the Space Shuttle Endeavour took off on the Shuttle Radar Topography Mission. Using a special 200-foot arm with radar antenna at each end, the Endeavour scanned 80% of the Earth's land surface. Traveling at 17,000 mph, it orbited Earth 16 times a day for 11 days. The project provided scientists with 9.8 terabytes of high definition radar data—more than 15,000 CDs could hold! Over the next three years, scientists used the data to create computer-generated images for the most detailed maps ever made of Earth.

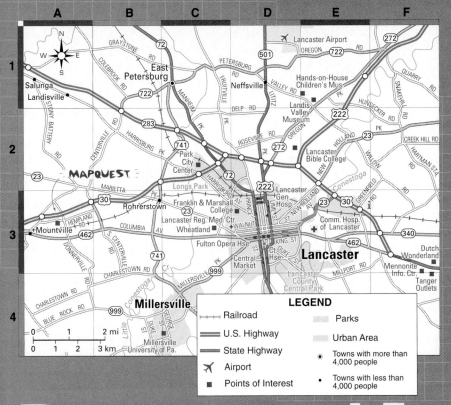

LEGEND

┝┼┼┼ Railroad		Parks
═══ U.S. Highway		Urban Area
─── State Highway	◉	Towns with more than 4,000 people
✈ Airport	•	Towns with less than 4,000 people
■ Points of Interest		

READING A MAP

DIRECTION Maps usually have a **compass rose** that shows you which way is north. On most maps, like this one, it's straight up. The compass rose on this map is in the upper left corner.

DISTANCE Of course the distances on a map are much shorter than the distances in the real world. The **scale** shows you how to estimate the real distance. This map's scale is in the lower left corner.

PICTURES Maps usually have little pictures or symbols to represent real things like roads, towns, airports, or other points of interest. The map **legend** (or **key**) tells what they mean.

FINDING PLACES Rather than use latitude and longitude to locate features, many maps, like this one, use a **grid system** with numbers on one side and letters on another. An **index**, listing place names in alphabetical order, gives a letter and a number for each. The letter and number tell you which square to look for a place on the map's **grid**. For example, Landisville can be found at A-1 on this map.

USING THE MAP People use maps to help them travel from one place to another. What if you lived in East Petersburg and wanted to go to the Hands-on-House Children's Museum? First, locate the two places on the map. East Petersburg is in C-1, and Hands-on-House is in E-1. Next, look at the roads that connect them and decide on the best route. (There could be several different ways to go.) One possibility is to take Route 722 northeast to Petersburg Road. Take that east to Valley Road. And, finally, travel southeast on Valley Road until you get to the museum.

83

EARTHQUAKES

Earthquakes may be so weak that they are hardly felt, or strong enough to do great damage. There are thousands of earthquakes each year, but most are too small to be noticed. About 1 in 5 can be felt, and about 1 in 500 causes damage.

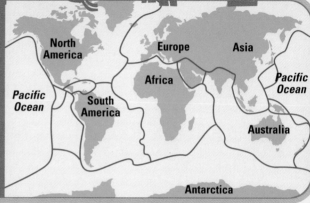

What Causes Earthquakes? The Earth's outer layer, its **crust**, is divided into huge pieces called **plates** (see map). These **plates**, made of rock, are constantly moving—away from each other, toward each other, or past each other. A crack in Earth's crust between two plates is called a **fault**. Many earthquakes occur along faults where two plates collide as they move toward each other or grind together as they move past each other. Earthquakes along the **San Andreas Fault** in California are caused by the grinding of two plates.

Measuring Earthquakes

The Richter scale goes from 0 to more than 8. These numbers indicate the strength of an earthquake. Each number means the quake releases about 30 times more energy than the number below it. An earthquake measuring 6 on the scale is about 30 times stronger than one measuring 5 and 900 times stronger than one measuring 4. Earthquakes that are 4 or above are considered major. (The damage and injuries caused by a quake also depend on other things, such as whether the area is heavily populated and built up.)

MAJOR EARTHQUAKES

The earthquakes listed here are among the largest and most destructive recorded in the past 100 years.

Year	Location	Magnitude	Deaths (approximate)
2003	China (western)	6.8	266
2002	Afghanistan (northern)	6.1	1,000+
2001	India (western)	7.9	30,000+
1999	Turkey (western)	7.4	17,200+
1998	Afghanistan (northeastern)	6.9	4,700+
	Afghanistan (northeastern)	6.1	2,323
1995	Japan (Kobe)	6.9	5,502
1994	United States (Los Angeles area)	6.8	61
1993	India (southern)	6.3	9,748
1990	Iran (western)	7.7	40,000+
1989	United States (San Francisco area)	7.1	62
1988	Soviet Armenia	7.0	55,000
1985	Mexico (Michoacan)	8.1	9,500
1976	China (Tangshan)	8.0	255,000
1970	Peru (northern)	7.8	66,000
1939	Chile (Chillan)	8.3	28,000
1927	China (Nan-Shan)	8.3	200,000
1923	Japan (Yokohama)	8.3	143,000
1920	China (Gansu)	8.6	200,000
1906	Chile (Valparaiso)	8.6	20,000
	United States (San Francisco)	8.3	3,000+

VOLCANOES

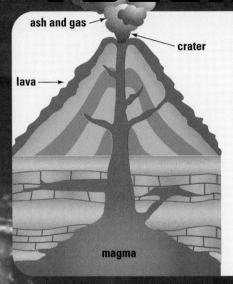

ash and gas

crater

lava

magma

A volcano is a mountain or hill with an opening on top known as a **crater**. Hot melted rock (**magma**), gases, ash, and other material from inside the Earth mix together a few miles underground, rising up through cracks and weak spots in the mountain. Every once in a while, the mixture may blast out, or erupt, through the crater. The magma is called **lava** when it reaches the air. This red-hot lava may have a temperature of over 2,000° Fahrenheit. The hill or mountain is made of lava and other materials that come out of the opening, and then cool and harden.

Some islands are really the tops of undersea volcanoes. The Hawaiian islands developed when volcanoes erupted under the Pacific Ocean.

SOME FAMOUS VOLCANIC ERUPTIONS

Year	Volcano (place)	Deaths (approximate)
79	Mount Vesuvius (Italy)	16,000
1586	Kelut (Indonesia)	10,000
1792	Mount Unzen (Japan)	14,500
1815	Tambora (Indonesia)	10,000
1883	Krakatau or Krakatoa (Indonesia)	36,000
1902	Mount Pelée (Martinique)	28,000
1980	Mount St. Helens (U.S.)	57
1982	El Chichón (Mexico)	1,880
1985	Nevado del Ruiz (Colombia)	23,000
1986	Lake Nyos (Cameroon)	1,700
1991	Mt. Pinatubo (Philippines)	800

Where is the Ring of Fire?

The hundreds of active volcanoes found on the land near the edges of the Pacific Ocean make up what is called the **Ring of Fire**. They mark the boundary between the plates under the Pacific Ocean and the plates under the continents around the ocean. (The plates of the Earth are explained on page 84, with the help of a map.) The Ring of Fire runs all along the west coast of South and North America, from the southern tip of Chile to Alaska. The ring also runs down the east coast of Asia, starting in the far north in Kamchatka. It continues down past Australia.

DID YOU KNOW? One of the largest volcanic eruptions in modern times took place August 26-27, 1883. The explosion of **Krakatau**, a volcanic island in Indonesia, was heard 3,000 miles away. Underwater earthquakes from the eruption created huge waves that traveled 8,000 miles. At least 36,000 people were killed, most by the big waves. The fine dust from the eruption was seen around the world and stayed in the air for 3 years. The result was colder temperatures, including what was called "the year without summer."

EARLY EXPLORATION

AROUND 1000	**Leif Ericson,** from Iceland, explored "Vinland," which may have been the coasts of northeast Canada and New England.
1271-95	**Marco Polo** (Italian) traveled to India, China, and Indonesia.
1492	**Christopher Columbus** (Italian) sailed four times from Spain to America and started colonies there.
1504	**Vasco da Gama** (Portuguese) sailed around the Cape of Good Hope to East Africa and India.
1497-98	**Juan Ponce de León** (Spanish) explored and named Florida.
1513	**Vasco Núñez de Balboa** (Spanish) explored Panama and reached the Pacific Ocean.
1513	**Ferdinand Magellan** (Portuguese) sailed from Spain around the tip of South America and across the Pacific to the Philippines, where he died. His expedition continued around the world.
1519-21	**Hernando Cortés** (Spanish) explored and conquered Mexico.
1519-36	**Hernando de Soto** (Spanish) explored the southeastern United States and the lower Mississippi Valley.
1539-42	**Samuel de Champlain** (French) traced the course of the St. Lawrence River and explored the northeastern United States.
1609-10	**Henry Hudson** (English), sailing from Holland, explored the Hudson River, Hudson Bay, and Hudson Strait.

All About... LEWIS AND CLARK

It's been 200 years since Meriwether Lewis and William Clark set out across the uncharted western lands of North America. They started near St. Louis in 1804. President Thomas Jefferson called the brave group "The Corps of Discovery." They were to explore for the U.S. the vast unknown territory between the Mississippi and the Rocky Mountains which Jefferson had bought from France a year before (in the "Louisiana Purchase"). In addition to political and military uses, they hoped to find a water route to the Pacific.

Jefferson appointed Captain Lewis, his personal secretary and an Army veteran, to head the expedition. As co-commander Lewis chose his friend Clark, another soldier, who was a skilled boatman and mapmaker. Together they led a group of 30 to 40 adventurers in a winding route more than 8,000 miles to the Rockies and over them to the Pacific coast of the Oregon Territory—and back! Among hazards they faced on the long trip (2 years, 4 months, 9 days) were winter cold and storms, mountains, rapids, bears, diseases, and unknown Indian tribes. While risking their lives they also took time to learn about Indian customs and record descriptions of more than 300 species of previously unknown plants and animals.

Sacagawea, a Shoshone Indian woman, was a valuable guide and translator. Among other things, she helped the expedition trade for the horses they needed to cross the Rockies.

Health

What's the longest muscle in the body?
•••
page 89

Surprising Facts About the Body

Your brain has about 100 billion nerve cells-called neurons—which gather and transmit electrochemical signals.

The brain makes up only about 2% of the body's weight, but it uses 20% of the oxygen and blood supply.

Adults blink every 4 to 6 seconds on average. Newborns only blink every minute or two—about what is needed to clean and lubricate the eye. The blink of an eye really is fast—it takes about 0.3 seconds!

An adult has about 5 feet of large intestine and 25 feet of the much narrower small intestine.

An adult has 6 quarts of blood that circulates through the whole body three times each minute. That means the blood travels about 12,000 miles per day—enough to cross the U.S. four times.

Babies are born with over 300 bones. Many of them fuse together as we grow up—and we end up with a total of 206.

Humans usually have 12 sets of ribs, but about 1 out of every 20 people is born with at least one extra rib.

More than half of an adult's 206 bones are in the hands and feet. There are 27 bones in each hand and 26 in each foot—for a total of 106.

The smallest bone in your body is in the ear. This bone, called the stirrup bone, is only about a tenth of an inch long.

The biggest bone in your body is the femur, or thigh bone. It's about one-fourth of your height.

The "funny bone" is not funny at all—it's *humerus* (the Latin name for the bone). The ulnar nerve running along your arm rests against the humerus bone; that's why it hurts a little when you hit it.

The lighter half-moon shape at the base of your fingernails actually has a name; it's called a lunula (LOON-yuh-luh).

Your body's 650 muscles make up about half of your weight.

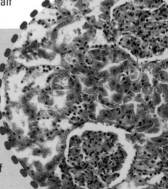

By age 13, most people have 28 teeth (babies have 20). Around age 18, four more "wisdom" teeth usually grow in, to make a full set of 32 teeth.

DID YOU KNOW? *In addition to the names you already know, the noises your body makes all have more formal or medical names. For example, a burp is an **eructation** (ear-uk-TAY-shun); a hiccup is a **singultus** (SIN-gul-tas); a sneeze is a **sternutation** (stern-you-TAY-shun); a stomach growl is a **borborygmus** (bor-buh-RIG-mus); and a yawning and stretching is **pandiculation** (pan-dik-you-LAY-shun).*

BODY BASICS:

Your body is made up of many different parts that work together every minute of every day and night. It is more amazing than any machine or computer. Even though everyone's body looks different outside, people have the same parts inside. Each system of the body has its own job. Some of the systems also work together to keep you healthy and strong.

CIRCULATORY SYSTEM In the circulatory system, the **heart** pumps **blood**, which then travels through tubes, called **arteries**, to all parts of the body. The blood carries the oxygen and food that the body needs to stay alive. **Veins** carry the blood back to the heart.

DIGESTIVE SYSTEM The digestive system moves food through parts of the body called the **esophagus**, **stomach**, and **intestines**. As the food passes through, some of it is broken down into tiny particles called **nutrients**, which the body needs. Nutrients enter the bloodstream, which carries them to all parts of the body. The digestive system then changes the remaining food into waste that is eliminated from the body.

ENDOCRINE SYSTEM
The endocrine system includes **glands** that are needed for some body functions. There are two kinds of glands. **Exocrine** glands produce liquids such as sweat and saliva. **Endocrine** glands produce chemicals called hormones. **Hormones** control body functions, such as growth.

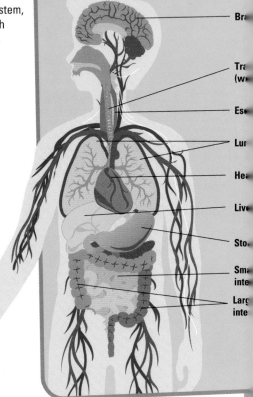

Br
Tra
(w
Es
Lur
Hea
Liv
Sto
Sma
inte
Larg
inte

NERVOUS SYSTEM The nervous system enables us to think, feel, move, hear, and see. It includes the **brain**, the **spinal cord**, and **nerves** in all parts of the body. Nerves in the spinal cord carry signals back and forth between the brain and the rest of the body. The brain tells us what to do and how to respond. It has three major parts. The **cerebrum** controls thinking, speech, and vision. The **cerebellum** is responsible for physical coordination. The **brain stem** controls the respiratory, circulatory, and digestive systems.

RESPIRATORY SYSTEM The respiratory system allows us to breathe. Air comes into the body through the nose and mouth. It goes through the **windpipe** (or **trachea**) to two tubes (called **bronchi**), which carry air to the **lungs**. Oxygen from the air is taken in by tiny blood vessels in the lungs. The blood then carries oxygen to the cells of the body.

WHAT THE BODY'S SYSTEMS DO

SKELETAL SYSTEM The skeletal system is made up of the **bones** that hold your body upright. Some bones protect organs, such as the ribs that cover the lungs.

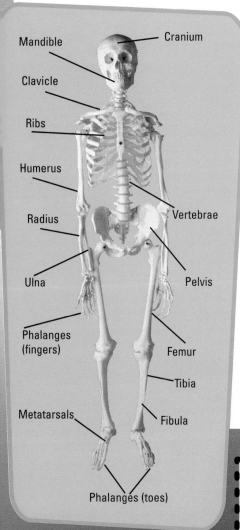

- Mandible
- Cranium
- Clavicle
- Ribs
- Humerus
- Radius
- Vertebrae
- Ulna
- Pelvis
- Phalanges (fingers)
- Femur
- Tibia
- Metatarsals
- Fibula
- Phalanges (toes)

MUSCULAR SYSTEM Muscles are made up of elastic fibers There are three types of muscle: **Skeletal, smooth,** and **cardiac.** The skeletal muscles help the body move—they are the large muscles we can see. Smooth muscles are found in our digestive system, blood vessels, and air passages. Cardiac muscle is found only in your heart. Smooth and cardiac muscles are **involuntary** muscles—they do their job without us having to think about them.

REPRODUCTIVE SYSTEM Through the reproductive system, adult human beings are able to create new human beings. Reproduction begins when a **sperm** cell from a man fertilizes an **egg** cell from a woman.

URINARY SYSTEM This system, which includes the **kidneys**, cleans waste from the blood and regulates the amount of water in the body.

IMMUNE SYSTEM The immune system protects your body from diseases by fighting against certain substances that come from outside, or **antigens.** This happens in different ways. For example, white blood cells called **B lymphocytes** learn to fight certain viruses and bacteria by producing **antibodies,** which spread around the body to attack them. Sometimes, as in **allergies,** the immune system makes a mistake and creates antibodies to fight a substance that's really harmless.

DID YOU KNOW? LONGEST MUSCLE

The longest muscle in the body is the sartorius (from the Latin word for "tailor"), running from the front of the hip to the knee. It allows us to get into and out of the cross-legged position—the way tailors used to sit to when they sewed.

WE ARE WHAT WE EAT

Have you ever noticed the labels on the packages of food you and your family buy? The labels provide information people need to make healthy choices about the foods they eat. Below are some terms you may see on labels.

NUTRIENTS ARE NEEDED

Nutrients are the parts of food the body can use for growth, for energy, and for repairing itself. Carbohydrates, fats, proteins, vitamins, minerals, and water are different kinds of nutrients found in food. **Carbohydrates** and **fats** provide energy. **Proteins** aid growth and help maintain and repair the body. **Vitamins** help the body use food, help eyesight and skin, and aid in fighting off infections. **Minerals** help build bones and teeth and aid in such functions as muscle contractions and blood clotting. **Water** helps with growth and repair of the body. It also helps the body digest food and get rid of wastes.

CALORIES COUNT

A **calorie** is a measure of how much energy we get from food. The government recommends the number of calories that should be taken in each day. Kids aged 7 to 12 and teenaged girls should eat about 2,200 calories daily. Teenaged boys need around 2,800. Active people—who play sports, for instance—may need more.

To maintain a **healthy weight,** it is important to balance the calories in the food you eat with the calories you use up. The more active you are, the more calories your body burns. If you eat more calories than your body uses, you will gain weight.

Junk food is a term for foods (such as candy, soda, and most desserts) that have lots of calories but not many nutrients.

Nutrition Facts

Serving Size 1/2 cup (1 oz.) = (30g)
Servings per container 14

Amount Per Serving	Cereal	Cereal w/ 1/2 cup Lowfat Milk
Calories	100	150
Calories from Fat	10	25

	% Daily Value**	
Total Fat 1g*	2%	4%
Saturated Fat 0g	0%	5%
Cholesterol 0mg	0%	3%
Sodium 50mg	2%	5%
Total Carbohydrates 20g	7%	9%
Dietary Fiber 2g	8%	8%
Sugars 5g		
Protein 4g		
Vitamin A	0%	6%
Vitamin C	0%	2%
Calcium	0%	15%
Iron	2%	4%

* Amount in Cereal. One half cup lowfat milk contributes an additional 50 calories, 1.5g total fat (1g saturated fat), 9 mg cholesterol, 60mg sodium, 6g total carbohydrates (6g sugars), and 3g protein.
** Percents (%) of a Daily Value are based on a 2,000 calorie diet. Your Daily Values may vary higher or lower depending on your calorie needs:

Nutrient	Calories	2,000	2,500
Total Fat	Less than	65g	80g
Sat Fat	Less than	20g	25g
Cholesterol	Less than	300mg	300mg
Sodium	Less than	2,400mg	2,400mg
Total Carbohydrates		300g	375g
Dietary Fiber		25g	30g

Calories per gram:
Fat 9 • Carbohydrate 4 • Protein 4

SOME LOWER-FAT FOODS

chicken or turkey hot dog
tuna fish canned in water
baked potato
pretzels
apple
plain popcorn (with no butter)
skim milk or 1% or 2% milk

SOME FATTY FOODS

beef or pork hot dog
fried hamburger
french fries
potato chips
tuna fish canned in oil
buttered popcorn
whole milk

A LITTLE FAT GOES A LONG WAY

A little bit of fat keeps your body warm. It gives the muscles energy. It helps keep the skin soft and healthy. But the body needs only a small amount to do all these things. Less than one-third of your calories should come from fat, if you're over two years old.

Cholesterol. Eating too much fat can make some people's bodies produce too much **cholesterol** (ka-**less**-ter-all). This waxy substance can build up over the years on the inside of arteries. Too much cholesterol keeps blood from flowing freely through the arteries and can cause serious health problems such as heart attacks.

DID YOU KNOW? In 2002, the National Center for Health Statistics reported that an estimated 8.8 million U.S. kids age 6-19 were overweight. Being overweight increases a risk of developing high blood pressure, diabetes, and heart disease. Starting in 2004, the Los Angeles school district, second largest in the U.S., banned the sale of soda—which is high in calories and low in nutrition—at all of its middle and high schools (it was already not allowed at elementary schools).

Which Foods Are the Right Foods?

To stay healthy, it is important to eat the right foods and to exercise. To help people choose the right foods for good health and fitness, the U.S. government developed the food pyramid shown below. The food pyramid shows the groups of foods that everyone should eat every day.

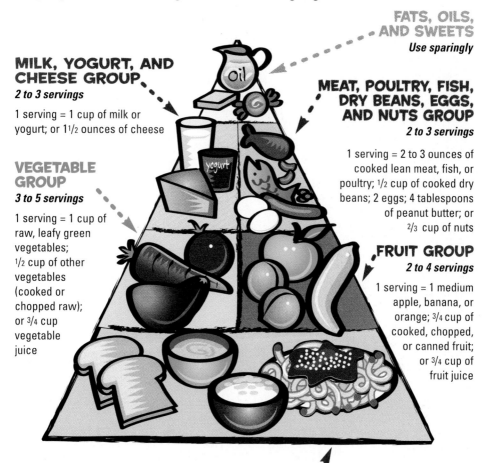

FATS, OILS, AND SWEETS
Use sparingly

MILK, YOGURT, AND CHEESE GROUP
2 to 3 servings

1 serving = 1 cup of milk or yogurt; or 1½ ounces of cheese

MEAT, POULTRY, FISH, DRY BEANS, EGGS, AND NUTS GROUP
2 to 3 servings

1 serving = 2 to 3 ounces of cooked lean meat, fish, or poultry; ½ cup of cooked dry beans; 2 eggs; 4 tablespoons of peanut butter; or ⅔ cup of nuts

VEGETABLE GROUP
3 to 5 servings

1 serving = 1 cup of raw, leafy green vegetables; ½ cup of other vegetables (cooked or chopped raw); or ¾ cup vegetable juice

FRUIT GROUP
2 to 4 servings

1 serving = 1 medium apple, banana, or orange; ¾ cup of cooked, chopped, or canned fruit; or ¾ cup of fruit juice

BREAD, CEREAL, RICE, AND PASTA GROUP
6 to 11 servings

1 serving = 1 slice of bread; 1 ounce of ready-to-eat cereal; or ½ cup of cooked cereal, rice, or pasta

The foods at the bottom of the pyramid are the ones everyone needs to eat in the biggest amounts. At the top are the foods to be eaten in the smallest amounts. The number of servings needed depends on your age and body size. Younger, smaller people need fewer servings. Older, larger people need more.

SUPER SNACKS

Hungry right now? Here are some treats you can make yourself—or with a little help. Be sure to ask permission and have an adult at hand.

APPLE CRISP ALA NOW!

You'll need: **granola mix, applesauce, cinnamon**

Mix about a half cup of applesauce, along with a quarter cup of granola, into bowl or big cup. Sprinkle lightly with cinnamon, and dig in!

TOASTED PUMKIN SEEDS

You'll need: **pumpkin seeds, salt**

After you carve your Halloween pumpkin, put the seeds into a colander or strainer and wash away all the pulp and stringy stuff. Pat the seeds dry with paper towels. Have an adult heat the oven to 350°F. Spread your seeds out on a cookie sheet in a single layer. Sprinkle a little salt over them. Have an adult put the tray into the oven—and when the seeds are dry and light brown, have the adult take it out. Don't forget to let them cool before you eat them!

BANANA SMASH

You'll need: **a small banana, applesauce, plain yogurt**

Put some applesauce (around a quarter cup or so should do it) and some plain yogurt (a teaspoon or so) in a bowl or big cup. Peel the banana, mash it up in the cup with the applesauce and yogurt, and eat.

TRAIL MIX

You'll need: **any kind of dry cereal (oat, corn, wheat); chocolate chips, raisins, or any kind of dried fruit pieces; peanuts or any kind of chopped nut**

For a great on-the-go snack, mix any combination of these ingredients (or other dry things you think might taste good) in equal amounts in a container. A small plastic bagful is easy to carry and will give you energy no matter where you go or what you're doing.

STAY HEALTHY WITH EXERCISE

Daily exercise makes you feel good. It also helps you think better, sleep better, feel more relaxed, and stay at a healthy weight. Regular exercise will make you stronger and help you improve at physical activities. About three-quarters of ninth graders say they get enough exercise. Do you?

Breathing deeply during exercise gets more oxygen into your lungs with each breath. Your heart pumps more oxygen-filled blood all through your body with each beat. Muscles and joints get stronger and more flexible as you use them.

Here are some activities, with a rough idea of how many calories a 100-pound person would burn per minute while doing them:

ACTIVITY	CALORIES PER MINUTE
Jogging (6 miles per hour)	8
Jumping rope (easy)	7
Playing basketball	7
Playing soccer	6
Bicycling (9.4 miles per hour)	5
Skiing (downhill)	5
Raking the lawn	4
Rollerblading (easy)	4
Walking (4 miles per hour)	4
Bicycling (5.5 miles per hour)	3
Swimming (25 yards per minute)	3
Walking (3 miles per hour)	3

Lefty slugger Babe Ruth ▶

A FEW FACTS ABOUT LEFTIES

Three of the last four presidents were left-handed. Ronald Reagan, George H.W. Bush, and Bill Clinton. Presidents James Garfield, Herbert Hoover, Harry Truman, and Gerald Ford were also left-handed. Other left-handers include Julius Caesar, Leonardo Da Vinci, Queen Elizabeth II, Babe Ruth, Paul McCartney—and Kermit the Frog.

About 10% to 13% of people are left-handed.

The official handshake for both the Boy Scouts and Girl Scouts is done with the left hand.

Throughout history left-handedness has been associated with evil or clumsiness. For sailors a "left-handed ship" means an unlucky ship. The Latin word for left is similar to the English word "sinister." Also, gauche, the word for "left" in French, is used to mean "awkward" in English. A "left-handed compliment" is an insult disguised as a compliment. In surfing, skateboarding, and snowboarding, riding "goofy-foot," means riding with the left foot in back.

Items such as scissors, power tools, can openers, telephones, even keyboards (the enter key and number pad are on the right) are made for right-handed people. It is hard to find a left-handed guitar.

International Left Handers Day is on August 13.

WEB SITE There are stores and Web sites that sell products made especially for left-handed people. For examples, go to *http://www.dmoz.org/Shopping/Niche/Left-Handed_Products/*

With the letters half covered, you can still read the name of this book. Or *can* you?

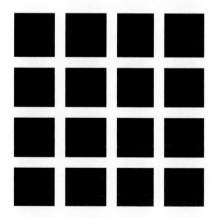

Do you see the gray dots?

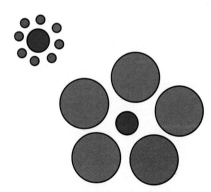

Which blue circle is bigger?

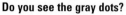

Holidays

When is Elephant Appreciation Day?
page 95

HOLiDAYS iN THE UNiTED STATES

There are no official holidays for the whole U.S. Each state can decide which holidays to celebrate. But most states celebrate the holidays listed below. These are the federal holidays, when workers for the federal government get the day off. Many offices, and most banks and schools, are closed on these days. Presidents' Day, Memorial Day, and Columbus Day are often celebrated on the nearest Monday.

NEW YEAR'S DAY Countries the world over celebrate the new year, although not always on January 1. For example, Chinese New Year falls between January 21 and February 19.

MARTIN LUTHER KING JR. DAY Observed on the third Monday in January, this holiday marks the birth (January 15, 1929) of the African-American civil rights leader Rev. Martin Luther King Jr. In 2004, it will be celebrated on January 19.

WASHINGTON'S BIRTHDAY OR **PRESIDENTS' DAY** On the third Monday in February (February 16, 2004), Americans celebrate the births of both George Washington (born February 22, 1732) and Abraham Lincoln (born February 12, 1809).

MEMORIAL DAY OR **DECORATION DAY** Memorial Day, observed on the last Monday in May (May 31, 2004), is set aside to remember men and women who died serving in the military.

FOURTH OF JULY OR **INDEPENDENCE DAY** July 4 is the anniversary of the day in 1776 when the American colonies signed the Declaration of Independence. Kids and grownups celebrate with bands and parades, picnics, barbecues, and fireworks.

LABOR DAY Labor Day, the first Monday in September, honors the workers of America. It was first celebrated in 1882. It falls on September 1 in 2003 and September 6 in 2004.

COLUMBUS DAY Celebrated on the second Monday in October, Columbus Day is the anniversary of October 12, 1492, the day Christopher Columbus was traditionally thought to have arrived in the Americas (on the island of San Salvador). It falls on October 13 in 2003 and October 11 in 2004.

VETERANS DAY Veterans Day, November 11, honors veterans of wars. First called Armistice Day, it marked the armistice (agreement) that ended World War I. This was signed on the 11th hour of the 11th day of the 11th month of 1918.

THANKSGIVING Thanksgiving was first observed by the Pilgrims in 1621 as a harvest festival and a day for thanks and feasting. In 1863, Abraham Lincoln revived the tradition. It comes on the fourth Thursday in November— November 27 in 2003 and November 25 in 2004.

CHRISTMAS Christmas is both a religious holiday and a legal holiday. It is celebrated on December 25.

ELECTION DAY Election Day, the first Tuesday after the first Monday in November (November 4 in 2003 and November 2 in 2004), is also a holiday in some states.

OTHER SPECIAL HOLIDAYS

VALENTINE'S DAY February 14 is a day for sending cards or gifts to people you love.

MOTHER'S DAY AND FATHER'S DAY Mothers are honored on the second Sunday in May. Fathers are honored on the third Sunday in June.

HALLOWEEN In ancient Britain, Druids wore grotesque costumes on October 31 to scare off evil spirits. Today, "trick or treating" children collect candy or money for UNICEF, the United Nations Children's Fund.

HANUKKAH (ALSO CHANUKAH) This eight-day Jewish festival begins on December 19 in 2003 and December 7 in 2004. It recalls when the Jews, in 165 B.C., recaptured the Temple of Jerusalem and dedicated it to God. Today, people light candles—starting with one on the first night and then an additional one each night, until the menorah, an eight-branched candle holder, is completely filled. And children get gifts!

KWANZAA This seven-day African-American festival begins on December 26. It celebrates seven virtues: unity, self-determination, collective work and responsibility, cooperative economics, purpose, creativity, and faith.

UNUSUAL HOLIDAYS

If going back to school gets you down, you can cheer up by observing **National Waffle Week**, the first week of September. If you like animals, **National Dog Week**, held the last full week in September, may be more your style. There are hundreds of odd holidays you probably never heard of. Here are a few (dates are for 2004):

January 21 — Squirrel Appreciation Day

February 15 — National I Want Butterscotch Day

March 15 — Act Happy Day (3rd Mon. in March)

April 10 — National Siblings Day

May 1 — Mother Goose Day

June 19 — Join Hands Day (3rd Sat. in June)

July 7 — Father-Daughter Take a Walk Together Day

August 7 — National Mustard Day (1st Sat. in August)

September 22 — Elephant Appreciation Day

October 31 — National Knock-Knock Day

November 26 — Buy Nothing Day (the day after Thanksgiving)

December 11 — Day of the Horse (2nd Sat. in December)

HOLIDAYS AROUND THE WORLD

BOXING DAY December 26 is a holiday in Britain, and also in Australia, Canada, and New Zealand. On this day, at one time, Christmas gifts were given out in boxes to servants, tradespeople, and the poor.

CANADA DAY Canada's national holiday, July 1, commemorates the union of Canadian provinces in 1867.

CHINESE NEW YEAR China's biggest holiday falls between January 21 and February 19 every year. Celebrations include parades, fireworks, and traditional meals. It comes on January 22 in 2004.

CINCO DE MAYO Mexicans remember May 5, 1867, when Mexico defeated its French rulers and became independent.

SHICHI-GO-SAN (SEVEN-FIVE-THREE) This Japanese festival is held near November 15, for boys ages 3 and 5, and girls ages 3 and 7. Dressed in fine clothes, they visit a shrine to give thanks for their health. Afterwards, their brightly colored paper bags—decorated with cranes and turtles, symbols of long life—are filled with candy and toys which they share.

CALENDAR BASICS

Holidays and calendars go hand in hand. Using a calendar, you can see what day of the week it is, and watch out for the next special day. Calendars divide time into days, weeks, months, and years. A year is the time it takes for one revolution of Earth around the Sun. Early calendars were lunar—based on the movements of the Moon across the sky. The ancient Egyptians were probably the first to develop a solar calendar, based on the movements of Earth around the Sun.

The Julian and Gregorian Calendars

In 46 B.C., the emperor Julius Caesar decided to use a calendar based on movements of the Sun. This calendar, called the **Julian calendar**, fixed the normal year at 365 days and added one day every fourth year (leap year). It also established the months of the year and the days of the week.

In A.D. 1582, the Julian calendar was revised by Pope Gregory XIII, because the year was 11 minutes, 14 seconds too long. This added up to about 3 extra days every 400 years. To fix it, he made years ending in 00 leap years only if they can be divided by 400. Thus, 2000 is a leap year, but 2100 will not be. The **Gregorian calendar** is the one used today in most of the world.

Jewish, Islamic, and Chinese Calendars

The **Jewish calendar**, which began almost 6,000 years ago, is the official calendar of Israel. The year 2003 is the same as 5763–5764 on the Jewish calendar, which starts at Rosh Hashanah, usually in September. The **Islamic calendar** started in A.D. 622. The year 2003 is equivalent to 1423–1424 on the Islamic calendar, which begins with the month of Muharram, usually in February or March. The **Chinese calendar** has years named after animals. There are 12 of them: Rat, Ox, Tiger, Rabbit, Dragon, Snake, Horse, Sheep, Monkey, Rooster, Dog, and Pig. On February 1, 2003, the Year of the Sheep began. On January 22, 2004, the Year of the Monkey starts.

WHERE DO THE NAMES OF THE MONTHS COME FROM?

January—named for the Roman god Janus, guardian of gates (often shown with two faces, looking backward and forward)
February—named for Februalia, a Roman time of sacrifice
March—named for Mars, the Roman god of war (the end of winter meant fighting could begin again)
April—"aperire," Latin for "to open," as in flower buds
May—named for Maia, the goddess of plant growth
June—"Junius," the Latin word for the goddess Juno
July—named after the Roman ruler Julius Caesar
August—named for Augustus, the first Roman emperor
September—"septem," the Latin word for seven
October—"octo," the Latin word for eight
November—"novem," the Latin word for nine
December—"decem," the Latin word for ten

BIRTHSTONES

MONTH	BIRTHSTONE
January	Garnet
February	Amethyst
March	Aquamarine
April	Diamond
May	Emerald
June	Pearl
July	Ruby
August	Peridot
September	Sapphire
October	Opal
November	Topaz
December	Turquoise

Homework Help

Here's a useful way to keep your months straight:

**30 days hath September,
April, June, and November
All the rest have 31,
Except the second month alone.
February has 28 days time,
Til leap year makes it 29.**

Did You KNOW?

The Roman calendar used to begin in March. When Julius Caesar started a new calendar, in 46 B.C., he kept the old names for the seventh, eighth, ninth, and tenth months—which are 9th to 12th in our calendar today.

Homework Help

Where should you look first when doing research? ••• *page 98*

If you need to study for an exam, write a research paper, or do a diorama, there are helpful hints in this chapter.

In other chapters, you can find lots of information on topics you may write about or study in school. Facts About Nations, pages 150-169, and Facts About U.S. States, pages 268-284, are good places to look. For math tips and formulas, look up the chapter on Numbers. For good books to read, and write about, see the Books chapter. Plus, there are many other study and learning tips throughout the book. Look for the "Homework Help" icon! ▶

THOSE TRICKY TESTS

GETTING READY

Being prepared for a test can relieve some of your jitters and can make test taking a lot easier! Here are some tips to help you prepare.

▶ Take good notes in class and keep up with assignments, so you don't have to learn material at the last minute! Just writing down the notes helps you remember the information.

▶ Make a study schedule and stick to it! Don't watch TV or listen to distracting music while studying.

▶ Start reviewing early if you can—don't wait until the night before the test.

▶ Go over the headings, summaries, and questions in each chapter to review key points. Read your notes and highlight the most important topics.

▶ Take study breaks so you can concentrate and stay alert.

▶ Get a good night's sleep and eat a good breakfast before the test.

THE BIG EVENT

Follow these suggestions for smooth sailing during test time:

▶ Take a deep breath and relax! That will help calm your nerves.

▶ Skim through the entire exam so you know what to expect and how long it may take.

▶ As you start each part, read directions carefully.

▶ Read each question carefully before answering. For a multiple choice question, check every possible answer before you decide on one. The best answer could be the last one!

▶ Don't spend too much time on any one question. Skip hard questions and go back to them at the end.

▶ Keep track of time so you can pace yourself. Use any time left at the end to go back and review your answers. Make sure you've written the answer you meant to select.

PICKING A TOPIC

Sometimes you not only have to research a topic and write about it—you have to pick the topic in the first place. Here are a few tips to keep in mind.

▶ **Start out by brainstorming.** In other words, let your brain flow freely with ideas of ALL kinds and write them all down. Even if an idea seems doubtful, write it down anyway. You can be more picky later on.

▶ **Focus on subjects you like.** If you're already interested in something, like soccer or Abraham Lincoln or Sherlock Holmes, you'll enjoy writing about it and probably do a better job.

▶ **It could even be something unfamiliar.** Writing on a subject you don't know anything about is a great way to learn.

▶ **Consider topics that are current.** You might want to pick a topic that's in the news. For example, Why We Should Recycle or Affirmative Action. You'll find plenty of information that way!

DOING RESEARCH

Once you pick a topic, the next step is to read all about it. Try to find information from as many sources as you can. If you can't come up with at least a few sources, then the topic is too narrow. If you're overwhelmed with information about the topic, maybe you'll need to narrow it down.

▶ **Encyclopedias are a good place to start.** They can give you a good overview of the subject.

▶ **The electronic catalog** of your school or town library will probably be your main source for finding material about your subject. Keep in mind that books are not as current as magazines and newspapers, but can still give you information you can use.

▶ **Check your library's indexes** for magazine or newspaper articles. *The Reader's Guide to Periodic Literature* can be a big help in finding articles; there's even an online version.

▶ You can also use **the Internet** as a research tool. For more details, see "Research on the Internet" (page 54).

▶ Don't be afraid to ask **the librarian** for help if you get stuck!

▶ As you read each source, **write down the facts and ideas** that you may need, using a separate 3x5 index card for each one.

▶ **Make sure** your cards show the title and author for each source and the page numbers for where you found the particular information.

Hint: Use quotation marks when you think it is important to use the same words as the author. When you rephase or rethink the idea in your own words, you don't have to use quotation marks.

~ESEARCH PAPER

WRITING IT DOWN

Now that you know how to pick your topic and research it, it's time to organize your facts and write about them.

See which cards you still need and try to put them in the order you want to use. **Develop a rough outline** of your main ideas in the order in which they'll appear.

Now you're ready for the **first draft**. It can be a rough draft that gets your ideas down while they're fresh. You can worry about the exact wording, the spellings, and so forth later on.

Your paper should contain three main parts:

INTRODUCTION The introduction, or first paragraph, explains your topic and your point of view on it. It should draw readers into the paper and let them know what to expect.

BODY The body of the paper develops your ideas. Use specific facts, examples, and details to make your points clear and convincing. Use separate paragraphs for each new idea and use words and phrases that link one paragraph to the next so your ideas flow smoothly.

CONCLUSION Summarize your main points in the final paragraph, or conclusion.

Put your first draft aside for a few days, then go back and re-read it. You'll be able to make corrections more easily after seeing it with fresh eyes. After you're done making your **revisions**, read the paper (slowly!) to check for misspellings and mistakes in grammar or punctuation.

SHOWING YOUR SOURCES

► It is important in a paper to show what sources you used. This can be done with **footnotes** that go on the same page as the information itself and say where you got each key fact or quote.

► Whether you use footnotes or not, you may need to do a **bibliography** at the end. This is a list of all the sources you used to prepare the report—even some that you may not have actually ended up using in what you wrote.

Hint: You usually will not have a reason to use the same wording as your source. If you do, make it clear, and use quotation marks.

► Your teacher will tell you what format to use for showing your sources. Here are samples of what you might put in your bibliography for a book, magazine article, or Internet source you used.

FOR A BOOK: *Author(s). title (italicized or underlined). city published: publisher, year.*
Jaffa, Harry V. *A New Birth of Freedom: Abraham Lincoln and the Coming of the Civil War.* Lanham, Md.: Rowman & Littlefield Publishers, 2000.

FOR A MAGAZINE OR NEWSPAPER ARTICLE: *Author. article title (in quotation marks). name of publication (in italics). date of issue: article page numbers.*
Wahl, Grant. "Eyes on the Prize: Real Madrid, the most compelling club soccer team ever, comes to U.S. TV." *Sports Illustrated.* May 5, 2003: 25.

FOR ON-LINE (INTERNET): *Author. title of page used (in quotation marks). website address (http://…). date.*
Environmental Protection Agency. "Municipal Solid Waste—Reduce, Reuse, and Recycle." *http://www.epa.gov/epaoswer/non-hw/muncpl/reduce.htm.* October 29, 2002

HOW TO MAKE A DIORAMA

A diorama is a small model of a real-life scene that has lifelike details and a realistic background. It could be anything from the habitat of a white Bengal tiger (see below) to a Native American village to a spaceship landing on the Moon.

After you choose the scene that you want to re-create, make a base for the model using a thin piece of board or cardboard, a shoebox, or a larger box. Make sure your base is the right size—the pieces of your model will look too cluttered if the base is too small or too empty if the base is too big. Here are some other tips to keep in mind when you're doing the layout:

▶ Put the buildings or vehicles in the scene at an angle to the sides of the base.

▶ Put bigger items in the back, leaving the front of the scene clear and easy to see.

▶ To draw attention to one particular part of the scene, have all the figures look in the same direction as the section you want to highlight. That way, the viewer's eyes will also focus there.

▶ Keep the scene "balanced"—don't put all the larger items on one side and the smaller items on the other.

After you finish the layout, gather all the figures and materials together that you want to use. Some of the supplies you might need include a shoe box or a slightly larger box, crayons or markers, paste or a glue stick, a pencil, scissors, tape, thread, a darning needle, a hole punch, acrylic paint, and pipe cleaners.

▶ If you use cutouts made of thin paper for the figures, paste them onto poster board or thin cardboard (like an old cereal box) so they stand up better.

▶ Hang flying animals or fish from the top of a box using invisible thread, tape, or pipe cleaners.

▶ Green and brown pipe cleaners work well as plants, and cotton puffs make great clouds or snow!

Make sure you use the same care and attention with the little details in the small items and figures as you use with the larger items—like the buildings and vehicles—so the overall look is complete and well thought out.

▼ *Diorama showing the habitat of a white Bengal tiger*

Inventions

What is nanotechnology? page 103

A lot of the world's inventions came before history was written. These include the wheel, pottery, many tools, and the ability to make fire. More recent inventions help us to travel faster, communicate better, and live longer.

INVENTIONS HELP US LIVE HEALTHIER AND LONGER LIVES

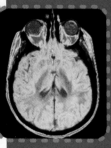

▲ A brain scan made with a CAT scanner

YEAR	INVENTION	INVENTOR (COUNTRY)
1780	bifocal lenses for glasses	Benjamin Franklin (U.S.)
1819	stethoscope	René T.M.H. Laënnec (France)
1842	anesthesia (ether)	Crawford W. Long (U.S.)
1895	X ray	Wilhelm Roentgen (Germany)
1922	insulin	Sir Frederick G. Banting (Canada)
1929	penicillin	Alexander Fleming (Scotland)
1954	antibiotic for fungal diseases	R. F. Brown & E. L. Hazen (U.S.)
1955	polio vaccine	Jonas E. Salk (U.S.)
1973	CAT scanner	Godfrey N. Hounsfield (England)
1978	artificial heart	Robert K. Jarvik (U.S.)
1987	meningitis vaccine	Connaught Lab (U.S.)
2002	iBOT stair-climbing wheelchair	Dean Kamen (U.S.)

INVENTIONS TAKE US FROM ONE PLACE TO ANOTHER

YEAR	INVENTION	INVENTOR (COUNTRY)
1785	parachute	Jean Pierre Blanchard (France)
1807	steamboat (practical)	Robert Fulton (U.S.)
1829	steam locomotive	George Stephenson (England)
1885	automobile (gasoline)	Karl Benz (Germany)
1885	bicycle (modern)	James Starley (England)
1885	motorcycle	Gottlieb Daimler (Germany)
1891	escalator	Jesse W. Reno (U.S.)
1891	submarine (modern)	John Holland (U.S.)
1895	diesel engine	Rudolf Diesel (Germany)
1903	propeller airplane	Orville & Wilbur Wright (U.S.)
1939	helicopter	Igor Sikorsky (U.S.)
1939	jet airplane	Hans van Ohain (Germany)
1973	Jet Ski®	Clayton Jacobsen II (U.S)
1980	rollerblades	Scott Olson (U.S.)
2001	Segway™ Human Transporter (HT)*	Dean Kamen (U.S.) ▶

*A self-balancing transportation device.

INVENTIONS HELP US COMMUNICATE WITH ONE ANOTHER

YEAR	INVENTION	INVENTOR (COUNTRY)
105	paper	Ts'ai Lun (China)
1447	moveable type	Johann Gutenberg (Germany)
1795	modern pencil	Nicolas Jacques Conté (France)
1837	telegraph	Samuel F.B. Morse (U.S.)
1845	rotary printing press	Richard M. Hoe (U.S.)
1867	typewriter	Christopher L. Sholes, Carlos Glidden, & Samuel W. Soulé (U.S.)
1870s	telephone*	Antonio Meucci (Italy), Alexander G. Bell (U.S.)
1876	telephone	Alexander G. Bell (U.S.)
1888	ballpoint pen	John Loud (U.S.)
1913	modern radio receiver	Reginald A. Fessenden (U.S.)
1937	xerography copies	Chester Carlson (U.S.)
1942	electronic computer	John V. Atanasoff & Clifford Berry (U.S.)
1944	auto sequence computer	Howard H. Aiken (U.S.)
1947	transistor	William Shockley, Walter H. Brattain, & John Bardeen (U.S.)
1955	fiber optics	Narinder S. Kapany (England)
1965	word processor	IBM (U.S.)
1968	computer mouse	Douglas Engelbart (U.S)
1979	cellular telephone	Ericsson Company (Sweden)
1987	laptop computer	Sir Clive Sinclair (England) ▶
1994	digital camera	Apple Computer, Kodak (U.S.)
2002	wind-up cell phone	Motorola (U.S.) & Freeplay Energy Group (England)

*Meucci developed a version of the telephone (early 1870s); Bell received a patent for another version (1876).

INVENTIONS MAKE OUR LIVES EASIER

YEAR	INVENTION	INVENTOR (COUNTRY)
1800	electric battery	Alessandro Volta (Italy)
1834	refrigeration	Jacob Perkins (England)
1846	sewing machine	Elias Howe (U.S.)
1851	cylinder (door) lock	Linus Yale (U.S.)
1879	practical lightbulb	Thomas A. Edison (U.S.)
1886	dishwasher	Josephine Cochran (U.S.)
1891	zipper	Whitcomb L. Judson (U.S.)
1901	washing machine	Langmuir Fisher (U.S.)
1903	windshield wipers	Mary Anderson (U.S.)
1907	vacuum cleaner	J. Murray Spangler (U.S.) ▶
1911	air conditioning	Willis H. Carrier (U.S.)
1924	frozen packaged food	Clarence Birdseye (U.S.)
1947	Tupperware	Earl Silas Tupper (U.S.)
1948	Velcro	Georges de Mestral (Switzerland)
1958	laser	A. L. Schawlow & C. H. Townes (U.S.)
1963	pop-top can	Ermal C. Fraze (U.S.)
1969	cash machine (ATM)	Don Wetzel (U.S.)
1971	food processor	Pierre Verdon (France)
1980	Post-its	3M Company (U.S.)
1981	Polartec fabric	Malden Mills (U.S.)
2002	robot vacuum	iRobot Corp. (U.S.)

INVENTIONS ENTERTAIN US

YEAR	INVENTION	INVENTOR (COUNTRY)
1709	piano	Bartolomeo Cristofori (Italy)
1877	phonograph	Thomas A. Edison (U.S.)
1877	microphone	Emile Berliner (U.S.)
1888	portable camera	George Eastman (U.S.)
1893	moving picture viewer	Thomas A. Edison (U.S.)
1894	motion picture projector	Charles F. Jenkins (U.S.)
1899	tape recorder	Valdemar Poulsen (Denmark)
1923	television*	Vladimir K. Zworykin* (U.S.)
1963	steel tennis racquet	René Lacoste (France)
1969	videotape cassette	Sony (Japan) ▶
1972	compact disc (CD)	RCA (U.S.)
1972	video game (Pong)	Noland Bushnell (U.S.)
1972	Hacky Sack	John Stalberger & Mike Marshall
1979	Walkman	Sony (Japan)
1995	DVD (digital video disk)	Matsushita (Japan)

Others who helped invent television include Philo T. Farnsworth (1926) and John Baird (1928).

INVENTIONS HELP MAKE LIFE SAFER

YEAR	INVENTION	INVENTOR (COUNTRY)
1752	lightning rod	Benjamin Franklin (U.S.)
1815	safety lamp for miners	Sir Humphry Davy (England)
1852	elevator brake	Elisha G. Otis (U.S.)
1863	fire extinguisher	Alanson Crane (U.S.) ▶
1923	automatic traffic signal	Garrett A. Morgan (U.S.)
1952	airbag	John Hetrick (U.S.)
1969	battery operated smoke detector	Randolph Smith & Kenneth House (U.S.)
1971	Kevlar (strong material used for helmets, bullet-proof vests)	Stephanie Louise Kwolek & Herbert Blades (U.S.)

Did You Know?

WORLD'S SMALLEST MICROCHAIN DRIVE

*Sandia National Laboratories in Livermore, California, may be the biggest and the best at making things small. Scientists there made this chain and gears out of silicon. It may may look like an ordinary bicycle chain and sprocket—but each link in the chain would fit on a human hair! The diameter of a hair is about 70 microns. A micron is one millionth of a meter. Tiny motors called **Microelectromechanical systems (MEMS)** could be used to drive these chains and gears to operate switches, cameras, sensors, and other new devices made with nanotechnology (technology on a tiny scale).*

To learn more about inventions and the people who created them, or to make your own invention, visit

National Inventors Hall of Fame
221 S. Broadway, Akron, Ohio 44308
Phone: (330) 762-4463.
E-mail: museum@invent.org
WEB SITE *http://www.invent.org*

INVENTIONS HELP US EXPAND OUR UNIVERSE

YEAR	INVENTION	INVENTOR (COUNTRY)
1250	magnifying glass	Roger Bacon (England) ▶
1590	2-lens microscope	Zacharias Janssen (Netherlands)
1608	telescope	Hans Lippershey (Netherlands)
1714	mercury thermometer	Gabriel D. Fahrenheit (Germany)
1926	rocket engine	Robert H. Goddard (U.S.)
1930	cyclotron (atom smasher)	Ernest O. Lawrence (U.S.)
1943	Aqua Lung	Jacques-Yves Cousteau & Emile Gagnan (France)
1977	space shuttle	NASA (U.S.)
2001	EZ-Rocket (reusable rocket engines)	Jeff Greason (U.S.)

BRIGHT IDEAS FROM KIDS

Christine Haas, 14, of Clovis, California, won first prize in the 2002 **Discovery Channel Young Scientist Challenge** (DCYSC). She created a a natural mosquito poison from the flowers of the California buckeye tree. Christine lives in an area with a lot of range land, where livestock graze, and mosquitos breed in the water. Ranchers don't want to put poisons into the water for fear of harming their animals. Christine's invention could do the trick. Her prize was a $15,000 scholarship and the title "America's Top Young Scientist of the Year." For more information, visit

WEB SITE *http://school.discovery.com/sciencefaircentral/dysc/accept/accept.html*

First prize at the Bayer/National Science Foundation Awards for 2002 went to middle schoolers **Patricia Rincon, Lauren Rushing, Joel Anderson, Patrick Hall**, and their coach, teacher Joe Ann Clark, from Brandon, Mississippi. The seventh-graders took on the suburban problem of runaway shopping carts by inventing a set of brakes for them. Like a self-propelled lawn mower, the carts move when a bar attached to the handle is squeezed and stop when the handle is released. In addition to a week-long trip to Disney World, each student won $5,000 in U.S. Savings Bonds. For more information on the contest, now called the Christopher Columbus Awards, go to

WEB SITE *http://www.nsf.gov/od/lpa/events/bayernsf/intro.htm*

FAST FORWARD!

How fast can you move forward through time, putting the inventions listed below in the right place on the timeline?

A-laser, **B**-space shuttle, **C**-bifocal glasses, **D**-propeller airplane, **E**-practical lightbulb

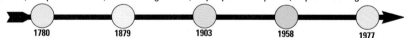

1780   1879   1903   1958   1977

Think you got that right? How about this one:

A-typewriter, **B**-moveable type, **C**-rollerblades, **D**-lightning rod, **E**-television, **F**-mercury thermometer, **G**-Segway Human Transport, **H**-videotape cassette **I**-telegraph, **J**-telescope

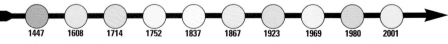

1447   1608   1714   1752   1837   1867   1923   1969   1980   2001

ANSWERS ON PAGES 314-317. FOR MORE PUZZLES GO TO **WWW.WORLDALMANACFORKIDS.COM**

Language

WORDS ABOUT WORDS

What letter of the alphabet is used the most? **page 106**

An **acronym** is an abbreviation formed from the first letters or syllables of a group of words.

"Radar" comes from "radio detection and ranging"

An **anagram** is a word or phrase made by rearranging the letters from another word or phrase, or perhaps from nonsense letters.

From "Presbyterians" you can get the anagram "Britney Spears."

Antonyms are words that have opposite meanings.

happy and sad
courageous and cowardly

A **cliché** is a saying or expression that has been used so often by so many people, it has lost its interest.

The early bird gets the worm
Pretty as a picture

An **eponym** is a word that comes from the name of a person or thing.

Braille, a system of raised dots that enable blind people to read by touch, was named for its creator, Louis Braille.

A **euphemism** is a pleasant word or phrase used in place of a harsher word or phrase.

Instead of "used car": pre-owned vehicle
Instead of "died": passed away

Homophones are words that sound alike but have different meanings and spellings.

by/bye/buy,
night/knight,
plain/plane,
weak/week

A **palindrome** is a word, phrase, or sentence that has exactly the same letters when spelled backward or forward.

evil olive
Was it a rat I saw?
Step on no pets.

A **pseudonym** is a name someone makes up and uses to hide his or her true identity.

Daniel Handler, the author of *A Series of Unfortunate Events*, uses the pseudonym Lemony Snicket.

A **pun** is the use of a word with two different meanings, in a way that's humorous.

The baker said, "I think I'll loaf around all day."
These bananas look appealing!

Synonyms are words that have the same or almost the same meanings.

happy and cheerful
puzzled and perplexed

THE ENGLISH

FACTS ABOUT ENGLISH

► According to the Oxford English Dictionary, the English language contains between one quarter of a million (250,000) and three quarters of a million (750,000) words. The number depends on whether you count different meanings of the same word as separate words and whether you include many obscure technical terms that are usually not in a dictionary.

► Worldwide, one out of four people can speak English to some extent.

► The most frequently used letters of the alphabet are E, T, A, and O, in that order.

► Here is a list of 30 of the most commonly used English words: the, of, and, a, to, in, is, that, it, was, he, for, as, on, with, his, be, at, you, I, are, this, by, from, had, have, they, not, or, one

► The English language has borrowed many words from different languages. Here are a few:
    Alligator comes from the Spanish word *el legarto*, which means "the lizard."
    Crayon comes from the French word *crayon*, which means "pencil."
    Volcano comes from the Italian word *vulcano*.
    Tsunami (tidal wave) comes from the Japanese words *tsu*, which means "harbor," and *nami*, which means "wave."
    Bungalow comes from the Hindi word *bangla*, which means "little house."

NEW WORDS

English is always changing as new words are born and old ones die out. Many new words come from the field of electronics and computers, from the media, or from slang.

anime: a style of animation originating in Japan that uses stark colorful graphics and shows lively characters in action-filled plots, often with fantastic or futuristic themes ("A favorite anime TV series is *Yu-Gi-Oh!*")

hottie: a physically attractive person ("Lots of girls think Justin Timberlake is a hottie.")

noogie: the act of rubbing your knuckles on a person's head so as to cause slight pain. ("If my brother gives me another noogie I'll scream!")

webcam: a camera used in sending live images over the World Wide Web. ("My sister likes to watch the Giant Panda webcam at Washington's National Zoo.")

IN OTHER WORDS: IDIOMS

Idioms are phrases that mean more than their words put together. Here are some:

buying a pig in a poke—"buying something without seeing it"—At country fairs in England years ago, dishonest men would put a cat in a burlap bag and try to sell it as a young pig. If a suspicious buyer wanted to see the pig, the seller would be forced to "let the cat out of the bag" (another idiom, meaning "to expose a secret"). Poke, meaning "bag or sack," is not heard much anymore, but it is the source of the word "pocket."

in a pickle—"in an awkward or embarrassing situation"—Meats and vegetables can be preserved by soaking them in barrels of a salty solution called pickle. The Dutch had a phrase meaning "sitting in the pickle," which was borrowed into English about 500 years ago.

raining cats and dogs—"raining very heavily"—Centuries ago, people thought certain animals had magical powers. Sailors believed cats had something to do with rainstorms. Dogs and wolves were symbols of winds in Norse mythology.

LANGUAGE

GETTING TO THE ROOT

Many English words and parts of words can be traced back to Latin or Greek. If you know the meaning of a word's parts, you can probably guess what it means. A **root** (also called a stem) is the part of the word that gives its basic meaning, but can't be used by itself. Roots need other word parts to complete them: either a **prefix** at the beginning, or a **suffix** at the end, or sometimes both. The following tables give some examples of Greek and Latin roots, prefixes, and suffixes.

LATIN

root	basic meaning	example
-aqua-	water	aquarium
-ject-	to throw	reject
-mem-	to keep in mind	memory
-port-	to carry	transport
-scrib-/ -script-	to write	prescription

prefix	basic meaning	example
co-	together	cooperate
de-	away, off	defrost
inter-	between, among	international
pre-	before	prevent
re-	again, back	rewrite
sub-	under	subway

suffix	basic meaning	example
-able/-ible	capable or worthy of	workable
-fy/-ify	make or cause to become	horrify
-ly	like, to the extent of	highly
-ous	full of	wondrous
-ty/-ity	state of, power to	purity

GREEK

root	basic meaning	example
-chron-	time	chronology
-bio-	life	biology
-dem-	people	democracy
-phon-	sound	telephone
-psych-	mind, soul, spirit	psychology
-scope-	to see	telescope

prefix	basic meaning	example
a-/an-	without, not	anaerobic, amoral
auto-	self	autopilot
geo-	Earth	geography
micro-	small	microscope
tele-	far off	television

suffix	basic meaning	example
-ism	act, state, theory of	realism
-ist	one who believes in, practices	capitalist
-graph	write, draw, describe, record	photograph
-logy	talk, speech, study	biology
-meter	measure, measuring device	kilometer

Did You KNOW?

Many English words were borrowed from Latin, the language of the ancient Romans—who themselves borrowed from the ancient Greeks. As the Romans conquered more territory, their language spread with them. Many words came into English directly from Latin, especially those used in law and science. Other words were borrowed from languages based on Latin.

In different parts of Europe, Latin developed over time into the languages we know as the "Latin" (or "Romance," from Romans) languages: primarily French, Italian, Portuguese, and Spanish. In 1066, the French-speaking Normans conquered England. For more than 200 years after that, French was the language of the government and of upper society. Many French words (like government!) came into English during this period.

Would you have guessed that Mandarin, the principal language of China, is the most common spoken language in the world? You may find more surprises in the chart below, which lists languages spoken in 2000 by at least 100,000,000 native speakers (those for whom the language is their first language, or mother tongue) and some of the places where each one is spoken.

Konnichi wa! (Japanese)

LANGUAGE	WHERE SPOKEN	NATIVE SPEAKERS
Mandarin	China, Taiwan	874,000,000
Hindi	India	366,000,000
English	U.S., Canada, Britain	341,000,000
Spanish	Spain, Latin America	322,000,000
Arabic	Arabian Peninsula	207,000,000
Bengali	India, Bangladesh	207,000,000
Portuguese	Portugal, Brazil	176,000,000
Russian	Russia	167,000,000
Japanese	Japan	125,000,000
German	Germany, Austria	100,000,000

LANGUAGE USED AT HOME	SPEAKERS OVER 5 YEARS OLD
❶ Speak only English	215,423,557
❷ Spanish	28,101,052
❸ Chinese	2,022,143
❹ French	1,643,838
❺ German	1,383,442
❻ Tagalog (Philippines)	1,224,241
❼ Vietnamese	1,009,627
❽ Italian	1,008,370
❾ Korean	894,063
❿ Russian	706,242
⓫ Polish	667,414
⓬ Arabic	614,582
⓭ Portuguese	564,630
⓮ Japanese	477,997
⓯ French Creole	453,368
⓰ Greek	365,436
⓱ Hindi	317,057
⓲ Persian	312,085
⓳ Urdu	262,900
⓴ Gujarathi	235,988
(spoken in India & parts of Africa)	

WHICH LANGUAGES ARE SPOKEN IN THE UNITED STATES?

Hello! (English)

Since the beginning of American history, immigrants have come to the United States from all over the world. They have brought their native languages with them.

¡Hola! That's how more than 28 million Americans say "hi" at home. Still, 215 million Americans only speak English.

The table at right lists the other most frequently spoken languages in the United States, as of the 2000 census.

¡Hola! (Spanish)

DID YOU KNOW?

- Because it is not related to any other language family, many people consider Basque to be the most difficult language to master. Basque is spoken in the Pyrenees Mountains, between France and Spain.

- At about 90 years old, Afrikaans is one of the world's youngest languages. A mixture of Dutch, German, and other languages, it is one of South Africa's two official languages, and is spoken by descendants of Dutch settlers.

- In many languages, the word for "mother" begins with the sound ma and the word for "father" begins with the sound da. But in the Georgian language, deda means "mother" and mama means "father."

LANGUAGE EXPRESS

Surprise your friends and family with words from other languages.

ENGLISH	SPANISH	FRENCH	GERMAN	CHINESE
January	enero	janvier	Januar	yi-yue
February	febrero	fevrier	Februar	er-yue
March	marzo	mars	Marz	san-yue
April	abril	avril	April	si-yue
May	mayo	mai	Mai	wu-yue
June	junio	juin	Juni	liu-yue
July	julio	juillet	Juli	qi-yue
August	agosto	aout	August	ba-yue
September	septiembre	septembre	September	jiu-yue
October	octubre	octobre	Oktober	shi-yue
November	noviembre	novembre	November	shi-yi-yue
December	diciembre	decembre	Dezember	shi er-yue
blue	azul	bleu	blau	lan
red	rojo	rouge	rot	hong
green	verde	vert	grun	lu
yellow	amarillo	jaune	gelb	huang
black	negro	noir	schwarz	hei
white	blanco	blanc	weiss	bai
happy birthday!	¡feliz cumpleaños!	bonne anniversaire!	Glückwunsch zum Geburtstag!	sheng-ri kuai le!
hello!	¡hola!	bonjour!	hallo!	ni hao!
good-bye!	¡adios!	au revoir!	auf Wiedersehen!	zai-jian!
one	uno	un	eins	yi
two	dos	deux	zwei	er
three	tres	trois	drei	san
four	cuatro	quatre	vier	si
five	cinco	cinq	funf	wu
six	seis	six	sechs	liu
seven	siete	sept	sieben	qi
eight	ocho	huit	acht	ba
nine	nueve	neuf	neun	jiu
ten	diez	dix	zehn	shi

- Some of the consonants in the Khoisan family of languages are pronounced with clicking sounds. These languages include Hottentot, Bushman, and Hatsa, and they are spoken by people in southern Africa (Namibia, South Africa, and Tanzania).
- Navajo words can mean different things depending on whether they are pronounced in a high, low, rising, or falling tone. The word tsin can mean "log," "stick," "tree," or "bone," depending on the tone in which it is spoken.
- The most frequently used languages on the Internet are: **1.** English, **2.** Japanese, **3.** Spanish, **4.** German, **5.** French.

All About... SLANG

What is slang? Your parents and teachers might say slang is bad or improper English, but a friend might consider slang to be poetic. And it is true that the sentence "When that school bell rings, I'm gonna bounce" gives you a more vivid image than the sentence "When school is over, I'm going to leave." Slang may be fine to use at times, but it is informal. Like casual clothes, it may not be right for every occasion.

American slang dates back to colonial times. We get the slang words *peepers* (eyes), *mug* (face), and *chops* (mouth) from criminals who were brought from England to the colonies between 1619 and 1772. The Civil War gave us the word *skedaddle*, which means "to run away." And we get the word *skivvies* (men's underwear) from World War II soldiers.

Today, thanks to hip-hop music, television, video, radio, film, and the Internet, slang gets around more than ever. A popular word nowadays is *phat*, which means excellent or superb. It comes from the word *emphatic*, and it also plays on the word *fat*.

SIGN LANGUAGE

Many people who are deaf or hearing-impaired, and cannot hear spoken words, talk with their fingers instead of their voices. To do this, they use a system of manual signs (the manual alphabet), or finger spelling, in which the fingers are used to form letters and words. Originally developed in France by Abbe Charles Michel De l'Epee in the late 1700s, the manual alphabet was later brought to the United States by Laurent Clerc (1785-1869), a Frenchman who taught people who were deaf.

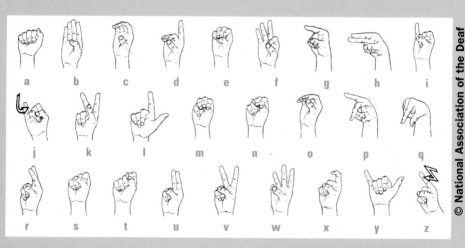

© National Association of the Deaf

▲ *American Manual Alphabet*

JOKES & RIDDLES

What's the difference between a jeweler and a jailer?
The jeweler sells watches and the jailer watches cells.

What is the center of gravity?
The letter "v."

What did one eye say to the other eye?
"Between you and me, there's something that smells."

How do dinosaurs pay their bills?
With Tyrannosaurus checks.

How do you make an egg laugh?
Tell it a yolk.

What's the hardest part about learning to inline skate?
The pavement.

What bird can lift the most?
A crane.

How do trees turn into petrified wood?
The wind makes them rock.

When does it rain money?
Whenever there's some change in the weather.

What has a head and a foot but no body?
A bed.

What clothes does a house wear?
Address, or a "coat of paint."

What should you do if you split your sides laughing?
Run fast until you get a stitch in it.

What's the longest word in the English language?
Smiles, because there is a mile between the first and last letter.

What needs at least two people to hold up its ends, but can't be lifted?
A conversation.

A man builds a house with all 4 sides facing south. A bear walks past the house. What color is the bear?
White; the house is built directly on the North Pole.

What has 4 legs, a back, but no body?
A chair.

If two's company and three's a crowd, what are four and five?
Nine.

If you were standing directly on Antarctica's South Pole facing north, which direction would you travel if you took one step backward?
North; from the South Pole, all directions are north.

In what year did Christmas Day and New Year's Day fall in the same year?
It happens every year.

Is an old hundred-dollar bill better than a new one?
It's 99 dollars better!

No sooner spoken than broken. What is it?
Silence.

Some months have 30 days, some months have 31 days; how many have 28?
They all do.

Forward I am heavy, but backward I am not. What am I?
A ton.

111

Military

SERIOUS BUSINESS

How fast can a B-1B Lancer fly? ... page 114

Soldiers risk their lives to fight for their nation or cause, often to defend the lives and freedom of others. Since the beginning of the Revolutionary War, more than 2.6 million U.S. soldiers have been killed or wounded in wars (almost as many people as now live in Arkansas). Today, about 1.5 million American men and women serve on active duty in the four major branches of the military—the Army, Navy, Air Force, and Marines.

In the Iraq war of 2003, U.S. special operations forces on the ground got information to help pinpoint military targets for bombing. This greatly reduced enemy resistance and meant fewer casualties for U.S.-led troops (about 170 deaths as of May). The newest technology also made it possible to bomb targets more precisely than in the past, so as to reduce the danger to civilians. However, large numbers of Iraqi soldiers and an unknown number of civilians did lose their lives.

Good intelligence and advanced technology have always been important, as well as clever tactics, and sometimes just plain stubbornness.

INTELLIGENCE

During World War II, U.S. military intelligence broke a Japanese naval code used to send secret messages by radio. Americans thus learned of a planned attack on the U.S.-held island of Midway, northwest of Hawaii. Planes from U.S. aircraft carriers were able to ambush the Japanese fleet before it got in shooting range of the island.

TECHNOLOGY

English forces in France used the longbow to defeat the French in the Battle of Agincourt, in 1415. Longbows, which were as tall as the archers themselves, could hurl heavy arrows 200 yards or more, or the length of two modern football fields.

TACTICS

The tactics of General Robert E. Lee led to a Southern victory in the Civil War Battle of Chancellorsville, Virginia, in May 1863. Trapped between two much larger Union forces, Lee divided his army into three parts and launched a surprise flanking attack that made the Northerners retreat.

STUBBORNNESS

Soldiers and civilians in the Russian city of Stalingrad (Volgograd) held off an invading German army in 1942–43. The Russians refused to surrender the city despite terrible casualties and hardships. Eventually, Russian troops launched a counterattack, and the Germans retreated.

OUT OF THE ORDINARY

WHAT ARE SPECIAL OPERATIONS? "Special operations" is a term for missions not part of normal warfare. In war, two large forces usually face each other, with thousands of troops fighting at once. "Special Ops" forces work in small units, often deep inside enemy territory. They can fight anywhere, from baking deserts to steaming jungles to snow-covered mountains. Most are parachute-trained, and some are trained in underwater operations. They know foreign languages. They are some of the finest troops in any army.

U.S. SPECIAL OPERATIONS FORCES The U.S. has the most special-operation forces in the world. The Army, Navy, Air Force, and Marines have units. All are under the Defense Department's Special Operations Command at MacDill Air Force Base in Florida.

Army The Army's Special Forces and Rangers are part of its 75th Regiment. Rangers specialize in larger-unit operations—like the raid on Taliban headquarters on October 19, 2001. More than 100 Rangers and other Special Forces troops took part in the first U.S. ground operations in Afghanistan. Their history goes back to "Roger's Rangers," a group of American frontiersmen who fought bravely in the French and Indian War (1754-63).

Formed in 1952, the Army's Special Forces **"Green Berets"** get their name from the caps they wear with their uniforms. They started wearing them in 1962, when John F. Kennedy was president. Today, the Army has four active-duty Special Forces Groups, with about 700 men each.

The basic unit of a Special Forces Group is the Alpha Detachment, or "A-Team." Each A-Team has a captain, a lieutenant, and 10 sergeants. Each member has one main specialty (operations, intelligence, medicine, weapons, demolitions, or radio operations) and is also trained in a second one. For example, a Green Beret might be a radio operator and also trained in medicine or in using explosives.

Air Force The Air Force has a variety of units that provide transportation and air cover for U.S. commandos. These units include the 1st Special Operations Wing and two Special Operations Squadrons.

Marines Every Marine Expeditionary Unit (of about 1,000 troops) has a Force Recon unit (about 150 troops) to act as its eyes and ears in the field.

Navy Organized during World War II, the Navy's SEALs were originally called underwater demolition teams, or UDTs. SEAL stands for "Sea-Air-Land," reminding us that these Navy warriors can fight anywhere they are needed.

THE RESCUE OF PRIVATE JESSICA LYNCH on April 1, 2003, was made by a Special Ops team of Army Rangers, Air Force pilots, Navy SEALs, and Marine commandos. She was being held as a prisoner of war in a hospital in the Iraqi city of An Nasiriya. An Iraqi named Mohammed saw Jessica there. He told U.S. forces about her and then went back to scout out the hospital's layout for them. Using his detailed maps, the soldiers were able to find the wounded POW and carry her out safely on a stretcher, in a nighttime raid that took just 25 minutes.

IN THE AIR

Here are some of the aircraft used by the U.S. in Afghanistan and in the war in Iraq.

B-2A SPIRIT This is the long-range "stealth bomber." Its shape, high-altitude flight, and stealth technology make it almost impossible for enemy radar to detect it. The B-2 can fly 6,000 miles without refueling. B-2s are part of the 509th Bomb Wing. Missions are usually flown from Whiteman Air Force Base in Missouri, but for operations in Iraq, they were based on Diego Garcia Island in the Indian Ocean. The B-2 can travel close to the speed of sound (about 700 mph) and fly as high as 50,000 feet. It carries a crew of two: a pilot and a bombardier. It is 69 feet long, 17 feet high, and weighs 336,500 lbs. fully loaded. Its wingspan is 172 feet.

B-1B LANCER These are long-range, multi-role bombers. Each B-1B can carry up to 84 500-pound bombs or 20 Cruise missiles. It is difficult for enemy radar to detect. The plane's four turbo-fan engines can push it as high as 30,000 feet, at speeds over 900 miles per hour. The B-1B carries a crew of four: a commander, a co-pilot, plus offensive and defensive systems officers. It is 146 feet long, 34 feet high, and weighs 190,000 lbs. (empty). Its wingspan is 137 feet.

RQ-1 PREDATOR This unmanned, propeller-driven aircraft is used mostly for observation. It has video cameras, an infrared camera (for night vision), and radar. It can see through dense clouds and smoke. It may carry Hellfire missiles to strike targets on the ground. The Predator is 27 feet long, weighs 950 pounds, and has a wingspan of 27 feet. It has a cruising range of 424 miles, at 84 miles per hour, and can fly as high as 25,000 feet. It has a crew of zero.

The RQ-4 Global Hawk is another plane without a pilot that was used in Iraq in 2003. Unlike the Predator, the Global Hawk is a jet-powered, high-altitude spy plane. It has a range of 4,000 miles and can fly as high as 60,000 feet. It has a wingspan of 116 feet and can stay in the air for 24 hours.

F-117A NIGHTHAWK This was the first plane to use "low-observable" technology. It's called the "stealth fighter," but it doesn't engage in battles with other planes. In Iraq, F-117s flew into heavily protected areas with two 2,000-pound laser-guided missiles, to take out difficult military targets like radar centers, ammunition factories, and Saddam Hussein's command bunker. F-117s are used at the beginning of a big attack to clear the way for other forces to follow. The F-117 is 63 feet long, 12 feet high, and has a wingspan of 43 feet. It weighs 52,500 pounds (empty) and flies just under the speed of sound.

USS Harry S. Truman

AT SEA

AIRCRAFT CARRIER Six carriers were deployed in the Persian Gulf or eastern Mediterranean Sea during the war with Iraq. They were the *USS Abraham Lincoln, USS Theodore Roosevelt, USS Harry S. Truman, USS Constellation, USS Kitty Hawk,* and *USS Nimitz.* These ships are designed to carry up to 80 airplanes, which take off from and land on their huge decks. The *USS Abraham Lincoln*, stationed in the Persian Gulf, had 1,600 missions flown from its deck to Iraq. Carriers are the heart of the modern navy. They are so expensive to build (nearly $5 billion!), though, that very few countries have them. A modern carrier is about as long as the Empire State Building is tall (1,092 feet) and its flight deck is 4.5 acres. A carrier is sometimes called a "floating city" because it can hold 6,000 people and has many of the same services as a regular town—restaurants, stores, gyms, a barbershop, a drug store, a dentist, a TV station, a hospital, and even a brig (jail). Because most carriers are nuclear powered, they can be at sea for months without refueling. This lets military planners be prepared for air strikes almost anywhere in the world.

ON THE GROUND

M1 ABRAMS MAIN BATTLE TANK The Abrams tank is called the backbone of the armored forces of the U.S. military. Along with the M-2 Bradley Infantry Fighting Vehicle (an armored troop carrier), it was the main ground force in Iraq in 2003. It is named after General Creighton W. Abrams, a famous tank commander of World War II and later Army chief of staff. The Abrams tank carries a crew of four (commander, gunner, loader, and driver) and weighs more than 60 tons. It uses a lot of fuel—about 3 gallons per mile—but it's a highly mobile vehicle that can fire shells while moving at fast speeds over rough ground. The tank also has special vision devices that allow its gunner to see a target at night. Over 8,000 of them have been built, not only for the United States, but also for some of its allies.

STRYKER MOBILE GUN SYSTEM This vehicle looks like a tank, but it isn't. A tank runs on treads, but this runs on eight wheels like a truck. It's lighter than a tank and can go faster, speeding along at over 60 miles an hour. It also can go over 300 miles without refueling—

much farther than a tank. It's also quieter, which means the enemy is less likely to hear it coming. The Stryker is small enough to be carried in a C-130 transport plane, something a tank can't do. The first Strykers were delivered in the summer of 2002, making it one of the newest vehicles added to the U.S. armored forces. These state-of-the-art machines weren't used in Iraq. They were set to be battle-ready by the end of May 2003.

Money

How long does the average dollar bill last? page 118

HISTORY of MONEY

Why Did People Start Using Money? At first, people bartered, which means they traded goods they had for things they needed. A farmer who had cattle might want to have salt to preserve meat, or cloth to make clothing. For this farmer, a cow became a "medium of exchange"—a way of getting things the farmer did not make or grow. Cattle became a form of money. Whatever people agreed to use for trade became the earliest kinds of money.

What Objects Have Been Used as Money?

► knives, rice, and spades in China around 3000 B.C.

► cattle and clay tablets in Babylonia around 2500 B.C.

► wampum (beads) and beaver fur by Native Americans of the northeast around A.D. 1500

► tobacco by early American colonists around 1650

► whales' teeth by the Pacific peoples on the island of Fiji, until the early 1900s

Wampum used by Native Americans

Why Did Governments Start Issuing Money? Governments were interested in issuing money because the money itself had value. If a government could gain control over the manufacture of money, it could increase its own wealth—often simply by making more money.

The first government to make coins that looked alike and use them as money is thought to be the Greek city-state of Lydia in the 7th century B.C. These Lydian coins were actually bean-shaped lumps made from a mixture of gold and silver.

By the Middle Ages (about A.D. 800-1100), gold had become a popular medium for trade in Europe. But gold was heavy and difficult to carry, and the cities and the roads of Europe at that time were dangerous places to carry large amounts of gold. So merchants and goldsmiths began issuing notes promising to pay gold to the person carrying the note. These "promissory notes" were the beginning of paper money in Europe. In the early 1700s, France's government became the first in Europe to issue paper money that looked alike. Paper money was probably also invented in China, where the explorer Marco Polo saw it in the 1280s.

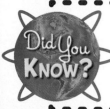

Did You Know?

Anybody have change for $100,000? That's the biggest U.S. bill ever made, and it has a picture of President Woodrow Wilson. There also are bills for $10,000 (showing former Treasury Secretary Salmon Chase), $5,000 (President James Madison), $1,000 (President Grover Cleveland), and $500 (President William McKinley). The $100,000 bill was not available to the public. It was only for certain bank transactions. Though they aren't made anymore, the other bills can still be used!

Money Around the World

When you go to a foreign country, one of the first things you may notice is what the money looks like. Many countries have colorful bills in different shapes and sizes. They often show queens or presidents or other famous people. But you also may find a rhinoceros, tiger, or elephant (India), a sea turtle (Brazil), cows and fruit (Nigeria), a map of the North Pole (Norway), or even schoolchildren (Taiwan).

All About... THE EURO

Citizens of 12 countries in Europe (see bottom of page) were excited about the crisp new paper money and sparkling new coins they had starting in January 2002. This new currency, called the euro, is good in all 12 countries. Switching to the euro was a big job. In a short time, banks had to get money worth 600 billion euros into the hands of 300 million people. There were 15 billion banknotes printed, showing structures such as gateways and bridges. For the 50 billion coins, the front (obverse) side has the word "euro" and a map of the euro area. On the other side (reverse), each euro country has a national symbol, such as the Irish harp for Ireland, and a portrait of the king for Spain.

Many Germans are sad to see their marks disappear. People in France and Italy miss their francs and lire. But now money flows easily from one country to another. This makes it easier to complete big financial deals between countries. And think how much easier it is for tourists. They can use the same kind of money to pay for a slice of pizza whether it's in Italy or in Belgium. Americans in Europe can easily figure what something costs because the euro and U.S. dollar are worth about the same— the euro equaled about $1.07 in spring 2003.

WHAT ARE EXCHANGE RATES?

When one country exports goods to another, the payment from the country buying the goods must be changed into the currency of the country selling them. People traveling to other countries usually need to convert their money into the local currency. In some countries, like Canada, stores will accept U.S. money for purchases, but will give change in Canadian money. How do they know how much change to give you? An exchange rate—that gives the price of one currency in terms of another—is used. For example, in April 2003 one U.S. dollar could buy 1.45 Canadian dollars.

Here are the exchange rates in 1990 and 2003 between the U.S. dollar and the currency of some of the country's biggest trading partners.

What A U.S. Dollar Bought

COUNTRY	IN 1990	IN 2003
Canada	1.2 Canadian dollars	1.45 Canadian dollars
Great Britain	0.56 pound	0.64 pound
European Union*	—	0.93 euros
Japan	144.8 yen	120.7 yen
Mexico	2.8 pesos	10.6 pesos

$5   603.5 YEN

United States   Japan

*The euro is used in Austria, Belgium, Finland, France, Germany, Greece, Ireland, Italy, Luxembourg, the Netherlands, Portugal, and Spain. Three EU countries—Denmark, Great Britain, and Sweden— have kept their own currencies.

MAKING MONEY

WHAT IS THE U.S. MINT?

The U.S. Mint, founded in 1792, is part of the Treasury Department. The Mint makes all U.S. coins and safeguards the nation's $100 million in gold and silver **bullion** (uncoined bars of metal). Reserves of these precious metals are held at West Point, New York, and Fort Knox, Kentucky. The Mint turns out coins at four production facilities (Denver, Philadelphia, San Francisco, and West Point). For more information, visit the U.S. Mint's website at

WEB SITE *http://www.usmint.gov*

WHAT KINDS OF COINS DOES THE MINT MAKE?

Branches of the U.S. Mint in Denver and Philadelphia currently make coins for "circulation," or everyday use. In 2002, these two facilities made nearly 14.5 billion coins, including more than 7 billion pennies! A tiny "D" or "P" near the year, called a mint mark, tells you which one made the coin. A Lincoln cent or "penny" with no mint mark was probably made at the Philadelphia Mint, which has by tradition never marked pennies. The U.S. Mint also makescommemorative coins in honor of events, like the Olympics, or people, like Christopher Columbus.

WHAT IS THE BUREAU OF ENGRAVING AND PRINTING?

The Bureau of Engraving and Printing (BEP), established in 1862, is also part of the Treasury Department. The BEP designs and prints all U.S. paper money. It also prints U.S. postage stamps and other official certificates. The BEP's production facilities in Washington, D.C., and Ft. Worth, Texas, made more than 7 billion bills in 2002. About 95% of them are used to replace worn out money. Even though bills are made of a special paper that is 75% cotton and 25% linen, they wear out pretty fast if they are used a lot. The $1 bill only lasts an average of 18 months, while $50 and $100 bills last about 9 years. For more information visit the BEP's website at

WEB SITE *http://www.moneyfactory.com*

WHOSE PORTRAITS ARE ON OUR MONEY?

The table below shows which presidents and other famous Americans appear on the front of all U.S. money.

Denomination	Portrait	Denomination	Portrait
1¢	Abraham Lincoln, 16th President	$2	Thomas Jefferson, 3rd President
5¢	Thomas Jefferson, 3rd President	$5	Abraham Lincoln, 16th President
10¢	Franklin D. Roosevelt, 32nd President	$10	Alexander Hamilton, 1st Treasury Secretary
25¢	George Washington, 1st President		
50¢	John F. Kennedy, 35th President	$20	Andrew Jackson, 7th President
$1 (COIN)	Sacagawea, Native American woman	$50	Ulysses S. Grant, 18th President
$1 (BILL)	George Washington, 1st President	$100	Benjamin Franklin, inventor, U.S. patriot

U.S. STATE QUARTERS

From 1999 to 2008, five new quarter designs are being minted each year. George Washington will stay on the front, but a design honoring one of the 50 states will appear on the back. The quarters for each state are coming out in the order in which the states joined the Union. By the end of 2002, these were Delaware, Pennsylvania, New Jersey, Georgia, Connecticut, Massachusetts, Maryland, South Carolina, New Hampshire, Virginia, New York, North Carolina, Rhode Island, Vermont, Kentucky, Tennessee, Ohio, Louisiana, Indiana, and Mississippi. In 2003, Illinois, Alabama, Maine, Missouri, and Arkansas were coming out. Michigan, Florida, Texas, Iowa, and Wisconsin are due in 2004.

HOW MUCH MONEY IS IN CIRCULATION?

As of June 2002, the total amount of money in circulation in the United States came to $625,742,394,425. More than 30 billion dollars was in coins, the rest in paper money.

All About...
THE COLOR OF MONEY

U.S. money has been green for so long that people call it by slang terms like "lettuce," "greenbacks," "mint leaves," and "the long green." People from countries with colorful money think U.S. bills are "boring." So it sounded exciting when the Treasury Department in 2002 announced it was going to start printing U.S. money in different colors. Sadly, the new colors are no big deal. The new $20 bills will use slight background tints that you may hardly notice (see below). New $10 and $5 bills will also soon be made with slight tints. The reason is that laser printers, color copiers, and scanners have given criminals new high-tech tools to make fake, or counterfeit, money. The U.S. Secret Service—which was founded to stop counterfeiters (and now also protects the president)—estimates that $47.5 million in fake money was used in 2001. The government hopes the new colored money will be much harder to copy accurately.

COIN CHALLENGES

In 3 moves, turning over 2 coins each time, can you get all 3 coins to come up tails?

Did you do it? OK, now try the "nine coin challenge." You have to make 8 jumps of one coin over another, like in checkers, and end up with only one coin in the center square. (Take jumped coins off the board as you go.) **Hint:** If you work 'round the clock, you might solve this puzzle!

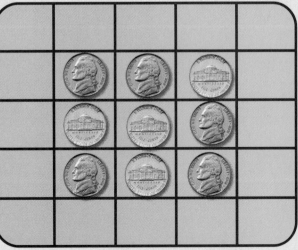

ANSWERS ON PAGES 314-317. FOR MORE PUZZLES GO TO WWW.WORLDALMANACFORKIDS.COM

Movies & TV

What octopus plays the clarinet? ••• page 122

20 MOVIE HITS
(2002 AND EARLY 2003)

Lord of the Rings: The Two Towers

Agent Cody Banks (PG)
Bend It Like Beckham (PG-13)
Big Fat Liar (PG)
Daredevil (PG-13)
Harry Potter and the Chamber of Secrets (PG)
Holes (PG)

Ice Age (PG)
The Jungle Book 2 (G)
Like Mike (PG)
Lilo & Stitch (PG)
The Lizzie McGuire Movie (PG)
Lord of the Rings: The Two Towers (PG-13)
The Rookie (G)
Scooby-Doo (PG)
Spider-Man (PG-13)
Spirited Away (PG)
Star Wars: Episode II—Attack of the Clones (PG)
Tuck Everlasting (PG)
What a Girl Wants (PG)
X2: X-Men United (PG-13)

20 POPULAR KIDS VIDEOS OF 2002

Atlantis: The Lost Empire
Big Fat Liar
Cinderella II: Dreams Come True
The Count of Monte Cristo
Harry Potter and the Sorcerer's Stone
Ice Age
Jimmy Neutron: Boy Genius
Lilo & Stitch
The Lord of the Rings:
    The Fellowship of the Ring
Mary-Kate & Ashley: Getting There
Mary-Kate & Ashley: When in Rome

Monsters, Inc.
The Princess Diaries
The Rookie
Scooby-Doo
Snow Dogs
Spider-Man
Spirit: Stallion
    of the Cimarron
Star Wars:
    Episode II—Attack of the Clones
The Time Machine

SOME POPULAR MOVIES

SNOW WHITE AND THE SEVEN DWARFS (1937) Walt Disney turned this classic fairy tale into the first-ever full-length animated film. It's still popular today.

THE WIZARD OF OZ (1939) As color came to the movies, Dorothy, played by Judy Garland, met a scarecrow, a tin woodsman, and a cowardly lion in the land of Oz.

SINGIN' IN THE RAIN (1952) In the most famous scene in this movie musical, the star, Gene Kelly, splashes through puddles as he dances down the street in the pouring rain.

THE SOUND OF MUSIC (1965) This musical tells the story of Maria Von Trapp, whose plans to become a nun change when she becomes the governess to seven motherless children and falls in love with their father.

STAR WARS (1977) Luke Skywalker, Princess Leia, and others battle Darth Vader and his dark Empire in a thriller set in outer space. The sequels *The Empire Strikes Back*

(1980) and *The Return of the Jedi* (1983) were also hits. In 1999, a "prequel" was released, *Episode I—The Phantom Menace. Episode II—Attack of the Clones* opened in May 2002.

HARRY POTTER AND THE SORCERER'S STONE (2001) The adventures of Harry, Hermione, and Ron first came to the big screen in this long-awaited movie, first in a series based on J. K. Rowling's Harry Potter books.

SHREK (2001) A big, green, moody ogre finds love and friendship in a very cracked fairy tale. This hilarious film uses the voices of Mike Myers, Eddie Murphy, Cameron Diaz, and John Lithgow.

MONSTERS, INC. (2001) Top-scarer James P. "Sulley" Sullivan (voice by John Goodman) and his one-eyed sidekick Mike Wazowski (Billy Crystal) save Monstropolis by discovering that laughter is more powerful than fear.

HOLES

Camp Green Lake isn't green and it doesn't have a lake. It's a desert wasteland filled with venomous creatures. That's the backdrop of the popular Disney Pictures adventure movie *Holes.* It stars Shia LaBeouf (of the *Even Stevens* TV series) as Stanley Yelnats IV, who was sentenced to months of detention at the camp for a crime he didn't commit—stealing sneakers. Stanley—also known as Caveman—is always in the wrong place at the wrong time. His bad luck stems from an ancient family curse beginning with his "no-good-dirty-rotten-pig-stealing great-great grandfather." The story of the Yelnats family curse unfolds in flashbacks, in one of the movie's many subplots.

Shia LaBeouf (left) and Khleo Thomas

The camp's mean director, called The Warden (played by Sigourney Weaver), and her right-hand men, Mr. Sir (Jon Voight) and Dr. Pendanski (Tim Blake Nelson), use a strange system to help the prisoners reform. Stanley and his fellow "inmates"are forced to dig holes to build character. Under strict supervision, they dig holes exactly five feet wide and five feet deep, day after day in the hot sun. Nobody knows the real reason they're digging, but they think it's strange that they must immediately report anything "special" they might find. Stanley and the other boys from D-Tent—X-Ray, Armpit, ZigZag, Magnet, Squid, and Zero (played by 14-year-old Khleo Thomas)—have to stick together to figure out what's hidden in the holes and break his family curse forever.

The movie is based on a popular book by Louis Sachar, who also wrote the screenplay. The novel *Holes* won many awards, including the 1999 Newbery Medal and a 1998 National Book Award. The song "Dig It" (sung by the D-Tent Boys) from the movie is also a chart-topper.

All About... SPONGEBOB

Who lives in a pineapple under the sea? That would be SpongeBob SquarePants. But you probably know this already—even if you're not one of the more than 60 million "kids" (a third of whom are between the ages of 18 and 48!) who watch Nickelodeon's *SpongeBob SquarePants* each month. The show, which first aired in 1999, is the most popular animated kids' show on TV today. In 2002, *TV Guide* named SpongeBob the #9 greatest cartoon character of all time (Bugs Bunny was #1).

He's absorbent and yellow. Though sponges *are* found in the sea, that's about where scientific reality ends with SpongeBob. He looks more like the kind of sponge you'd wipe your kitchen counter with. In the town of Bikini Bottom (on the ocean floor), his best friend is a talking starfish and his neighbor is Squidward, an octopus who plays the clarinet. A squirrel named Sandy Cheeks, who comes from Texas, lives there too, in a special glass dome.

If nautical nonsense is something you wish . . . you can thank Stephen Hillenburg (right). He's the one who created this happy-go-lucky invertebrate and the wacky world of Bikini Bottom. Hillenburg knows very well how silly and unscientific his show is, because he studied marine biology in college. Before settling on a sponge, Stephen thought about making a jellyfish his star. SpongeBob was going to be called "SpongeBoy," but that name was already taken. After making 65 half-hour episodes, Stephen quit TV to work on a "SpongeBob" movie. Look for it in 2004.

Most Popular Cable TV Shows in 2002-2003
(Source: Nielsen Media Research; as of April 20, 2003)

AGES 6-11
1. SpongeBob SquarePants
2. The Adventures of Jimmy Neutron: Boy Genius
3. The Fairly OddParents
4. All Grown Up
5. All That

AGES 12-17
1. Lizzie McGuire
2. Yu Yu Hakusho
3. Sister, Sister
4. Smart Guy
5. Rurouni Kenshin

Most Popular Network TV Shows in 2002-2003
(Source: Nielsen Media Research; as of April 20, 2003)

AGES 6-11
1. American Idol
2. The Simpsons
3. Wonderful World of Disney
4. Malcolm in the Middle
5. Survivor: Thailand

AGES 12-17
1. American Idol
2. The Simpsons
3. Joe Millionaire
4. Malcolm in the Middle
5. Oliver Beene

PEOPLE TO WATCH

Hilary Duff

Hilary Duff caught the acting bug early on and has been going strong ever since. The multi-talented teenager stars in the hit Disney TV series *Lizzie McGuire*, for which she was nominated as Favorite Television Actress at Nickelodeon's 16th Annual Kids' Choice Awards in 2003. Her show won the award as Favorite Television Series. Hilary also starred in *the Lizzie McGuire Movie*, and in *Agent Cody Banks*, both released in spring 2003. She made her singing debut with the single "I Can't Wait" on the *Lizzie McGuire* soundtrack from Walt Disney Records. She also performs a single called "Why Not" on the movie soundtrack.

Hilary was born in Houston, Texas, on September 28, 1987. She splits her time between homes in Houston and Los Angeles, along with her parents, sister Haylie, and two dogs. When she has free time between acting and singing gigs, Hilary does volunteer work for Kids With a Cause and the Audrey Hepburn Children's Fund, both of which help abused and suffering children around the world. She also loves swimming, dancing, rollerblading, and just hanging out with her friends. What's next for this busy young star? Hilary fans can look for her line of clothing in spring 2004. She's busy designing styles and picking out fabrics and colors with two designers at NTD Apparel.

Shia LaBeouf

After watching his friend act on *Dr. Quinn Medicine Woman* one night, Shia LaBeouf decided that he could do just as good a job. The next day, he looked in the Yellow Pages for an agent, and the rest is history. Now he's starring in his own TV series, *Even Stevens* (he plays Louis Stevens, the youngest brother in the Stevens family and a class clown). He was nominated for a Young Artist Award in 2000.

Shia, who was named after his grandfather, was born on June 11, 1986, in Los Angeles. He seemed destined to become a performer—his grandfather was a comedian and his father was a chicken trainer in the circus! Shia says he gets his comedic talents from both his parents, who helped him develop his stand-up comedy routine.

Before he got an agent, Shia would perform his routine at coffee clubs. But now he's too busy for stand-up comedy. Besides his own TV series, he starred in three movies in 2003: *Holes, When Harry Met Lloyd: Dumb and Dumberer,* and *Charlie's Angels: Full Throttle.* Shia also finds time to surf and is developing his own clothing line. He and his pal A.J. Trauth, who plays Alan Twitty on *Even Stevens,* decided to become fashion designers so they could buy new surfboards. He might be a household name, but in some ways he's still a typical California teen!

Museums

The word museum comes from a Greek word that means "temple of the Muses." Muses were the Greek goddesses of art and science.

The oldest museum in the U.S. is The Charleston Museum, founded in South Carolina in 1773. The U.S. now has about 16,000 museums. Some are described here. For others, look in the Index under "Museums." You can also check out the Association of Children's Museums on the Internet at

WEB SITE http://www.childrensmuseums.org

Where does the name Pez come from?
page 126

All About...
THE SMITHSONIAN INSTITUTION

In 1835, the people of the United States received a unique gift from an English scientist. In his will, James Smithson left $508,318 to the U.S. to set up an institution for the "increase and diffusion of knowledge." No one knew exactly what he had in mind or why he was interested in giving money to this new foreign country. At first, nobody knew what to do about the gift. President Andrew Jackson was not even sure if it was legal for him to accept it. He had Congress pass a measure allowing him to do so. After a long time Congress passed in 1846 another bill, signed by President James Polk, establishing the Smithsonian. The Smithsonian's original building, known as "the castle," wasn't finished until 1855.

Today, the Smithsonian is the biggest museum complex in the world. It holds more than 142 million artworks, objects, and specimens, such as the 1813 flag that inspired Francis Scott Key to write "The Star-Spangled Banner," the Wright brothers' first airplane, the Hope Diamond, dresses worn by U.S. First Ladies, and much more. There are museums devoted to aviation and space exploration, American history, the arts, natural history, postal history, cultural history, and other fields. In addition to its 16 museums and 7 research centers, the Smithsonian also includes the National Zoo. Nearly 30 million people visited the Smithsonian's museums in 2001, and about another 3 million went to its zoo.

Admission is free for all Smithsonian museums in Washington, D.C.

Check out the Smithsonian's "Not Just for Kids" page to visit the **Hands On History** and **Hands On Science Centers**, the **American History by the Letter**, and **The Lemelson Center for the Study of Invention and Innovation** student page.

WEB SITE http://americanhistory.si.edu/notkid/index.htm

LIVING HISTORY EXHIBITS

These places to visit have been restored or re-created to look the way they did many years ago. Museum staff wear costumes and show what life use to be like.

Colonial Williamsburg, Williamsburg, Virginia. Learn about life in the American colonies in this restored version of Williamsburg, which was the capital of Virginia (1699 to 1780). Nearby is a re-creation of **Jamestown**, the first permanent English settlement in America.

Yorktown Victory Center, Yorktown, Virginia. Witness life during the American Revolution in this re-created Continental Army camp and farm from the 1700s.

St. Augustine Historic District

Historic Allaire Village, Wall, New Jersey. Blacksmiths, carpenters, and other workers demonstrate their trades in this restored village from the 1830s.

Lower East Side Tenement Museum, New York, New York. Learn about the lives of 4 immigrant families who lived her and worked in the garment industry at different times between the 1870s and 1930s.

St. Augustine Historic District, St. Augustine, Florida. Visit the oldest permanent European settlement in America— and the Castillo de San Marcos, a fort built between 1672 and 1695.

Stuhr Museum of the Prairie Pioneer, Grand Island, Nebraska. This restored railroad town, Pawnee-Indian earth lodge, and pioneer settlement captures the flavor of life in Nebraska at the end of the 1800s.

ETHNIC MUSEUMS

These museums show the culture and history of different groups.

Freer Gallery of Art and Arthur M. Sackler Gallery, Washington, D.C. • Displays art from China, Japan, India, and other Asian countries.

The Jewish Museum, New York, New York • Has exhibits covering many centuries of Jewish history and culture.

National Museum of the American Indian, New York, New York • Has displays on the ways of life and the history of Native Americans.

The Heard Museum, Phoenix, Arizona • Displays art by Native Americans, primarily from the southwestern U.S., such as the Apache, Hopi, and Navajo.

The Latin American Art Museum, Miami, Florida • Celebrates artwork, music, poetry, and dance performances by Hispanic and Latin American artists of today.

Charles H. Wright Museum of African American History, Detroit, Michigan • Features a large model of a slave ship, inventions by African Americans, music by black composers, and the space suit worn by the first U.S. black female astronaut.

DID YOU KNOW? **100 YEARS OF FLIGHT** *On December 17, 2003, the 100th anniversary of the Wright Brothers' historic flight, the National Air and Space Museum planned to open its Udvar-Hazy Center at the Washington Dulles International Airport. The 760,057-square-foot building will be home to 200 aircraft and 135 spacecraft, many of them too big for the museum on the National Mall. Exhibits will include the first U.S. Space Shuttle, Enterprise, and the Lockheed SR-71 Blackbird—a spy plane that flew 3 times the speed of sound.*

ODD MUSEUMS

At the **BURLINGAME MUSEUM OF PEZ MEMORABILIA** in Burlingame, California, you can find just about every plastic Pez candy dispenser ever made. They are a for sale. Prices range from $2.00 for Pez currently sold in stores to $1,300 for a special Mar Poppins dispenser.

WEB SITE *http://www.burlingamepezmuseum.com*

DID YOU KNOW? Pez started out as an aid to smokers trying to quit. The headless dispenser was made to look like a cigarette lighter. The name Pez was created from the German word for peppermint (**p**f**e**f**f**e**r**min**z**).

The **NATIONAL YO-YO MUSEUM** in Chico, California, claims to have the world's biggest working wooden yo-yo—it weighs 256 pounds and has a diameter of 50 inches.

WEB SITE *http://www.nationalyoyo.org*

The **DEVIL'S ROPE MUSEUM** in McLean, Texas, is a whole museum dedicated to preserving the many kinds of "devil's rope," or barbed wire, that fenced the west. The museum is located on Old Route 66 (see page 233).

WEB SITE *http://www.barbwiremuseum.com*

The **WORLD KITE MUSEUM AND HALL OF FAME,** in Long Beach, Washington, has more than 1,300 kites, including a collection of 700 kites from Japan, China, and Malaysia.

WEB SITE *http://www.worldkitemuseum.com*

MUSEUMS OF ALL KINDS

The National Watch and Clock Museum, Columbia,
Pennsylvania, has one of the world's biggest collections devoted to timekeeping. The 12,000 pieces include many clocks from the 17th to the 19th centuries. You'll also find a 1,000-year-old Chinese incense clock and a modern cesium clock so accurate that it will only gain or lose 1 second in 130,000 years!

The National Cowboy and Western Heritage Museum,
Oklahoma City, Oklahoma. The American Cowboy gallery traces the history and culture of this way of life from Spanish colonial times to the 20th century. There are also galleries for Western art and sculpture. Other galleries depict Native American life and customs and life on the frontier.

The San Francisco Maritime Museum,
San Francisco, California. Come aboard one of the largest collections of historic ships in the world. In addition to the tall sailing ships, you can tour a 1915 steam ship or the nearby USS *Pampanito*, a World War II submarine.

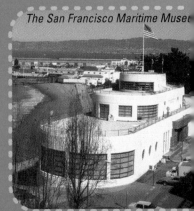

The San Francisco Maritime Muset

The Center for Puppetry Arts, Atlanta, Georgia.
This museum has more than 900 puppets and 1,000 posters in its permanent collection. From January 2003 to January 2004, there will be a special exhibit called "Puppetry in Focus: Treasures from our Global Collection." It features more than 50 puppets from the Czech Republic, Egypt, India, Indonesia, Japan, Mexico, Russia, and other countries.

Where can you find a didgeridoo? ... page 127

Music & Dance

MUSICAL INSTRUMENTS

There are many kinds of musical instruments. Instruments in an orchestra are divided into four groups, or sections: string, woodwind, brass, and percussion.

PERCUSSION INSTRUMENTS

make sounds when they are struck. This group includes drums, cymbals, triangles, gongs, bells, xylophones, and glockenspiels. Keyboard instruments, like the piano, are sometimes thought of as percussion instruments.

snare drum ▶

WOODWINDS are

long and round and hollow inside. They make sounds when air is blown into them through a mouth hole or a reed. The clarinet, flute, oboe, bassoon, and piccolo are woodwinds.

▲ clarinet

BRASSES

are hollow inside. They make sounds when air is blown into a mouthpiece shaped like a cup or a funnel. The trumpet, French horn, trombone, and tuba are brasses.

▲ trumpet

▲ violin

STRINGED INSTRUMENTS

make sounds when the strings are either stroked with a bow or plucked with the fingers. The violin, viola, cello, bass, and harp are used in an orchestra. The guitar, banjo, and mandolin are other stringed instruments.

INSTRUMENTS FROM ALL OVER

AUSTRALIA—The **didgeridoo** is a large tube of eucalyptus wood or bamboo. Players must breathe in through the nose while blowing out through the mouth. It has a deep, buzzing sound.

CHINA—The **erhu** is played with a bow, like a violin, but it only has two strings. Its sound box is covered with snakeskin. While the bow of a violin plays on top of the strings, the erhu is played with the bow between its two strings.

The didgeridoo ▲

IRELAND—The **bodhrán** is a frame drum (something like a tambourine) with a wooden body and a goatskin covering. It is played with a short double-ended stick called a *cipin* or *tipper*. Frame drums are found elsewhere around the world, but most are played with the hands.

MIDDLE EAST—The **oud** is played in many Arab countries of North Africa and the Middle East. It has a short neck, with a body shaped like half a pear. There are five pairs of strings. The oud gets its name from the Arabic *al-oud* (branch of wood).

127

MUSIC AND MUSIC MAKERS

▶**POP** Pop music (short for popular music) puts more emphasis on melody (tune) than does rock and has a softer beat. **Famous pop singers:** Frank Sinatra, Barbra Streisand, Madonna, Michael Jackson, Mariah Carey, Brandy, 'N Sync, Destiny's Child, Jennifer Lopez, Britney Spears.

▶**RAP and HIP-HOP** In rap, words are spoken or chanted to a fast, hip-hop beat, with the emphasis on rhythm rather than melody. Rap was created in inner cities. The lyrics show strong feelings and may be about anger and violence. Hip-hop often includes "samples," which are pieces of music from other songs. **Famous rappers:** Eminem, Coolio, LL Cool J, TLC, The Fugees, Will Smith, Nelly, Jay-Z, Nas.

▶**JAZZ** Jazz has its roots in the work songs, spirituals, and folk music of African-Americans. It began in the South in the early 1900s. **Famous jazz artists:** Louis Armstrong, Fats Waller, Jelly Roll Morton, Duke Ellington, Benny Goodman, Billie Holiday, Sarah Vaughan, Ella Fitzgerald, Dizzy Gillespie, Charlie Parker, Miles Davis, John Coltrane, Thelonious Monk, Wynton Marsalis.

▶**ROCK** (also known as Rock 'n' Roll) Rock music, which started in the 1950s, is based on black rhythm and blues and country music. It often uses electronic instruments and equipment. Folk rock, punk, heavy metal, and alternative music are types of rock music. **Famous rock musicians:** Elvis Presley, Bob Dylan, Chuck Berry, The Beatles, Janis Joplin, The Rolling Stones, Joni Mitchell, Bruce Springsteen, Pearl Jam, Matchbox 20.

▶**BLUES** The music called "the blues" developed from work songs and religious folk songs (spirituals) sung by African-Americans. It was introduced early in the 1900s by African-American musicians. Blues songs are usually sad. (A type of jazz is also called "the blues.") **Famous blues performers:** Ma Rainey, Bessie Smith, Billie Holiday, B. B. King, Muddy Waters, Robert Johnson, Howling Wolf, Etta James.

Alan Jackson ▲

TOP ALBUMS of 2002

1. *The Eminem Show,* Eminem
2. *Nellyville,* Nelly
3. *Let Go,* Avril Lavigne
4. *Home,* Dixie Chicks
5. *8 Mile* soundtrack, Eminem and others
6. *M!ssundaztood,* Pink
7. *Ashanti,* Ashanti
8. *Drive,* Alan Jackson
9. *O Brother, Where Art Thou?* soundtrack, various artists
10. *Up!,* Shania Twain

The Rock and Roll Hall of Fame and Museum, in Cleveland, Ohio, honors rock-and-roll musicians with exhibits and multi-media presentations. Musicians cannot be included until 25 years after their first record. AC/DC, The Clash, Elvis Costello and the Attractions, The Police, and The Righteous Brothers were among performers added in 2003.

▶**COUNTRY** American country music is based on Southern mountain music. Blues, jazz, and other musical styles have also influenced it. Country music became popular through the *Grand Ole Opry* radio show in Nashville, Tennessee, during the 1920s. **Famous country artists:** Hank Williams, Willie Nelson, Vince Gill, Reba McEntire, Tim McGraw, Faith Hill, Lee Ann Womack, Billy Gilman, Alan Jackson, Shania Twain, Dixie Chicks.

▶**CLASSICAL** Often more complex than other types of music, classical music is based on European musical traditions that go back several hundred years. Common forms of classical music include the symphony, chamber music, opera, and ballet music. **Some early classical composers:** Johann Sebastian Bach, Ludwig van Beethoven, Johannes Brahms, Franz Joseph Haydn, Wolfgang Amadeus Mozart, Frederic Chopin.

Some modern composers: Aaron Copland, Virgil Thomson, Igor Stravinsky.

▶**OPERA** An opera is a play sung to music. The words of an opera are called the libretto, and a long song sung by one character (like a speech in a play) is called an aria. **Some famous operas:** *The Barber of Seville* (Gioacchino Rossini); *Carmen* (Georges Bizet); *La Boheme (*Giacomo Puccini*)*; *La Traviata* (Giuseppe Verdi); *Porgy and Bess* (George Gershwin).

▶**CHAMBER** Chamber music is written for a small group of musicians, often only three (a trio) or four (a quartet), to play together. In chamber music, each instrument plays a separate part. A string quartet (music written for two violins, viola, and cello) is an example of chamber music. Other instruments, such as a piano, are sometimes part of a chamber group.

SYMPHONY

A symphony is music written for an orchestra. The sections of a symphony are called movements.

VOICE

Human voices have a range in pitch from low to high. For men, the low end is called the bass (pronounced like base), followed by baritone, and tenor. The range for women goes from contralto (the lowest) up to alto, mezzo-soprano, and soprano. The next time you listen to a singer, try to figure out his or her range.

MUSICAL NOTATION

These are some of the symbols composers use when they write music.

treble clef	𝄞	half note	♪
bass clef	𝄢	quarter note	♩
sharp	♯	eighth note	♪
flat	♭	sixteenth note	♬
natural	♮	whole rest	▬
whole note	o	half rest	▬

american musicals

American musical theater uses singing, dancing, and music to tell stories in exciting ways. Broadway, New York City's theater district, is the musical capital of the world. Some musicals start as movies, or are made into movies. A few famous musicals are listed here. The date after the show's name is the year it opened on Broadway.

Annie (1977), by Charles Strouse and Martin Charnin. Here's how Little Orphan Annie was adopted by Daddy Warbucks. One featured song: "Tomorrow." Tony Award 1977.

Beauty and the Beast (1994), by Alan Menkin, Howard Ashman, and Tim Rice. First it was a story. Then it was a movie in French. Then it became an animated movie musical. Finally the tale of Belle and the Beast she came to love is brought to life on a stage.

Cats (1982), by Andrew Lloyd Webber. Based on poems about all kinds of cats written by T.S. Eliot, this play closed in 2000 after a record 7,485 performances. Its best-known song was "Memory." Tony Award 1983.

The Lion King (1997), by Elton John, Tim Rice, Mark Mancina, Roger Allers, and Irene Meechi. Based on the animated Disney movie, this show uses masks and puppets to tell the story of animals progressing through "The Circle of Life." Tony Award 1998.

The Producers (2001), by Mel Brooks. What happens when you set out to make a flop? That's what the producers plan as a crazy way to get rich quick. Based on Mel Brooks's 1967 film of the same name, *The Producers* won a record 12 Tony Awards in 2001.

West Side Story (1957), by Leonard Bernstein and Stephen Sondheim. This groundbreaking show used music and dance to update the story of Romeo and Juliet to the West Side of Manhattan in New York City.

A MUSICAL REVOLUTION?

For each clue, find an instrument in that instrument group that fits. When you're done, the letters in the circles will give you the answer to the question in the title. The first instrument has been filled in for you.

CLUES: 1-string, 2-string, 3-woodwind, 4-percussion, 5-brass, 6-woodwind, 7-percussion, 8-brass, 9-woodwind, 10-woodwind, 11-string

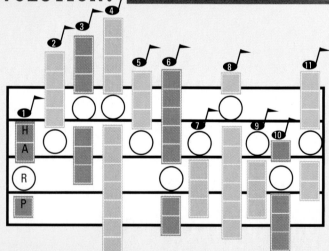

ANSWERS ON PAGES 314-317. FOR MORE PUZZLES GO TO
WWW.WORLDALMANACFORKIDS.COM

Dance

Dancers perform patterns of movement, usually to music or rhythm. Dance may be a form of art, or part of a religious ceremony. Or it may be done just for entertainment.

►BALLET Ballet is a kind of dance based on formal steps. The movements are often graceful and flowing. Ballets are almost always danced to music, are performed for an audience, and often tell a story. In the 15th century, ballet was part of the elaborate entertainment performed for the rulers of Europe. In the 1600s, professional dance companies existed, but without women; women's parts were danced by men wearing masks. In the 1700s dancers wore bulky costumes and shoes with high heels. Women danced in hoopskirts—and so did men! In the 1800s ballet steps and costumes began to look the way they do now. Many of the most popular ballets today date back to the middle or late 1800s.

►BALLROOM DANCING Ballroom, or social, dancing involves dances done for fun by ordinary people. Social dancing has been around since at least the Middle Ages, when it was popular at fairs and festivals. In the 1400s social dance was part of fancy court pageants. It developed into ballroom dances like the minuet and the waltz during the 1700s. More recent dances include the Charleston, lindy, twist, and tango, as well as disco dancing, break dancing, line dancing, and dances such as the macarena and electric slide.

►MODERN DANCE Modern dance differs from classical ballet. It is often less concerned with graceful, flowing movement and with stories. Modern dance steps are often not performed in traditional ballet. Dancers may put their bodies into awkward, angular positions and turn their backs on the audience. Many modern dances are based on ancient art, such as Greek sculpture, or on dance styles found in Africa and Asia.

►FOLK DANCE Folk dance is the term for a dance that is passed on from generation to generation and is part of the culture or way of life of people from a particular country or ethnic group. Virginia reel (American), czardas (Hungarian), jig, and the Israeli hora are some folk dances.

Some Famous Ballets

THE SLEEPING BEAUTY This 1890 ballet was the first ballet Anna Pavlova saw when she was a young girl in Russia, and it inspired her to become one the greatest ballerinas of all time. It carries the audience into a mystical world where spells are cast and a fairy comes to the aid of a handsome prince. Tchaikovsky composed the beautiful score.

SWAN LAKE First danced in St. Petersburg, Russia, in 1895 to music by Tchaikovsky. Perhaps the most popular ballet ever, *Swan Lake* is the story of a prince and his love for a maiden who was turned into a swan by an evil magician.

GISELLE *Giselle* is a classic romantic ballet that is as popular now as when it was first performed over 160 years ago (1841). It combines drama and dancing with mystery, romance, and magic. Adolphe Adam composed the music.

THE RIVER This 1970 ballet by Alvin Ailey is danced to music by the jazz musician Duke Ellington. It has been described as a celebration of life.

a ballet dancer ►

Nations

Where do Le come from page 155

KIDS
AROUND THE WORLD

EGYPT

Even though it is mostly desert, Egypt is an agricultural country because of the fertile area around the Nile River. It is a major producer of cotton and corn. Most Egyptians are Muslims—people who practice the religion known as Islam. Family life is important to Egyptians. From a young age, boys and girls there are raised very differently. Boys work with their fathers in the fields or in their businesses, while the girls help take care of the children and do household chores like sewing and cooking. Except for working at carpet weaving and other crafts—such as these girls are doing—girls aren't usually seen in public places of business.

GUATEMALA

Guatemala is a mostly rural country in Central America, with mountains, lakes, and jungles. Maya Indians make up nearly half of the population; the rest are mainly people of mixed Indian and Spanish descent called mestizos. Most are Catholic. Spanish is the official language, but 20 Mayan languages are also widely spoken. The customs and traditions of the Mayans are still a big part of the culture. Their hand-woven clothing is very bright and colorful, like the clothes these boys are wearing. The patterns on the clothing can tell a lot about people's lives, such as which village they are from and whether or not they are married.

JAPAN

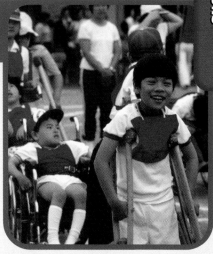

Japan is made up of four large islands and lots of smaller ones. Most of the people live in big cities such as Tokyo and Osaka. Japanese is the official language, but many people speak English when conducting business. Most people are Buddhist and also practice the Japanese religion Shinto. The Japanese love to read and are proud of their 100% literacy rate. The main part of their diet is rice and fish, but fast food like McDonald's is very popular among young people. Japanese kids also love baseball and Western music, and like to dress in jeans and T-shirts. Children have 240 school days every year, including a half-day on Saturdays (compared to about 180 a year in the U.S.).

NIGERIA

Nigeria has more people than any other country in Africa. Nigerians have big families, and they value family life and education. Christianity and Islam are the major religions. Western culture has influenced many areas of their life, from business to music to food. The children like to watch American shows on satellite TV. But they still like dressing in their colorful native costumes. Nigerians love soccer and other competitive sports, and they enjoy meeting friends and shopping in the markets. These markets are colorful and crowded. Besides fruits and vegetables, they sell live chickens, goats, and cows!

RUSSIA

Russia is almost twice as big as the U.S. and extends over two continents (Europe and Asia), but has fewer people. Most Russians live in the western part and three out of four live in cities, often in apartment buildings. Russia was part of the former Soviet Union, a Communist country, and the government controlled many aspects of life. Now it is a democracy, but the economy is not doing well and times are hard. All over Russia, "Day of Knowledge" celebrations are held for students on September 1, the traditional start of the school year. Politicians—even the President—give speeches at schools around the country. If the first falls on a day off, kids still go to their schools for concerts, games, sports, and other activities. Chess, gymnastics, ice hockey, soccer, skiing, and skating are some of the most popular activities for kids in Russia.

Maps & Flags
of the Nations of the World

Maps showing the continents and nations of the world appear on pages 134-145. Flags of the nations appear on pages 146-149. A map of the United States appears on pages 264-265.

AUSTRALIA

★ National Capital

★ State Capital

• Other City

1:40,886,000

0   250   500 mi

0   250   500 km

Two-Point Equidistant Projection

© MAPQUEST.COM

PACIFIC ISLANDS

★ National Capital

★ Territorial Capital

● Other City

1:84,569,000

| 0 | 500 | 1,000 mi |

| 0 | 500 | 1,000 km |

Miller Projection

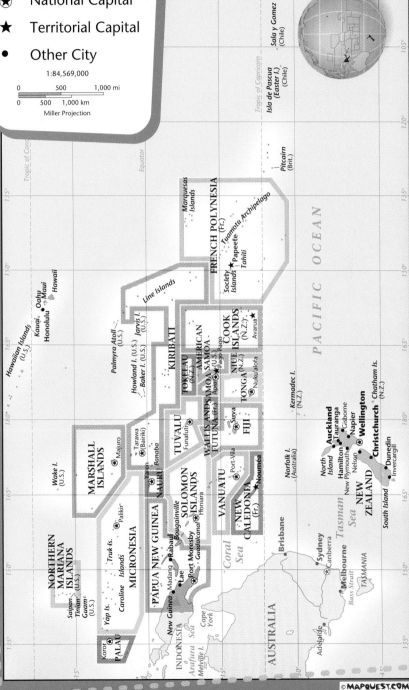

Tropic of Capricorn

Sala y Gomez
(Chile)

Isla de Pascua
(Easter I.)
(Chile)

Tropic of Cancer

Equator

Pitcairn
(Brit.)

Marquesas
Islands

FRENCH POLYNESIA
(Fr.)

Tuamotu Archipelago

Society ★ Papeete
Islands   Tahiti

PACIFIC OCEAN

Hawaiian Islands
(U.S.)

Kauai● Oahu● Maui
Honolulu Hawaii

Line Islands

Palmyra Atoll
(U.S.)

Howland I. (U.S.)
Baker I. (U.S.)

Jarvis I.
(U.S.)

KIRIBATI

TOKELAU
(N.Z.)

AMERICAN
SAMOA
(U.S.)

COOK
ISLANDS
(N.Z.)
Avarua ★

Pago Pago

WALLIS AND SAMOA
FUTUNA (Fr.) Apia ★

NIUE
(N.Z.)

TONGA
Nuku'alofa ★

Kermadec I.
(N.Z.)

MARSHALL
ISLANDS
● Majuro

Tarawa
★ (Bairiki)

TUVALU
Funafuti ★

Banaba

Yaren
NAURU ★

Suva
FIJI

Chatham Is.
(N.Z.)

Auckland
Tauranga
Gisborne
Hamilton ● Napier
New Plymouth ● Wellington
Nelson ● Christchurch
Dunedin ●
Invercargill

North
Island

NEW
ZEALAND

South Island

Norfolk I.
(Australia)

Wake I.
(U.S.)

NORTHERN
MARIANA
ISLANDS

Saipan
Tinian (U.S.)
Guam
(U.S.)

Truk Is.
Yap Is.
Caroline Islands ★ Palikir

MICRONESIA

Koror
PALAU

New Guinea

INDONESIA

Arafura
Sea

Melville I.

PAPUA NEW GUINEA

Madang ● Lae
Port Moresby ★
Guadalcanal

Rabaul ●
Bougainville

SOLOMON
ISLANDS
Honiara ★

VANUATU
Port-Vila ★

NEW
CALEDONIA
(Fr.)
★ Nouméa

Coral
Sea

Cape
York

AUSTRALIA

Brisbane ●

Sydney ●
Canberra ★
Melbourne ●

Tasman
Sea

Bass Strait
TASMANIA

Adelaide ●

© MAPQUEST.COM

SWEDEN

NORWAY

GREAT BRITAIN

ICELAND

Arctic Circle

Denmark Strait

Cape Farewell

Greenland Sea

Spitsbergen

GREENLAND (KALAALLIT NUNAAT) (Den.)

Tasiilaq

Nuuk (Godthaab)

Labrador Sea

Davis Strait

Hebron

Schefferville

Happy Valley–Goose Bay

Labrador City

NEWFOUNDLAND

Island of Newfoundland

St. Anthony

Corner Brook

St. John's

St. Pierre & Miquelon Is. (Fr.)

Anticosti Is.

Sept-Îles

QUÉBEC

Chibougamau

CANADIAN SHIELD

Belcher Is.

James Bay

ONTARIO

Moosonee

Povungnituk

Ungava Peninsula

Hudson Strait

Pangnirtung

Iqaluit

Baffin Island

Baffin Bay

Pond Inlet

Arctic Bay

Nord

Cape Morris Jessup

Knud Rasmussen Land

Qaanaaq (Thule)

Alert

Ellesmere I.

Grise Fiord

Queen Elizabeth Islands

Resolute

Repulse Bay

Southampton I.

Hudson Bay

Churchill

York Factory

Lake Winnipeg

MANITOBA

Thompson

Flin Flon

La Ronge

Prince Albert

Uranium City

SASK.

Saskatoon

Regina

North Pole

Arctic Ocean

Victoria I.

Cambridge Bay

Kugluktuk

Banks I.

Holman

Sachs Harbour

Great Bear L.

Déline

NUNAVUT

NORTHWEST TERRITORIES

Yellowknife

Ft. Smith

Hay River

Ft. Simpson

Great Slave L.

Mackenzie

CANADA

ALBERTA

Ft. McMurray

Peace River

Edmonton

La Loche

Jasper

Calgary

ROCKY

GREAT

Beaufort Sea

Inuvik

Fort McPherson

BROOKS RANGE

Point Barrow

Barrow

Kotzebue

Point Hope

Nome

Bethel

RUSSIA

Bering Strait

Bering Sea

ALASKA

Fairbanks

Fort Yukon

Yukon

ALASKA RANGE

Mt. McKinley 6,194 m. (20,320 ft.)

Kenai

Anchorage

Seward

Valdez

Kodiak

Gulf of Alaska

Arctic Circle

Dawson

Mayo

Carmacks

YUKON

Whitehorse

Watson Lake

BRITISH COLUMBIA

Prince George

Williams Lake

RANGE

COAST MOUNTAINS

Skagway

Juneau

Sitka

Yakutat

Mt. Logan 5,959 m. (19,551 ft.)

Ketchikan

Prince Rupert

Kitimat

Queen Charlotte Is.

Vancouver I.

Vancouver

Victoria

NEW. P.E.I.

N.S.

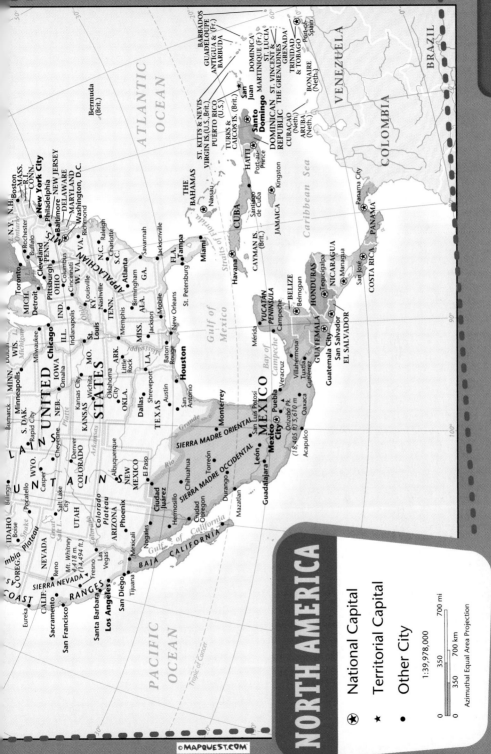

NORTH AMERICA

✪ National Capital

★ Territorial Capital

• Other City

1:39,978,000

0   350   700 mi

0   350   700 km

Azimuthal Equal Area Projection

©MAPQUEST.COM

ATLANTIC OCEAN

PACIFIC OCEAN

Caribbean Sea

Gulf of Mexico

Bay of Campeche

Gulf of California

Straits of Florida

UNITED STATES

MEXICO

CANADA

BRAZIL

VENEZUELA

COLOMBIA

CUBA

HAITI
DOMINICAN REPUBLIC

JAMAICA

THE BAHAMAS

BELIZE
GUATEMALA
EL SALVADOR
HONDURAS
NICARAGUA
COSTA RICA
PANAMA

Bermuda (Brit.)

BARBADOS
GUADELOUPE (Fr.)
ANTIGUA & BARBUDA
DOMINICA
MARTINIQUE (Fr.)
ST. LUCIA
ST. VINCENT & THE GRENADINES
GRENADA
TRINIDAD & TOBAGO
BONAIRE (Neth.)
CURAÇAO (Neth.)
ARUBA (Neth.)

ST. KITTS & NEVIS
VIRGIN IS.(U.S./Brit.)
PUERTO RICO (U.S.)
TURKS & CAICOS IS. (Brit.)
CAYMAN IS. (Brit.)

SIERRA MADRE ORIENTAL
SIERRA MADRE OCCIDENTAL
YUCATÁN PENINSULA
BAJA CALIFORNIA
APPALACHIAN
ROCKY MOUNTAINS
Colorado Plateau
SIERRA NEVADA
COAST RANGES
Columbia Plateau
Great Salt L.
Snake
Platte
Arkansas
Rio Grande
Mississippi

N.Y., N.H., Boston MASS.
R.I.
CONN.
New York City
NEW JERSEY
Philadelphia
DELAWARE
Baltimore MARYLAND
Washington, D.C.
Richmond
VA.
W. VA.
PENN.
Pittsburgh
OHIO
Columbus
Cincinnati
Cleveland
Detroit
MICH.
Toronto
Buffalo
Rochester
Ontario
Michigan
WIS.
Milwaukee
Minneapolis
MINN.
S. DAK.
N. DAK.
Bismarck
Billings
MONT.
IDAHO
Boise
Pocatello
WYO.
Casper
Cheyenne
Denver
COLORADO
NEB.
Omaha
IOWA
ILL.
Chicago
IND.
Indianapolis
St. Louis
MO.
KANSAS
Wichita
Kansas City
Oklahoma City
OKLA.
ARK.
Little Rock
Memphis
TENN.
Nashville
KY.
Louisville
N.C. Raleigh
Charlotte
S.C.
GA.
Atlanta
Birmingham
ALA.
MISS.
Jackson
LA.
Baton Rouge
New Orleans
Shreveport
TEXAS
Dallas
Austin
San Antonio
Houston
Oklahoma
Savannah
Jacksonville
FLA.
Tampa
St. Petersburg
Miami
Charlotte
Columbia
NEVADA
Reno
Sacramento
San Francisco
Eureka
CALIF.
Fresno
Mt. Whitney 4,418 m. (14,494 ft.)
Las Vegas
Salt Lake City
UTAH
ARIZONA
Phoenix
Santa Barbara
Los Angeles
San Diego
Tijuana
Mexicali
Nogales
NEW MEXICO
Albuquerque
El Paso
Ciudad Juárez
Chihuahua
Hermosillo
Ciudad Obregón
Durango
Mazatlán
Torreón
León
Guadalajara
Monterrey
San Luis Potosí
Puebla
Mexico City
Orizaba Pk. (18,405 ft.) 5,610 m
Acapulco
Oaxaca
Veracruz
Mérida
Campeche
Villahermosa
Tuxtla Gutiérrez
Belmopan
Guatemala City
San Salvador
Tegucigalpa
Managua
San José
Panama City
Panama
Havana
Santiago de Cuba
Kingston
Nassau
Port-au-Prince
Santo Domingo
San Juan
Santo Domingo
Port-of-Spain

Tropic of Cancer

CARIBBEAN SEA

ATLANTIC OCEAN

PACIFIC OCEAN

TRINIDAD AND TOBAGO

Equator

PANAMA

Panama City

Santa Marta
Barranquilla
Cartagena
Sincelejo
Montería
Coro
Maracaibo
Cabimas
L. Maracaibo
Valledupar
Valera
Mérida
San Cristóbal
Bucaramanga
Barrancabermeja
Cúcuta
Manizales
Pereira
Armenia
Ibagué
Cali
Palmira
Buenaventura
Popayán
Pasto

MEDELLIN

Bogotá

Tunja
Villavicencio

COLOMBIA

ANDES MTS.

Valencia
Maracay
Caracas
Barquisimeto
San Fernando de Apure
Puerto Ayacucho

VENEZUELA

LLANOS

El Tigre
Maturín
Cumaná
Ciudad Bolívar
Ciudad Guayana

Georgetown
New Amsterdam
Paramaribo
Kourou
Cayenne

GUYANA
SURINAME
FRENCH GUIANA (Fr.)

GUIANA HIGHLANDS

Boa Vista

Negro R.

Orinoco R.

Atabapo R.

ECUADOR

Esmeraldas
Portoviejo
★ **Quito**
Ambato
▲ Chimborazo 20,702 ft. 6,310 m.
Guayaquil
Machala
Tumbes
Talara
Sullana
Piura
Chiclayo
Trujillo
Chimbote
Cajamarca
Cuenca

PERU

Iquitos
Yurimaguas
Huánuco
Cerro de Pasco
Huancayo
Ayacucho
Ica
Callao
★ **Lima**
Arequipa
Puno

Marañón R.
Ucayali R.
Huallaga R.
Patitumayo R.

Benjamin Constant
Cruzeiro do Sul
Rio Branco
Pucallpa
▲ Mt. Huascarán 22,205 ft. 6,768 m.

AMAZON BASIN

SELVAS

Manaus

Purus R.
Juruá R.
Madeira R.
Amazon R.
Tapajós R.

Santarém

Belém

Marajó I.

Macapá

Imperatriz

São Luís

Parnaíba
Teresina
Fortaleza
Natal
João Pessoa
Recife
Maceió
Aracaju
Campina Grande
Juàzeiro do Norte

Salvador
Ilhéus
Itabuna
Feira de Santana
Vitória da Conquista
Montes Claros
Governador Valadares
Vitória

BRAZIL

BRAZILIAN HIGHLANDS

Tocantins R.

São Francisco R.

Araguaia R.

Xingu R.

Gurupi
Anápolis
Goiânia
São José do Rio Prêto
Uberlândia
Ribeirão
Brasília ★
Belo

MATO GROSSO PLATEAU

Cuiabá
Corumbá
Campo Grande

Paraguay R.

CHACO

BOLIVIA

Santa Cruz
Cochabamba
Sucre
Potosí
Oruro
La Paz
Tarija

Trinidad
Guajará-Mirim
Porto Velho
Riberalta
Cobija
Puerto Maldonado

Guaporé R.
Mamoré R.
Beni R.

ALTIPLANO

L. Titicaca
Juliaca
Cusco

Tacna
Arica
Iquique

DESERT

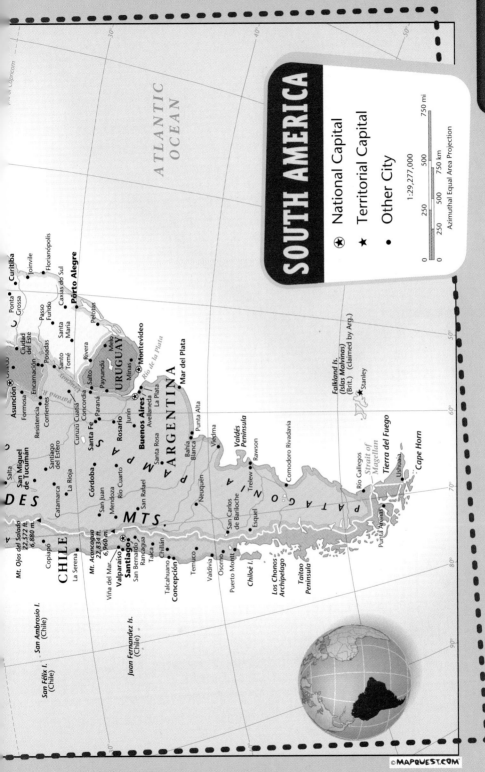

SOUTH AMERICA

⊛ National Capital
★ Territorial Capital
• Other City

1:29,277,000

Azimuthal Equal Area Projection

0   250   500   750 km
0   250   500   750 mi

ATLANTIC OCEAN

Tropic of Capricorn

Curitiba
Joinville
Florianópolis
Ponta Grossa
Passo Fundo
Caxias do Sul
Pôrto Alegre
Pelotas
Santa Maria

Ciudad del Este
Encarnación
Posadas
Santo Tomé
Formosa
Resistencia
Corrientes
Asunción ⊛
Paraná R.
Curuzú Cuatiá
Concordia
Salto
Paysandú
Rivera
Minas
URUGUAY
Montevideo ⊛
Río de la Plata
Mar del Plata

Paraná
Santa Fe
Rosario
Junín
Buenos Aires ⊛
La Plata
Avellaneda
Santa Rosa
Punta Alta
Viedma
Bahía Blanca

ARGENTINA

Córdoba
Río Cuarto
San Juan
Mendoza
San Rafael
Neuquén

Salta
San Miguel de Tucumán
Santiago del Estero
Catamarca
La Rioja

San Carlos de Bariloche
Esquel

P A T A G O N I A

Valdés Peninsula
Rawson
Trelew
Comodoro Rivadavia

Río Gallegos
Punta Arenas
Ushuaia

Strait of Magellan
Tierra del Fuego
Cape Horn

Falkland Is.
(Islas Malvinas)
(Brit.) (claimed by Arg.)
★ Stanley

D E S   M T S.

Mt. Ojos del Salado
22,572 ft.
6,880 m.

Mt. Aconcagua
22,834 ft.
6,960 m.

CHILE
Copiapó
La Serena
Viña del Mar
Valparaíso
Santiago ⊛
San Bernardo
Rancagua
Talca
Chillán
Talcahuano
Concepción
Temuco
Valdivia
Osorno
Puerto Montt
Chiloé I.
Los Chonos Archipelago
Taitao Peninsula

San Félix I.
(Chile)

San Ambrosio I.
(Chile)

Juan Fernández Is.
(Chile)

©MAPQUEST.COM

139

EUROPE

★ National Capital

● Other City

1:22,107,000

| 0 | 250 | 500 mi |
| 0 | 250 | 500 km |

Azimuthal Equal Area Projection

ICELAND
Reykjavík ★ Akureyri
Arctic Circle

Tror

Bodø

Norwegian Sea

Faroe Is.
(Den.)

Trondheim

NORWAY
Bergen

Sundsvall

SWEDEN

Shetland Is.
(Brit.)

Oslo ★

Uppsala
Stockholm
Linköping

Stavanger

Orkney
Is.

Skagerrak

Göteborg

Gotlan

Öla

Hebrides

Aberdeen

Glasgow
Edinburgh
Belfast

GREAT BRITAIN
Newcastle
(UNITED KINGDOM)

Jutland Århus
Copenhagen Helsingborg
DENMARK Malmö
Odense

North
Sea

Bal

Dublin ★
IRELAND
Cork

Irish
Sea

Liverpool Leeds
Manchester Sheffield

Hamburg

Gdańsk
Szczecin

Birmingham
Cardiff Bristol

NETHERLANDS
Amsterdam ★

Bremen
Hannover

Berlin ★
GERMANY

Poznań

Land's End
Portsmouth

London ★
Rotterdam
Antwerp

Essen
Cologne

Leipzig

Dresden

Kc

English Channel
Channel Is.
(Brit.) Le Havre

Brussels ★
Lille
BELGIUM Liège

Bonn
Frankfurt

Prague ★
CZECH REP.

Wroc

Katowic

Brest
Rouen
LUXEMBOURG
Paris ★ Luxembourg ★

Mannheim
Stuttgart

Brno

Ostrav

ATLANTIC
OCEAN

Nantes
Loire

Strasbourg
Dijon

Munich

Linz

SLOVA

Vienna ★ Bratisla

Cape Finisterre

FRANCE

Bern ★ Zurich
Geneva SWITZERLAND

LIECHTENSTEIN
AUSTRIA
Graz

Budap
HUNG

Bay
of
Biscay

Bordeaux

Vigo
Gijón

Bilbao

Lyon
ALPS

Mt. Blanc
4807 m
(15,771 ft)

Milan

SLOVENIA
Ljubljana

Pécs

Ljubljana

Zagreb

Porto

Valladolid

PYRENEES

Toulouse

Turin
Verona Venice

Genoa

DINARIC

CROATIA BOSNIA &
HERZEGOV

Pro

PORTUGAL
Lisbon ★

IBERIAN

Zaragoza

Pico de Aneto
3404 m
(11,168 ft)

Marseille
Toulon

Nice

MONACO
Ligurian Sea

APENNINES

SAN
MARINO

Sarajevo

Split

Badajoz

Tagus

Madrid ★

PENINSULA

ANDORRA

Corsica
(Fr.)

Elba

VATICAN
CITY ★ ★ Rome

Dubrovnik
Podgor

Cape
St. Vincent

Córdoba
Sevilla

SPAIN

Valencia
Alicante

Granada

Majorca
Palma
Minorca

Balearic Is.
(Sp.)

Sardinia
(It.)

Balearic Sea

Tyrrhenian
Sea

Naples

Salerno

ITALY

Bari

Cadiz
Málaga

Strait of
Gibraltar

GIBRALTAR (Brit.)

Cagliari

Co
Ioni
Sec

Mediterranean

Rabat ★
Casablanca

MOROCCO

Algiers ★

Tunis ★

ATLAS MOUNTAINS
ALGERIA

TUNISIA

Palermo

Catania ▲ Mt. Etna
3323 m
(10,902 ft)
Sicily

Valletta ★
MALTA

Sea

North Cape
mmerfest

Barents Sea

Nar'yan-Mar

Pechora

Murmansk

KOLA PENINSULA
Apatity

Ukhta

R U S S I A

Serov

Arkhangel'sk

Berezniki

Petropavl

Oulu

Belomorsk

SVykivkar

Yekaterinburg

FINLAND

Kotlas

Perm'

Chelyabinsk

Lake Onega

Petrozavodsk

Kirov

Qostanay

Tampere
Lahti

Lake Ladoga

Vologda

Izhevsk

Ufa

Magnitogorsk

Helsinki

St. Petersburg

Cherepovets

Naberezhnyye Chelny

EUROPEAN

Velikiy Novgorod

Yaroslavl'

Kazan

Tallinn

ESTONIA
Tartu

Pskov

Ivanovo

Nizhniy Novgorod

Tver

Ul'yanovsk

Tol'yatti

Orenburg

Orsk

LATVIA

Moscow

Saransk

Samara

Daugavpils

Ryazan'

Penza

Aktobe

THUANIA

Vitsyebsk

Smolensk

Tula

Oral

KAZAKHSTAN

unas
rad

Mahilyow

Lipetsk

Tambov

Ural

Minsk

Bryansk

Voronezh

Saratov

Hrodna

BELARUS

Homyel'

Kursk

Aral Sea

Brest

Volgograd

rsaw

AND

Kiev

Kharkiv

Atyraü

UZBEKISTAN

UKRAINE

Dnieper

Luhans'k

L'viv

Donets'k

Astrakhan'

ATHIAN
šice

Chernivtsi

Dnipropetrovs'k

Don

Aktaü

Dniester

MOLDOVA

Zaporizhzhia

Rostov na Donu

Caspian

Debrecen

Iaşi

Kryvyy Rih

Mariupol'

ROMANIA

Chişinău

Mykolaiv

Sea of Azov

Stavropol'

Grozniy

Makhachkala

TURKMENISTAN

mişoara

Odesa

CRIMEA

Krasnodar

Sea

Ploieşti

Simferopol'

Turkmenbashy

Bucharest

Constanţa

Sevastopol'

CAUCASUS

GEORGIA

grade

Danube

Black Sea

T'bilisi

Baku

BULGARIA

Varna

ARMENIA

AZERBAIJAN

&
EGRO

Sofia

Burgas

Trabzon

Yerevan

Skopje

Plovdiv

Tabriz

Tehran

EDONIA

Istanbul

ITA
KAN
NSULA

Thessaloniki

Ankara

TURKEY

IRAN

Larisa

REECE

Izmir

Adana

IRAQ

as

Athens

PONNESE

Cyclades

Baghdad

Rhodes

Nicosia

SYRIA

Euphrates

Sea of Crete

CYPRUS

LEBANON

Crete

Iraklion

Beirut

Damascus

Persian Gulf

© MapQuest.com

ATLANTIC OCEAN

IRELAND

PORTUGAL
SPAIN
MOROCCO
ALGERIA
TUNISIA

GREAT BRITAIN
NORWAY
SWEDEN
FINLAND
FRANCE
GERMANY
BEL. NETH. DEN.
SWITZ.
CZECH REP.
AUS.
POLAND
LITH. LAT.
ESTONIA
St. Petersburg
BELARUS
Moscow
HUNG.
SERB. & MONT.
ROM.
MOL.
UKRAINE
BUL.
GREECE
ITALY
ALB.

Barents Sea
Murmansk
Arkhangel'sk

R U S S

URAL MOUNTAINS

Yekaterinburg
Chelyabinsk
Magnitogorsk
Omsk
Novosibirs
To
Pavlod

Izmir
Istanbul
Ankara
TURKEY

Black Sea
GEORGIA
T'bilisi
ARMENIA
Yerevan
AZERBAIJAN
Baku

Caspian Sea
Volgograd
Astrakhan'
Volga

Astana
KAZAKHSTAN
Karaganda
Semey
(Semipalatinsk)

Aral Sea
Lake Balkhash

CYPRUS
Nicosia
LEBANON
Beirut
Tel Aviv
Jerusalem
ISRAEL
Damascus
SYRIA
Amman
JORDAN
IRAQ
Baghdad
Al Basrah
SAUDI ARABIA
KUWAIT
Kuwait City
Manama
BAHRAIN
QATAR
Riyadh
Mecca
Jeddah
Doha
Abu Dhabi
UNITED ARAB EMIRATES
Muscat
OMAN

Tabriz
TURKMENISTAN
Ashgabat
Tehran
Mashhad
Esfahan
IRAN
Shiraz
Kerman

UZBEKISTAN
Tashkent
Dushanbe
Bishkek
Almaty
KYRGYZSTAN
Kashi
TAJIKISTAN
AFGHANISTAN
Kabul
Qandahar
Islamabad
Srinagar
Amritsar
Lahore
PAKISTAN
Sukkur
New Delhi
Delhi
Hyderabad
Karachi

Takla Mar Desert
XIZAN (TIBE
HIMALAYA
NEPAL
Kathmandu
Lucknov
Jaipur
Kanpur
Ganc

LIBYA

CHAD

EGYPT
Sinai

AFRICA
SUDAN

Red Sea
Nile

ERITREA
ETHIOPIA
DJI.
Aden
Gulf of Aden
SOMALIA

Sanaa
YEMEN

Socotra (Yemen)

Persian Gulf
Gulf of Oman

Arabian Sea

Ahmadabad
INDIA
Nagpur

Mumbai
Hyderabad

Bangalore
Madras (Chennai)
Kochi
Madurai
SRI LANKA
Colombo

Lakshadweep (India)

Male
MALDIVES

Mediterranean Sea
Tropic of Cancer
Equator

INDIAN OCEAN

ASIA

⊛ National Capital

★ Territorial Capital

• Other City

1:51,084,000

0   500   1,000 mi

0   500   1,000 km

Two-Point Equidistant Projection

rth Pole
North Pole
CTIC
EAN
Chukchi
Sea
ALASKA
Bering
Sea
East
Siberian
Sea
Anadyr
Laptev
Sea
KAMCHATKA
PENINSULA
Magadan
Petropavlovsk-
Kamchatskiy
Yakutsk
Sea of
Okhotsk
SIBERIA
Sakhalin
Kuril
Islands
(Russia)
oyarsk **Bratsk**
Komsomolsk
na Amure
Blagoveshchensk
Khabarovsk
znetsk
Lake
Baikal
Chita
Sapporo
Irkutsk
Ulan-Ude
Harbin
Vladivostok
JAPAN
Sendai
Ulaanbaatar
Changchun
Sea of
Japan
(East Sea)
Tokyo
MONGOLIA
Shenyang
Pyongyang
Yokohama
GOBI DESERT
N. KOREA
Kyoto
Hohhot
Huang
Beijing
Dalian
Kobe
Osaka
ä
Tianjin
Seoul
Hiroshima
Jinan
S. KOREA
IANG
Taiyuan
Qingdao
Nagasaki
Yellow
PACIFIC
Lanzhou
Zhengzhou
Sea
OCEAN
CHINA
Xi'an
Nanjing
Shanghai
East
erest
Chengdu
Wuhan
China
m.
Chang
Changsha
Wenzhou
Sea
S ft.)
Chongqing
Fuzhou
Okinawa (Japan)
Lhasa
Xiamen
Taipei
HUTAN
Kunming
Guangzhou
TAIWAN
mphu
Nanning
Hong Kong
Philippine
LADESH
(Xianggang)
Sea
Dhaka
Hanoi
Macao
cutta)
Mandalay
Gulf
LUZON
of
of
LAOS
Tonkin
Manila
gal
MYANMAR
Vientiane
Da Nang
PHILIPPINES
(BURMA)
South
Yangon
THAILAND
VIETNAM
China
Cebu
(Rangoon)
Sea
MINDANAO
Bangkok
CAMBODIA
Davao
man
Phnom
Ho Chi Minh City
Sulu
ands
Penh
Sea
ndia)
Andaman
Kota Kinabalu
Celebes
Sea
Manado
NEW GUINEA
icobar
Bandar Seri Begawan
Sea
Irian
slands
BRUNEI
Jaya
(India)
Kuching
MALAYSIA
BORNEO
Medan
Kuala
SINGAPORE
Banda
Lumpur
Singapore
INDONESIA
Sea
Arafura
SUMATRA
Banjarmasin
Sea
Padang
Java
Timor
Palembang
Makassar
Sea
Dili
Jakarta
Surabaya
EAST
JAVA
TIMOR
Bandung
Kupang
AUSTRALIA

©MAPQUEST.COM

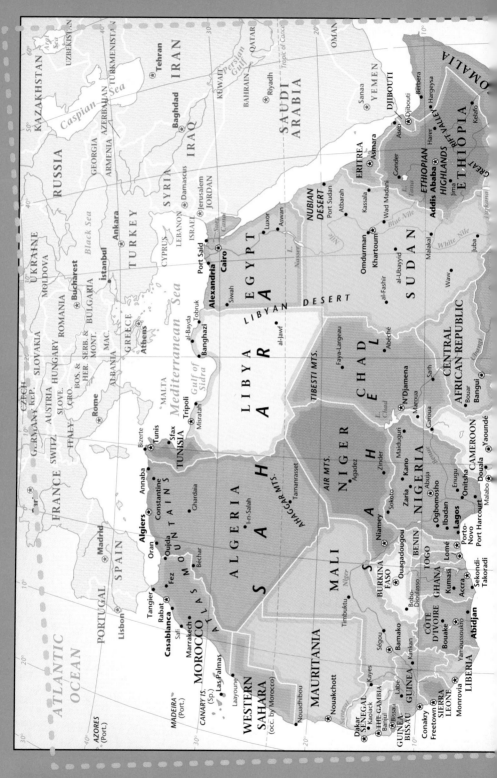

KAZAKHSTAN

Aral Sea

UZBEKISTAN

TURKMENISTAN

Caspian Sea

Tehran

IRAN

RUSSIA

GEORGIA

ARMENIA AZERBAIJAN

Baghdad

IRAQ

KUWAIT

Persian Gulf

BAHRAIN

QATAR

Riyadh

SAUDI ARABIA

OMAN

YEMEN

Sanaa

DJIBOUTI

Djibouti

Berbera

Hargeysa

SOMALIA

Aseb

ERITREA

Asmara

Aswan

Gonder

Kelafo

ETHIOPIAN HIGHLANDS

GREAT RIFT VALLEY

ETHIOPIA

Addis Ababa

Harer

Jima

UKRAINE

MOLDOVA

Black Sea

Ankara

TURKEY

Istanbul

Bucharest

ROMANIA

BULGARIA

SERB. & MONT.

MAC.

ALBANIA

GREECE

Athens

CYPRUS

LEBANON

Damascus

SYRIA

ISRAEL

Jerusalem

JORDAN

Suez Canal

Port Said

Cairo

Alexandria

EGYPT

Siwah

Luxor

L. Nasser

Nile

NUBIAN DESERT

Port Sudan

Atbarah

Kassala

Wad Madani

Blue Nile

Omdurman

Khartoum

al-Ubayyid

SUDAN

Malakal

Juba

White Nile

Waw

al-Fashir

Abéché

CENTRAL AFRICAN REPUBLIC

Bangui

Bouar

CZECH REP.

SLOVAKIA

AUSTRIA

HUNGARY

SWITZ.

SLOVE.

CRO.

BOS. & HER.

ITALY

Rome

Mediterranean Sea

MALTA

Tripoli

Misratah

Gulf of Sidra

Banghazi

al-Bayda

Tobruk

LIBYAN DESERT

LIBYA

SAHARA

TIBESTI MTS.

Faya-Largeau

L. Chad

CHAD

N'Djamena

Sarh

Maroua

Garoua

CAMEROON

Yaoundé

Douala

Malabo

SAHEL

FRANCE

SPAIN

Madrid

PORTUGAL

Lisbon

ATLANTIC OCEAN

AZORES (Port.)

MADEIRA (Port.)

CANARY IS. (Sp.)

Las Palmas

Laayoune

WESTERN SAHARA (occ. by Morocco)

Tangier

Rabat

Casablanca

Safi

Marrakech

MOROCCO

Fez

Oujda

Oran

Algiers

Constantine

Annaba

Bizerte

Tunis

Sfax

TUNISIA

ATLAS MOUNTAINS

Béchar

Ghardaia

I-n-Salah

ALGERIA

HAGGAR MTS.

Tamanrasset

Agadez

AIR MTS.

NIGER

Zinder

Maiduguri

Kano

Zaria

Sokoto

Abuja

NIGERIA

Enugu

Onitsha

Ibadan

Ogbomosho

Lagos

Porto-Novo

Port Harcourt

BENIN

TOGO

Lomé

GHANA

Accra

Kumasi

Sekondi-Takoradi

Abidjan

CÔTE D'IVOIRE

Bouake

Yamoussoukro

LIBERIA

Monrovia

SIERRA LEONE

Freetown

Conakry

GUINEA

Labé

Kankan

Bobo-Dioulasso

BURKINA FASO

Ouagadougou

Niamey

Niger

Ségou

Bamako

Kayes

MALI

Timbuktu

MAURITANIA

Nouakchott

Nouadhibou

Senegal

Dakar

SENEGAL

Kaolack

THE GAMBIA

Banjul

GUINEA-BISSAU

Bissau

Kanfan

MAURITANIA

144

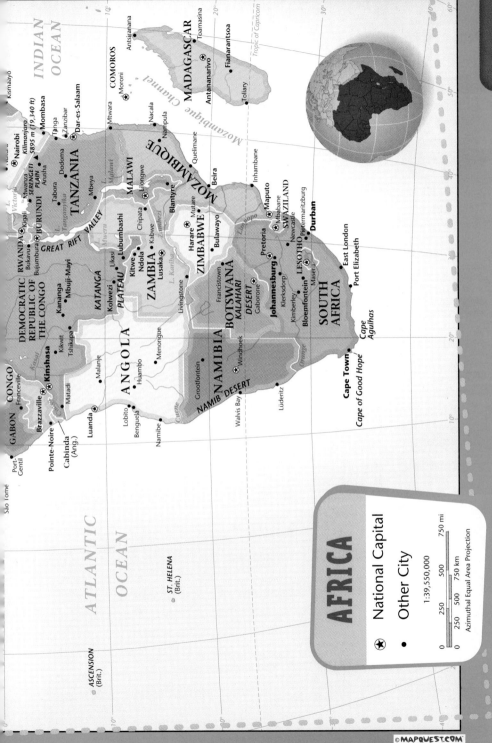

INDIAN OCEAN

Kismaayo

RWANDA
BURUNDI

Kigali ✪
Bukavu

Bujumbura ✪

Nairobi ✪
Kilimanjaro
5895 m (19,340 ft)
Mombasa
Tanga
Zanzibar
Dar-es-Salaam

Mwanza
SERENGETI
PLAIN

Dodoma
Arusha
Tabora

TANZANIA

Mbeya

L. Victoria

L. Tanganyika

DEMOCRATIC
REPUBLIC OF
THE CONGO

GREAT RIFT VALLEY

Kananga
Mbuji-Mayi

KATANGA
PLATEAU

Likasi
Kolwezi
Lubumbashi

Kitwe
Ndola
Lusaka ✪

ZAMBIA

Chipata

L. Malawi

MALAWI

Lilongwe

Blantyre

Mtwara

Nacala
Nampula

Quelimane

MOZAMBIQUE

Mozambique Channel

COMOROS
Moroni

MADAGASCAR

Antsiranana
Toamasina

Antananarivo ✪

Fianarantsoa

Toliary

Tropic of Capricorn

Beira

Inhambane

Harare ✪
Mutare

ZIMBABWE
Bulawayo

Maputo ✪

SWAZILAND
Mbabane ✪

Newcastle

Pietermaritzburg
Durban

Kikwit
Tshikapa

Kinshasa ✪

Brazzaville ✪

CONGO

GABON

Franceville

Port-
Gentil

Sao Tome

ASCENSION
(Brit.)

ST. HELENA
(Brit.)

Pointe-Noire
Cabinda
(Ang.)

Luanda

Lobito
Benguela
Namibe

ANGOLA
Malanje
Huambo
Menongue

Matadi

Livingstone

Francistown

BOTSWANA
KALAHARI
DESERT
Gaborone ✪

Grootfontein

NAMIBIA

Windhoek ✪

NAMIB DESERT

Walvis Bay

Lüderitz

Kimberley
Klerksdorp

Johannesburg
Bloemfontein ✪

Pretoria ✪

LESOTHO
Maseru ✪

SOUTH
AFRICA

Cape
Aguilhas

Cape Town
Cape of Good Hope

East London
Port Elizabeth

Kabwe

Kariba

Limpopo

Orange

Cunene

ATLANTIC OCEAN

©MAPQUEST.COM

AFRICA

✪ National Capital

• Other City

1:39,550,000

0   250   500   750 mi
0 250 500 750 km

Azimuthal Equal Area Projection

AFGHANISTAN

ALBANIA

ALGERIA

ANDORRA

ANGOLA

ANTIGUA AND BARBUDA

ARGENTINA

ARMENIA

AUSTRALIA

AUSTRIA

AZERBAIJAN

THE BAHAMAS

BAHRAIN

BANGLADESH

BARBADOS

BELARUS

BELGIUM

BELIZE

BENIN

BHUTAN

BOLIVIA

BOSNIA AND HERZEGOVINA

BOTSWANA

BRAZIL

BRUNEI

BULGARIA

BURKINA FASO

BURUNDI

CAMBODIA

CAMEROON

CANADA

CAPE VERDE

CENTRAL AFRICAN REPUBLIC

CHAD

CHILE

CHINA

COLOMBIA

COMOROS

CONGO, DEMOCRATIC REP. OF THE

CONGO, REP. OF THE

COSTA RICA

CÔTE D'IVOIRE

CROATIA

CUBA

CYPRUS

CZECH REPUBLIC

DENMARK

DJIBOUTI

DOMINICA

DOMINICAN REPUBLIC

FLAGS of the NATIONS of the WORLD
(East Timor–Liechtenstein)

 EAST TIMOR

 ECUADOR

 EGYPT

 EL SALVADOR

 EQUATORIAL GUINEA

 ERITREA

 ESTONIA

 ETHIOPIA

 FIJI

 FINLAND

 FRANCE

 GABON

 THE GAMBIA

 GEORGIA

 GERMANY

 GHANA

 GREECE

 GRENADA

 GUATEMALA

 GUINEA

 GUINEA-BISSAU

 GUYANA

 HAITI

 HONDURAS

 HUNGARY

 ICELAND

 INDIA

 INDONESIA

 IRAN

 IRAQ

 IRELAND

 ISRAEL

 ITALY

 JAMAICA

 JAPAN

 JORDAN

 KAZAKHSTAN

 KENYA

 KIRIBATI

 NORTH KOREA

 SOUTH KOREA

 KUWAIT

 KYRGYZSTAN

 LAOS

 LATVIA

 LEBANON

 LESOTHO

 LIBERIA

 LIBYA

 LIECHTENSTEIN

FLAGS of the NATIONS of the WORLD
(Lithuania–Saudi Arabia)

LITHUANIA

LUXEMBOURG

MACEDONIA

MADAGASCAR

MALAWI

MALAYSIA

MALDIVES

MALI

MALTA

MARSHALL ISLANDS

MAURITANIA

MAURITIUS

MEXICO

MICRONESIA

MOLDOVA

MONACO

MONGOLIA

MOROCCO

MOZAMBIQUE

MYANMAR (BURMA)

NAMIBIA

NAURU

NEPAL

NETHERLANDS

NEW ZEALAND

NICARAGUA

NIGER

NIGERIA

NORWAY

OMAN

PAKISTAN

PALAU

PANAMA

PAPUA NEW GUINEA

PARAGUAY

PERU

PHILIPPINES

POLAND

PORTUGAL

QATAR

ROMANIA

RUSSIA

RWANDA

ST. KITTS AND NEVIS

ST. LUCIA

ST. VINCENT AND
THE GRENADINES

SAMOA

SAN MARINO

SÃO TOMÉ AND PRÍNCIPE

SAUDI ARABIA

FLAGS of the NATIONS of the WORLD
(Senegal–Zimbabwe)

SENEGAL

SERBIA & MONTENEGRO

SEYCHELLES

SIERRA LEONE

SINGAPORE

SLOVAKIA

SLOVENIA

SOLOMON ISLANDS

SOMALIA

SOUTH AFRICA

SPAIN

SRI LANKA

SUDAN

SURINAME

SWAZILAND

SWEDEN

SWITZERLAND

SYRIA

TAIWAN

TAJIKISTAN

TANZANIA

THAILAND

TOGO

TONGA

TRINIDAD AND TOBAGO

TUNISIA

TURKEY

TURKMENISTAN

TUVALU

UGANDA

UKRAINE

UNITED ARAB EMIRATES

UNITED KINGDOM (GREAT BRITAIN)

UNITED STATES

URUGUAY

UZBEKISTAN

VANUATU

VATICAN CITY

VENEZUELA

VIETNAM

YEMEN

ZAMBIA

ZIMBABWE

Facts About Nations

There are 193 nations in the world. The information for each of them goes across two pages. The left page gives the name and capital of each nation, its location, and its area. On the right page, the population column tells how many people lived in each country in 2003, according to estimates. The currency column shows the name of each nation's money and how much one United States dollar was worth there at the start of 2003. The language column gives official languages and other common languages.

KEY TO THE DOTS

- Africa
- Asia
- Australia
- Europe
- North America
- Pacific Islands
- South America

NATION	CAPITAL	LOCATION OF NATION	AREA
Afghanistan	Kabul	Southern Asia, between Iran and Pakistan	250,000 sq. mi. (647,500 sq. km.)
Albania	Tiranë	Eastern Europe, between Greece and Serbia & Montenegro	11,100 sq. mi. (28,750 sq. km.)
Algeria	Algiers	North Africa on the Mediterranean Sea, between Libya and Morocco	919,600 sq. mi. (2,381,740 sq. km.)
Andorra	Andorra la Vella	Europe, in the mountains between France and Spain	174 sq. mi. (450 sq. km.)
Angola	Luanda	Southern Africa on the Atlantic Ocean, north of Namibia	481,400 sq. mi. (1,246,700 sq. km.)
Antigua and Barbuda	St. John's	Islands on eastern edge of the Caribbean Sea	174 sq. mi. (440 sq. km.)
Argentina	Buenos Aires	Fills up most of the southern part of South America	1,068,300 sq. mi. (2,766,890 sq. km.)
Armenia	Yerevan	Western Asia, north of Turkey and Iran, west of the Caspian Sea	11,500 sq. mi. (29,800 sq. km.)
Australia	Canberra	Continent south of Asia, between Indian and Pacific Oceans	2,967,910 sq. mi. (7,686,850 sq. km.)
Austria	Vienna	Central Europe, north of Italy	32,380 sq. mi. (83,860 sq. km.)
Azerbaijan	Baku	Western Asia, north of Iran, on the Caspian Sea	33,440 sq. mi. (86,600 sq. km.)
The Bahamas	Nassau	Islands in the Atlantic Ocean, east of Florida	5,380 sq. mi. (13,940 sq. km.)
Bahrain	Manama	In the Persian Gulf, near the coast of Qatar	240 sq. mi. (620 sq. km.)

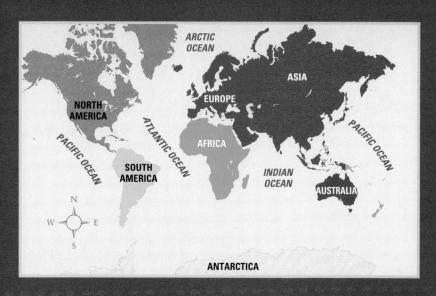

POPULATION	CURRENCY	LANGUAGE	DID YOU KNOW?
23,897,000	$1 = 4,726 afghanis	Afghan Persian (Dari), Pashtu	A new government is rebuilding after the 2002 defeat of the Taliban.
3,166,000	$1 = 133.94 leks	Albanian, Greek	The Roman Emperor Constantine came from Illyria, ancient name for Albania.
31,800,000	$1 = 78.93 dinars	Arabic, French, Berber Dialects	The Casbah, a 16th-century fortress, is in Algiers.
69,000	$1 = .96 euros	Catalan, French, Castilian	This tiny nation has a police force, but no regular army.
13,625,000	$1 = 58.86 kwanzas	Portuguese, African dialects	In the 1400s, the Portuguese began trading slaves in Angola.
68,000	$1 = 2.67. East Carribean dollars	English	Most of the people of these islands trace their roots to West Africa.
38,428,000	$1 = 3.33 pesos	Spanish, English, Italian	Mount Aconcagua (22,834 ft) is the tallest peak in the western hemisphere.
3,061,000	$1 = 558.14 drams	Armenian	Dating to 783 B.C., Yerevan is one of the oldest continuously occupied towns.
19,731,000	$1 = 1.76 Australian dollars	English, aboriginal languages	Australia boasts over 7,000 beaches—more than any other nation.
8,166,000	$1 = .96 euro	German	The Schottengymnasium, a school in Vienna, has been open since 1155.
8,370,000	$1 = 4,913 manats	Azeri, Russian, Armenian	Nine out of 10 Azerbaijanis are Muslims.
314,000	Bahamas dollar Same value as U.S. dollar	English, Creole	Only about 40 of the Bahamas' 700-plus islands are inhabited.
724,000	$1 = .38 dinars	Arabic, English, Farsi, Urdu	In 2002 women in Bahrain were allowed to vote for the first time.

NATION	CAPITAL	LOCATION OF NATION	AREA
Bangladesh	Dhaka	Southern Asia, nearly surrounded by India	56,000 sq. mi. (144,000 sq. km.)
Barbados	Bridgetown	Island in the Atlantic Ocean, north of Trinidad	165 sq. mi. (430 sq. km.)
Belarus	Minsk	Eastern Europe, east of Poland	80,200 sq. mi. (207,600 sq. km.)
Belgium	Brussels	Western Europe, on the North Sea, south of the Netherlands	11,780 sq. mi. (30,510 sq. km.)
Belize	Belmopan	Central America, south of Mexico	8,860 sq. mi. (22,960 sq. km.)
Benin	Porto-Novo	West Africa, on the Gulf of Guinea, west of Nigeria	43,480 sq. mi. (112,620 sq. km.)
Bhutan	Thimphu	Asia, in the Himalaya Mountains, between China and India	18,000 sq. mi. (47,000 sq. km.)
Bolivia	La Paz	South America, in the Andes Mountains, next to Brazil	424,160 sq. mi. (1,098,580 sq. km.)
Bosnia and Herzegovina	Sarajevo	Southern Europe, on the Balkan Peninsula	19,740 sq. mi. (51,130 sq. km.)
Botswana	Gaborone	Southern Africa, between South Africa and Zambia	231,800 sq. mi. (600,370 sq. km.)
Brazil	Brasília	Occupies most of the eastern part of South America	3,286,490 sq. mi. (8,511,970 sq. km.)
Brunei	Bandar Seri Begawan	On the island of Borneo, northwest of Australia in the Pacific Ocean	2,230 sq. mi. (5,770 sq. km.)
Bulgaria	Sofia	Eastern Europe, on the Balkan Peninsula, bordering the Black Sea	42,820 sq. mi. (110,910 sq. km.)
Burkina Faso	Ouagadougou	West Africa, between Mali and Ghana	105,900 sq. mi. (274,200 sq. km.)
Burundi	Bujumbura	Central Africa, northwest of Tanzania	10,750 sq. mi. (27,830 sq. km.)
Cambodia	Phnom Penh	Southeast Asia, between Vietnam and Thailand	69,900 sq. mi. (181,040 sq. km.)
Cameroon	Yaoundé	Central Africa, between Nigeria and Central African Republic	183,570 sq. mi. (475,440 sq. km.)
Canada	Ottawa	Occupies the northern part of North America, north of the United States	3,851,810 sq. mi. (9,976,140 sq. km.)
Cape Verde (not on map)	Praia	Islands off the western tip of Africa	1,560 sq. mi. (4,030 sq. km.)
Central African Republic	Bangui	Central Africa, south of Chad	240,530 sq. mi. (622,984 sq. km.)

POPULATION	CURRENCY	LANGUAGE	DID YOU KNOW?
146,736,000	$1 = 57.9 takas	Bangla, English	Annual flooding of the Ganges River covers about 30% of the country.
270,000	$1 = 1.99 Barbados dollars	English	It's named for its bearded fig trees (from the Spanish *barbados,* 'bearded ones').
9,895,000	$1 = 1,930 rubles	Byelorussian, Russian	Belarrusian bibles were some of the first books printed in Eastern Europe.
10,318,000	$1 = .96 euro	Flemish (Dutch), French, German	Brussels sprouts have been grown near Brussels for some 400 years.
256,000	$1 = 1.97 Belize dollars	English, Spanish, Mayan, Garifuna	Belize is Central America's only country without a Pacific coast.
6,736,000	$1 = 629.76 CFA francs	French, Fon, Yoruba	Sandbanks make access to the coast of Benin difficult.
2,257,000	$1 = 48 ngultrums	Dzongkha, Tibetan	Traditional clothing in this Buddhist nation has not changed for centuries.
8,808,000	$1 = 7.51 Bolivianos	Spanish, Quechua, Aymara	The country is named after the independence fighter Simon Bolivar.
4,161,000	$1 = 1.87 mark	Serbo-Croatian	Before its independence in 1992, the country was part of Yugoslavia.
1,785,000	$1 = 5.39 pulas	English, Setswana	The average baby born in Botswana will live about 35 years.
178,470,000	$1 = 3.44 reals	Portuguese, Spanish, English	Brazil produces about 40 percent of the world's coffee.
358,000	$1 = 1.74 Brunei dollars	Malay, English, Chinese	Tiny Brunei once ruled over all of Borneo and part of the Philippines.
7,897,000	$1 = 1.88 leva	Bulgarian	In the Middle Ages, Bulgaria became an important center of Slavic culture.
13,002,000	$1 = 629.76. CFA francs	French, tribal languages	This nation won independence from France as Upper Volta, in 1947.
6,825,000	$1 = 1,034 francs	Kirundi, French, Swahili	The pygmy Twa people were the first people to live in this region.
14,144,000	$1 = 3,835 riels	Khmer, French	About 90% of the people in this country are Buddhists.
16,018,000	$1 = 629.76 CFA francs	English, French	Mt. Cameroon (13,350 ft.) is the highest mountain in West Africa.
31,510,000	$1 = 1.56 Canadian dollars	English, French	About 85% of all Canadians live within 200 miles. of the U.S. border.
463,000	$1 = 108.95 escudos	Portuguese, Crioulo	Pico do Cano is the only volcano still active on these volcanic islands.
3,865,000	$1 = 629.76 CFA francs	French, Sangho, Arabic, Hunsa, Swahili	Diamonds are the leading export of this developing nation.

NATION	CAPITAL	LOCATION OF NATION	AREA
Chad	N'Djamena	North Africa, south of Libya	496,000 sq. mi. (1,284,000 sq. km.)
Chile	Santiago	Along the western coast of South America	292,260 sq. mi. (756,950 sq. km.)
China	Beijing	Occupies most of the mainland of eastern Asia	3,705,410 sq. mi. (9,596,960 sq. km.)
Colombia	Bogotá	Northwestern South America, southeast of Panama	439,740 sq. mi. (1,138,910 sq. km.)
Comoros	Moroni	Islands between Madagascar and the east coast of Africa	840 sq. mi. (2,170 sq. km.)
Congo, Democratic Republic of the	Kinshasa	Central Africa, north of Angola and Zambia	905,570 sq. mi. (2,345,410 sq. km.)
Congo, Republic of the	Brazzaville	Central Africa, east of Gabon	132,000 sq. mi. (342,000 sq. km.)
Costa Rica	San José	Central America, south of Nicaragua	19,700 sq. mi (51,100 sq. km.)
Côte d'Ivoire (Ivory Coast)	Yamoussoukro	West Africa, on the Gulf of Guinea, west of Ghana	124,500 sq. mi. (322,460 sq. km.)
Croatia	Zagreb	Southern Europe, south of Hungary	21,830 sq. mi. (56,540 sq. km.)
Cuba	Havana	In the Caribbean Sea, south of Florida	42,800 sq. mi. (110,860 sq. km.)
Cyprus	Nicosia	Island in the Mediterranean Sea, off the coast of Turkey	3,570 sq. mi. (9,250 sq. km.)
Czech Republic	Prague	Central Europe, south of Poland, east of Germany	30,350 sq. mi. (78,870 sq. km.)
Denmark	Copenhagen	Northern Europe, between the Baltic Sea and North Sea	16,640 sq. mi. (43,090 sq. km.)
Djibouti	Djibouti	North Africa, on the Gulf of Aden, across from Saudi Arabia	8,500 sq. mi. (22,000 sq. km.)
Dominica	Roseau	Island in the Caribbean Sea	290 sq. mi. (750 sq. km.)
Dominican Republic	Santo Domingo	On an island, along with Haiti, in the Caribbean Sea	18,810 sq. mi. (48,730 sq. km.)
East Timor	Dili	Part of an island in the South Pacific Ocean, north of Australia	5,740 sq. mi. (14,880 sq. km.)
Ecuador	Quito	South America, on the equator, bordering the Pacific Ocean	109,480 sq. mi. (283,560 sq. km.)
Egypt	Cairo	Northeastern Africa, on the Red Sea and Mediterranean Sea	386,660 sq. mi. (1,001,450 sq. km.)

POPULATION	CURRENCY	LANGUAGE	DID YOU KNOW?
8,598,000	$1 = 629.76 CFA francs	French, Arabic, Sara, Sango	Chad has cave paintings that are over 5,000 years old.
15,805,000	$1 = 713.78 pesos	Spanish	This "Shoestring Republic" is 2,650 mi. long but an average of 110 mi. wide.
1,304,196,000 (incl. Taiwan)	$1 = 8.28 yuan	Mandarin, Yue, Wu, Hakka	The Great Wall of China once extended some 1,500 mi.
44,222,000	$1 = 2,851 pesos	Spanish	This is the only South American country with Caribbean and Pacific coasts.
768,000	$1 = 470.35 francs	Arabic, French, Comorian	Ylang-ylang, a major export, is a perfume made from a native tree.
52,771,000	$1 = 360 Congolese francs	French	In 2002, a volcanic eruption destroyed the large city of Goma.
3,724,000	$1 = 629.76 CFA francs	French, Lingala, Kikongo	Bantu peoples of the Congo have lived there since before A.D. 1000.
4,173,000	$1 = 379.16 colones	Spanish	More than 725 species of birds are native to Costa Rica.
16,631,000	$1 = 629.76 CFA francs	French, Dioula	This nation is the world's leading producer of cocoa beans.
4,428,000	$1 = 7.22 kunas	Serbo-Croatian	Dubrovnik has a drugstore that first opened in 1317.
11,300,000	$1 = 1 peso	Spanish	Cuba's 2-inch-long bee hummingbird is the world's smallest bird.
802,000	$1 = .55 pound	Greek, Turkish, English	Center of a kingdom in the 7th century B.C., Nicosia is one of the world's oldest cities.
10,236,000	$1 = 30.1 koruny	Czech, Slovak	Prague is home to Europe's oldest synagogue (c. 1270).
5,364,000	$1 = 7.13 kroner	Danish, Faroese	Legos (from the Danish Leg Godt—"play well") come from Denmark.
703,000	$1 = 175 Djibouti francs	French, Arabic, Afar, Somali	Djibouti is on a dangerous strait, the Bab al-Mandab ("gate of tears").
70,000	$1 = 2.67 EC dollars	English, French patois	Dominica was sighted and named by Christopher Columbus in 1493.
8,745,000	$1 = 20 pesos	Spanish	Pico Duarte (10,417 ft.) is the highest peak in the West Indies.
778,000	U.S. dollar	English, Portuguese, Bahasa Indonesia, Tetum	East Timor became independent in May 2002.
13,003,000	U.S. dollar	Spanish, Quechua	Quito is the oldest capital city in South America.
71,931,000	$1 = 4.59 pounds	Arabic, English, French	About 20,000 ships go through Egypt's Suez Canal each year.

NATION	CAPITAL	LOCATION OF NATION	AREA
El Salvador	San Salvador	Central America, southwest of Honduras	8,120 sq. mi. (21,040 sq. km.)
Equatorial Guinea	Malabo	West Africa, on the Gulf of Guinea, off the west coast of Cameroon	10,830 sq. mi. (28,050 sq. km.)
Eritrea	Asmara	Northeast Africa, north of Ethiopia	46,840 sq. mi. (121,320 sq. km.)
Estonia	Tallinn	Northern Europe, on the Baltic Sea, north of Latvia	17,460 sq. mi. (45,230 sq. km.)
Ethiopia	Addis Ababa	East Africa, east of Sudan	435,190 sq. mi. (1,127,130 sq. km.)
Fiji	Suva	Islands in the South Pacific Ocean, east of Australia	7,050 sq. mi. (18,270 sq. km.)
Finland	Helsinki	Northern Europe, between Sweden and Russia	130,130 sq. mi. (337,030 sq. km.)
France	Paris	Western Europe, between Germany and Spain	211,210 sq. mi. (547,030 sq. km.)
Gabon	Libreville	Central Africa, on the Atlantic coast, south of Cameroon	103,350 sq. mi. (267,670 sq. km.)
The Gambia	Banjul	West Africa, on the Atlantic Ocean, surrounded by Senegal	4,400 sq. mi. (11,300 sq. km.)
Georgia	Tbilisi	Western Asia, south of Russia, on the Black Sea	26,900 sq. mi. (69,700 sq. km.)
Germany	Berlin	Central Europe, northeast of France	137,890 sq. mi. (357,020 sq. km.)
Ghana	Accra	West Africa, on the southern coast	92,100 sq. mi. (238,540 sq. km.)
Greece	Athens	Southern Europe, in the southern part of the Balkan Peninsula	50,940 sq. mi. (131,940 sq. km.)
Grenada	Saint George's	Island on the eastern edge of the Caribbean Sea	130 sq. mi. (340 sq. km.)
Guatemala	Guatemala City	Central America, southeast of Mexico	42,040 sq. mi. (108,890 sq. km.)
Guinea	Conakry	West Africa, on the Atlantic Ocean, north of Sierra Leone	94,930 sq. mi. (245,860 sq. km.)
Guinea-Bissau	Bissau	West Africa, on the Atlantic Ocean, south of Senegal	13,950 sq. mi. (36,120 sq. km.)
Guyana	Georgetown	South America, on the northern coast, east of Venezuela	83,000 sq. mi. (214,970 sq. km.)
Haiti	Port-au-Prince	On an island, along with Dominican Republic, in the Caribbean Sea	10,710 sq. mi. (27,750 sq. km.)

POPULATION	CURRENCY	LANGUAGE	DID YOU KNOW?
6,515,000	$1 = 8.75 colones	Spanish	*Casamiento,* a mixture of rice and beans, is a common everyday food.
494,000	$1 = 629.76 CFA francs	Spanish, French, Fang, Bubi	Malabo is located on an island in the Gulf of Guinea.
4,141,000	$1 = 13.5 nakfa	Tigrinya, Tigre, Kunama, Afar	Eritrea was once a colony of Italy.
1,323,000	$1 = 15.02 krooni	Estonian, Russian	Estonia is the smallest and farthest north of the 3 Baltic States.
70,678,000	$1 = 8.35 birr	Amharic, Tigrinya, Orominga	Ethiopia was once part of the ancient African Kingdom of Aksum.
839,000	$1 = 2.06 Fiji dollars	English, Fijian, Hindustani	Only about 100 of Fiji's more than 300 islands and islets are inhabited.
5,207,000	$1 = .96 euro	Finnish, Swedish	Tarja Halonen, Finland's first woman president, took office in 2000.
60,144,000	$1 = .96 euro	French	France produces over 360 kinds of cheese, from cows, goats, or sheep.
1,329,000	$1 = 629.76 CFA francs	French, Bantu dialects	Libreville (French for "freetown") was founded in 1849 for freed slaves.
1,426,000	$1 = 23 dalasi	English, Mandinka, Wolof	The Gambia is surrounded on three sides by the country of Senegal.
5,126,000	$1 = 2.11 laris	Georgian, Russian	The Georgian language has its own unique alphabet.
82,476,000	$1 = .96 euro	German	Aside from Russia, Germany is the most populous country in Europe.
20,922,000	$1 = 8,400 cedis	English, Akan, Ewe, Moshi-Dagomba, Ga	Ghana's Lake Volta is one of the largest man-made lakes in the world.
10,976,000	$1 = .96 euro	Greek, English, French	Athens is the site of the 2004 Summer Olympics.
89,260	$1 = 2.67 EC dollars	English, French patois	Grenada is the smallest independent nation in the western hemisphere.
12,347,000	$1 = 7.72 quetzals	Spanish, Mayan languages	Guatemala was the center of the Mayan Empire (3rd-10th cent. A.D.).
8,480,000	$1 = 1,971 francs	French, tribal languages	Common animals in Guinea include parrots, snakes, and crocodiles.
1,493,000	$1 = 629.76 CFA francs	Portuguese, Crioulo	At carnival time people wear masks of sharks, hippos, and bulls.
765,000	$1 = 179 Guyana dollars	English, Amerindian dialects	Dense forest makes up about 75% of this sparsely populated country.
8,326,000	$1 = 36 gourdes	Haitian Creole, French	Haiti is the 2nd-oldest republic, after the U.S., in the western hemisphere.

NATION	CAPITAL	LOCATION OF NATION	AREA
Honduras	Tegucigalpa	Central America, between Guatemala and Nicaragua	43,280 sq. mi. (112,090 sq. km.)
Hungary	Budapest	Central Europe, north of Serbia & Montenegro	35,920 sq. mi. (93,030 sq. km.)
Iceland	Reykjavik	Island off the coast of Europe, in the North Atlantic Ocean	40,000 sq. mi. (103,000 sq. km.)
India	New Delhi	Southern Asia, on a large peninsula on the Indian Ocean	1,269,350 sq. mi. (3,287,590 sq. km.)
Indonesia	Jakarta	Islands south of Southeast Asia, along the equator	705,190 sq. mi. (1,826,440 sq. km.)
Iran	Tehran	Southern Asia, between Iraq and Pakistan	636,000 sq. mi. (1,648,000 sq. km.)
Iraq	Baghdad	In the Middle East, between Syria and Iran	168,750 sq. mi. (437,070 sq. km.)
Ireland	Dublin	Off Europe's coast, in the Atlantic Ocean, west of Great Britain	27,140 sq. mi. (70,280 sq. km.)
Israel	Jerusalem	In the Middle East, between Jordan and the Mediterranean Sea	8,020 sq. mi. (20,770 sq. km.)
Italy	Rome	Southern Europe, jutting out into the Mediterranean Sea	116,310 sq. mi. (301,230 sq. km.)
Jamaica	Kingston	Island in the Caribbean Sea, south of Cuba	4,240 sq. mi. (10,990 sq. km.)
Japan	Tokyo	Four big islands and many small ones, off the east coast of Asia	145,880 sq. mi. (377,840 sq. km.)
Jordan	Amman	In the Middle East, south of Syria, east of Israel	35,300 sq. mi. (91,540 sq. km.)
Kazakhstan	Astana	Central Asia, south of Russia	1,049,200 sq. mi. (2,717,300 sq. km.)
Kenya	Nairobi	East Africa, on the Indian Ocean, south of Ethiopia	224,960 sq. mi. (582,650 sq. km.)
Kiribati	Tarawa	Islands in the middle of the Pacific Ocean, near the equator	280 sq. mi. (720 sq. km.)
Korea, North	Pyongyang	Eastern Asia, in the northern part of the Korean Peninsula	46,540 sq. mi. (120,540 sq. km.)
Korea, South	Seoul	Eastern Asia, south of North Korea, on the Korean Peninsula	38,020 sq. mi. (98,480 sq. km.)
Kuwait	Kuwait City	In the Middle East, on the northern end of the Persian Gulf	6,880 sq. mi. (17,820 sq. km.)
Kyrgyzstan	Bishkek	Western Asia, between Kazakhstan and Tajikistan	76,600 sq. mi. (198,500 sq. km.)

POPULATION	CURRENCY	LANGUAGE	DID YOU KNOW?
6,491,000	$1 = 16.92 lempiras	Spanish	The marimba is Honduras's most popular musical instrument.
9,877,000	$1 = 225.89 forints	Hungarian (Magyar)	Budapest is sometimes called the Paris of Eastern Europe.
290,000	$1 = 81.03 kronur	Icelandic (Islenska)	85% of Iceland's homes are heated by underground (geothermal) energy.
1,065,462,000	$1 = 47.98 rupees	Hindi, English	Indian civilization began at least 5,000 years ago.
219,883,000	$1 = 8929.57 rupiah	Bahasa Indonesian, English, Dutch	Indonesia is home to the komodo dragon, largest lizard in the world.
68,920,000	$1 = 7,971 rials	Persian (Farsi), Turkic, Luri	Until the 1930's Iran was known as Persia.
24,175,000	$1 = .31 dinar	Arabic, Kurdish	The ancient Sumerians invented cuneiform, an early form of writing.
3,956,000	$1 = .96 euro	English, Gaelic	Ireland is known as the "emerald isle," for its brilliant green grass.
6,433,000	$1 = 4.79 new shekels	Hebrew, Arabic, English	The Dead Sea (-1,348 ft.) is the lowest point on the Earth's surface.
57,423,000	$1 = .96 euro	Italian, German, French, Slovene	The Renaissance, the 15th-16th-century revival of learning, began in Italy.
2,651,000	$1 = 49.85 Jamaican dollars	English, Jamaican, Creole	Reggae, a mixture of native, rock, and soul music, is from Jamaica.
127,654,000	$1 = 119.73 yen	Japanese	Japan is in one of earth's most active earthquake zones.
5,473,000	$1 = .71 dinar	Arabic, English	Philadelphia was the ancient name for Amman, Jordan's modern capital.
15,433,000	$1 = 155.85 tenges	Kazakh, Russian	The shrinking Aral Sea was once the world's 4th-largest lake.
31,987,000	$1 = 77.58 shillings	Swahili, English	The Kenyan Highlands are one of the most productive agricultural regions in Africa.
98,550	$1 = 1.76 Australian dollars	English, Gilbertese	The nation's 33 islands are scattered over 2 million sq. mi. of ocean.
22,664,000	$1 = 2.2 won	Korean	Settled in 1122 B.C., Pyongyang is the oldest city on the Korean Peninsula.
47,700,000	$1 = 1,196.89 won	Korean	The Korean language is written in Han'gul, a language script created in the 1400s.
2,521,000	$1 = .3 dinar	Arabic, English	Kuwait gets its water supply by removing the salt from seawater.
5,138,000	$1 = 46.2 soms	Kyrgyz, Russian	At over 5,250 ft., Ysyk Köl is one of the world's highest lakes.

NATION	CAPITAL	LOCATION OF NATION	AREA
Laos	Vientiane	Southeast Asia, between Vietnam and Thailand	91,400 sq. mi. (236,800 sq. km.)
Latvia	Riga	On the Baltic Sea, between Lithuania and Estonia	24,900 sq. mi. (64,590 sq. km.)
Lebanon	Beirut	In the Middle East, between the Mediterranean Sea and Syria	4,000 sq. mi. (10,400 sq. km.)
Lesotho	Maseru	Southern Africa, surrounded by the nation of South Africa	11,720 sq. mi. (30,350 sq. km.)
Liberia	Monrovia	Western Africa, on the Atlantic Ocean, southeast of Sierra Leone	43,000 sq. mi. (111,370 sq. km.)
Libya	Tripoli	North Africa, on the Mediterranean Sea, to the west of Egypt	679,360 sq. mi. (1,759,540 sq. km.)
Liechtenstein	Vaduz	Southern Europe, in the Alps between Austria and Switzerland	60 sq. mi. (160 sq. km.)
Lithuania	Vilnius	Northern Europe, on the Baltic Sea, east of Poland	25,200 sq. mi. (65,200 sq. km.)
Luxembourg	Luxembourg	Western Europe, between France and Germany	1,000 sq. mi. (2,590 sq. km.)
Macedonia	Skopje	Southern Europe, north of Greece	9,780 sq. mi. (25,330 sq. km.)
Madagascar	Antananarivo	Island in the Indian Ocean, off the east coast of Africa	226,660 sq. mi. (587,040 sq. km.)
Malawi	Lilongwe	Southern Africa, south of Tanzania and east of Zambia	45,750 sq. mi. (118,480 sq. km.)
Malaysia	Kuala Lumpur	Southeast tip of Asia and the north coast of the island of Borneo	127,320 sq. mi. (329,750 sq. km.)
Maldives	Male	Islands in the Indian Ocean, south of India	115 sq. mi. (300 sq. km.)
Mali	Bamako	West Africa, between Algeria and Mauritania	480,000 sq. mi. (1,240,000 sq. km.)
Malta	Valletta	Island in the Mediterranean Sea, south of Italy	120 sq. mi. (320 sq. km.)
Marshall Islands	Majuro	Chain of small islands in the middle of the Pacific Ocean	70 sq. mi. (181 sq. km.)
Mauritania	Nouakchott	West Africa, on the Atlantic Ocean, north of Senegal	398,000 sq. mi. (1,030,700 sq. km.)
Mauritius (not on map)	Port Louis	Islands in the Indian Ocean, east of Madagascar	720 sq. mi. (1,860 sq. km.)
Mexico	Mexico City	North America, south of the United States	761,610 sq. mi. (1,972,550 sq. km.)

POPULATION	CURRENCY	LANGUAGE	DID YOU KNOW?
5,657,000	$1 = 7,600 kips	Lao, French, English	In the 1300s, Laos was named the Kingdom of the Million Elephants.
2,307,000	$1 = .59 lat	Lettish, Lithuanian	Riga Castle, now the residence of Latvia's president, dates from 1330.
3,653,000	$1 = 1,507.39 pounds	Arabic, French, English, Armenian	Beirut is found in recorded history as early as the 15th century B.C.
1,802,000	$1 = 8.45 maloti	English, Sesotho	Diamonds are Lesotho's chief export.
3,367,000	Same value as U.S. dollar	English, tribal languages	Liberia's pygmy hippopotamus is half the size of the common hippo.
5,551,000	$1 = 1.23 dinars	Arabic, Italian, English	Much of Libya lies within the great Sahara Desert.
33,150	$1 = 1.4 Swiss francs	German, Alemanic dialect	The postal system in this tiny country is administered by Switzerland.
3,444,000	$1 = 3.31 litas	Lithuanian, Polish, Russian	A Lithuanian-American, Valdas Adamkus, became president in 1998.
453,000	$1 = .96 euro	French, German	Four Holy Roman emperors came from this tiny duchy.
2,056,000	$1 = 61.6 denars	Macedonian, Albanian	Skopje was rebuilt after an earthquake in 1963 destroyed over half of the city.
17,404,000	$1 = 6,380 Malagasy francs	Malagasy, French	The island is home to the lemur, one of its many unique wild animals.
12,105,000	$1 = 86.66 kwachas	English, Chichewa	Lakes cover nearly one-fourth of Malawi.
24,425,000	$1 = 3.8 ringgits	Malay, English, Chinese dialects	The Petronas Towers in the capital are the tallest buildings in the world.
318,000	$1 = 12.8 rufiyaa	Maldivian, Divehi, English	None of the more than 1,000 islands of the country is larger than 5 sq. mi in area.
13,007,000	$1 = 629.76 CFA francs	French, Bambara	Timbuktu was a great learning center in the 15th and 16th centuries.
394,000	$1 = .4 Maltese lira	Maltese, English	Valletta is a 16th-century fortress-city built by the Knights of St. John.
56,430	U.S. dollar	English, Marshallese	More than 800 species of fish thrive in the waters of the Marshalls.
2,893,000	$1 = 261.75 ouguiyas	Hasaniya Arabic, Wolof, Pular	Little plant life and few animals exist in the Sahara in northern Mauritania.
1,221,000	$1 = 29.15 Mauritian rupees	English, French, Creole, Hindi	The island of Mauritius is almost entirely surrounded by coral reefs.
103,457,000	$1 = 10.39 new pesos	Spanish, Mayan dialects	The advanced civilizations of Mexico included the Maya and the Aztec.

NATION	CAPITAL	LOCATION OF NATION	AREA
Micronesia	Palikir	Islands in the western Pacific Ocean	270 sq. mi. (700 sq. km.)
Moldova	Chisinau	Eastern Europe, between Ukraine and Romania	13,000 sq. mi. (33,700 sq. km.)
Monaco	Monaco	Europe, on the Mediterranean Sea, surrounded by France	3/4 of a sq. mi. (2 sq. km.)
Mongolia	Ulaanbaatar	Central Asia between Russia and China	604,000 sq. mi. (1,565,000 sq. km.)
Morocco	Rabat	Northwest Africa, on the Atlantic Ocean and Mediterranean Sea	172,410 sq. mi. (446,550 sq. km.)
Mozambique	Maputo	Southeastern Africa, on the Indian Ocean	309,500 sq. mi. (801,590 sq. km.)
Myanmar (Burma)	Yangon (Rangoon)	Southern Asia, to the east of India and Bangladesh	262,000 sq. mi. (678,500 sq. km.)
Namibia	Windhoek	Southwestern Africa, on the Atlantic Ocean, west of Botswana	318,700 sq. mi. (825,420 sq. km.)
Nauru	Yaren district	Island in the western Pacific Ocean, just below the equator	8 sq. mi. (21 sq. km.)
Nepal	Kathmandu	Asia, in the Himalaya Mountains, between China and India	54,400 sq. mi. (140,800 sq. km.)
Netherlands	Amsterdam	Northern Europe, on the North Sea, to the west of Germany	16,030 sq. mi. (41,530 sq. km.)
New Zealand	Wellington	Islands in the Pacific Ocean east of Australia	103,740 sq. mi. (268,680 sq. km.)
Nicaragua	Managua	Central America, between Honduras and Costa Rica	50,000 sq. mi. (129,490 sq. km.)
Niger	Niamey	North Africa, south of Algeria and Libya	489,000 sq. mi. (1,267,000 sq. km.)
Nigeria	Abuja	West Africa, on the southern coast between Benin and Cameroon	356,670 sq. mi. (923,770 sq. km.)
Norway	Oslo	Northern Europe, on the Scandinavian Peninsula	125,180 sq. mi. (324,220 sq. km.)
Oman	Muscat	On the Arabian Peninsula, southeast of Saudi Arabia	82,030 sq. mi. (212,460 sq. km.)
Pakistan	Islamabad	South Asia, between Iran and India	310,400 sq. mi. (803,940 sq. km.)
Palau	Koror	Islands in North Pacific Ocean, southeast of Philippines	180 sq. mi. (460 sq. km.)
Panama	Panama City	Central America, between Costa Rica and Colombia	30,200 sq. mi. (78,200 sq. km.)

POPULATION	CURRENCY	LANGUAGE	DID YOU KNOW?
109,000	U.S. dollar	English, Trukese, Pohnpeian, Yapese	Micronesia is made up of more than 600 islands and islets.
4,267,000	$1 = 13.9 lei	Moldovan, Russian	Moldova was at times part of Romania and the Soviet Union.
32,130	$1 = .96 euro	French, English, Italian	Citizens are barred from gambling in the country's world-famous casinos.
2,594,000	$1 = 1,125 tugriks	Khalkha Mongolian	By 1222, Mongol leader Genghis Khan ruled most of Asia and Russia.
30,566,000	$1 = 10.2 dirhams	Arabic, Berber dialects	Morocco has the broadest plains and highest mountains in North Africa.
18,863,000	$1 = 23,655 meticals	Portuguese, native dialects	Decades of civil war have left over a million landmines buried here.
49,485,000	$1 = 6.27 kyats	Burmese	Myanmar is widely known as the Land of Golden Pagodas.
1,987,000	$1 = 8.51 dollars	Afrikaans, English, German	Windhoek is situated on a plateau more than a mile above sea level.
12,570	$1 = 1.76 Australian dollars	Nauruan, English	Australian currency is the legal tender (money) used in Nauru.
25,164,000	$1 = 76.5 rupees	Nepali, many dialects	A mysterious creature called the yeti is said to roam Nepal's mountain peaks.
16,149,000	$1 = .96 euro	Dutch	Nowadays in the Netherlands, wooden shoes are worn mostly by farmers.
3,875,000	$1 = 1.89 NZ dollars	English, Maori	The 3 *Lord of the Rings* movies were filmed in New Zealand.
5,466,000	$1 = 14.57 gold cordobas	Spanish	The country's Caribbean and Pacific coasts are more than 200 mi. long.
11,972,000	$1 = 629.76 CFA francs	French, Hausa, Djerma	Niger was once part of noted ancient and medieval African empires.
124,009,000	$1 = 130.4 nairas	English, Hausa, Yoruba, Ibo	Nigeria is the biggest oil-producing country in Africa.
4,533,000	$1 = 6.95 kroner	Norwegian	The UN ranks Norway as the world's top country in "quality of life."
2,851,000	$1 = .38 rial Omani	Arabic	The average annual rainfall in Oman is generally less than 4 in. (100 mm.).
153,578,000	$1 = 58.14 rupees	Urdu, English, Punjabi, Sindhi	K2, the world's 2nd-highest peak (28,250 ft), is in Pakistan's Hindu Kush.
19,720	U.S. dollar	English, Palauan	The islands of Palau are old coral reefs that have risen above the sea.
3,120,000	$1 = 1 balboa	Spanish, English	Richard Halliburton swam the Panama Canal in 1928, paying a toll of 36 cents.

NATION	CAPITAL	LOCATION OF NATION	AREA
Papua New Guinea	Port Moresby	Part of the island of New Guinea, north of Australia	178,700 sq. mi. (462,840 sq. km.)
Paraguay	Asunción	South America, between Argentina and Brazil	157,050 sq. mi. (406,750 sq. km.)
Peru	Lima	South America, along the Pacific coast, north of Chile	496,230 sq. mi. (1,285,220 sq. km.)
Philippines	Manila	Islands in the Pacific Ocean, off the coast of Southeast Asia	115,830 sq. mi. (300,000 sq. km.)
Poland	Warsaw	Central Europe, on the Baltic Sea, east of Germany	120,730 sq. mi. (312,680 sq. km.)
Portugal	Lisbon	Southern Europe, on the Iberian Peninsula, west of Spain	35,670 sq. mi. (92,390 sq. km.)
Qatar	Doha	Arabian Peninsula, on the Persian Gulf	4,420 sq. mi. (11,440 sq. km.)
Romania	Bucharest	Southern Europe, on the Black Sea, north of Bulgaria	91,700 sq. mi. (237,500 sq. km.)
Russia	Moscow	Stretches from Eastern Europe across northern Asia to the Pacific Ocean	6,592,800 sq. mi. (17,075,200 sq. km.)
Rwanda	Kigali	Central Africa, northwest of Tanzania	10,170 sq. mi. (26,340 sq. km.)
Saint Kitts and Nevis	Basseterre	Islands in the Caribbean Sea, near Puerto Rico	100 sq. mi. (260 sq. km.)
Saint Lucia	Castries	Island on eastern edge of the Caribbean Sea	240 sq. mi. (620 sq. km.)
Saint Vincent and the Grenadines	Kingstown	Islands on eastern edge of the Caribbean Sea, north of Grenada	150 sq. mi. (390 sq. km.)
Samoa (formerly Western Samoa)	Apia	Islands in the South Pacific Ocean	1,100 sq. mi. (2,860 sq. km.)
San Marino	San Marino	Southern Europe, surrounded by Italy	23 sq. mi. (60 sq. km.)
São Tomé and Príncipe	São Tomé	In the Gulf of Guinea, off the coast of West Africa	390 sq. mi. (1,000 sq. km.)
Saudi Arabia	Riyadh	Western Asia, occupying most of the Arabian Peninsula	756,990 sq. mi. (1,960,580 sq. km.)
Senegal	Dakar	West Africa, on the Atlantic Ocean, south of Mauritania	75,750 sq. mi. (196,190 sq. km.)
Serbia and Montenegro	Belgrade, Podgorica	Europe, on Balkan Peninsula, west of Romania and Bulgaria	39,520 sq. mi. (102,350 sq. km.)
Seychelles (not on map)	Victoria	Islands off the coast of Africa, in the Indian Ocean	180 sq. mi. (460 sq. km.)

POPULATION	CURRENCY	LANGUAGE	DID YOU KNOW?
5,711,000	$1 = 3.95 kinas	English, Motu	Wild animals there include the tree kangaroo, wallaby, wild pig, and dingo.
5,878,000	$1 = 7,290 guarani	Spanish, Guarani	The Itaipú dam, on the border with Brazil, is the world's biggest hydroelectric plant.
27,167,000	$1 = 3.5 new soles	Spanish, Quechua, Aymara	The warm ocean current known as El Niño appears every few years off the coast of Peru.
79,999,000	$1 = 53.5 pesos	Pilipino, English	Most Filipinos live on the 11 largest of the country's 7,100 islands.
38,587,000	$1 = 3.82 zlotys	Polish	Pope John Paul II was born in Poland in 1920.
10,062,000	$1 = .96 euro	Portuguese	Port wine is named for Oporto, Portugal's second largest city.
610,000	$1 = 3.64 riyals	Arabic, English	The government gets 90% of its revenue from selling oil.
22,334,000	$1 = 33,500 lei	Romanian, Hungarian	The Danube Delta is Europe's youngest land geologically.
143,246,000	$1 = 31.88 rubles	Russian, many others	Record lows of –90° F have been recorded in the region of Siberia.
8,387,000	$1 = 500 francs	French, English, Kinyarwanda,	The source of the Nile River has been located in Rwanda.
38,760	$1 = 2.67 EC dollars	English	In 1493, Columbus named St. Kitts for his patron, St. Christopher.
149,000	$1 = 2.67 EC dollars	English, French patois	Bananas are the principal export of this island country.
120,000	$1 = 2.67 EC dollars	English, French patois	Soufrière, an active volcano in the north, last erupted in 1979.
178,000	$1 = 3.22 tala	English, Samoan	Most Samoans live in small seashore villages of 100-500 people.
28,120	$1 = .96 euro	Italian	San Marino claims to be Europe's oldest country, founded in A.D. 301.
161,000	$1 = 9,019.7 dobras	Portuguese	Portugal ruled these islands for nearly 300 years—until 1975.
24,217,000	$1 = 3.75 riyals	Arabic	Mecca, the birthplace of Muhammad, is the holiest city of Islam.
10,095,000	$1 = 629.76 CFA francs	French, Wolof	Senegal is among the world's largest producers of peanuts.
10,527,000	$1 = 58.98 new dinars	Serbo-Croatian, Albanian	In 2003, Yugoslavia turned into a union of its last 2 republics, Serbia and Montenegro.
34,000	$1 = 5.62 rupees	English, French, Creole	This group of about 115 islands is the smallest country in Africa.

NATION	CAPITAL	LOCATION OF NATION	AREA
Sierra Leone	Freetown	West Africa, on the Atlantic Ocean, south of Guinea	27,700 sq. mi. (71,740 sq. km.)
Singapore	Singapore	Mostly on one island, off the tip of Southeast Asia	250 sq. mi. (650 sq. km.)
Slovakia	Bratislava	Eastern Europe, between Poland and Hungary	18,860 sq. mi. (48,850 sq. km.)
Slovenia	Ljubljana	Eastern Europe, between Austria and Croatia	7,820 sq. mi. (20,250 sq. km.)
Solomon Islands	Honiara	Western Pacific Ocean	10,980 sq. mi. (28,450 sq. km.)
Somalia	Mogadishu	East Africa, east of Ethiopia	246,200 sq. mi. (637,660 sq. km.)
South Africa	Pretoria (admin.) Cape Town (legisl.)	At the southern tip of Africa	471,010 sq. mi. (1,219,910 sq. km.)
Spain	Madrid	Europe, south of France, on the Iberian Peninsula	194,890 sq. mi. (504,780 sq. km.)
Sri Lanka	Colombo	Island in the Indian Ocean, southeast of India	25,330 sq. mi. (65,610 sq. km.)
Sudan	Khartoum	North Africa, south of Egypt, on the Red Sea	967,500 sq. mi. (2,505,810 sq. km.)
Suriname	Paramaribo	South America, on the northern shore, east of Guyana	63,040 sq. mi. (163,270 sq. km.)
Swaziland	Mbabane	Southern Africa, almost surrounded by South Africa	6,700 sq. mi. (17,360 sq. km.)
Sweden	Stockholm	Northern Europe, on the Scandinavian Peninsula	173,730 sq. mi. (449,960 sq. km.)
Switzerland	Bern (admin.) Lausanne (judicial)	Central Europe, in the Alps, north of Italy	15,940 sq. mi. (41,290 sq. km.)
Syria	Damascus	In the Middle East, north of Jordan and west of Iraq	71,500 sq. mi. (185,180 sq. km.)
Taiwan	Taipei	Island off southeast coast of China	13,890 sq. mi. (35,980 sq. km.)
Tajikistan	Dushanbe	Asia, west of China, south of Kyrgyzstan	55,300 sq. mi. (143,100 sq. km.)
Tanzania	Dar-es-Salaam	East Africa, on the Indian Ocean, south of Kenya	364,900 sq. mi. (945,090 sq. km.)
Thailand	Bangkok	Southeast Asia, south of Laos	198,000 sq. mi. (514,000 sq. km.)
Togo	Lomé	West Africa, between Ghana and Benin	21,930 sq. mi. (56,790 sq. km.)

POPULATION	CURRENCY	LANGUAGE	DID YOU KNOW?
4,971,000	$1 = 2,010 leones	English, Mende, Temne, Krio	Crocodiles and hippos are found in the rivers of Sierra Leone.
4,609,000	$1 = 1.74 Singapore dollars	Chinese, Malay, Tamil, English	Singapore is the world's 2nd most densely populated country.
5,402,000	$1 = 39.62 koruny	Slovak, Hungarian	Bratislava served as the capital of Hungary from 1541 to 1784.
1,984,000	$1 = 221.15 tolars	Slovenian, Serbo-Croatian	Slovenia is the most prosperous of the former Yugoslav republics.
477,000	$1 = 7.36 Solomon dollars	English, Melanesian	The islands' mountains are of volcanic origin and heavily wooded.
9,890,000	$1 = 2,620 shillings	Somali, Arabic, Italian, English	Frankincense and myrrh are the major forest products of Somalia.
45,026,000	$1 = 8.43 rand	Afrikaans, English, Ndebele, Sotho	South Africa has a total of 11 official languages, 9 of them native.
41,060,000	$1 = .96 euro	Castilian Spanish, Catalan, Galician	Bullfighting is the national sport of Spain.
19,065,000	$1 = 96.6 rupees	Sinhala, Tamil, English	The Temple of the Tooth in Kandy is said to contain one of Buddha's teeth.
33,160,000	$1 = 258.7 dinars	Arabic, Nubian, Ta Bedawie	Sudan is the largest country in Africa in total area.
436,000	$1 = 2,178.5 guilders	Dutch, Sranang Tongo	Most of Suriname's people are of East Indian origin.
1,077,000	$1 = 8.45 emalangeni	English, siSwati	4 out of 10 adults in Swaziland have the AIDS virus.
8,876,000	$1 = 8.73 kronor	Swedish	One of the world's oldest parliaments, the Riksdag dates back to 1435.
7,169,000	$1 = 1.4 francs	German, French, Italian, Romansch	Switzerland has not fought in a foreign war since 1515.
17,800,000	$1 = 51.58 pounds	Arabic, Kurdish, Armenian	Syria was once part of the empire of Alexander the Great.
22,603,000	$1 = 34.71 new Taiwan dollars	Mandarin Chinese, Taiwanese	Mainland China claims this country as one of its provinces.
6,245,000	$1 = 3.25 somoni	Tajik, Russian	The Nurek Dam in Tajikistan is the highest in the world (984 ft.).
36,977,000	$1 = 978 shillings	Swahili, English	Mount Kilimanjaro is 19,340 ft. high, the highest mountain in Africa.
62,833,000	$1 = 42.99 bahts	Thai, English	Thailand is the world's largest exporter of rice and farmed shrimp.
4,909,000	$1 = 629.76 CFA francs	French, Ewe, Kabye	Togo is a leading world producer of phosphates.

NATION	CAPITAL	LOCATION OF NATION	AREA
Tonga	Nuku'alofa	Islands in the South Pacific Ocean	290 sq. mi. (750 sq. km.)
Trinidad and Tobago	Port-of-Spain	Islands off the north coast of South America	1,980 sq. mi. (5,130 sq. km.)
Tunisia	Tunis	North Africa, on the Mediterranean, between Algeria and Libya	63,170 sq. mi. (163,610 sq. km.)
Turkey	Ankara	On the southern shore of the Black Sea, partly in Europe and partly in Asia	301,380 sq. mi. (780,580 sq. km.)
Turkmenistan	Ashgabat	Western Asia, north of Afghanistan and Iran	188,500 sq. mi. (488,100 sq. km.)
Tuvalu	Funafuti Atoll	Chain of islands in the South Pacific Ocean	10 sq. mi. (26 sq. km.)
Uganda	Kampala	East Africa, south of Sudan	91,140 sq. mi. (236,040 sq. km.)
Ukraine	Kiev	Eastern Europe, south of Belarus and Russia	233,100 sq. mi. (603,700 sq. km.)
United Arab Emirates	Abu Dhabi	Arabian Peninsula, on the Persian Gulf	32,000 sq. mi. (82,880 sq. km.)
United Kingdom (Great Britain)	London	Off the northwest coast of Europe	94,530 sq. mi. (244,820 sq. km.)
United States	Washington, D.C.	In North America; 48 of 50 states between Canada and Mexico	3,717,810 sq. mi. (9,629,090 sq. km.)
Uruguay	Montevideo	South America, on the Atlantic Ocean, south of Brazil	68,040 sq. mi. (176,220 sq. km.)
Uzbekistan	Tashkent	Central Asia, south of Kazakhstan	172,740 sq. mi. (447,400 sq. km.)
Vanuatu	Port-Vila	Islands in the South Pacific Ocean	5,700 sq. mi. (14,760 sq. km.)
Vatican City		Surrounded by the city of Rome, Italy	1/5 sq. mi. (1/2 sq. km.)
Venezuela	Caracas	On the northern coast of South America, east of Colombia	352,140 sq. mi. (912,050 sq. km.)
Vietnam	Hanoi	Southeast Asia, south of China, on the eastern coast	127,240 sq. mi. (329,560 sq. km.)
Yemen	Sanaa	Asia, on the southern coast of the Arabian Peninsula	203,850 sq. mi. (527,970 sq. km.)
Zambia	Lusaka	Southern Africa, east of Angola	290,580 sq. mi. (752,610 sq. km.)
Zimbabwe	Harare	Southern Africa, south of Zambia	150,800 sq. mi. (390,580 sq. km.)

POPULATION	CURRENCY	LANGUAGE	DID YOU KNOW?
108,000	$1 = 2.23 pa'angas	Tongan, English	Tonga is ruled by a King and a prime minister he appoints for life.
1,303,000	$1 = 6.16 Trinidad dollars	English, Hindi, French, Spanish	Trinidad gave birth to calypso, a popular folk music of the Caribbean.
9,832,000	$1 = 1.34 dinar	Arabic, French	Pirates from Tunisia roamed the seas until the early 1800s.
71,325,000	$1 = 1,639,344.26 Turkish liras	Turkish, Kurdish, Arabic	More than 20 of Turkey's mountains are over 10,000 ft.
4,867,000	$1 = 5,200 manats	Turkmen, Russian, Uzbek	The Kara Kum Desert occupies 80% of the area of Turkmenistan.
11,310	$1 = 1.76 Australian dollars	Tuvaluan, English	Tuvalu has the world's 2nd-smallest population, after Vatican City.
25,827,000	$1 = 1,850 shillings	English, Luganda, Swahili	More than half the population of Uganda is under the age of 15.
48,523,000	$1 = 5.33 hryvnia	Ukrainian, Russian	In the 1840s, Russian rulers banned the Ukrainian language from schools.
2,995,000	$1 = 3.67 dirhams	Arabic, Persian, English, Hindi	A hereditary ruler, or emir, governs each of the 7 states of this country.
59,251,000	$1 = .62 pound	English	England, Northern Ireland, Scotland, and Wales make up the United Kingdom.
294,043,000	U.S. dollar	English, Spanish	The Statue of Liberty, erected in New York Harbor in 1886, was a gift from France.
3,415,000	$1 = 27.25 pesos	Spanish	More than 90% of Uruguay's people are of European descent.
26,093,000	$1 = 1,030 soms	Uzbek, Russian	The tomb of the Mongol conqueror Tamerlane is in Samarkand.
212,000	$1 = 133.3 vatus	French, English, Bislama	Espiritu Santo, Vanuatu's biggest island, was a key U.S. base during World War II.
900	$1 = .96 euro	Italian, Latin	The Vatican's Swiss Guards wear a style of uniform that dates from the 1500s.
25,699,000	$1 = 1406.47 bolivares	Spanish	Angel Falls, the world's highest waterfall, drops 3,212 ft.
81,377,000	$1 = 15,403 dong	Vietnamese, French, Chinese	France took over Vietnam in 1854 and ruled there until 1954.
20,010,000	$1 = 178.01 rials	Arabic	The city of Aden is Yemen's principal port and commercial center.
10,812,000	$1 = 4,375 kwacha	English, native languages	The Zambezi, Africa's 4th-longest river, rises in Zambia.
12,891,000	$1 = 55.45 Zimbabwe dollars	English, Shona, Sindebele	The lake behind Kariba Dam is the world's largest-capacity reservoir.

United Nations

A COMMUNITY OF NATIONS

The United Nations (UN) was started in 1945 after World War II. The first members of the UN were 50 nations that met in San Francisco, California. They signed an agreement known as the UN Charter. By early 2003, the UN had 191 independent countries as members—including East Timor, which joined in 2002. Only two independent nations—Taiwan and Vatican City—were not members.

The UN Charter lists these purposes:
- to keep worldwide peace and security
- to develop friendly relations among countries
- to help countries cooperate in solving problems
- to promote respect for human rights and basic freedoms
- to be a center that helps countries achieve their goals

FAST FACTS ABOUT THE UN

UN Day is celebrated every year on October 24, the day the UN Charter was ratified by a majority of nations.

- The flags of all 191 members—from Afghanistan to Zimbabwe—fly in front of UN Headquarters in New York and UN European Headquarters in Geneva, Switzerland.

- Six official languages are used at the United Nations—Arabic, Chinese, English, French, Russian, and Spanish.

- The UN is the world's only organization permitted to issue postage stamps. Usually only countries are allowed to do that. UN stamps, can be used only to send mail from UN offices in New York, Geneva, and Vienna.

- The land and buildings of the UN Headquarters in New York City are officially international territory. The 18 acres of land were donated by John D. Rockefeller Jr. in 1945.

- The UN's office in Vienna, Austria, is the home of the United Nations Office for Outer Space Affairs (UNOOSA), which is responsible for promoting international cooperation in the peaceful uses of outer space.

Did You KNOW?

Before there was a UN, there was the League of Nations, a similar organization founded in 1919, after World War I, in an effort "to promote international cooperation and to achieve peace and security." The U.S. never joined. After failing to prevent World War II, the League of Nations disbanded, transferring all of its assets to the UN in 1946. Beneath the foundation stone of the Palais des Nations, the UN's European Headquarters in Geneva, Switzerland, is a box containing a list of League of Nations members as of 1929 and coins from each country.

Flags fly at the UN

UN PEACEKEEPERS

The Security Council sets up and directs UN peacekeeping missions, to try to stop people from fighting while the countries or groups try to work out their differences. The map below shows the location of 13 peacekeeping missions that were operating in January 2003. These peacekeepers wear blue helmets or berets with white UN letters. In 2001 the UN approved a special mission for Afghanistan, the International Security Assistance Force (ISAF). In early 2003, more than 4,000 troops were based in Kabul, with support from 22 countries. These troops work under UN authority, but don't wear UN berets.

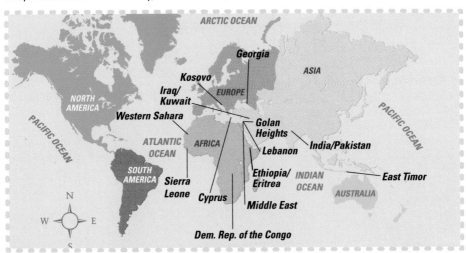

How THE UN IS ORGANIZED

GENERAL ASSEMBLY What It Does: discusses world problems, admits new members, appoints the secretary-general, decides the UN budget **Members:** All members of the UN belong to the General Assembly; each country has one vote.

SECURITY COUNCIL What It Does: handles questions of peace and security **Members:** Five permanent members (China, France, Great Britain, Russia, U.S.), each of whom can veto any proposed action; ten elected by the General Assembly for two-year terms. In early 2003 the ten were Bulgaria, Cameroon, Guinea, Mexico, and Syria (ending 2003) and Angola, Chile, Germany, Pakistan, and Spain (ending 2004).

ECONOMIC AND SOCIAL COUNCIL What It Does: deals with issues related to trade, economic development, industry, population, children, food, education, health, and human rights **Members:** Fifty-four member countries elected for three-year terms.

INTERNATIONAL COURT OF JUSTICE (WORLD COURT) located at The Hague, Netherlands **What It Does:** highest court for disputes between countries **Members:** Fifteen judges, each from a different country, elected to nine-year terms.

SECRETARIAT What It Does: carries out day-to-day operations of the UN **Members:** UN staff, headed by the secretary-general.

For more information about the UN, you can write to:
Public Inquiries Unit, United Nations, Room GA-57, New York, NY 10017
Website: www.un.org

Numbers

NUMERALS IN ANCIENT CIVILIZATION

How many zeros are there in 1 trillion?
•••
page 173

People have been counting since the earliest of times. This is what some numerals looked like in different cultures.

MODERN	1	2	3	4	5	6	7	8	9	10	20	50	100
Egyptian	I	II	III	IIII	III over II	III III	IIII III	IIII IIII	IIII IIIII	∩	∩∩	∩∩∩∩∩	9
Babylonian	Y	YY	YYY	ᵞᵞᵞ	ᵞᵞᵞᵞ	ᵞᵞᵞ	ᵞᵞᵞ	ᵞᵞᵞ	ᵞᵞᵞ	⟨	⟪	⟪⟪	Y⟪
Greek	A	B	Γ	Δ	E	F	Z	H	θ	I	K	N	P
Mayan	•	••	•••	••••	—	•̲	••̲	•••̲	••••̲	═	◉̇	◉̈	◉̄
Chinese	一	二	三	四	五	六	七	八	九	十	二十	五十	百
Hindu	I	੨	੩	੮	੫	੬	੭	੮	੯	10	੨o	੮o	100
Arabic	1	٢	٣	٣	٦	٤	٧	٨	٩	١o	٢o	٤o	1oo

ROMAN NUMERALS

Roman numerals are still used today. The symbols used for different numbers are the letters I (1), V (5), X (10), L (50), C (100), D (500), and M (1,000). If one Roman numeral is followed by a larger one, the first is subtracted from the second. For example, IV means 5 – 1 = 4. Think of it as "one less than five." On the other hand, if one Roman numeral is followed by another that is equal or smaller, add them together. Thus, XII means 10 + 1 + 1 = 12. Can you put the year you were born in Roman numerals?

According to legend, Rome was founded in 753 B.C. Can you put that year into Roman numerals?

1	I	14 XIV	90 XC
2	II	15 XV	100 C
3	III	16 XVI	200 CC
4	IV	17 XVII	300 CCC
5	V	18 XVIII	400 CD
6	VI	19 XIX	500 D
7	VII	20 XX	600 DC
8	VIII	30 XXX	700 DCC
9	IX	40 XL	800 DCCC
10	X	50 L	900 CM
11	XI	60 LX	1,000 M
12	XII	70 LXX	2,000 MM
13	XIII	80 LXXX	3,000 MMM

▼ The Colosseum

ANSWERS ON PAGES 314-317.
FOR MORE PUZZLES GO TO
WWW.WORLDALMANACFORKIDS.COM

THE PREFIX TELLS THE NUMBER

After each number are one or more prefixes used to form words that include that number. Knowing what the prefix stands for can help you understand the meaning of the word. For example, a monorail has one track. A pentagon has five sides. September gets its name from the calendar used in Roman times, when it was the seventh month (the Roman year began in March). An octopus has eight arms.

▲ *A tricycle*

1	uni-, mon-, mono-	unicycle, unicorn, monarch, monorail
2	bi-	bicycle, binary, binoculars, bifocals
3	tri-	tricycle, triangle, trilogy, trio
4	quadr-, tetr-	quadrangle, quadruplet, tetrahedron
5	pent-, quint-	pentagon, pentathlon, quintuplet
6	hex-, sext-	hexagon, sextuplet, sextet
7	hept-, sept-	heptathlon, septuplet
8	oct-	octave, octet, octopus, octagon
9	non-	nonagon, nonet
10	dec-	decade, decibel, decimal
100	cent-	centipede, century
1000	kilo-	kilogram, kilometer, kilowatt
million	mega-	megabyte, megahertz, megapixel
billion	giga-	gigabyte, gigawatt

▼ *A monorail*

BIG NUMBERS

Below are the words for some numbers, plus the number of zeros needed when each number is written out.

ten	1 zero	10
hundred	2 zeros	100
thousand	3 zeros	1,000
ten thousand	4 zeros	10,000
hundred thousand	5 zeros	100,000
million	6 zeros	1,000,000
ten million	7 zeros	10,000,000
hundred million	8 zeros	100,000,000
billion	9 zeros	1,000,000,000
trillion	12 zeros	1,000,000,000,000
quadrillion	15 zeros	1,000,000,000,000,000
quintillion	18 zeros	1,000,000,000,000,000,000
sextillion	21 zeros	1,000,000,000,000,000,000,000
septillion	24 zeros	1,000,000,000,000,000,000,000,000

A googol

There are words for even bigger numbers. For example, a googol has 100 zeros, and a googolplex is equal to the number 1 followed by a googol of zeros!

How Many SIDES and FACES Do They Have?

When a figure is flat (two-dimensional), it is a plane figure. When a figure takes up space (three-dimensional), it is a solid figure. The flat surface of a solid figure is called a face. Plane and solid figures come in many different shapes.

TWO-DIMENSIONAL

square

circle

triangle

The flat surface of a cube is a square.

THREE-DIMENSIONAL

cube

sphere

tetrahedron (pyramid)

WHAT ARE POLYGONS?

A polygon is a two-dimensional figure with three or more straight sides (called line segments). A square is a polygon. Polygons have different numbers of sides—and each has a different name. If the sides are all the same length and all the angles between the sides are equal, the polygon is called regular. If the sides are of different lengths or the angles are not equal, the polygon is called irregular. At right are some regular and irregular polygons.

NAME & NUMBER OF SIDES	REGULAR	IRREGULAR
TRIANGLE – 3	△	◁
QUADRILATERAL OR TETRAGON – 4	□	▱
PENTAGON – 5	⬠	⬠
HEXAGON – 6	⬡	⬡
HEPTAGON – 7	⬣	⬣
OCTAGON – 8	⯃	⬡
NONAGON – 9	⬡	⬠
DECAGON – 10	◯	⬡

WHAT ARE POLYHEDRONS?

A polyhedron is a three-dimensional figure with four or more faces. Each face on a polyhedron is a polygon. Below are some polyhedrons with many faces.

tetrahedron 4 faces	hexahedron 6 faces	octahedron 8 faces	dodecahedron 12 faces	icosahedron 20 faces

◀ *Great Pyramid of Khefren*

↑ **FINDING THE AREA OF A FIGURE CAN BE EASY,**
↑ **IF YOU KNOW THE NOT-SO-SECRET FORMULA.**

AREA OF A SQUARE:

A plane figure with four sides is called a **quadrilateral.** A square is a quadrilateral with four right angles and four *equal* sides, like the figure you see here. To find the area for a square, use this formula: **SIDE x SIDE** (**SIDE x SIDE** can also be written as s², pronounced "side squared"). The sides of this square are each 3 centimeters long. So the area is 3 x 3, or 9. These are no longer centimeters but **square centimeters**, like the smaller squares inside the big one.

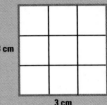

3 cm

3 cm

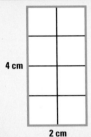

4 cm

2 cm

AREA OF A RECTANGLE:

Rectangles are another type of quadrilateral. They have four right angles, but unlike a square, the sides are not all equal.
To find the area of a rectangle, multiply **BASE x HEIGHT** (length x width). This rectangle has a base of 4 centimeters and a height of 2 centimeters. Its area is 8 square centimeters.

AREA OF A PARALLELOGRAM:

Parallelograms are quadrilaterals that have parallel opposite sides, but no right angles. The formula for the area of parallelogram is the same as for a rectangle—**BASE X HEIGHT.**

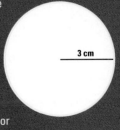

height 2 cm

base 4 cm

AREA OF A TRIANGLE:

3 cm

2 cm

A triangle is a three-sided plane figure. The prefix "tri" means three, which refers to the three points where the sides of a triangle meet.
To find the area for a triangle use **1/2 x (BASE x HEIGHT)** (first multiply the base by the height, then multiply that number by 1/2).
This triangle has a base of 2 centimeters and a height of 3 centimeters. So the area will be 3 square centimeters.

AREA OF A CIRCLE:

The distance around a circle is called its **circumference.** All the points on the circumference are an equal distance from the center. That distance from center to circumference is called the **radius.** A **diameter** is any straight line that has both ends on the circle and passes through its center. It's twice as long as the radius.
To find the circle's area you need to use π—a number called **pi** (π) that equals about 3.14. The formula for area is:
π x RADIUS x RADIUS (or **π x RADIUS SQUARED**).
For instance, this circle has a radius of 3 centimeters, so its area = π x 3 x 3, or about π x 3²; that is, 3.14 x 9. This comes to 28.26 square centimeters.

3 cm

DID YOU KNOW? *The Greek letter **pi** (π) stands for the number you get when you divide the circumference of a circle by its diameter. It is always the same, no matter how big the circle is! The Babylonians discovered this in 2000 B.C. Actually, no one can say exactly what the value of π is. When you divide the circumference by the diameter it does not come out even, and you can keep going as many places as you want: 3.14159265…it goes on forever.*

MULTIPLICATION TABLE

x	0	1	2	3	4	5	6	7	8	9	10	11	12
0	0	0	0	0	0	0	0	0	0	0	0	0	0
1	0	1	2	3	4	5	6	7	8	9	10	11	12
2	0	2	4	6	8	10	12	14	16	18	20	22	24
3	0	3	6	9	12	15	18	21	24	27	30	33	36
4	0	4	8	12	16	20	24	28	32	36	40	44	48
5	0	5	10	15	20	25	30	35	40	45	50	55	60
6	0	6	12	18	24	30	36	42	48	54	60	66	72
7	0	7	14	21	28	35	42	49	56	63	70	77	84
8	0	8	16	24	32	40	48	56	64	72	80	88	96
9	0	9	18	27	36	45	54	63	72	81	90	99	108
10	0	10	20	30	40	50	60	70	80	90	100	110	120
11	0	11	22	33	44	55	66	77	88	99	110	121	132
12	0	12	24	36	48	60	72	84	96	108	120	132	144

Homework Help

Here are a few hints to help make memorizing this table more manageable:

► First, you can skip half the other numbers! If you know that 2 x 3 = 6, you also know that 3 x 2 = 6. Changing the order of the numbers being multiplied doesn't change the result—that's the commutative property.

► You don't have to memorize the row for zero or one. Any time you multiply a number by zero, the answer is zero: 7 x 0 = 0. Multiplying a number by 1 doesn't change its value: 7 x 1 = 7.

► Now you have only 66 "items" to memorize. You can find them in the triangle in the chart above. And some of them are easy to learn.

► Multiplying by 5 and 10 is like *counting* by 5 or 10. Start with 25, for example: 5 x 5 = 25. To multiply 5 by 6, simply add 5 to get 30. Then 35, 40, and so on. All multiplication is really a series of additions: 3 x 5 is the same as 5 + 5 + 5 = 15. To multiply a number by 10, just add a 0 to it: 8 x 10 = 80.

► Multiplying by 11 may seem tough, but it really isn't. Multiply any number from 1 to 9 by 11, and you'll always get double that number: 2 x 11 = 22; 3 x 11 = 33.

Here's a finger trick that only works for multiplying by 9. Spread your fingers out in front of you. Your left pinky is 1, your left ring finger is 2, and so on. Your right pinky is 10. To find the answer to 9 x 4, fold down your 4th finger (left index finger). Look to the left of the folded finger. You have 3 still sticking out. To the right of the folded finger, you have 6 fingers out (your left thumb, plus the 5 on your right hand.). The answer is 36.

Here's a useful way to remember the order of operations you need to follow when working on math problems like $2^2 \times (1 + 3) - 1 = 15$. Do any operation with parentheses first, then any involving exponents. Multiplication and division come next, followed by addition and subtraction—from left to right in both cases. Just remember the sentence: "**P**lease **E**xcuse **M**y **D**ear **A**unt **S**ally".
P = parentheses, E = exponents, M = multiplication, D = division, A = addition, S = subtraction

QUICK THINKING, OR JUST A GOOD GAUSS?

One of the most famous mathematicians in history was Carl Friedrich Gauss. There's a story that when Gauss was just starting school, his teacher wanted to keep the students busy so he gave them what he thought was a hard—or at least time-consuming—problem: add up all the whole numbers from 1 to 100 (that is, find the sum of $1 + 2 + 3 + 4 + 5$ and so on up to 100). Gauss finished in just a few seconds. How did he work so fast? He thought of a trick to make the problem easy. He realized that you could group the numbers in 50 pairs: 1 and 100, 2 and 99, 3 and 98, 4 and 97, and so on. Each pair added up to 101, and since there are 50 pairs, the answer must be 50 x 101, or 5050.

OPERATION: GIANT SQUID

Wind your way through this large mollusk and discover the length of the largest specimen ever found. Add, subtract, multiply, or divide the numbers as you go. When you get to the end, you'll know how many feet long this creature of the deep measured.

ANSWERS ON PAGES 314-317. FOR MORE PUZZLES GO TO WWW.WORLDALMANACFORKIDS.COM

Population

Which state ranks 25th in population?
page 179

WHERE DO PEOPLE LIVE?

In 1959 there were five billion people in the world. In 1999 the number hit six billion. According to the latest estimates by the UN, the world population is expected to grow to almost nine billion by 2050. This is a lot, but not as much as the UN predicted before. The UN expects that fewer people will be born and the AIDS epidemic in many countries will be worse than was once thought.

LARGEST CITIES IN THE WORLD

Here are the ten cities that had the most people, as of 2001. Numbers include people from the built-up area around each city (metropolitan area), not just the city. (See page 179 for big U.S. cities by themselves.)

CITY, COUNTRY	POPULATION
Tokyo, Japan	26,444,000
Mexico City, Mexico	18,066,000
São Paulo, Brazil	17,962,000
New York City, U.S.	16,732,000
Mumbai (Bombay), India	16,086,000
Los Angeles, U.S.	13,213,000
Kolkata (Calcutta), India	13,058,000
Shanghai, China	12,887,000
Dhaka, Bangladesh	12,519,000
Delhi, India	12,441,000

LARGEST COUNTRIES
(Most People, 2003)

COUNTRY	POPULATION
China	1,304,196,000*
India	1,065,462,000
United States	294,043,000
Indonesia	219,883,000
Brazil	178,470,000
Pakistan	153,578,000
Bangladesh	146,736,000
Russia	143,246,000
Japan	127,654,000
Nigeria	124,009,000
Mexico	103,457,000
Germany	82,476,000
Vietnam	81,377,000
Philippines	79,999,000
Egypt	71,931,000
Turkey	71,325,000
Ethiopia	70,678,000
Iran	68,920,000
Thailand	62,833,000
France	60,144,000
United Kingdom	59,251,000
Italy	57,423,000
Dem. Rep. of the Congo	52,771,000
Ukraine	48,523,000
South Korea	47,700,000

*This list comes from the United Nations, which includes Taiwan in its figure for China.

SMALLEST COUNTRIES
(Fewest People, 2003)

COUNTRY	POPULATION
Vatican City	900
Tuvalu	11,305
Nauru	12,570
Palau	19,717
San Marino	28,119
Monaco	32,130
Liechtenstein	33,145

POPULATION OF THE UNITED STATES 2002

Estimated U.S. Population on July 1, 2002: 288,368,698.

Rank & State Name	Population	Rank & State Name	Population
1 California	35,116,033	27 Oregon	3,521,515
2 Texas	21,779,893	28 Oklahoma	3,493,714
3 New York	19,157,532	29 Connecticut	3,460,503
4 Florida	16,713,149	30 Iowa	2,936,760
5 Illinois	12,600,620	31 Mississippi	2,871,782
6 Pennsylvania	12,335,091	32 Kansas	2,715,884
7 Ohio	11,421,267	33 Arkansas	2,710,079
8 Michigan	10,050,446	34 Utah	2,316,256
9 New Jersey	8,590,300	35 Nevada	2,173,491
10 Georgia	8,560,310	36 New Mexico	1,855,059
11 North Carolina	8,320,146	37 West Virginia	1,801,873
12 Virginia	7,293,542	38 Nebraska	1,729,180
13 Massachusetts	6,427,801	39 Idaho	1,341,131
14 Indiana	6,159,068	40 Maine	1,294,464
15 Washington	6,068,996	41 New Hampshire	1,275,056
16 Tennessee	5,797,289	42 Hawaii	1,244,898
17 Missouri	5,672,579	43 Rhode Island	1,069,725
18 Maryland	5,458,137	44 Montana	909,453
19 Arizona	5,456,453	45 Delaware	807,385
20 Wisconsin	5,441,196	46 South Dakota	761,063
21 Minnesota	5,019,720	47 Alaska	643,786
22 Colorado	4,506,542	48 North Dakota	634,110
23 Alabama	4,486,508	49 Vermont	616,592
24 Louisiana	4,482,646	50 District of Columbia	570,898
25 South Carolina	4,107,183	51 Wyoming	498,703
26 Kentucky	4,092,891		

▼ New York City, the largest city in the U.S.

LARGEST CITIES IN THE UNITED STATES

Cities grow and shrink in population. At right is a list of the largest cities in the United States in 2000 compared with their populations in 1950. Which seven cities increased in population? Which three decreased?

RANK & CITY	2000	1950
1 New York, NY	8,008,278	7,891,957
2 Los Angeles, CA	3,694,820	1,970,358
3 Chicago, IL	2,896,016	3,620,962
4 Houston, TX	1,953,631	596,163
5 Philadelphia, PA	1,517,550	2,071,605
6 Phoenix, AZ	1,321,045	106,818
7 San Diego, CA	1,223,400	334,387
8 Dallas, TX	1,188,580	434,462
9 San Antonio, TX	1,144,646	408,442
10 Detroit, MI	951,270	1,849,568

COUNTING PEOPLE

Every 10 years the Census Bureau takes a census to try and count the people in the United States and learn some basic things about the population.

As of April 1, 2000, the total U.S. population was 281,421,906, according to the Census Bureau's numbers. Were you counted? Census takers tried to visit and count people who did not send back their forms. They think they did a good job.

Why is the census needed?

▶ The census provides a picture of the people that helps researchers as well as businesses plan their sales. Where do people live? How old are they? How many kids do they have? Do they own their home? Were they born in the U.S.? What is their background?

▶ The population of a state determines how many representatives it has in the U.S. House.

▶ Census information helps the federal government in Washington, D.C., decide which public services must be provided and where.

CENSUS FACTS

From Census 2000	From the Census for 1900
There were 281 million people.	There were 76 million people.
There were 96 males for every 100 females.	There were 104 males for every 100 females.
About half the people were under 35.	About half the people were under 22.
One out of five were under 15.	One out of three were under 15.
About 12 percent were 65 or older,	About 4 percent were 65 or older.
Half the households had three people or less.	Half the households had six people or more.
Two-thirds of the homes were owner-occupied.	More than half of the homes were rented.
Four out of five people lived in or near cities.	Seven out of 10 people lived in rural areas.

Who Are We?

Census 2000 was the first time a census allowed Americans to identify themselves as being of more than one race. Almost seven million people made that choice. That is about 2 percent of the total population of the United States. This list shows the percentage of Americans that felt they belonged in each of the racial groups listed here.

▶ Hispanics are the fastest-growing minority in the U.S., up almost 58% since 1990.

▶ In 2000, 1 out of 4 Americans was non-white; in 1900, only 1 out of 8 was non-white.

RACE	PERCENT OF POPULATION
One race	97.6%
White	75.1%
Black or African American	12.3%
American Indian and Alaska Native	0.9%
Asian	3.6%
Native Hawaiian and Other Pacific Islander	0.1%
Some other race	5.5%
Two or more races	2.4%
Hispanic or Latino	12.5%
Not Hispanic or Latino	87.5%
(Hispanics may be of any race.)	

DID YOU KNOW? *The town of Edgar Springs, Missouri (pop. 190), now has the honor of being the population center of the U.S. That's the spot where a model of the country would balance if each American weighed the same. Since 1790, this spot has moved to the west and then to the south, as people spread out across the country.*

MEXICO

The Many Faces of America:
IMMIGRATION

▼ Immigrants entering the U.S. at Ellis Island, early 1900s

The number of people in the U.S. who were born in another country (foreign-born) reached 32.5 million in 2002, or 11.5 percent of the population. This percent has been rising since 1970, when it was down to 4.7 percent, and is the highest since 1930. In the early 1900s, most immigrants came from Europe; in 2002 52% of the foreign-born population were from Latin America, and 26% were born in Asia.

Immigrants come for various reasons, such as to live in freedom, to escape poverty or oppression, and to make better lives for themselves and their children. But some people were brought here by force. In the 1600s, the British began shipping Africans to the American colonies to work as slaves. One out of every three people living in the southern colonies in the 1700s was a slave.

What Countries Do Immigrants Come From?

Below are some of the countries immigrants came from in 2001. Immigration from all countries to the U.S. totaled 1,064,318 in 2001.

	Number	Percent of total
Mexico	206,426	19.4
India	70,290	6.6
China	56,426	5.3
Philippines	53,154	5.0
Vietnam	35,531	3.3
El Salvador	31,272	2.9
Cuba	27,703	2.6
Haiti	27,120	2.5
Bosnia-Herzegovina	23,640	2.2
Canada	21,933	2.1
Dominican Republic	21,313	2.0
Ukraine	20,975	2.0
Korea	20,742	1.9
Russia	20,413	1.9
Nicaragua	19,896	1.9

Where Do Immigrants Settle?

In 2002, about 70% of the immigrants from Mexico went to live in California and Texas. About one-third of the immigrants from India went to California and New Jersey. Florida received almost 80% of the immigrants from Cuba, 63% of immigrants from Haiti, and about half of those from Nicaragua. Half of the immigrants from the Dominican Republic chose New York.

California
282,957

New York
114,116

Florida
104,715

Texas
86,315

This bar chart shows the states that received the highest number of immigrants in 2001.

New Jersey
59,920

Illinois
48,296

Charlotte
ton

Halifax

NTIC

EAN

New Orleans

San Antonio

Houston

Tampa

West Palm Beach

A CITIZENSHIP TEST

When immigrants wanting to be U.S. citizens are interviewed, they may be asked any of 100 questions. Here are some of them. How many can you answer correctly?

1. Why did the Pilgrims come to America?
2. What was the name of their ship?
3. What country did we fight in the Revolutionary War?
4. Who was president during the Civil War?
5. What are the two major political parties in the U.S. today?
6. In what month do we vote for the president?
7. In what month is the new president inaugurated?
8. How many senators are there in Congress?
9. For how long do we elect each senator?
10. Who said, "Give me liberty or give me death"?

Answers are on pages 314-317.

The Statue of Liberty

When most immigrants arrived in New York by ship they were greeted by the Statue of Liberty in the Harbor. "Lady With the Lamp" was given to the U.S. by France and has served as a welcome to Americans-to-be since 1886. In 1903, a poem by Emma Lazarus, "The New Colossus," was inscribed at the base of the statue. It reads in part:

"Give me your tired, your poor, Your huddled masses yearning to breathe free..."

COUNTING THE FIRST AMERICANS

American Indians, or Native Americans, lived in North and South America long before the first Europeans. Their ancestors are thought to have arrived more than 20,000 years ago, probably from Northeast Asia.

How many American Indians were here in the 1400s? It is estimated that at least 850,000, perhaps many more, lived then in what is now the United States. But no one really knows.

How many American Indians are in the U.S. now? During the 17th, 18th, and 19th centuries, disease and wars with white settlers and soldiers killed huge numbers of Indians. By 1910 there were only about 220,000 left in the United States. Since then, the American Indian population has increased dramatically. According to Census 2000, the total number of Native Americans was about 2.5 million (not including those who listed themselves as of more than one race).

In 1924, the U.S. Congress approved a law giving citizenship to all Native Americans.

Ten Largest Native American Tribes in the U.S.

These figures do not include those affiliated with more than one tribe or listing more than one race.

Cherokee	281,069	Choctaw	87,349
Navajo	269,202	Pueblo	59,533
Sioux	108,272	Apache	57,060
Chippewa	105,907	Lumbee	51,913
Latin American Indian	104,354	Eskimo	45,919

Prizes & Contests

NOBEL PRIZES

Where is the All-American Soap Box Derby held?
page 187

The Nobel Prizes are named after Alfred B. Nobel (1833-1896), a Swedish scientist who invented dynamite, and left money to be given every year to people who have helped humankind. The Nobel Peace Prize goes to people who the judges think did the most during the past year to help achieve peace. Prizes are also given for physics, chemistry, medicine-physiology, literature, and economics. The 2002 Peace Prize went to former U.S. President Jimmy Carter for his efforts to "find peaceful solutions to international conflicts, to advance democracy and human rights, and to promote economic and social development."

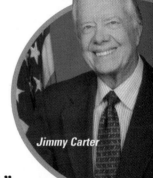

Jimmy Carter

PAST WINNERS OF THE NOBEL PEACE PRIZE INCLUDE:

◄ **2001** United Nations (UN); Kofi Annan, UN secretary-general

2000 Kim Dae Jung, South Korean president

1999 Médecins Sans Frontières (Doctors Without Borders), an organization that gives medical help to disaster and war victims

1994 Yasir Arafat, Palestinian leader; Shimon Peres, foreign minister of Israel; Yitzhak Rabin, prime minister of Israel

1993 Nelson Mandela, leader of South African blacks; Frederik Willem de Klerk, president of South Africa

1986 Elie Wiesel, Holocaust survivor and author

1983 Lech Walesa, leader of the Polish trade union Solidarity

1979 Mother Teresa, founder, in India, of a religious order that cares for the sick and dying

1976 Betsy Williams and Mairead Corrigan, co-founders of a movement for peace in Northern Ireland

1973 Henry Kissinger, U.S. secretary of state; Le Duc Tho, North Vietnamese foreign minister (declined the prize)

1964 Martin Luther King Jr., civil rights leader

1952 Albert Schweitzer, missionary, surgeon

1919 Woodrow Wilson, U.S. president and founder of the League of Nations

1906 Theodore Roosevelt, U.S. president and peace negotiator

1905 Baroness Bertha von Suttner, an early advocate of peace through international cooperation

Other winners of Nobel Prizes have included:

Toni Morrison, 1993 Nobel Prize in Literature Born in Lorain, Ohio, in 1931, Toni Morrison is known for writing both fiction and nonfiction on African-American themes. Her books include *Beloved, The Song of Solomon,* and *Tar Baby.*

Francis Crick, James Watson, and Maurice Wilkins, 1962 Nobel Prize in Medicine These scientists (Watson is American, the others British) won the prize for discovering the double helix structure of DNA. They made the discovery in 1953. James Watson loved to read *The World Almanac* when he was young.

Wilhelm Conrad Roentgen, 1901 Nobel Prize in Physics Born in Germany in 1845, Roentgen became world famous for his 1895 discovery of X rays, which are sometimes called "Roentgen rays."

Toni Morrison

THE MEDAL OF HONOR

The Medal of Honor is given by the U.S. government for bravery in war against an enemy. The first medals were awarded in 1863. Since that time, more than 3,400 people have received the award.

PULITZER PRIZES

The Pulitzer Prizes are named after Joseph Pulitzer (1847–1911), a journalist and newspaper publisher, who gave the money to set them up. They are given for excellence in journalism, drama, literature, and music.

SPINGARN MEDAL

The Spingarn Medal was set up in 1914 by Joel Elias Spingarn, leader of the National Association for the Advancement of Colored People (NAACP). It is awarded every year by the NAACP for achievement by an African-American. Here are some winners:

2002: U.S. Representative John Lewis

2000: TV personality Oprah Winfrey

1994: Writer and poet Maya Angelou

1991: General Colin Powell

1985: Actor Bill Cosby

1979: Civil rights activist Rosa Parks

1975: Baseball player Hank Aaron

1957: Civil rights leader Martin Luther King Jr.

1946: Justice Thurgood Marshall

1923: Agricultural researcher George Washington Carver

I was born in 1928 in St. Louis, Missouri, and I was raised in the Arkansas countryside. I wrote a famous book about my life, called *I Know Why the Caged Bird Sings.* I am one of the first African-American women to write a best-seller. I am also a poet, historian, actress, playwright, producer, director, civil rights activist, and winner of a Spingarn Medal. I wrote a poem for President Clinton's inauguration in 1993, and read it at the ceremony.

Answer: Maya Angelou

ENTERTAINMENT AWARDS

The Oscar ceremonies are watched on TV by hundreds of millions of people around the world. Among other entertainment awards given every year are the Grammys and the MTV Video Music Awards.

ACADEMY AWARDS

The Oscars are awarded every year by the Academy of Motion Picture Arts and Sciences for the best in movies. Here are some of the films and people that won Oscars for 2002:

Best Picture: *Chicago*

Best Actor: Adrien Brody, *The Pianist*

Best Actress: Nicole Kidman, *The Hours*

Best Supporting Actor: Chris Cooper, *Adaptation*

Best Supporting Actress: Catherine Zeta-Jones, *Chicago*

Best Director: Roman Polanski, *The Pianist*

Best Original Screenplay: *Spirited Away*

MTV VIDEO MUSIC AWARDS

The MTV Video Music Awards are presented each year in a variety of music video categories. Here are some winners for 2002:

Best Video of the Year: Eminem, "Without Me"

Best New Artist: Avril Lavigne, "Complicated"

Best Male Video: Eminem, "Without Me"

Best Female Video: Pink, "Get the Party Started"

Best Group Video: No Doubt, featuring Bounty Killer, "Hey Baby"

Best Pop Video: No Doubt, featuring Bounty Killer, "Hey Baby"

Best Rock Video: Linkin Park, "In the End"

Best Hip Hop Video: Jennifer Lopez, featuring Ja Rule, "I'm Real (Remix)"

GRAMMY AWARDS

Grammys are given out each year by the National Academy of Recording Arts and Sciences. Some of the winners for 2002 were:

Record of the Year (single): "Don't Know Why," Norah Jones

Album of the Year: *Come Away With Me,* Norah Jones

Song of the Year: "Don't Know Why," written by Jesse Harris

New Artist: Norah Jones

Pop Vocal Album: *Come Away With Me,* Norah Jones

Pop Female Performance: "Don't Know Why," Norah Jones

Pop Male Performance: "Your Body Is a Wonderland," John Mayer

Pop Duo or Group: "Hey Baby," No Doubt

Traditional R&B Album: *Voyage to India,* India.Arie

▲ *Norah Jones*

Contemporary R&B Album: *Ashanti,* Ashanti

Rock Album: *The Rising,* Bruce Springsteen

Rock Song: "The Rising," written by Bruce Springsteen

Rap Album: *The Eminem Show,* Eminem

Female Rap Soloist: "Scream a.k.a. Itchin'," Missy Elliott

Male Rap Soloist: "Hot in Herre," Nelly

Country Album: *Home,* Dixie Chicks

Country Song: "Where Were You (When The World Stopped Turning)," written by Alan Jackson

Spoken Word Album for Children: *There Was an Old Lady Who Swallowed a Fly,* Tom Chapin

Musical Album for Children: *Monsters, Inc.— Scream Factory Favorites,* Riders in the Sky

Film or TV Song: "If I Didn't Have You," written by Randy Newman

185

Bee a Winner

If you have a knack for spelling or an interest in world geography, then these two national contests may be for you.

NATIONAL SPELLING BEE

The National Spelling Bee was started in Louisville, Kentucky, by the *Courier-Journal* in 1925. Newspapers across the U.S. run local spelling bees for kids ages 15 and under. Winners may qualify to compete in the Scripps Howard National Spelling Bee held every year in Washington, D.C., in late May or early June. If you're interested, ask your school principal to contact your local newspaper.

Competing against 249 other contestants, 13-year-old Pratyush Buddiga got through 11 rounds, including a new 25-word written test added for *round 2* in 2002. His winning word was *prospicience* (meaning "foresight"). A student at Mountain Ridge Middle School in Colorado Springs, Colorado, Pratyush brought home an engraved trophy and $12,000 in cash. His family, friends, and teachers were very proud of him!

Here are some of the words Pratyush spelled on his way to the top. Some of them are just a little bit difficult!

ROUND	SPELLING WORD	ROUND	SPELLING WORD
1	tergiversation	7	oubliette
2	(written round)	8	troching
3	deuterogamy	9	repoussage
4	grobian	10	paraclete
5	thremmatology	11	prospicience
6	amole		

WEB SITE http://www.spellingbee.com

NATIONAL GEOGRAPHIC BEE

Each year thousands of schools in the U.S. participate in the National Geographic Bee using materials prepared by the National Geographic Society. Since it started in 1989, millions of students have competed in this contest for a $25,000 college scholarship and the honor of being a national champion.

In 2002 the winner was 10-year-old Calvin McCarter from Jennison, Michigan. Calvin was a fifth grader and home-schooled. Besides geography, he enjoys playing the piano, collecting stamps, and playing soccer and baseball. Second place went to 14-year-old Matthew Russell from Bradford, Pennsylvania. In third place was 14-year-old Erik Miller from Kent, Washington.

WINNING QUESTION: *Lop Nur, a marshy depression at the east end of the Tarim Basin, is a nuclear test site for which country?*

ANSWER: *China*

If you want to enter this contest, you must be in grades 4 through 8. School-level bees are followed by state-level bees and then the national competition. For more information, ask your school principal to write to: National Geographic Bee; National Geographic Society; 1145 17th Street NW; Washington, D.C. 20036-4688. The registration deadline each year is October 15.

WEB SITE http://www.nationalgeographic.com

READY, SET, GO...

ALL-AMERICAN SOAP BOX DERBY

Every summer, kids from all over the U.S. and as far away as Germany, Japan, and the Philippines head to Akron, Ohio, for the All-American Soap Box Derby. These gravity-powered coasters have been raced there since 1934. The kids build (with help from adults) and race their own cars in local events to earn their way to the "Derby Downs" track in Akron. The three divisions are Stock (for first-time builders ages 9-16), Super Stock (for experienced builders ages 9-16), and Masters (for advanced builders ages 11-16). The nationals are a week-long event, with lots of festivities leading up to the finals.

In 2002, gold winners' jackets went to Megan Thomas, age 10 (Stock); Josh Esque, age 13 (Super Stock); and Samantha Underwood, age 14 (Masters); all of Akron, Ohio. Winners also receive college scholarships, trophies, and other prizes.

To find out how to get started, contact the All-American Soap Box Derby in Akron (http://aasbd.org) or the Regional Director of your state. After registering with your local Derby program, the next step is to look at the list of racing products to design and build your own racer. Then it's a real race to the finish line!

Akron is also home to the National Super Kids Classic, a soap box derby held for kids with disabilities. This race is usually held in August.

WEB SITE http://www.nationalsuperkids.com

WORLD CHAMPIONSHIP
SHOVEL RACES

The snow may be cold, but the speeds are hot at this unusual race. Every year at Angelfire Resort in New Mexico, racers fly down a 1,000-foot course sitting on scoop shovels—and reach speeds of 60 miles per hour! In the modified speed class, the racers look more like jets or dragsters, and can go nearly 80 mph!

Anthony Anaya

How did this strange competition get started? Nearly 30 years ago, ski lift operators started racing each other down the mountain once the lifts had closed. Their game snowballed into one of the most bizarre—even Xtreme—winter sports. The racers compete for the fastest shovel, the fastest modified shovel, and the wackiest shovel. In the modified shovel classes, high-tech or wacky sleds with runners can be built—but there must be a shovel touching the snow. Wacky entries have included a furnished living room, a big Bart Simpson, and even a giant chicken sandwich!

Standard shovel winners at the 2003 Championships, held February 1-2, included Erin Gaffney, age 7, 31 mph (Little Scoops); James Adkins, age 13, 58 mph (Youth); and Gail Boles, age 40, 63 mph (Adult). The modified shovel winner was Anthony Anaya, age 44, at 73 mph.

187

Religion

What does "Islam" mean? page 189

How did the universe begin? Why are we here on Earth? What happens to us after we die? For most people, religion is a way of answering questions like these. Believing in a God or gods, or in a higher power, is one way of making sense of the world around us. Religions can also help guide people's lives. About six billion people all over the world are religious believers.

Different religions have different beliefs. For example, Christians, Jews, and Muslims all believe in one God, while Hindus believe in many gods. On this page and the next are some facts about the world's major religions.

BUDDHISM

WHO STARTED BUDDHISM? Gautama Siddhartha (the Buddha), around 525 B.C.

WHAT WRITINGS ARE THERE? The three main collections of Buddhist writings are called the **Tripitaka**, or "Three Baskets." Many of these writings are called **sutras** or "teachings."

WHAT DO BUDDHISTS BELIEVE? Buddha taught that life is filled with suffering. In order to be free of that suffering, believers have to give up worldly possessions and worldly goals and try to achieve a state of perfect peace known as *nirvana*.

HOW MANY ARE THERE? In 2002, there were more than 360 million Buddhists in the world, 98% of them in Asia.

WHAT KINDS ARE THERE? There are two main kinds of Buddhists. **Theravada** ("Path of the Elders") **Buddhism**, the older kind, is more common in the southern part of Asia. **Mahayana** ("Great Vessel") **Buddhism** is more common in northern Asia.

CHRISTIANITY

WHO STARTED CHRISTIANITY? Jesus Christ, in the first century. He was born in Bethlehem between 8 B.C. and 4 B.C. and died about A.D. 29.

WHAT WRITINGS ARE THERE? The **Bible**, including the Old Testament and New Testament, is the main religious writing of Christianity.

WHAT DO CHRISTIANS BELIEVE? That there is one God. That Jesus Christ is the Son of God, who came on Earth, died to save humankind, and rose from the dead.

HOW MANY ARE THERE? Christianity is the world's biggest religion. In 2002, there were more than two billion Christians, in nearly all parts of the world. More than one billion of the Christians were **Roman Catholics**, who follow the leadership of the pope in Rome. Other groups of Christians include **Orthodox Christians**, who accept most of the same teachings as Roman Catholics but follow different leadership, and **Protestants**, who often disagree with Catholic teachings. Protestants rely especially on the Bible itself. They belong to many different group or "denominations."

HINDUISM

WHO STARTED HINDUISM? Aryan beliefs spread into India, around 1500 B.C. These beliefs were mixed with the beliefs of the people who already lived there.

WHAT WRITINGS ARE THERE? The **Vedas** are the most important writings in Hinduism. They include ancient hymns and rules for religious ceremonies. Other writings include the teachings of the **Upanishads** and a long poem about war, the **Bhagavad Gita**.

WHAT DO HINDUS BELIEVE? Hindus believe there are many gods and many ways of worshipping and that people die and are reborn many times as other living things. They also believe there is a universal soul, known as *Brahman*. The goal of life is to escape the cycle of birth and death and become part of the *Brahman*. This is done by leading a good life.

HOW MANY ARE THERE? In 2002, there were about 830 million Hindus, mainly in India and places where people from India have gone to live.

WHAT KINDS ARE THERE? There are many kinds of Hindus, who worship different gods or goddesses.

ISLAM

WHO STARTED ISLAM? Muhammad, the Prophet, in A.D. **610**.

WHAT WRITINGS ARE THERE? The **Koran** (al-Qur'an in Arabic) sets out the main beliefs and practices of Islam, the religion of Muslims.

WHAT DO MUSLIMS BELIEVE? People who believe in Islam are known as Muslims. The word "Islam" means submission to God. Muslims believe that there is no other god than the one God; that Muhammad is the prophet and lawgiver of his community; that they should pray five times a day, fast during the month of Ramadan, give to the poor, and once during their life make a pilgrimage to Mecca in Saudi Arabia if they can afford it.

HOW MANY ARE THERE? In 2002, there were more than one billion Muslims, mostly in parts of Africa and Asia. The two main branches are: **Sunni Muslims**, who make up over 80% of all Muslims today, and **Shiite Muslims**, who broke away in a dispute over leadership after Muhammad died in 632.

JUDAISM

WHO STARTED JUDAISM? Abraham is considered to be the founder of Judaism. He lived around 1300 B.C.

WHAT WRITINGS ARE THERE? The most important is the **Torah**, the first five books of the Old Testament of the Bible.

WHAT DO JEWS BELIEVE? Jews believe that there is one God who created the universe and rules over it, and that they should be faithful to God and carry out God's commandments.

HOW MANY ARE THERE? In 2002, there were about 14.5 million Jews living around the world. Many live in Israel and the United States.

WHAT KINDS ARE THERE? In the United States and Europe there are three main forms: **Orthodox**, **Conservative**, and **Reform**. Orthodox Jews are the most traditional. They follow strict laws about how they dress, what they can eat, and how they conduct their lives. Conservative Jews follow many of the traditions. Reform Jews are the least traditional.

MAJOR HOLY DAYS FOR
CHRISTIANS, JEWS, AND MUSLIMS

CHRISTIAN HOLY DAYS

	2003	2004	2005
Ash Wednesday	March 5	February 25	February 9
Good Friday	April 18	April 9	March 25
Easter Sunday	April 20	April 11	March 27
Easter for Orthodox Churches	April 27	April 11	May 1
Christmas	December 25	December 25	December 25

JEWISH HOLY DAYS

The Jewish holy days begin at sundown the night before the first full day of the observance. The date of these evenings are listed below.

	2003-4 (5763)	2004-5 (5764)	2005-6 (5765)
Rosh Hashanah (New Year)	September 26	September 15	October 3
Yom Kippur (Day of Atonement)	October 5	September 24	October 12
Hanukkah (Festival of Lights)	December 19	December 7	December 2
Passover	April 5	April 23	April 12

ISLAMIC (MUSLIM) HOLY DAYS

	2003-4 (1424)	2004-5 (1425)	2005-6 (1426)
Muharram 1 (New Year)	March 4	February 21	February 10
Mawlid (Birthday of Muhammad)	May 13	May 1	April 21
Ramadan 1	October 26	October 15	October 4
Eid al-Adha (Dhûl-Hijjah 10)	February 1	January 20	January 10

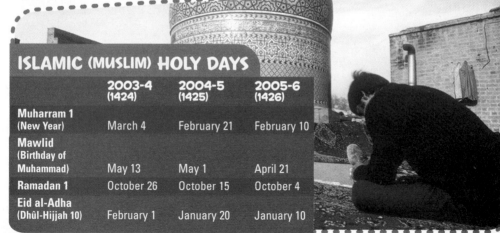

MAJOR HOLY DAYS FOR
BUDDHISTS AND HINDUS

BUDDHIST HOLY DAYS Not all Buddhists use the same calendar to determine holidays and festivals. Here are some well-known Buddhist observances and the months in which they may fall:

Nirvana Day, mid-February: marks the death of Siddhartha Gautama (the Buddha).

Vesak or Visakah Puja (Buddha Day), April/May: the most important holiday. Celebrates the birth, enlightenment, and death of the Buddha.

Asalha Puja (Dharma Day), July: commemorates the Buddha's first teaching, in which he revealed the Four Noble Truths.

Magha Puja or Sangha Day, February: commemorates the day when 1,250 of Buddha's disciples *(sangha)* visited him without being called.

Vassa (Rains Retreat), July-October: a 3-month period during Asia's rainy season, when monks stay inside and study. Other people try to live simply and give up bad habits. Sometimes called "Buddhist Lent."

The Dalai Lama

HINDU HOLY DAYS Different Hindu groups use different calendars. Here are a few of the many Hindu festivals and the months in which they may fall:

Maha Shivaratri, February/March: festival dedicated to Shiva, creator and destroyer.

Holi, March/April: festival of spring.

Ramanavami, March/April: anniversary of the birth of Rama, who is Vishnu in human form.

Diwali, October/November: Hindu New Year, the "Festival of Lights."

RELIGIOUS MEMBERSHIP IN THE UNITED STATES

The two largest religious groups in the U.S. are Protestants followed by Roman Catholics. The pie chart below shows how many people belong to these and other main religious groups. These numbers are recent estimates; no one knows exactly how many people belong to each group.

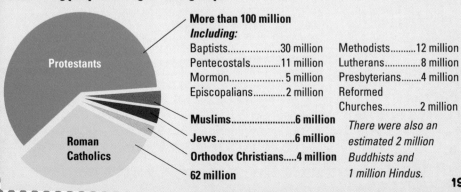

Protestants

Roman Catholics

More than 100 million
Including:

Baptists	30 million	Methodists	12 million
Pentecostals	11 million	Lutherans	8 million
Mormon	5 million	Presbyterians	4 million
Episcopalians	2 million	Reformed Churches	2 million

Muslims ...... 6 million

Jews ...... 6 million

Orthodox Christians ..... 4 million

62 million

There were also an estimated 2 million Buddhists and 1 million Hindus.

191

| 12 |
| Mg |
| 24.305 |

Atomic Weight ■ Noble Gases

25	26	27	28	29	30	31	32	33	Se
Mn	Fe	Co	Ni	Cu	Zn	Ga	Ge	As	
54.938	55.847	58.933	58.69	63.546	65.39	69.72	72.61	74.922	

| Cr |
| 51.996 |

V

43	44
Tc	Ru
(98)	101.07

Pd Ag Cd
107.87 112.4

In

Ca Sc
40.08 44.9

Rb Sr
5.47

Science

WHAT EVERYTHING IS MADE OF

Everything we see and use is made up of basic ingredients called elements. There are more than 100 elements. Most have been found in nature. Some are created by scientists in labs.

What is a "thunderegg"?
page 194

Elements Found in Earth's Crust
(percent by weight)

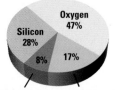

Oxygen 47%
Silicon 28%
17%
8%
Aluminum
Iron, Calcium, Sodium, Potassium, Others

Elements Found in the Atmosphere
(percent by volume)

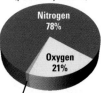

Nitrogen 78%
Oxygen 21%
1% Argon, Carbon Dioxide, Others

Homework Help

IT ALL STARTS WITH AN ATOM

The smallest possible piece of an element that has all the properties of the original element is called an **atom**. Each tiny atom is made up of even smaller particles called **protons, neutrons,** and **electrons**. These are made up of even smaller particles called **quarks**.

To tell one element from another, scientists count the number of protons in an atom. The total number of protons is called the element's **atomic number**. All of the atoms of an element have the same number of protons and

electrons, but some atoms have a different number of neutrons. For example, carbon-12 has six protons and six neutrons, and carbon-13 has six protons and seven neutrons.

We call the amount of matter in an atom its **atomic mass.** Carbon-13 has a greater atomic mass than carbon-12. The average atomic mass of all of the different atoms of the same element is called the element's **atomic weight**. Every element has a different atomic number and a different atomic weight.

CHEMICAL SYMBOLS ARE SCIENTIFIC SHORTHAND

When scientists write the names of elements, they often use a symbol instead of spelling out the full name. The symbol for each element is one or two letters. Scientists write O for oxygen and He for helium. The symbols usually come from the English name for the element (C for carbon). The symbols for some of the elements come from the element's Latin name. For example, the symbol for gold is Au, which is short for *Aurum*, the Latin word for gold.

How Elements are Named
How many of these elements have you heard of?

NAME	SYMBOL	WHAT IT IS	WHEN FOUND	NAMED FOR
Aluminum	Al	metal	1825	*alumen*, Latin word for "alum"
Americium	Am	radioactive metal	1944	America
Einsteinium	Es	radioactive metal	1952	Albert Einstein
Helium	He	gas	1868	the Greek workd *helios*, meaning sun
Iodine	I	nonmetallic solid	1811	the Greek word *iodes*, meaning violet
Iridium	Ir	transitional metal	1804	the Latin word *iridis*, meaning rainbow
Mercury	Hg	transitional metal	B.C.	the Roman god Mercury
Neon	Ne	gas	1898	the Greek word *neon*, meaning new
Strontium	Sr	alkaline earth metal	1808	Strontian, town in Scotland
Uranium	U	radioactive metal	1789	the planet Uranus

Elements are named after places, scientists, figures in mythology, or properties of the element. But no element gets a name until the International Union of Pure and Applied Chemistry (IUPAC) accepts it. In all, 109 elements have been named. Several others have been reported, but not named and not yet confirmed.

All About... COMPOUNDS

Carbon, hydrogen, nitrogen, and oxygen are the most common chemical elements in the human body. Many other elements may be found in small amounts. These include calcium, iron, phosphorous, potassium, and sodium.

When elements join together, they form compounds. Water is a compound made up of hydrogen and oxygen. Salt is a compound made up of sodium and chlorine.

Common Name	Contains the Compound	Contains the Elements
Aspirin	acetylsalicylic acid	carbon, oxygen, hydrogen
Baking soda	sodium bicarbonate	sodium, hydrogen, carbon, oxygen
Bleach (liquid)	sodium hypochlorite	sodium, chlorine, oxygen
Chalk	calcium carbonate	calcium, carbon, oxygen
Rust	iron oxide	iron, oxygen
Sugar	sucrose	carbon, hydrogen, oxygen
Vinegar	acetic acid	carbon, hydrogen, oxygen

MINERALS, ROCKS, and GEMS

WHAT ARE MINERALS?

Minerals are solid materials that were never alive. All the land on our planet—even the ocean floor—rests on a layer of rock made up of minerals. Minerals have also been found on other planets, on our moon, and in meteorites that landed on Earth. Some minerals, such as gold and silver, are made up entirely of one element. But most are formed from two or more elements joined together.

The most common mineral is **quartz**, which is made of silicon and oxygen and is found all over the world. **Sand** is made up mostly of quartz. **Graphite**, which is used in pencils, is another common mineral. Other minerals, like **diamonds**, are very rare and valuable. Diamonds and graphite are different forms of the same element—carbon!

WHAT ARE ROCKS?

Rocks are combinations of minerals. There are three kinds:

1 IGNEOUS ROCKS—rocks that form from melted minerals deep in the Earth that cool and become solid. Granite is an igneous rock made from quartz, feldspar, and mica.

2 SEDIMENTARY ROCKS—rocks that usually form in the beds of seas, lakes, and rivers from tiny pieces of other rocks, sand, and shells packed together. It takes millions of years to form sedimentary rocks. Limestone, sandstone, and shale are kinds of sedimentary rock.

3 METAMORPHIC ROCK—Over millions of years, the heat and pressure inside Earth can change the minerals in rocks. This changed rock is called a metamorphic rock. Marble is a metamorphic rock formed from limestone.

WHAT ARE GEMS?

Most **gems** are minerals that have been cut and polished to be used as jewelry or other kinds of decoration. Some gems are not minerals. A pearl is not a mineral; it comes from an oyster, which is a living thing. The most valued gems are minerals called **precious stones,** such as those listed here.

GEM NAME	MINERAL	ELEMENT IT IS MADE OF	USUAL COLORS
Diamond	carbon	carbon	bluish white
Emerald	beryl	beryllium, silicon, aluminum, oxygen	green
Ruby	corundum	aluminum, oxygen	red
Sapphire	corundum	aluminum, oxygen	blue

Did You KNOW?

THUNDEREGGS Geodes, or thundereggs, are dull, rounded hollow rock formations, partly (or completely) filled with layers of colored quartz crystals. This rock, which is the state stone of Oregon, takes its nickname from the Native American belief that "thunder spirits" threw them down from the mountains. The world's biggest geode was discovered in Spain in 2000. It is 26 feet long and 5.6 feet high!

Thunderegg

WHAT IS DNA?

Every cell in every living thing (or organism) has **DNA**, a molecule that holds all the information about that organism. Lengths of connected DNA molecules, called **genes**, are like tiny pieces of a secret code. They determine what each organism is like in great detail. Almost all the DNA and genes come packaged in rod-like structures called **chromosomes**—humans have 46. There are 22 almost identical pairs, plus the X and Y chromosomes, which determine if a human is male (one X chromosome and one Y chromosome) or female (two X chromosomes).

Genes are passed on from parents to children, and no two organisms (except clones or identical twins) have the same DNA. Many things—the color of our eyes or hair, whether we're tall or short, our chances of getting certain diseases—depend on the genes we get from our parents.

What Makes Us Human

The human genome is the DNA code for our species—it's what makes us human beings. In 2000, the U.S. Human Genome Project identified the 3.1 billion separate codes in human DNA. In early 2003, researchers succeeded in mapping out all the human chromosomes.

The human genome contains about 30,000 to 40,000 genes. That's not many more genes than a roundworm—about 20,000—and it's fewer than the 50,000-plus genes of a rice plant! But unlike the genes of most living things, human genes are able to produce more than one kind of protein. Proteins perform most life functions and make up a large part of cellular structures.

By studying human genes, scientists can learn more about hereditary diseases and get a better idea of how humans evolved.

All About... CLONING

A **clone** is an organism that has developed from a cell of just one other organism. It has the exact same DNA as its parent. Scientists have been able to clone mammals artificially. The most famous clone was a sheep named Dolly, born in Scotland in 1996. In February 2003, after developing arthritis and a lung disease, Dolly was euthanized ("put to sleep"). She was young by sheep standards, and scientists were not sure whether her bad health came from being a clone. Labs that have cloned other mammals, including cattle and goats, say that the ones that live to adulthood seem normal in every way they can measure.

In February 2002, researchers in Texas announced the birth of "CC" (carbon copy), the world's first cloned cat. CC has the same DNA as Rainbow, the cat she was cloned from. But they look different, because calico patterns are affected by growth in the womb, not just genes. They differ in other ways too. CC is playful and curious, while Rainbow is shy. CC is slim, while Rainbow is chunky.

Researchers are also trying to clone extinct animals—such as the Tasmanian tiger and mammoths—using DNA from specimens kept in museums or found frozen in glaciers. Most scientists say that cloning dinosaurs—as in the movie *Jurassic Park*—is probably impossible, however, because they won't be able to find remains with enough intact dinosaur DNA.

Is human cloning possible? Perhaps, but many people believe it would be wrong, for ethical reasons and because of the risk of health problems.

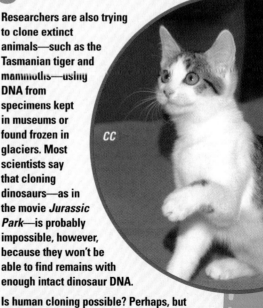

CC

Some Famous Scientists

Tim Berners-Lee (1955–), a British computer whiz who radically changed the history of computing and communication when he invented the World Wide Web in 1989. Since then he has worked to make the web grow as a source of information about everything under the sun. He works at a laboratory in Massachusetts.

Marie Curie (1867–1934), a Polish-French physical chemist known for discovering radium, which is used to treat some diseases. She won the Nobel Prize for chemistry in 1911. She and her husband, Pierre Curie, also won the Nobel Prize for physics in 1903 for their work in radiation.

Charles Darwin (1809–1882), a British scientist best known for his theory of evolution. According to this theory, living creatures slowly developed over millions of years into the forms they have today.

Thomas Edison (1847–1931), Ohio-born inventor who only attended school for three months. He created devices that transformed society, such as a reliable electric lightbulb, the electric generator, phonograph, wireless telegraph, motion-picture projector, and alkaline, iron-nickel batteries.

Albert Einstein (1879–1955), a German-American physicist who developed a revolutionary theory about the relationships between time, space, matter, and energy. He won a Nobel Prize in 1921.

Albert Einstein

Gertrude Elion (1918-1999), U.S. chemist who played a key role in developing drugs to treat leukemia and viral diseases. She never earned a Ph.D., but she received many honorary degrees and, in 1988, won the Nobel Prize in Physiology or Medicine.

Rosalind Franklin (1920–1958), British chemist whose X-ray photographs played a key role in determining the "double helix" structure of DNA. After helping determine the structure of DNA, Franklin turned her attention to viruses and made important discoveries there too.

Galileo Galilei (1564-1642), Italian astronomer and physicist who established basic principles of physics. Using a telescope he built, he was the first person to see the moons of Jupiter and craters and mountains on our Moon. He argued that the Eath moves around the Sun.

Galileo Galilei

Johannes Kepler (1571–1630), German astronomer who developed three laws of planetary motion. He was the first to propose a force (later named gravity) that governs planets' orbits around the sun.

Ada Lovelace (1815–1852), British mathematical genius who is considered the first computer programmer. She designed a "language" for the first computing machine (invented by Charles Babbage).

Sir Isaac Newton (1642–1727), a British scientist famous for many revolutionary discoveries. He worked out the basic laws of motion and gravity. He also showed that sunlight is made up of all the colors of the rainbow. He invented the branch of mathematics called calculus, but he kept this discovery quiet. Soon after, a German philosopher and mathematician named Gottfried von Leibniz (1646–1716) also worked out a system of calculus, and made it widely known.

Sir Isaac Newton

Wolfgang Pauli (1900–1958), Austrian-American physicist who invented a famous rule of physics. It says two electrons cannot occupy the same energy state in an atom at the same time. This helps explain why objects do not blend into each other. In 1931 he proposed the existence of a tiny particle, called a neutrino. Scientists confirmed 25 years later that it exists.

SCIENCE MUSEUMS

If you like exhibits you can touch interact with, here are a few museums that you might like to visit:

Exploratorium, San Francisco, California. Since 1969 this museum has been famous for all of its "hands-on" exhibits, which help visitors learn about animal behavior, electricity, hearing, heat and temperature, color, light, motion, sound and music, weather, and more.

WEB SITE http://www.exploratorium.edu

Franklin Institute Science Museum, Philadelphia, Pennsylvania. Benjamin Franklin has his own exhibit hall where visitors can experiment with some of his inventions. The bioscience exhibit invites people to listen to their own heartbeats and experience what it's like inside a human heart. "It's All in the Brain" helps visitors experience how the brain reacts to the outside world.

WEB SITE http://www.fi.edu

The Liberty Science Center, Jersey City, New Jersey, includes a dark "touch tunnel" you can crawl through guided by your sense of touch, a bug zoo with living crawly creatures, some of which you can hold, a water-sand table that shows how water currents and erosion shape shorelines, a climbing wall, a "virtual reality" sports exhibit, and many other fun displays.

WEB SITE http://www.lsc.org

The Museum of Natural Science, Houston, Texas, has a paleontology exhibit that includes a model of a giant pterosaur—as far as we know, the biggest flying creature ever to live. It had a 35-foot wingspan, about that of a fighter jet. Other great exhibits include a "whisper dish" that lets whispers be heard across a room and a "neon refinery" that uses neon tubes to show how a real oil refinery works.

WEB SITE http://www.hmns.org

The Museum of Science and Industry, Chicago, Illinois, is the largest science museum in a single building in the Western Hemisphere. It has more than 800 exhibits. Among these is the Great Train Story, a 3,500-sq.-ft. model train display, elaborately depicting a journey from Seattle to Chicago.

WEB SITE http://www.msi.chicago.org

The Ontario Science Centre, Toronto, Ontario, Canada, has scads of informative and occasionally wacky exhibits, including the "Amazing Aging Machine," a computer with special imaging software that shows how you may look when you're 30 or 60 years older, and a Van de Graaf generator—a giant silver ball—that demonstrates electrical effects by making your hair stand up.

WEB SITE http://www.ontariosciencecentre.ca

▼ Van de Graaf generator at the Ontario Science Centre

SCIENCE Q & A

WHY DO PLANTS NEED SUNLIGHT? Sunlight—along with water and carbon dioxide, a gas found in the air—is necessary for photosynthesis. That's the process by which plants make their food. In fact, the word *photosynthesis* means putting together (*synthesis*) with light (*photo*). Leaves are the food factories in plants, where photosynthesis takes place. Chlorophyll, a chemical that gives leaves their green color, plays a key role in the process. Photosynthesis also releases oxygen into the atmosphere—a good thing, since that's what people breathe! In winter when there is less sunlight, photosynthesis slows down and then stops, and plants live off the food they have stored. When the green chlorophyll goes out of the leaves, they take on the color of other chemicals in them—that's how trees get their beautiful autumn leaves.

WHAT ARE CLOUDS MADE OF? Clouds are made up of a great many tiny droplets of water. The droplets are small enough that they don't fall to the ground, but there are enough of them that they can be seen. Clouds also contain dust, which the droplets stick to. Sometimes people "seed" clouds with dust, to help large drops of water form so that it will rain.

WHY IS COLD IN THE WINTER AND HOT IN THE SUMMER?
Imagine a line running through the center of Earth from the North Pole to the South Pole. Earth rotates around this line (its axis). But the Earth's axis is not perpendicular (straight up) in relation to its orbit. It's tilted about 23.5 degrees. This tilt doesn't change, but as the Earth moves around its orbit, either the North Pole or the South Pole is closer to the Sun. For the Northern Hemisphere, the warmest days of the year come in June, July, and August. As the Earth moves through its orbit, the northern half of the planet faces the Sun more directly. On June 21, the **Summer Solstice,** the Sun is the nearest it will come to appearing directly overhead. More direct sunlight heats the air, the land, and the water—making it warmer in summer.

As the Earth continues through its yearlong orbit, its northern half eventually points away from the Sun. In the Northern Hemisphere this means that the Sun will start to appear lower in the sky. The heat energy from the Sun is less intense coming in from an angle—it's spread out over more area. (Try shining a flashlight on a piece of paper. Does the light on the paper look brighter when you shine the light straight down or from an angle?) On December 21 or 22, the **Winter Solstice,** the Sun is the lowest it will be in the sky. For the Southern Hemisphere, the Solstices are reversed. Australia's summer begins in December!

HOW DO FISH BREATHE? Like humans and other animals, fish need to take in oxygen. But they get it in a different way—through their *gills,* which are located on either side of the fish, just behind the mouth. When fish open their mouths, water comes in; when they close their mouths the water is pumped over the gills. (This is how it works for most fish; sharks and some other species don't have as good a pumping system and so they need to keep swimming to force water over the gills.) The gills have surfaces with many tiny blood vessels—capillaries—and when the water passes over these surfaces, the oxygen in the water passes into the blood of the fish (as it does in people's lungs). The gills are delicate structures, held up by the water. When a fish is taken out of water, the gills collapse and the fish suffocates.

WHY IS THE SKY BLUE?

Sunlight makes the sky blue. Light from the Sun is actually white until it reaches Earth's atmosphere. Then it hits water vapor, dust, and other particles in the air and scatters in different directions. White light is made up of all the colors of the spectrum. Since blue is scattered much more than any other color, blue is what we see when we look up at a clear sky. During sunrises and sunsets, we see red and orange because, with the Sun closer to the horizon, the light has to travel through much more of the atmosphere, and the blue is scattered before it gets to us, so that what's left is primarily red and orange light.

WHAT CAUSES THUNDER?

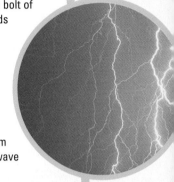

Lightning does. In an instant, a bolt of lightning can heat the air around it up to 60,000°F. The heated air expands violently, like an explosion. As the air expands it also cools quickly and starts to contract. This quick expansion and contraction air creates the shock waves we hear as thunder.

Think of popping a balloon. When you blow it up, you are putting the air under pressure. Why? Because air molecules in the balloon are packed more tightly than they are in the air around it. The rubber keeps the air inside the balloon from spreading out. When the balloon breaks, the air expands rapidly (like the air superheated by lightning). The molecules from inside the balloon push against those on the outside—creating a shock wave that you hear as a "pop."

WHAT DO CATS USE THEIR WHISKERS FOR?

Cats' whiskers are very sensitive to touch. Cats can use them to help find their way around in the dark. (Cheetahs, which are less active at night than many other species of cats, have less-developed whiskers.) Also, the size of a cat's whiskers is directly proportional to the size of the cat. So perhaps the whiskers help them know when a space is too tight, so that they don't try to squeeze into it and get caught.

CAN A BASEBALL PITCHER REALLY MAKE A BALL CURVE?

Pitchers can make a ball curve as much as $17\frac{1}{2}$ inches from its path. A snap of the wrist puts extra *spin* on the ball. As it spins, the stitches on one side move with the airflow around it. The stitches on the other side move against the airflow. When stitches and air move together, the flow is faster. The increased speed reduces the air pressure on that side. On the opposite side, the air pressure is increased. The ball moves—curves—toward the side of the ball with the lower pressure.

WHAT CAUSES RAINBOWS?

The light we usually see (visible light) is made up of different frequencies, or colors, in a certain range, called the *spectrum*. The colors of the visible spectrum are red, orange, yellow, green, blue, indigo, and violet. White light is a mixture of all these colors. A *prism* can separate the frequencies mixed in a beam of white light. When you see a rainbow, the tiny water droplets in the air act as many tiny prisms, separating the Sun's white light into the colors of the spectrum.

Homework Help

Here's a useful way to remember the order of the colors of the spectrum. Remember the name ROY G. BIV

R = red, O = orange, Y = yellow, G = green, B = blue, I = indigo, V = violet

FIZZ ROCKET

Did you ever see a rocket taking off? It climbs into the sky on a pillar of fire. But how exactly does it work? You can get an idea by building your own rocket and launching it. (For safety reasons, be sure to have an adult with you when you're doing this.)

WHAT YOU NEED:

► A 35-mm film canister with a cap that fits *inside* the rim—a photography store may have extra ones they'll give you if you explain it's for a science project.

► A fizzing antacid tablet, the kind sold to cure upset stomachs.

► Paper—a few sheets of normal printer paper are fine.

► Scissors and tape.

► A cup of water.

► Goggles or sunglasses or something similar to wear as eye protection.

WHAT TO DO:

❶ Make the body of the rocket—a cylinder—by cutting a strip of paper, then taping it to the film canister. *Make sure the cap end is at the bottom!*

❷ Make a nose cone for the rocket by cutting a circle out of the paper, then cutting a wedge out of the circle.

❸ When you tape together the edges of the wedge, you'll get a cone.

❹ Have fun with your rocket design—you can add fins if you want. Try short or tall rockets, and make the nose cone more or less pointed.

❺ Take your rocket outside and put on your eye protection.

❻ With the rocket pointing down, fill the canister about one-third full of water.

❼ Drop half the antacid tablet in the canister. Then quickly put the cap back on, turn the rocket right side up, and put it on the ground for blasting off.

❽ Stand back and see how high it goes!

WHAT HAPPENED?

Rockets—yours and the ones NASA sends into space—work because of Newton's Third Law of Motion: for every action there is an equal and opposite reaction. In the fizz rocket, the antacid tablet dissolves in the water and releases bubbles of gas. In a balloon, which is elastic, the gas would blow up the balloon. But the film canister in the rocket isn't elastic; the bubbles build up pressure until finally they pop out the cap. The cap and water rush out in a downward direction, and the rocket blasts off in the opposite direction—toward the sky. Real rockets, of course, use a different fuel, but the same basic principle.

Space

What planet is 5,000 light-years away?
•••
page 203

THE SOLAR SYSTEM

Nine planets, including Earth, travel around the Sun. These planets, together with the Sun, make up the solar system.

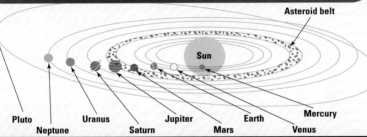

Asteroid belt

Sun

Pluto　　Uranus　　　　Jupiter　　　　Earth　　　Mercury
　Neptune　　　　Saturn　　　Mars　　　Venus

THE SUN IS A STAR

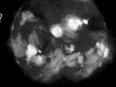

Did you know that the Sun is a star, like the other stars you see at night? It is a typical, medium-size star. But because the Sun is much closer to our planet than any other star, we can study it in great detail. The diameter of the Sun is 864,000 miles—more than 100 times Earth's diameter. The gravity of the Sun is nearly 28 times the gravity of Earth.

How Hot Is the Sun? The surface temperature of the sun is close to 10,000°F, and it is believed that the Sun's inner core may reach temperatures around 30 million degrees! The Sun provides enough light and heat energy to support all forms of life on our planet.

THE PLANETS ARE IN MOTION

The planets move around the Sun along elliptical paths called **orbits**. One complete path around the Sun is called a **revolution**. Earth takes one year, or 365¼ days, to make one revolution around the Sun. Planets that are farther away from the Sun take longer. Some planets have one or more **moons**. A moon orbits a planet in much the same way that the planets orbit the Sun.

Each planet also spins (or rotates) on its **axis**. An axis is an imaginary line running through the center of a planet. The time it takes Earth to rotate on its axis equals one day.

Homework Help

Here's a useful way to remember the names of planets in order of their usual distance from the Sun. Think of this sentence: **M**y **V**ery **E**xcellent **M**other **J**ust **S**ent **U**s **N**ine **P**izzas

M = Mercury, **V** = Venus, **E** = Earth, **M** = Mars, **J** = Jupiter, **S** = Saturn, **U** = Uranus, **N** = Neptune, **P** = Pluto.

THE PLANETS

1 MERCURY

Average distance from the Sun: 36 million miles
Diameter: 3,032 miles
Average temp.: 333° F
Surface: silicate rock
Time to revolve around the Sun: 88 days
Time to rotate on its axis: 58 days, 15 hours, 36 minutes
Number of moons: 0

DID YOU KNOW? *Mercury is the closest planet to the Sun, but it gets very cold there. Since Mercury has almost no atmosphere, most of its heat escapes at night, and temperatures can fall to –300°F.*

2 VENUS

Average distance from the Sun: 67 million miles
Diameter: 7,521 miles
Average temp.: 867° F
Surface: silicate rock
Time to revolve around the Sun: 224.7 days
Time to rotate on its axis: 243 days
Number of moons: 0

DID YOU KNOW? *Venus spins in the opposite direction of Earth's rotation. On Venus, the Sun actually rises in the west!*

3 EARTH

Average distance from the Sun: 93 million miles
Diameter: 7,926 miles
Average temp.: 59° F
Surface: water, basalt and granite rock
Time to revolve around the Sun: 365 ¼ days
Time to rotate on its axis: 23 hours, 56 minutes, 4.2 seconds
Number of moons: 1

DID YOU KNOW? *Earth's atmosphere is made up mostly of nitrogen (78%) and oxygen (21%). It helps protect us from harmful solar radiation and meteors.*

4 MARS

Average distance from the Sun: 142 million miles
Diameter: 4,213 miles
Average temp.: –81° F
Surface: iron-rich basaltic rock
Time to revolve around the Sun: 687 days
Time to rotate on its axis: 24 hours, 37 minutes, 22 seconds
Number of moons: 2

DID YOU KNOW? *Mars has its own Grand Canyon, called Valles Marineris. It stretches about 2,500 miles across the planet.*

5 JUPITER

Average distance from the Sun: 484 million miles
Diameter: 88,732 miles
Average temp.: –162° F
Surface: liquid hydrogen
Time to revolve around the Sun: 11.9 years
Time to rotate on its axis: 9 hours, 55 minutes, 30 seconds
Number of moons: 60

DID YOU KNOW? *The Great Red Spot we can see on Jupiter is actually a huge storm that is 25,000 miles wide.*

6 SATURN

Average distance from the Sun: 888 million miles
Diameter: 74,975 miles
Average temp.: –218° F
Surface: liquid hydrogen
Time to revolve around the Sun: 29.5 years
Time to rotate on its axis: 10 hours, 39 minutes, 22 seconds
Number of moons: 31

DID YOU KNOW? *Saturn's biggest moon, Titan, is bigger than the planet Mercury.*

7 URANUS

Average distance from the Sun: 1.8 billion miles
Diameter: 31,763 miles
Average temp.: −323° F
Surface: liquid hydrogen and helium
Time to revolve around the Sun: 84 years
Time to rotate on its axis: 17 hours, 14 minutes
Number of moons: 21

DID YOU KNOW? *The blue color of Uranus is a result of methane gas in its atmosphere. Methane reflects blue light.*

8 NEPTUNE

Average distance from the Sun: 2.8 billion miles
Diameter: 30,603 miles
Average temp.: −330° F
Surface: liquid hydrogen and helium
Time to revolve around the Sun: 164.8 years
Time to rotate on its axis: 16 hours, 6 minutes
Number of moons: 8

DID YOU KNOW? *In millions of years, Neptune's largest moon, Triton, will get so close to Neptune that it may break up. The pieces would form into rings.*

9 PLUTO

Average distance from the Sun: 3.6 billion miles
Diameter: 1,413 miles
Average temp.: −369° F
Surface: rock and frozen gases
Time to revolve around the Sun: 247.7 years
Time to rotate on its axis: 6 days, 9 hours, 18 minutes
Number of moons: 1

DID YOU KNOW? *The first-ever mission to Pluto—New Horizons—was scheduled for a 2006 launch. The probe should reach Pluto by 2015!*

More PLANET FACTS

Largest planet: Jupiter
Smallest planet: Pluto
Planet closest to the Sun: Mercury
Planet closest to Earth: Venus (Every 19 months, Venus gets closer to Earth than any other planet ever does.)
Fastest-moving planet: Mercury (107,000 miles per hour)
Slowest planet: Pluto (10,600 mph)
Warmest planet: Venus
Coldest planet: Pluto
Shortest day: Mercury
Longest day: Jupiter

THE MOON

The moon is about 238,900 miles from Earth. It is 2,160 miles in diameter and has no atmosphere. The dusty surface is covered with deep craters. It takes the same time for the moon to rotate on its axis as it does to orbit Earth (27 days, 7 hours, 43 minutes). This is why one side of the moon is always facing Earth. The moon has no light of its own, but reflects light from the Sun. The fraction of the lighted part of the moon that we see at a certain time is called a *phase*. It takes the moon about 29½ days to go through all its phases. This is called a **lunar month.**

PHASES OF THE MOON

New Moon	Crescent Moon	First Quarter	Full Moon

Last Quarter	Crescent Moon	New Moon

Did You KNOW?
*There are now more than 100 known planets outside our solar system. The first **extrasolar** planet was discovered in 1995. Scientists found the most distant planet yet in January 2003. Known as OGLE-TR-56b, the planet is in the constellation Sagittarius—about 5,000 light-years from Earth!*

NOT JUST PLANETS

Comet Hale-Bopp

COMETS are fast-moving chunks of ice, dust, and rock that form huge gaseous heads as they move nearer to the Sun. One of the most well-known is **Halley's Comet**. It can be seen about every 76 years and will appear in the sky again in the year 2061.

ASTEROIDS (or minor planets) are solid chunks of rock or metal that range in size from small boulders to hundreds of miles across. **Ceres**, the largest, is about 600 miles in diameter. Thousands of asteroids orbit the Sun between Mars and Jupiter in what we call the **Asteroid Belt**.

SATELLITES are objects that move in an orbit around a planet. Moons are natural satellites. Artificial satellites, launched into orbit by humans, are used as space stations and observatories. They are also used to take pictures of Earth's surface and to transmit communications signals.

METEOROIDS are small pieces of stone or metal traveling in space. Most meteoroids are fragments from comets or asteroids that broke off from crashes in space with other objects. A few are actually chunks that blew off the Moon or Mars after an asteroid hit. When a meteoroid enters the Earth's atmosphere, it usually burns up completely. This streak of light is called a **meteor**, or "shooting star." If a piece of a meteroid survives its trip through our atmosphere and lands on Earth, it is called a **meteorite**.

WHAT IS AN ECLIPSE?

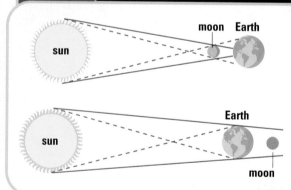

During a **solar eclipse,** the moon casts a shadow on Earth. A total solar eclipse is when the Sun is completely blocked out. When this happens, a halo of gas can be seen around the Sun. This is called the **corona**.

Sometimes Earth casts a shadow on the moon. During a total **lunar eclipse,** the moon remains visible, but it looks dark, often with a reddish tinge (from sunlight bent through Earth's atmosphere).

Upcoming total SOLAR ECLIPSES

TOTAL SOLAR ECLIPSES
November 23, 2003
Will be seen in Antarctica.
March 29, 2006
Will be seen across the Atlantic Ocean, Africa, and part of Asia.
August 1, 2008
Will be seen in northern Canada, Greenland, and Asia.

Upcoming total LUNAR ECLIPSES

TOTAL LUNAR ECLIPSES
November 8-9, 2003
Will be seen from Africa to Europe, western Asia, and eastern North America.
May 4, 2004
Will be seen in Europe, Africa, and parts of Asia and Australia.
October 28, 2004
Will be seen in North and South America, Europe, and Africa.

BIGQUESTIONS

DOES THE UNIVERSE GO ON FOREVER?

Most astronomers do not think the **universe** goes on forever. They do think it is expanding—getting bigger and bigger as time goes on. In fact, the universe is so big that astronomers measure many distances in **light-years**—the distance a beam of light would travel in a whole year, going at 186,000 miles a second. One light-year is trillions of miles, and astronomers think the universe is at least **billions of light-years across.**

WHAT IS A GALAXY?

A **galaxy** is a group of billions of stars held together by gravity. Galaxies also contain interstellar gas and dust. The universe may have about 50 billion galaxies. The one we live in is called the **Milky Way.** The Sun and most stars we see are just a few of the 200 billion stars in the Milky Way.

WHAT IS A NEBULA?

Historically, any fuzzy patch in the sky has been called a **nebula,** even galaxies and star clusters. **Planetary nebulas** come from the late stages of some stars, while star clusters and galaxies are star groupings. **Emission nebulas, reflection nebulas,** and dark dust clouds are regions of interstellar gas and dust that may be hundreds of light-years wide and are often birthplaces of stars. Emission nebulas give off a reddish glow, caused when their hydrogen gas is heated by newly formed, hot stars in the vicinity. Dust particles in some areas reflect hot blue starlight and appear as reflection nebulas. Dark dust clouds, though still mainly gas, contain enough dust to absorb starlight and appear as **dark nebulas.**

Crab Nebula

HOW FAR AWAY ARE THE STARS?

Our Sun is about 93 million miles away. The next closest star is Proxima Centauri, which is part of the triple star system of Alpha Centauri. Proxima is about 25 trillion miles, or 4.2 light-years, away and (unlike Alpha Centauri) cannot be seen by the unaided eye. But on a clear night you can see some stars much farther—up to 2.7 million light-years—away, even without a telescope or binoculars. This means you are seeing light from up to 2.7 million years ago. And with NASA's powerful Hubble Telescope you could see star explosions, called **supernovas,** up to 12 billion light-years away!

WHAT IS A BLACK HOLE?

A **black hole** is a region in space with gravity so strong that nothing can get out—not even light. Black holes are most likely formed when giant stars at least 20 times as massive as our Sun burn up their fuel and collapse, creating very dense cores. Scientists also think bigger, "supermassive" black holes may form from the collapse of many stars in the centers of galaxies. Astronomers can't see black holes, since they do not give off light. They watch for signs, such as effects on the orbits of nearby stars, or X-ray bursts from matter being sucked into the black hole.

HOW OLD IS THE UNIVERSE?

Scientists estimate the universe began about 13 to 14 billion years ago. Many believe it formed from the **Big Bang.** According to this theory, everything—all matter and energy—was packed together into a tiny space. This blew apart in a huge explosion, and the universe was born.

205

EXPLORING SPACE

American space exploration began in 1958, when the Explorer I satellite was launched into orbit and NASA (the National Aeronautics and Space Administration) was formed.

SEARCHING for LIFE

For years scientists have tried to discover whether there is life on other planets in our solar system or elsewhere. They look for signs of what is needed for life on Earth—basics like water and proper temperature.

NASA is searching for signs of life on Mars. This search will continue until at least 2013. Some spacecraft will fly around Mars taking pictures. Others will land there to study soil and rocks and look for living things.

NASA has a new telescope mission planned for 2005 called the Terrestrial Planet Finder. It will look for planets similar to Earth in other solar systems through a giant, space-based telescope.

Outside of NASA, another program is looking for life on other worlds. It is called SETI (Search for Extraterrestrial Intelligence). Most often it uses powerful radio telescopes to detect signs of life. Recently, however, astronomers began searching for light signals as signs of extraterrestrial life.

MARS PROBES

In the summer of 2003, NASA was slated to launch the twin Mars Exploration Rovers, which should arrive on different parts of Mars in January 2004. These robot "scientists" (one is shown here) will collect samples and search for signs of water. In early 2003, NASA and the LEGO company held a "Name the Mars Rovers" contest for kids.

The European Space Agency was set to launch the *Mars Express*—its first Mars probe—in the summer of 2003. It will orbit the planet and send its lander, Beagle 2, to the surface in December 2003 to test for signs of water.

The first Japanese Mars orbiter, *Nozomi,* was launched in 1998. Its purpose is to study the upper atmosphere of Mars. *Nozomi* used too much fuel correcting its course, so it had to slow down. It should reach Mars in early 2004.

Unmanned Missions
IN THE SOLAR SYSTEM

LAUNCH DATE

1962	**Mariner 2** First successful flyby of Venus.
1964	**Mariner 4** First probe to reach Mars, 1965.
1972	**Pioneer 10** First probe to reach Jupiter, 1973.
1973	**Mariner 10** Only U.S. probe to reach Mercury, 1974.
1975	**Viking 1 and 2** Landed on Mars in 1976.
1977	**Voyager 1** Reached Jupiter in 1979 and Saturn in 1980.
1977	**Voyager 2** Reached Jupiter in 1979, Saturn in 1981, Uranus in 1986, Neptune in 1989.
1989	**Magellan** Orbited Venus and mapped its surface.
1989	**Galileo** Reached Jupiter, 1995.
1996	**Mars Global Surveyor** Began mapping surface in 1999.
1996	**Mars Pathfinder** Landed on Mars, sent a roving vehicle (Sojourner) to explore the surface in 1997.
1997	**Cassini** Expected to reach Saturn in 2004.
2001	**Mars Odyssey** Began mapping and studying Mars in early 2002.

FIRST ASTRONAUTS IN SPACE

The start of the U.S. space program in 1958 was a response to the Soviet Union's launching of its satellite SPUTNIK I into orbit on October 4, 1957. In 1961, three years after NASA was formed, President John F. Kennedy promised Americans that the United States would land a person on the moon by the end of the 1960s. NASA landed men on the moon in July 1969. Since then, more than 400 astronauts have made trips into outer space. This time line shows some of their early flights.

1961 On April 12, Soviet cosmonaut Yuri Gagarin, in *Vostok 1*, became the **first human to orbit Earth**. On May 5, U.S. astronaut Alan B. Shepard Jr. of the *Mercury 3* mission became the **first American in space**.

1962 On February 20, U.S. astronaut John H. Glenn Jr. of *Mercury 6* became the **first American to orbit Earth**.

1963 From June 16 to 19, the Soviet spacecraft *Vostok 6* carried the **first woman in space**, Valentina V. Tereshkova.

1965 On March 18, Soviet cosmonaut Aleksei A. Leonov became the **first person to walk in space**. He spent 10 minutes outside the spaceship. On December 15, U.S. *Gemini 6A* and *7* (with astronauts) became the **first vehicles to rendezvous** (approach and see each other) **in space**.

1966 On March 16, U.S. *Gemini 8* became the **first craft to dock with** (become attached to) **another vehicle** (an unmanned *Agena* rocket).

1967 On January 27, a fire in a U.S. *Apollo* spacecraft on the ground killed astronauts Virgil I. Grissom, Edward H. White, and Roger B. Chaffee. On April 24, *Soyuz 1* crashed on Earth, killing Soviet cosmonaut Vladimir Komarov.

1969 On July 20, after successful flights of *Apollo 8, 9,* and *10,* U.S. *Apollo 11*'s **lunar module** *Eagle* **landed on the moon's surface** in the area known as the Sea of Tranquility. Neil Armstrong became the **first person ever to walk on the moon**.

1970 In April, *Apollo 13* astronauts returned safely to Earth after an explosion damaged their spacecraft and prevented them from landing on the moon.

1971 In July and August, U.S. *Apollo 15* astronauts tested the **Lunar Rover** on the moon.

1972 In December, *Apollo 17* was the sixth and **final U.S. space mission to land successfully on the moon**.

1973 On May 14, the U.S. put its **first space station**, **Skylab**, **into orbit**. The last Skylab crew left in January 1974.

1975 On July 15, the U.S. launched an *Apollo* spacecraft and the U.S.S.R. launched a *Soyuz* spacecraft. Two days later, the **American and Soviet crafts docked**, and for several days their crews worked and spent time together in space. This was NASA's last space mission with astronauts until the space shuttle.

SHUTTLES AND SPACE STATIONS

In the 1970s, NASA developed the space shuttle program. Earlier space capsules could not be used again after returning to Earth. In 1986, the Soviet Union launched its MIR space station. By the mid-1990s, the U.S. and Russia were sharing projects in space.

1977 — The first shuttle **Enterprise,** took off from the back of a 747 jet airliner.

1981 — **Columbia** was launched and became the first shuttle to reach Earth's orbit.

1983 — In April, NASA began using a third shuttle, **Challenger**.

1984 — In August, the shuttle **Discovery** was launched for the first time.

1985 — In October, the shuttle **Atlantis** was launched for the first time.

1986 — On January 28, after 24 successful missions, **Challenger** exploded 73 seconds after takeoff. Astronauts Dick Scobee, Michael Smith, Ellison Onizuka, Judith Resnik, Greg Jarvis, and Ron McNair, and teacher Christa McAuliffe died. In February, the Soviet space station **Mir** was launched into orbit.

1988 — In September new safety procedures led to a successful launch of **Discovery**.

1990 — On April 24, the **Hubble Space Telescope** was launched from **Discovery**.

1992 — In May, NASA launched a new shuttle, **Endeavour**.

1995 — In June, **Atlantis** docked with **Mir** for the first time.

1998 — In December, **Endeavour** was launched with **Unity**, a U.S.-built part of the International Space Station. The crew attached it to the Russian-built **Zarya** control module.

2000 — The first crew arrived at the International Space Station in November.

2001 — In February, **Atlantis** carried the lab module **Destiny** to the International Space Station. **Mir** parts splashed down in the Pacific in March, ending the 15-year Russian program.

2002 — In March, **Columbia** astronauts carried out the fourth repair/upgrade of the **Hubble Space Telescope**.

Disaster in Space

On February 1, 2003, after a 16-day scientific mission, space shuttle *Columbia* disintegrated during its reentry into the Earth's atmosphere, killing astronauts Rick Husband, William McCool, Michael Anderson, David Brown, Kalpana Chawla, Laurel Clark, and the first Israeli astronaut in space, Ilan Ramon. Wreckage from the shuttle fell across hundreds of miles in Texas and Louisiana. By examining the debris recovered, investigators at NASA hoped to find out the cause of the accident and make changes for the future.

INTERNATIONAL SPACE STATION

The International Space Station (ISS) is being built by 16 countries, including the U.S. and Russia, and is expected to be completed in 2006, if all goes well. The first crew of three astronauts lived and worked aboard the ISS for about four months starting in November 2000. The fifth crew returned to Earth in December 2002 , after almost six months in space. A sixth crew was sent up to replace them.

When it's finished, the ISS will weigh over 1 million pounds. It will be about a hundred yards square (356 feet wide and 290 feet long). That's four times bigger than the Russian *Mir* space station. There will be almost an acre of solar panels to supply electricity to the 52 computers and six scientific laboratories on board.

The ISS is orbiting the Earth at an altitude of 250 miles. To find out when you might be able to see it over your town, go to

WEB SITE http://spaceflight.nasa.gov/realdata/tracking/index.html

A DAY ABOARD THE INTERNATIONAL SPACE STATION

Space travel can be dangerous, but it can also be rewarding. On the space station itself there are many challenges that Earth-bound beings will never experience.

A "day" in space is not the same as a day on Earth: as the Space Station orbits the Earth, astronauts go through 15 dawns in 24 hours. But, in order to avoid permanent jet lag, they still wake up in the "morning" and begin their day as do humans on Earth.

Almost everything must be recycled—including food, air, and water from the shower. In fact, the only thing that doesn't get recycled is human waste, which is thrown out through a suction device connected to the space toilet. Lack of gravity affects everything. Food must be kept inside bags or weighted down by magnets so that it doesn't float away and possibly get caught in the controls for the Space Station. Astronauts have to exercise or they will lose their bone and muscle mass. They must sleep with their sleeping bag attached to a wall, or they will free-float and possibly get sucked into an air vent.

Astronauts work hard all day performing experiments, doing medical tests, checking equipment, and making repairs. At the end of the day, they get free time to read, write e-mails, view DVDs, or simply watch the Earth rotate, which they say is the most fun of all.

WHO AM I?

I was born on January 14, 1943, in Shanghai, China, but I consider Bethany, Oklahoma, my hometown. I have a Ph.D. in biochemistry, and in 1978 was picked by NASA to become an astronaut. I have been on five space flights, with a total of 5,354 hours in space, and I hold the record for the most flight hours in orbit by any woman in the world. In 1996 I spent 188 days on the Russian space station **Mir**, more days than any other U.S. astronaut. I am the only woman ever to receive the Congressional Space Medal of Honor, and I am now Chief Scientist at NASA.

Answer: Astronaut Shannon Lucid

CONSTELLATIONS

Ancient cultures used myths to explain how constellations came to be. The constellation of Cassiopeia looks like the letter "W" in the sky. In Greek mythology, Cassiopeia was an Ethiopian queen. She was the wife of Cepheus and the mother of Andromeda. According to tradition, when she died she was changed into the constellation that is named after her.

Andromeda

Cassiopeia

Cepheus

POLARIS
(North Star)

Ursa Minor
(Little Dipper)

Big Dipper

Ursa Major

THE ZODIAC

The **zodiac** is an imaginary belt that goes around the sky. The orbits of the Sun, the moon, and planets known to ancient peoples are within it. The zodiac is divided into 12 sections, which are called **signs of the zodiac**. The ancient Babylonians named each of the sections for a constellation that could be seen within its limits during ancient times.

ARIES (Ram)
March 21–April 19

TAURUS (Bull)
April 20–May 20

GEMINI (Twins)
May 21–June 21

CANCER (Crab)
June 22–July 22

LEO (Lion)
July 23–August 22

VIRGO (Maiden)
August 23–Sept. 22

LIBRA (Balance)
Sept. 23–Oct. 23

SCORPIO (Scorpion)
Oct. 24–Nov. 21

SAGITTARIUS (Archer)
Nov. 22–Dec. 21

CAPRICORN (Goat)
Dec. 22–Jan. 19

AQUARIUS (Water Bearer)
Jan. 20–Feb. 18

PISCES (Fishes)
Feb. 19–March 20

PLANETARY CROSS-SEARCH PUZZLE

Circle the names of all nine planets in the round word search. They run up, down, backward, forward, and diagonally. Then use the uncircled remaining letters to fill in the names of other things you might see in the sky. There's a clue under each word.

 Once used in thermometers.

 She's a really good tennis player.

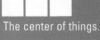 You live here.

 A kind of candy bar.

```
    A M A R S
  E J Y R U C R E M
 N T U H T R A E S L
 U S N P K I O T U L P
 T E A T I E S U N A R U
 P M T L T N V E N U S
  E O U Y E S W A L S
   N M R Y R T R O A
      N S I U
```

 The biggest planet.

A kind of car.

Third farthest.

He's king of the sea.

A famous dog.

The center of things.

It can be new or full.

Really famous people.

Another candy bar in the sky.

An artificial star.

Sports

What golfer uses her dad as a caddie?
•••
page 220

BASEBALL

The 2002 World Series featured two teams from California, and the first-ever meeting of two wildcard teams (teams that made the playoffs, but didn't win their divisions). The Anaheim Angels defeated the San Francisco Giants, 4-1, in Game 7 to win their first championship. Game 6 proved to be the turning point. Anaheim trailed by 5 runs after 6 innings. Behind 3 games to 2 and facing elimination, the Angels mounted a comeback as they had done in nearly half their games all season. Scott Spiezio hit a 3-run homer in the 7th and Darin Erstad led off with a homer in the 8th to bring the Angels within a run of tying the game and the Series. After singles by Tim Salmon and Garret Anderson, Troy Glaus hit a 2-run double to put the Angels ahead for good.

2002 MAJOR LEAGUE LEADERS

MVP AWARD
AL: Miguel Tejada, Oakland
NL: Barry Bonds, San Francisco

CY YOUNG AWARD (top pitcher)
AL: Barry Zito, Oakland
NL: Randy Johnson, Arizona

ROOKIE OF THE YEAR
AL: Eric Hinske, Toronto
NL: Jason Jennings, Colorado

BATTING CHAMPS
AL: Manny Ramirez, Boston, .349
NL: Barry Bonds, San Francisco, .370

HOME RUN LEADERS
AL: Alex Rodriguez, Texas, 57
NL: Sammy Sosa, Chicago, 49

EARNED RUN AVERAGE LEADERS
AL: Pedro Martinez, Boston, 2.26
NL: Randy Johnson, Arizona, 2.32

Barry Zito

COOL FEATS, FACTS, & FIRSTS

▶ On May 13, 1942, pitcher Jim Tobin of the Boston Braves hits 3 home runs in a game, becoming the first and only pitcher to do this.

▶ On May 2, 2002, Mike Cameron and Bret Boone of the Seattle Mariners each hit 2 home runs in the first inning of a game against the Chicago White Sox.

▶ On April 30, 2002, New York Mets pitcher Al Leiter beats the Arizona Diamondbacks, making him the first pitcher with wins against all 30 major league teams.

▶ On April 23, 1999, St. Louis Cardinals first baseman Fernando Tatis becomes the only player ever to hit 2 grand slams in the same inning.

LITTLE LEAGUE

Little League Baseball is the largest youth sports program in the world. It began in 1939 in Williamsport, Pennsylvania, with 45 boys playing on three teams. Now nearly three million boys and girls ages 5 to 18 play on 200,000 Little League teams in more than 80 countries.

WEB SITE http://www.littleleague.org

---- All About... BARRY BONDS ----

Eleven-time All-Star Barry Bonds is already being called one of the best players ever. The San Francisco Giants outfielder is a lock for the Hall of Fame. He's got the single-season home run record of 73. He's 4th on the all-time home run list (behind his godfather Willie Mays!) with 621 by the end of April 2003. He's won a record five MVP Awards. He's got more records than he can count. But Barry did something in 2002 that he had never done before—he played in the World Series. He hit four homers and batted .471 in the Fall Classic, though the Giants lost to the Angels in seven games.

Barry Lamar Bonds was born on July 24, 1964, in Riverside, California. He has been around baseball all of his life. When he was 4 years old, his father Bobby was a rookie for the San Francisco Giants (Bobby went on to be a 3-time All-Star). Barry went to Arizona State to play baseball instead of turning pro right away. He was drafted by Pittsburgh and got his first major league hit—a pinch-hit single—on April 20, 1986.

THE NEGRO LEAGUES

▼ Willie Mays (left) & Roy Campanella

In the early 20th century Major League Baseball, like America, was segregated. Black and Latino players weren't allowed in the majors. They formed their own teams and traveled around, playing exhibition games against each other and any other teams they could find. This was called "barnstorming." In the 1920s and 1930s, pro leagues such as the Negro National League, the Eastern Colored League, and the Negro American League were formed. The Homestead Grays (Pennsylvania), Pittsburgh Crawfords, and Kansas City Monarchs were some of the more successful teams. Famous players included Josh Gibson, a powerful home run hitter called the "black Babe Ruth"; James "Cool Papa" Bell, a base-stealer said to be so fast he could "turn out the light and get in bed before the room got dark"; and the legendary Leroy "Satchel" Paige, who pitched into his 50s. Hall of Fame players like Hank Aaron, Roy Campanella, and Willie Mays got their start in the Negro Leagues.

BASEBALL HALL OF FAME

The National Baseball Hall of Fame and Museum opened in 1939, in Cooperstown, New York. To be eligible for membership, players must be retired from baseball for five years. In 2003, Gary Carter and Eddie Murray were headed to Cooperstown.

WEB SITE *http://www.baseballhalloffame.org*

◄ Hall of Fame plaque for Hank Aaron, the all-time leader in home runs

BASKETBALL

Basketball began in 1891 in Springfield, Massachusetts, when Dr. James Naismith invented it, using peach baskets as hoops. At first, each team had nine players instead of five. Big-time pro basketball started in 1949, when the National Basketball Association (NBA) was formed. The Women's National Basketball Association (WNBA) began play in 1997.

HIGHLIGHTS OF THE 2002–2003 NBA SEASON

SCORING LEADER:
Tracy McGrady, Orlando Magic

Games: 75
Points: 2,407
Average: 32.1

REBOUNDING LEADER:
Ben Wallace, Detroit Pistons

Games: 73
Rebounds: 1,126
Average: 15.4

ASSISTS LEADER:
Jason Kidd, New Jersey Nets

Games: 80
Assists: 711
Average: 8.9

STEALS LEADER:
Allen Iverson, Philadelphia 76ers

Games: 82
Steals: 225
Average: 2.74

BLOCKED SHOTS LEADER:
Theo Ratliff, Atlanta Hawks

Games: 81
Blocks: 262
Average: 3.23

MOST VALUABLE PLAYER:
Tim Duncan, San Antonio Spurs
DEFENSIVE PLAYER OF THE YEAR:
Ben Wallace, Detroit Pistons
ROOKIE OF THE YEAR:
Amare Stoudemire
COACH OF THE YEAR:
Gregg Popovich

NBA Hall of Fame

The Naismith Memorial Basketball Hall of Fame in Springfield, Massachusetts. was founded in 1959 to honor great basketball players, coaches, referees, and others important to the history of the game. In the fall of 2002, the new Basketball Hall of Fame opened. This 80,000-square-foot building cost $45 million to build and includes many interactive exhibits and a theater. The 136-foot-tall spire has a 13-foot high lighted basketball which can be seen for miles. The 120-foot diameter "basketball" part of the building houses a full-size basketball court inside. The newest class headed for the Hall of Fame in September 2003 includes Robert Parish, James Worthy, famed broadcaster Chick Hearn, and famous Globetrotter Meadowlark Lemon.

WEB SITE http://www.hoophall.com

WHO AM I?

I was born on February 12, 1934, in Monroe, Louisiana. I wasn't the first to both coach and play on an NBA team. But in 1966, I became the first African-American to coach *any* pro sports team in the U.S. I was also the only player-coach to win two NBA titles, which I did in 1968 and 1969. I was a 5-time NBA MVP and am considered the best defensive center ever.

Answer: Bill Russell

The Harlem Globetrotters

When Abe Saperstein founded the Globetrotters in Chicago in 1927, they were a serious team. The fun-loving style of today's Globetrotters didn't develop until 1939. One night, with a 107-point lead, players clowned around and the crowd loved it! They began to work comic sketches and displays of basketball wizardry into their games every night. In the 1940s Reece "Goose" Tatum developed many routines and the role of the "Clown Prince"—later played by "Meadowlark" Lemon, then "Geese" Ausbie. Another famous trotter was "Curly" Neal, one of the world's greatest dribblers. Now in their 75th year, the Trotters have entertained more than 100 million fans in 115 countries. On November 13, 2000, Michigan State beat the Trotters, 72-68, snapping a 1,270-game winning streak. For the record, the Globetrotters once won 8,829 games in a row! Among sports stars who once played for the Globetrotters were NBA Hall of Famers Wilt Chamberlain and Connie Hawkins, baseball Hall of Fame pitcher Bob Gibson, and boxing great Sugar Ray Robinson.

HIGHLIGHTS OF THE
2002 WNBA SEASON

A year after ousting 4-time champion Houston, Lisa Leslie and the L.A. Sparks won their second WNBA title in a row. They defeated the New York Liberty, 69-66, in game 2 of the best-of-3 WNBA finals at the Staples Center in Los Angeles, August 31, 2002. Leslie, who led L.A. with 17 points, was named MVP of the Finals for the 2nd straight year. She also won her 3rd All-Star MVP Award in 2002.

The WNBA went through some changes after the 2002 season. The Miami and Portland teams went out of business. The Utah team moved to San Antonio, Texas, and became the Silver Stars. The Orlando team moved to Uncasville, Connecticut, and changed its name to the Connecticut Sun.

Most Valuable Player: Sheryl Swoopes, Houston Comets
Defensive Player of the Year: Sheryl Swoopes, Houston Comets
Rookie of the Year: Tamika Catchings, Indiana Fever
Coach of the Year: Marianne Stanley, Washington Mystics
Scoring Leader: Chamique Holdsclaw, Washington Mystics
Games: 20   Points: 397   Average: 19.9
Rebounding Leader: Chamique Holdsclaw, Washington Mystics
Games: 20   Rebounds: 232   Average: 11.6
Assists Leader: Ticha Penicheiro, Sacramento Monarchs
Games: 24   Assists: 192   Average: 8.0

◄ *Sheryl Swoopes*

COLLEGE BASKETBALL

The men's National Collegiate Athletic Association (NCAA) Tournament began i 1939. Today, it is a spectacular 65-team extravaganza. The Final Four weeken when the semi-finals and finals are played, is one of the most-watched sports competition in the U.S. The Women's NCAA Tournament began in 1982. Since then, the popularity of the women's game has grown by leaps and (re)bounds.

THE 2003 NCAA TOURNAMENT RESULTS

MEN'S FINAL FOUR
SEMI-FINALS:
Kansas 94, Marquette 61
Syracuse 95, Texas 84
FINALS:
Syracuse 81, Kansas 78
MOST OUTSTANDING PLAYER:
Carmelo Anthony, Syracuse

WOMEN'S FINAL FOUR
SEMI-FINALS:
Tennessee 66, Duke 56
Connecticut 71, Texas 69
FINALS:
Connecticut 73, Tennessee, 68
MOST OUTSTANDING PLAYER:
Diana Taurasi, Connecticut

THE JOHN R. WOODEN AWARD
Awarded to the nation's outstanding male college basketball player by the Los Angeles Athletic Club.
2003 winner: **T.J. Ford, Texas**

THE WADE TROPHY
Awarded to the nation's outstanding female college basketball player by the National Association for Girls and Women in Sport.
2003 winner: Diana Taurasi, Connecticut

CYCLING

The "modern" bicycle, with two wheels the same size, pedals, and a chain drive, appeared at the end of the 1800s. In fact, not until 1869 were they even called bicycles. Before that, the various two-wheeled inventions were known as "velocipedes." Clubs were formed and races held, but it was mostly a sport for the upper classes, who could afford bicycles. The world's most famous cycling race is the Tour de France. It was first held in 1903.

All About... Lance Armstrong

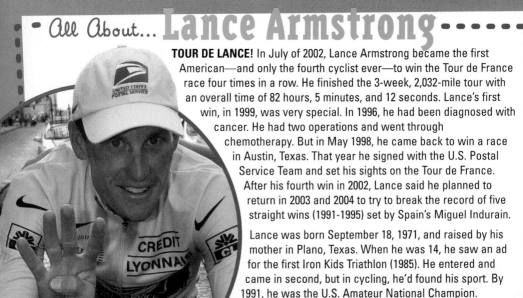

TOUR DE LANCE! In July of 2002, Lance Armstrong became the first American—and only the fourth cyclist ever—to win the Tour de France race four times in a row. He finished the 3-week, 2,032-mile tour with an overall time of 82 hours, 5 minutes, and 12 seconds. Lance's first win, in 1999, was very special. In 1996, he had been diagnosed with cancer. He had two operations and went through chemotherapy. But in May 1998, he came back to win a race in Austin, Texas. That year he signed with the U.S. Postal Service Team and set his sights on the Tour de France. After his fourth win in 2002, Lance said he planned to return in 2003 and 2004 to try to break the record of five straight wins (1991-1995) set by Spain's Miguel Indurain.

Lance was born September 18, 1971, and raised by his mother in Plano, Texas. When he was 14, he saw an ad for the first Iron Kids Triathlon (1985). He entered and came in second, but in cycling, he'd found his sport. By 1991, he was the U.S. Amateur National Champion.

FOOTBALL

American football began as a college sport. The first game that was like today's football took place between Yale and Harvard in New Haven, Connecticut, on November 13, 1875. The National Football League started in 1922. The rival American Football League began in 1960. The two leagues played the first Super Bowl in 1967. In 1970, the leagues merged. In 2002, the Houston Texans join the NFL, and the AFC and NFC were realigned into four divisions of four teams.

BUCCANEERS SUPER IN BIG GAME

On January 26, 2003, the Tampa Bay Buccaneers outscored and out-muscled the Oakland Raiders 48-21, in Super Bowl XXXVII, played in San Diego, California. The Raider offense had a lot of trouble with the tough Buccaneer defense. The Bucs had 5 sacks and 5 interceptions, and held Oakland to 19 rushing yards. Free safety Dexter Jackson earned MVP honors by twice intercepting Rich Gannon, the regular season MVP.

Rich Gannon ▶

2002 NFL Leaders & Awards

RUSHING YARDS: Ricky Williams, Miami Dolphins • 1,853
RUSHING TDs: Priest Holmes, Kansas City Chiefs • 21
RECEPTIONS: Marvin Harrison, Indianapolis Colts • 143
RECEIVING YARDS: Marvin Harrison, Indianapolis Colts • 1,722
RECEIVING TDs: Terrell Owens, San Francisco 49ers • 13
PASSING YARDS: Rich Gannon, Oakland Raiders • 4,689
PASSER RATING: Chad Pennington, New York Jets • 104.2
PASSING TDs: Tom Brady, New England Patriots • 28
PASS INTERCEPTIONS: (tie) Rod Woodson, Oakland Raiders; Brian Kelly, Tampa Bay Buccaneers • 8
SACKS: Jason Taylor, Miami Dolphins • 18.5

2002 Associated Press Awards

Most Valuable Player:
Rich Gannon, Oakland Raiders

Offensive Player of the Year:
Priest Holmes, Kansas City Chiefs

Defensive Player of the Year:
Derrick Brooks, Tampa Bay Buccaneers

Coach of the Year:
Andy Reid, Philadelphia Eagles

Offensive Rookie of the Year:
Clinton Portis, Denver Broncos

Defensive Rookie of the Year:
Julius Peppers, Carolina Panthers

Comeback Player of the Year:
Tommy Maddox, Pittsburgh Steelers

WEB SITE http://www.nfl.com

DID YOU KNOW? *The Green Bay Packers were sponsored by the Indian Packing Company and later the Acme Packing Company. Both companies eventually went out of business, but the name "Packers" stuck.*

"The Greatest Game Ever Played" **December 28, 1958, NFL Championship, New York City (Yankee Stadium): Baltimore Colts 23, New York Giants 17.** With a 14-3 lead in the 3rd quarter, the Colts had the ball on the Giants' 1-yard line and seemed to be on their way to an easy win. But the Giants made a determined goal-line stand, got the ball on their own 5-yard line, and drove downfield for a TD. In the 4th quarter, Frank Gifford caught a TD pass to give the Giants a 17-14 lead. But Colts star quarterback Johnny Unitas passed his team down the field, completing 3 to Ray Berry for 62 yards. With 7 seconds left, the Colts kicked a field goal to force the first post-season overtime. In the extra period, the Giants punted and Unitas went to work. He took the Colts 80 yards before fullback Alan "The Horse" Ameche bulled into the end zone from the 1-yard line, to end what many still call "the greatest game ever played."

"The Ice Bowl" **December 31, 1967, NFL Championship, Green Bay, Wisconsin: Green Bay Packers 21, Dallas Cowboys 17.** It was 13 degrees below zero, with a windchill of –46 when the game started. Incredibly, 50,000 fans packed the stadium. The Packers, who were going for their third championship in a row, figured they had the advantage because they were used to the cold. They grabbed an early 14-0 lead, but they too were affected by the cold. Two fumbles in the second half led to a touchdown and a field goal for Dallas. Green Bay was down 17-14, with 4:50 remaining. Future Hall of Famer Bart Starr led his team down inside the one-yard line. There were 16 seconds left in the game, and the temperature had fallen to –18. The field was frozen solid. After two running plays went nowhere, Green Bay was out of time-outs. Everyone expected Starr to try a pass. If it failed, the clock would stop, and they could kick a field goal to tie. But Starr took the snap and made his now-famous dive for the touchdown, and the NFL Championship.

"The Immaculate Reception" **December 23, 1972, AFC Divisional Playoffs, Pittsburgh: Pittsburgh Steelers 13, Oakland Raiders 7.** Down 7-6, with just over a minute left, the Steelers' Terry Bradshaw fired a pass downfield to halfback John Fuqua, who was hit hard by Raiders defender Jack Tatum just as the ball arrived. It hit one of the players and bounced in the air and, luckily for the Steelers, into the hands of rookie running back Franco Harris. After his "immaculate reception," Harris ran 42 yards for a touchdown with 5 seconds left.

"The Catch" **January 10, 1982, NFC Championship Game, San Francisco: San Francisco 49ers 28, Dallas Cowboys 27.** The 49ers and Cowboys traded the lead six times. With less than five minutes to go and behind 27-21, the 49ers got the ball on their own 11-yard line. Led by quarterback Joe Montana, the Niners were able to move the ball to the Cowboys' six-yard line with 58 seconds left. Montana connected with receiver Dwight Clark, whose leaping catch (now frequently replayed) for the winning TD sent the 49ers to their first Super Bowl.

"The Comeback" **January 3, 1993, AFC Wild Card Game, Orchard Park, New York: Buffalo Bills 41, Houston Oilers 38 (OT).** Down 35-3 early in the third quarter, Buffalo backup quarterback Frank Reich (starter Jim Kelly was injured) went to work. The Bills scored an amazing five straight TDs to go ahead 38-35. Reich threw four TD passes, three of them to wide receiver Andre Reed. Houston's Al Del Greco tied the game with a field goal as the fourth quarter ended. In overtime, Buffalo's Nate Odomes picked off a Warren Moon pass. That set up Steve Christie's field goal, to end one of the NFL's greatest comebacks.

Pro Football Hall of Fame
Football's Hall of Fame in Canton, Ohio, was founded in 1963 by the National Football League to honor outstanding players, coaches, and contributors.

The class of 2003, including running back Marcus Allen, defensive end Elvin Bethea, guard Joe DeLamielleure, receiver James Lofton, and coach Hank Stram, were to be inducted into the hall in August 2003. **WEB SITE** *http://www.profootballhof.com*

COLLEGE FOOTBALL

College football is one of America's most colorful and exciting sports. The National Collegiate Athletic Association (NCAA), founded in 1906, oversees college football today.

In the Fiesta Bowl in Tempe, Arizona, the Ohio State Buckeyes defeated the Miami Hurricanes, 31-24, in two overtimes to win the national championship on January 3, 2003.

2002 TOP 5 COLLEGE TEAMS
Chosen by the Associated Press Poll and the USA Today/ESPN Poll

Rank	AP	USA Today/ESPN
❶	Ohio St.	Ohio St.
❷	Miami (FL)	Miami (FL)
❸	Georgia	Georgia
❹	USC	USC
❺	Oklahoma	Oklahoma

HEISMAN TROPHY
The 2002 winner was quarterback **Carson Palmer** from the University of Southern California. The 6'5", 225-pound senior threw for 303 yards and a TD as the Trojans defeated the Iowa Hawkeyes, 38-17 in the Orange Bowl. Carson was born on December 27, 1979, in Laguna Niguel, California. He is the fifth Trojan to win the Heisman. In the 2003 NFL Draft, Carson was the #1 pick, taken by the Cincinnati Bengals.

GREAT COLLEGE FOOTBALL MOMENTS

January 2, 1984, Orange Bowl: Miami 31, Nebraska 30. The underdog Miami Hurricanes led the top-ranked, undefeated Nebraska Cornhuskers, 17-0. But the 'Huskers didn't give up—they even scored a TD on a trick play known as the "fumblerooski." The quarterback put the ball on the ground, where it was picked up by a lineman who ran it into the end zone. Miami still led 31-17 in the fourth quarter, but Nebraska scored two more TDs to pull within a point of the 'Canes. After their final score, Nebraska tried a two-point conversion that would have given them the win. But the quarterback's pass was blocked, and Miami got the victory and a national championship.

January 2, 1987, Fiesta Bowl: Penn State 14, Miami 10. The heavily favored Miami Hurricanes were ranked No. 1, and Penn State Nittany Lions were No. 2. Both teams had perfect 11-0 records going into the game, which would decide the national champion. Miami's offense outgained Penn State's 445 yards to 162. But Miami quarterback Vinny Testaverde was sacked four times and threw five interceptions, including one at the Penn State six-yard line with less than 20 seconds left.

January 3, 2003, Fiesta Bowl: Ohio State 31, Miami (FL) 24 (2OT). Defending national champ Miami had not lost in 34 straight games. Miami trailed most of the game until Todd Sievers tied it up at 17 with a field goal on the last play. In overtime, Miami scored as Ken Dorsey threw to tight end Kellen Winslow Jr. After an incomplete pass on 4th down, it seemed that Ohio State had lost. But a pass interference penalty was called on Miami, and three plays later Ohio State quarterback Craig Krenzel scored. In the second overtime, Maurice Clarett scored on a 5-yard run for Ohio State. Miami got to the 1-yard line, but couldn't score. Result: Buckeye Championship!

GOLF

Golf began in Scotland as early as the 1400s. The first golf course in the U.S. opened in 1888 in Yonkers, NY. The sport has grown to include both men's and women's professional tours. And millions play golf just for fun.

The men's tour in the U.S. is run by the Professional Golf Association (PGA). The four major championships (with the year first played) are:

British Open (1860)
United States Open (1895)
PGA Championship (1916)
Masters Tournament (1934)

The women's tour in the U.S. is guided by the Ladies Professional Golf Association (LPGA). The four major championships are:

United States Women's Open (1946)
McDonalds LPGA Championship (1955)
Nabisco Championship (1972)
*Women's British Open (1976)

*Replaced the du Maurier Classic as a major in 2001.

MAJOR WOW FOR WIE

In March 2003, crowds at the Kraft Nabisco Championship LPGA tour were wowed by 13-year-old golf sensation Michelle Wie, who finished ninth in her first major tournament. Not only is the 6-foot-tall eighth-grader from Hawaii taller than most people she meets, she can hit a ball farther than a lot of the best players in golf— about 300 yards! Michelle shot a third round 66 to set a record for an amateur playing in a major tournament. That score earned her the chance to play in the final group with Annika Sorenstam, one of the LPGA's best. Michelle started playing golf at age four, and won Hawaii's most important golf event—the Jennie K.—at 11 years old. She hopes to attend Stanford University, just like her idol, Tiger Woods. B.J., her father, admits she needs to work on her strategy, but says that all of the recent attention makes her work harder. And he should know—he's her caddie.

GYMNASTICS

It takes strength, coordination, and grace to become a top gymnast. Although the sport goes back to ancient Greece, modern-day gymnastics began in Sweden in the early 1800s. The sport has been part of the Olympics since 1896. The first World Gymnastic Championships were held in Antwerp, Belgium, in 1903. For the 100th anniversary in 2003, the competition was set to be held in Anaheim, California, August 15-24.

Men today compete in the All-Around, High Bar, Parallel Bars, Rings, Vault, Pommel Horse, Floor Exercises, and Team Combined. The women's events are the All-Around, Uneven Parallel Bars, Balance Beam, Floor Exercises, and Team Combined. In rhythmic gymnastics, women compete in All-Around, Rope, Hoop, Ball, Clubs, and Ribbon.

ICE HOCKEY

SPORTS

Ice hockey began in Canada in the mid-1800s. The National Hockey League (NHL) was formed in 1916. In 2002, the NHL had 30 teams—24 in the U.S. and 6 in Canada.

The Detroit Red Wings won their 10th Stanley Cup in 2002. Only Montreal (23) and Toronto (14) have won more NHL titles. The Red Wings lost the first game of the Cup final, then stormed back to defeat the Carolina Hurricanes four straight times. Detroit defenseman Nicklas Lidstrom became the first European player to win the Conn Smythe Trophy as most valuable player in the playoffs.

SEASON	WINNER	RUNNER-UP
1990-91	Pittsburgh Penguins	Minnesota North Stars
1991-92	Pittsburgh Penguins	Chicago Black Hawks
1992-93	Montreal Canadiens	Los Angeles Kings
1993-94	New York Rangers	Vancouver Canucks
1994-95	New Jersey Devils	Detroit Red Wings
1995-96	Colorado Avalanche	Florida Panthers
1996-97	Detroit Red Wings	Philadelphia Flyers
1997-98	Detroit Red WIngs	Washington Capitals
1998-99	Dallas Stars	Buffalo Sabres
1999-2000	New Jersey Devils	Dallas Stars
2000-2001	Colorado Avalanche	New Jersey Devils
2001-2002	Detroit Red Wings	Carolina Hurricanes

The Adventures of LORD STANLEY'S CUP

In 1892, Lord Stanley, the British governor general of Canada, bought a silver cup (actually a bowl) as an annual prize for the best amateur hockey team in Canada.

Today, NHL champions have their names engraved on one of the silver rings around the cup's base. When all the bands are filled, the oldest one is retired to the Hockey Hall of Fame and a new ring is added.

The Stanley Cup is the only professional sports trophy that each player on the winning team gets to take home. The Cup has had so many interesting adventures that it now travels with an escort from the Hockey Hall of Fame at all times. Here are a few cup stories:

► In 1905, the cup was left overnight on the Rideau Canal in Ottawa, Canada. It had been drop-kicked into the canal on a bet. Luckily, the water was frozen and the Ottawa players were able to get the cup back the next day.

► In 1924, some Montreal players on the way to a victory party took the cup out of the trunk to change a tire. When they got to the party they realized they had left the cup in a snow bank by the side of the road. It was still there when they went back for it.

► In 1997, the cup made its first trip to Russia, with Detroit players Slava Fetisov, Slava Kozlov, and Igor Larionov. They paraded it through Moscow's Red Square. Larionov, Pavel Datsyuk, and Maxim Kuznetsov took the cup back to Russia in 2002.

► On November 8, 2002, the Detroit Red Wings took the cup to visit President George W. Bush at the White House.

HIGHLIGHTS OF THE 2002-2003 NHL SEASON

POINTS LEADER: Peter Forseberg, Colorado Avalanche • games: 75, Points: 106 (29 goals)

GOALS LEADER: Milan Hejduk, Colorado Avalanche • games: 82, Goals: 50

ASSISTS LEADER: Peter Forseberg, Colorado Avalanche • games: 75, Assists: 77

GOALIE WINS: Martin Brodeur, New Jersey Devils • games: 73, Wins: 41

HOCKEY HALL OF FAME
The Hockey Hall of Fame in Toronto, Ontario, Canada, was opened in 1961 to honor hockey greats. **WEB SITE** http://www.hhof.com

THE OLYMPIC GAMES

The first Olympics were held in Greece more than 2,500 years ago. In 776 B.C. they featured just one event—a footrace. Boxing, wrestling, chariot racing, and the pentathlon (which consists of five different events) came later. The Olympic Games were held every four years for more than 1,000 years, until A.D. 393, when a Roman emperor stopped them.

2004 SUMMER OLYMPICS:
ATHENS, GREECE

The Olympic Games were born in ancient Greece, and the first modern Games were held in Athens in 1896. In 2004, 10,500 athletes and 3,000 officials representing 199 teams are expected to attend the 28th Olympiad from August 13 through the 29th. There will be 301 events in 28 sports. The mascots are Phevos and Athena, who are brother and sister. They are named after two ancient Greek gods: Phevos or Phoebus (a name for Apollo), god of light and music, and Athena, goddess of wisdom and the patron of the city of Athens. The emblem of the Athens Olympics is an olive wreath, or *kotinos*, which was the award given to winners in the ancient games. The next Olympics will be held in Turin, Italy (Winter 2006), and in Beijing, China (Summer 2008).

All About... SNOWBOARDING

The U.S. dominated the snowboarding halfpipe competition at the 2002 Olympics. Vermont's Kelly Clark, 18, won the women's competition, making her the first American gold medalist of the Games. In the men's event, Ross Powers, Danny Kass, and Jarret Thomas stomped the competition. Their tricks were sick, their air was big, and they took gold, silver, and bronze! In the men's parallel giant slalom, American Chris Klug took a bronze medal just 19 months after he had a life-saving liver transplant.

The history of snowboards goes back to 1965, when Sherman Poppen produced a "Snurfer." It was just two skis bolted together, with a rope on the front to hold on to. Jake Burton had a Snurfer when he was a teenager, and in 1977 he started a company—Burton Snowboards—to improve on the concept. It took more than 100 different designs before Burton got the "snowboard" he wanted. Out west, another pioneering "snow-surfer," Tom Sims—of Sims Snowboards—was building boards as well. But it wasn't until 1983, when Stratton Mountain Resort in Vermont finally allowed snowboards on the slopes, that the sport really began to grow. Other resorts soon followed, and today resorts that don't allow snowboards are rare. Snowboarding became an Olympic sport in 1998.

SOME MODERN OLYMPIC FIRSTS

1896 — The first modern Olympic Games were held in Athens, Greece. A total of 312 athletes from 13 nations participated in nine sports.

1900 — Women competed in the Olympic Games for the first time.

1908 — For the first time, medals were awarded to the first three people to finish each event—a gold for first, a silver for second, and a bronze for third.

1920 — The Olympic flag was raised for the first time, and the Olympic oath was introduced. The five interlaced rings of the flag represent: Africa, America, Europe, Asia, and Australia.

1924 — The first Winter Olympics, featuring skiing and skating events, were held.

The Olympic flame was introduced at the Olympic Games. A relay of runners carries a torch with the flame from Olympia, Greece, to the site of each Olympics.

1994 — Starting with the 1994 Winter Olympics, the winter and summer Games have alternated every two years, instead of being held in the same year, every fourth year.

2004 Summer Olympic Sports

Archery
Badminton
Baseball
Basketball
Boxing
Canoe/Kayak
 (slalom, sprint)
Cycling
 (road, mountain bike, track)
Diving
Equestrian
 (dressage, jumping, 3-day event)

Fencing
Field Hockey
Football (Soccer)
Gymnastics
 (artistic, rhythmic, trampoline)
Handball
Judo
Modern Pentathlon
 (show jumping, running, fencing, pistol shooting, swimming—one event per day for 5 days)
Rowing
Sailing
Shooting

Softball
Swimming
Synchronized Swimming
Table Tennis
 (Ping-Pong)
Taekwondo
Tennis
Track and Field
Triathlon
Volleyball
 (beach, indoor)
Water Polo
Weightlifting
Wrestling

WHO AM I?

I was born on September 12, 1913, in Oakville, Alabama. I am often said to be the greatest track and field athlete of all time. In college, I once set 3 world records in a span of 70 minutes. At the 1936 Summer Olympics in Berlin, Germany, I won 4 gold medals for the United States and set a world record in the 100-yard dash. For my athletic achievements on behalf of the nation, I was awarded the Medal of Freedom by President Gerald Ford in 1976.

Answer: Jesse Owens

SOCCER

Soccer, also called football outside the U.S., is the number one sport worldwide, played by the most people, and in almost every country. More than 240 million people play organized soccer, according to a 2000 survey done by FIFA (Fédération Internationale de Football Association), the sport's international governing body. That's one out of every 25 people on the planet. The survey also found that more than 20 million women play soccer. Countries with the highest number of regular adult soccer players were the United States, about 18 million; Indonesia, 10 million; Mexico, 7.4 million; China, 7.2 million; Brazil, 7 million; and Germany, 6.3 million.

THE WORLD CUP

Mia Hamm

Sixteen countries are scheduled to compete in the 2003 Women's World Cup in China, September 23 through October 11. On May 3, 2003, FIFA decided to move the event from Asia due to health concerns over the ongoing SARS epidemic in that region. The Asian Women's World Cup qualifying series was to have been in Bangkok, Thailand, in April 2003, but it was postponed. Officials named Australia, Brazil, or the United States as the most likely countries to host the 2003 World Cup. A decision on the new location of the World Cup was expected by June.

The U.S. hosted and won the 1999 World Cup. The U.S. also won the first-ever Women's World Cup in 1991. Norway won it in 1995. In 2003, the U.S. will have five returning veteran players from those two championship teams: Brandi Chastain, Joy Fawcett, Julie Foudy, Mia Hamm, and Kristine Lilly.

MEN'S WORLD CUP In 2002, soccer superpower Brazil won 7 straight matches, including a 2-0 win over Germany in the final on June 30. It was a record fifth World Cup championship for Brazil. The U.S. team had one of its best showings ever. The U.S. defeated Mexico, 2-0, before losing 1-0 to Germany in the quarterfinals. Brazilian forward Ronaldo won the Golden Shoe for most goals, 8, including 2 in the final. Germany's Oliver Kahn became the first goalkeeper to win the Golden Ball as the tournament's best player.

Held every four years, the Men's World Cup is the biggest soccer tournament in the world. The first World Cup was held in Uruguay in 1930. The next men's World Cup is scheduled to be held in 12 cities in Germany in 2006. The final will be held in Berlin.

WUSA–WOMEN'S UNITED SOCCER ASSOCIATION

The Carolina Courage defeated the Washington Freedom, 3-2, in the WUSA Founders Cup II, played in Atlanta on August 24, 2002. Carolina forward Birgit Prinz, who scored 1 goal and set up another, was MVP of the game. Philadelphia's Marinette Pichon was the 2002 WUSA MVP and Offensive Player of the Year. **WEB SITE** http://www.wusa.com

MLS–MAJOR LEAGUE SOCCER

In their fourth trip, the Los Angeles Galaxy won their first MLS Cup championship, October 20, 2002, at Gillette Stadium in Foxboro, Massachusetts. The Galaxy beat the New England Revolution, 1-0, in sudden death overtime. Carlos Ruiz scored the winning goal in the 113th minute and was named MVP of the game. Ruiz was also MVP of the season. **WEB SITE** http://www.mlsnet.com

SPECIAL OLYMPICS

The Special Olympics is dedicated to "empowering individuals with mental retardation." It is the world's largest program of sports training and athletic competition for children and adults with special needs. Founded in 1968, Special Olympics International has offices in all 50 U.S. states and Washington, D.C., and throughout the world. The organization offers training and competition to 1.5 million athletes in 150 countries.

The first Special Olympics competition took place in Chicago in 1968. After national events in individual countries, Special Olympics International holds World Games. These alternate between summer and winter sports every two years. In March 2001, more than 2,500 athletes and coaches from 80 countries gathered in Anchorage, Alaska, for the World Winter Games. More than 7,000 athletes from 160 countries were expected at the 2003 World Summer Games in Dublin, Ireland, the first to be held outside of the U.S.

SPECIAL OLYMPICS OFFICIAL SPORTS

▶ **Winter:** alpine and cross-country skiing, figure and speed skating, floor hockey, snowshoeing, snowboarding

▶ **Summer:** aquatics (swimming and diving), athletics (track and field), basketball, bowling, cycling, equestrian, golf, gymnastics, powerlifting, roller skating, soccer, softball, tennis, volleyball

▶ **Demonstration sports:** badminton, bocce, sailing

For more information, contact Special Olympics International Headquarters, 1325 G Street NW, Suite 500, Washington, D.C. 20005. Phone: (202) 628-3630.

WEB SITE http://www.specialolympics.org

SWIMMING

When the modern Olympic Games began in Athens, Greece, in 1896, the only racing stroke was the breaststroke. Today, men and women at the Olympics swim the backstroke, breaststroke, butterfly, and freestyle, in events ranging from 50 meters to 1,500 meters.

SOME GREAT U.S. OLYMPIC SWIMMERS

Mark Spitz made history by winning seven gold medals at the 1972 Games in Munich. He won 11 medals—nine gold—in his Olympic career.

Matt Biondi won seven medals—five gold—at the 1988 Olympics in Seoul. He won eight gold medals, 11 overall, in his Olympic career from 1984 to 1992.

Janet Evans, at age 17, won three golds at the 1988 Olympics in Seoul. In 1992 she won another gold and a silver at Barcelona.

Dara Torres won five golds at the 2000 Games in Sydney, the most by a U.S. woman at one Olympiad. Seven years after retiring, she returned to become the first American to swim in four Olympics (1984, 1988, 1992, 2000).

Modern tennis began in 1873. It was based on court tennis. In 1877 the first championships were held in Wimbledon, near London. In 1881 the first official U.S. men's championships were held at Newport, Rhode Island. Six years later, the first women's championships took place, in Philadelphia. The four most important ("grand slam") tournaments today are the Australian Open, the French Open, the All-England (Wimbledon) Championships, and the U.S. Open.

Grand Slam Tournaments

ALL-TIME GRAND SLAM SINGLES WINNERS

MEN	Australian	French	Wimbledon	U.S.	Total
Pete Sampras (b. 1971)	2	0	7	5	14
Roy Emerson (b. 1936)	6	2	2	2	12
Bjorn Borg (b. 1956)	0	6	5	0	11
Rod Laver (b. 1938)	3	2	4	2	11
Bill Tilden (1893-1953)	*	0	3	7	10
WOMEN					
Margaret Smith Court (b. 1942)	11	5	3	5	24
Steffi Graf (b. 1969)	4	6	7	5	22
Helen Wills Moody (1905-1998)	*	4	8	7	19
Chris Evert (b. 1954)	2	7	3	6	18
Martina Navratilova (b. 1956)	3	2	9	4	18

*Never played in tournament.

SERENA SUPREME

In June 2002, Serena Williams, then 20 years old, won the French Open, defeating her older sister Venus, then 22 and the world's #1 player. Serena had lost to Venus in five of their last six matches against each other. In July, Serena faced Venus again in the final at Wimbledon, where Venus had been champion in 2000 and 2001. Serena won 7-6 (7-4), 6-3. The sisters faced each other again at the U.S. Open final in September. As she had been at Wimbledon, Venus was going for her third straight title. But Serena dominated again, winning 6-4, 6-3.

Serena had sprained her ankle a week before the 2002 Australian Open, missing her chance at a true "Grand Slam" (winning all four grand slam tournaments in a single year) for 2002. But she completed her own version—a "Serena Slam"—in February 2003 by defeating Venus at the Australian Open. Never in history had sisters met in four straight grand slam tournaments. No sisters had ever been ranked #1 and #2, either. Serena is only the sixth woman ever to hold all four titles at once, and the first since Steffi Graf in 1988.

◀ Serena (right) and Venus Williams

X GAMES

The X Games, founded by ESPN television executive Ron Semiao, were first held in June 1995 in Newport, Rhode Island. They originally featured skateboarding and BMX biking events. Considered the Olympics of action sports, the X Games include both summer and winter competitions, each held annually in the United States. Star athletes include skateboarder Tony Hawk, street luger Biker Sherlock, and BMX (bicycle) freestyler Dave Mirra.

2003 WINTER X GAMES

The seventh annual Winter X Games were held January 30-February 2 in Aspen, Colorado, with about 250 athletes from all over the world competing for medals and $500,000 in prizes. Events included Snowboarding, Skiing, Snowmobiling, and the Motocross (off-road motorcycling). Among the highlights: Shaun White scooping up two gold medals in the Men's Slopestyle and Superpipe snowboarding, and Gretchen Bleiler winning gold for the Women's Snowboarding Superpipe. Tanner Hall struck gold for the second straight year in the Ski Slopestyle event, and Blair Morgan won his third straight gold medal in the Snowmobiling SnoCross.

SUMMER X GAMES

The Summer X Games, held every year since 1995, feature competitions such as Bicycle Stunt, Skateboarding, Downhill BMX, Motocross (off-road motorcycling), In-Line Skating, Wakeboarding, Street Luging, and Speed Climbing. At the 2002 X Games held in Philadelphia in August, Mike Metzger pulled off back-to-back flips to earn his gold in the Motocross, Matt Hoffman amazed the crowds with his no-handed 900 in the BMX Vert finals, and Brazilian Rodil de Araujo Jr. won three gold medals for skateboarding. Fifteen-year-old Japanese In-Line skater Takeshi Yasutoko won gold (the youngest skater to medal at the X Games), and 14-year-old American Tori Allen held on to win gold in Speed Climbing.

In 2003, the Summer X Games were set to be held in Los Angeles, California, August 14-18.

WEB SITE *http://expn.go.com*

All About... TONY HAWK

Born in Carlsbad, California, in 1968, Tony Hawk is probably the world's most famous skateboarder. Since 1978, he's won many championships, as well as nine Summer X Games medals (5 gold, 3 silver, 1 bronze). Tony also invented nearly 50 maneuvers. He was ESPN's Alternative Athlete of the Year in 1999. That was the year he did "The 9" (a 900 degree aerial spin—that's 2.5 times around) at the X Games in San Francisco. It's a move that was once thought to be impossible!

Tony retired from competition in 2000, but he's still very involved in skateboarding. In 2002, he launched (and performed in) the first-ever Boom Boom HuckJam Arena Tour featuring bands and top skateboard, BMX, and motocross athletes. Another North American HuckJam tour was planned for the fall of 2003.

Transportation

A SHORT HISTORY OF TRANSPORTATION
WIND, WHEELS, AND WATER

Which Wright brother flew first, Wilbur or Orville?
•••
page 232

Sagres Two, *three-masted bark, Portugal* ▶

5000 B.C.
People harness animal-muscle power. Oxen and donkeys carry heavy loads.

3500 B.C.
Egyptians create the first sailboat. Before this, people made rafts or canoes and paddled them with poles or their hands.

1450s
Portuguese build fast ships with three masts. These plus the compass usher in an age of exploration.

1730s
Stagecoach service begins in the U.S.

1830
Passenger rail service begins in England with the *Rocket,* a steam train built by George Stephenson. It goes about 24 miles an hour.

5000 B.C.

3500 B.C.
In Mesopotamia (modern-day Iraq), people invent vehicles with wheels. But the first wheels are made of heavy wood, and the roads are terrible.

1100 B.C.
Chinese invent the magnetic compass. It allows them to sail long distances.

1660s
Horse-drawn stagecoaches begin running in France. They stop at stages to switch horses and passengers—the first mass transit system.

1769
James Watt patents the first successful steam engine.

1807
Robert Fulton patents a highly efficient steamboat.

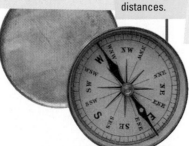

AGE OF MACHINES

1903
At Kitty Hawk, North Carolina, the Wright brothers fly the first powered heavier-than-air machine.

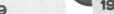

1939
The first practical helicopter and first jet plane are invented. The jet flies up to 434 mph. Jet passenger service began in 1958.

1981
The Space Shuttle *Columbia* is the first reusable spacecraft with a human crew.

1997
British driver Andy Green breaks the sound barrier on land for the first time, going 763 mph.

1839
Kirkpatrick Macmillan of Scotland invents the first pedaled bicycle.

1908
Henry Ford builds the first Model T, a practical car for the general public.

1961
Russian cosmonaut Yuri Gagarin orbits the Earth in a spaceship.

1862
Étienne Lenoir of Belgium builds the first car with an internal-combustion engine.

1869
Transcontinental railroad is completed at Promontory Point, Utah.

▼ *Replica of Union Pacific's Locomotive No. 119*

1947
Flying 700 mph, U.S. Air Force Capt. Charles "Chuck" Yeager breaks the sound barrier in the jet-powered Bell X-1.

1969
U.S. astronauts aboard *Apollo 11* land on the Moon.

2000
Amtrak runs its northeast high-speed *Acela* train. It can go 150 miles an hour.

IF AT FIRST YOU DON'T SUCCEED... *In 2002, after five failed attempts in 10 years, Chicago businessman Steve Fossett became the first person to fly around the world alone in a balloon. (Bertrand Piccard and Brian Jones had done it together in 1999.) Steve took off from western Australia in his balloon,* Spirit of Freedom, *on June 19. The balloon, filled with helium and hot air, was 140 ft. high and 60 ft. wide. His average altitude was 5 to 6 miles above sea level, where temperatures outside his closet-sized cabin were 30 to 50 degrees below zero. He traveled 21,110 miles in the balloon (a record), and stayed up for 14 days and 20 hours, landing back in Australia, in a remote desert area, on July 4.*

Did You Know?

TRAINS

▲ *Bullet trains, Tokyo Station*

The first successful steam locomotive was built in England in 1804. Richard Trevithick's engine pulled 24,000 pounds of iron, 70 men, and 5 wagons along a 9.5-mile track. In 1830 the **Baltimore and Ohio** introduced America's first steam locomotive, the **"Tom Thumb,"** to haul both passengers and freight. America's first transcontinental railroad was built from 1862 to 1869. Other railroad lines soon followed. In 1893, the first **electrified rail line** went into service, in Baltimore. **Diesel engines** were introduced in 1928, and **streamlined** trains began to appear in 1934.

The most famous modern high-speed train is the **Shinkansen (Bullet Train),** introduced in Japan in 1964. It can go as fast as 130 miles per hour. In 1981 France launched the **Train à Grande Vitesse (TGV),** which runs commercially at speeds of up to 186 mph. In the U.S. in 2000, Amtrak introduced **Acela Express** 150-mph high-speed service between Boston and Washington, D.C. Japan Railway is testing **Maglev** (MAGnetic LEVitation) trains. These use huge magnetic forces to lift trains above the track and send them forward on electical currents. The lack of friction helps them cruise at speeds of around 280 mph, and they have reached a record speed of 343 mph.

Autos

In 1886 **Gottlieb Daimler** patented a three-wheeled motor carriage in Germany. That same year, **Karl Benz** produced his first successful gasoline-powered vehicle. **John W. Lambert** of Ohio made the first gas-powered automobile in the U.S. in 1891.

Five years later, the **Duryea Brothers** of Springfield, Massachusetts, started the first car manufacturing company in the U.S. **Henry Ford** came soon after. His production of the Model T using an assembly line in 1913 revolutionized the automobile industry, making cars affordable for large numbers of people. Many improvements were made over the years, such as the first aerodynamically designed car, the **Chrysler Airflow** (1934), and air-conditioning, introduced by the Packard company in 1940. Ferdinand Porsche's **Volkswagen** "beetle," mass-produced after World War II, was one of the most popular cars in history.

▲ *1911 Ford Model T*

Today, fuel efficiency is a big goal. The most fuel-efficient cars sold today are **gas-electric hybrids**. These can get up to 60 miles per gallon, using both a gas and an electric engine. When the gas engine runs, it charges batteries for the electric engine, which is used for slow speeds or to boost the gas engine. A computer decides which engine to use.

Nonpolluting electric cars powered by **hydrogen fuel cells** are promising, but you won't see many on the road for a long time. A prototype built by Ford cost $5 million.

▶ *Isuzu 4200 R showcar*

AIR

EARLY AIRCRAFT

▲ *Boeing 747*

In 1783, the **Montgolfier brothers** flew the first hot air balloon over Paris. Another Frenchman, **Henri Giffard,** flew the first dirigible (blimp) in 1852. It was powered by steam. The first **heavier-than-air flying machine** was also steam-powered. **Samuel P. Langley** of the Smithsonian Institution in Washington, D.C., built a model plane with a 12-foot wingspan that flew nearly a mile in 1896. **Wilbur and Orville Wright** had also been experimenting with heavier-than-air machines. In 1903 they traveled from their bicycle shop in Dayton, Ohio, to Kitty Hawk, North Carolina. Here they made 4 successful manned flights on December 17, launching the air age.

MILESTONES IN AVIATION
Airlines were first developed in the U.S. to carry mail. **Transcontinental service** was launched in 1921, **bringing mail** from San Francisco to New York in 33 hours—3 times faster than by train. By 1926, regular airmail service was in place, and a pilot named Charles A. Lindbergh was flying the Chicago-to-St. Louis route. **Passenger service** was well under way by 1930.

Aircraft continued to get bigger and faster. In 1936, the DC-3 set a record flying from Los Angeles to Newark, New Jersey, in 13 hours and 4 minutes. In 1959 the **Boeing 707** was launched. It was the first successful passenger jet. The Boeing 707 could carry 180 passengers at 550 miles per hour—about 225 mph faster than propeller-powered airliners. One of the most famous airliners to be developed was the **Boeing 747** "jumbo jet," introduced in 1969. Cruising at 566 mph, it can carry about 500 passengers.

SEA

Ships are used for many activities, from fishing, to vacationing, to exploration, to war. But their most important job has always been carrying cargo. The Egyptians were building reed and wooden sailboats some 5,000 years ago. They also built wooden **barges** over 200 feet long that could carry close to 2,000,000 pounds of cargo.

By the 1500s, huge sailing ships called **galleons** were hauling cargo around the world. Spanish galleons carried gold, spices, and other riches back to Europe from South America. These ships had to be big and needed cannons to defend themselves from pirates. Later cargo ships did without cannons. **Packet ships** began regularly scheduled passenger service across the Atlantic in 1818. In the 1840s, the U.S. built the first **clipper ships.** With a slender hull and many sails, they were the fastest ships of the pre-steam era.

The **world's biggest ship** today is the supertanker *Jahre Viking*. It's 1,502 feet long. That's longer than the Empire State building is tall. The *Jahre Viking* can carry 4.2 million barrels of oil. The *Queen Mary 2*, scheduled to set sail for New York in December 2003, will be the largest passenger ship ever. It will be 23 stories high and 1,131 feet long. That's almost 150 feet longer than the height of Eiffel Tower.

▶ *A clipper ship*

WHY IS IT 4 A.M. IN LOS ANGELES WHEN IT'S 7 A.M. IN NEW YORK?

When the sun rises on the east coast, it's still dark in the central states, and the farther west you go, the farther away you are from daybreak. Before the mid-1800s, traveling east or west was so slow that it was possible to use the local time set by each city. But when the railroads came, people could travel hundreds of miles in a day. Organizing a schedule using many different times was nearly impossible. No one could ever agree what time it was! Railroads had to have a system of **standard time** and **time zones.** The familiar time zones of Eastern, Central, Mountain, and Pacific were adopted by railroads in the U.S. and Canada in 1883.

The next year, 24 international time zones—one for each hour of the day—were established. These begin at the **prime meridian,** the longitude line passing through Greenwich, England. Halfway around the world, in the Pacific Ocean, is the **International Date Line,** which roughly follows the 180th meridian and is in the 12th time zone. Cross the line going west, and it's tomorrow. Going east, the date is one day earlier.

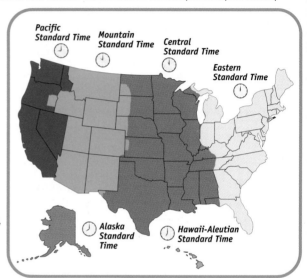

Pacific Standard Time Mountain Standard Time Central Standard Time Eastern Standard Time Alaska Standard Time Hawaii-Aleutian Standard Time

THE AIR AGE BEGINS

ORVILLE AND WILBUR WRIGHT were successful printers and bicycle makers in Dayton, Ohio, but what they really wanted to do was fly. On September 25, 1903, they arrived in Kitty Hawk, North Carolina, and started preparing for their historic flight. The brothers had been testing their aircraft in Kitty Hawk since 1900, but this time they felt the design would work.

THE 1903 FLYER was a skeletal flying machine built of spruce and ash. The 40-foot-long wings were covered with cotton cloth. It had a 12-horsepower gasoline engine and weighed just over 600 lbs. The Flyer was ready on December 14. Wilbur won a coin toss and took the controls. The first try was a failure. The Flyer stalled on takeoff and did not get off the ground. But three days later, the plane was ready for another attempt. It was Orville's turn to take the controls.

About 10:35 A.M. on December 17, the Flyer lifted into the air in the face of a gusting wind. For 12 breathtaking seconds, Orville flew the aircraft. It traveled 120 ft. before landing with a skid. The brothers flew three more times that morning. On the fourth flight, the Flyer was damaged, bringing an important day in aviation history to an end.

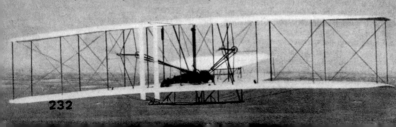

Travel

Where is the world's biggest Ferris wheel?
••• page 236

ROADSIDE AMERICA–ROUTE 66

More than any other invention, the automobile changed American society. Henry Ford's assembly-line production made cars so inexpensive that by the 1920s many Americans could afford one.

With cars came a new freedom. People wanted to go places—especially west. New and better roads had to be built. One of the most famous is a legendary road that passes diagonally through the heart of the country, from Chicago to Los Angeles. It started out as the National Old Trails Road. In 1926, when paving began, it became **Route 66**.

Beginning in the late 1950s, Route 66's 2,400 miles were bypassed section by section as interstate highways were built. When the last stretch of interstates was finished in 1984, Route 66 was officially retired and is now called **Historic Route 66**.

People still travel along Route 66. Billboards and giant statues advertise famous hotels, restaurants, and diners. If you take this route, here are just a few points of interest nearby:

ILLINOIS Since 1891, Funks Grove (near Bloomington) has been offering "Pure Maple Sirup." Yes, that *is* how they spell it.

MISSOURI Check out Meramec Caverns and the Jesse James Museum in Stanton, or the St. Louis Car Museum.

OKLAHOMA Near Tulsa, you can visit one of the world's largest gun collections at the J. M. Davis Arms and Historical Museum. See more than 20,000 guns, including a 500-year-old Chinese hand cannon and a rifle from 1570.

TEXAS As you cross the Texas Panhandle, you'll pass Tex, the 47-foot-tall cowboy, near the town of Canyon. In McLean, check out the Devil's Rope Museum (see page 126).

NEW MEXICO Take a detour to Four Corners Monument—the only place in the U.S. where you can stand in four states (Arizona, Colorado, New Mexico, and Utah) at once!

ARIZONA Near Flagstaff, visit the Grand Canyon, or Arizona's second most famous hole in the ground, Barringer Meteorite Crater (nearly a mile wide and 570 feet deep).

CALIFORNIA Near Barstow is the Calico Ghost Town, founded in 1881. The 500 nearby mines produced $86 million in silver and $45 million in borax (used mainly for cleaning products) before the town was abandoned in 1907.

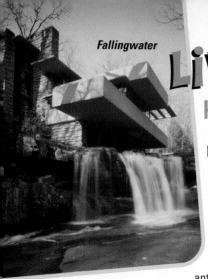
Fallingwater

LIVING IN STYLE!
HISTORIC AMERICAN HOMES AND HOTELS

Pack your suitcase. It's vacation time! How would you like to visit some of these cool places?

THE BREAKERS (NEWPORT, RI) In the late 1800s, the wealthiest families in America competed in building luxurious summer homes called "cottages." Railway heir Cornelius Vanderbilt II built The Breakers in 1895-96 to be the greatest of them all. This 70-room Italian Renaissance mansion features a state dining room fit for princes, and a reception room with antiques once owned by French Queen Marie Antoinette.

FALLINGWATER (MILL RUN, PA) Imagine living over a waterfall. You could if you stayed at Fallingwater, the vacation home designed by architect Frank Lloyd Wright in 1935 for the Edgar J. Kaufmann family of Pittsburgh. Rather than building a house with a view of the waterfall (as the family requested), Wright put the house *over* the falls. Fallingwater rises over 30 feet above the waterfall of a stream called Bear Run, and several balconies stretch out over the stream.

GRAND HOTEL (MACKINAC ISLAND, MI) Guests have stayed at the 300-room Grand Hotel since 1887. Its 660-foot-long front porch comes into view as you approach from Lake Michigan. You might feel as if you've traveled back in time when you've taken the ferry to Mackinac Island. You can visit historical sites and see how people lived in the late 1800s. Private motorized vehicles are barred, and people get around by horse and carriage or bicycle.

HEARST CASTLE (SAN SIMEON, CA) Newspaper publisher William Randolph Hearst called it "La Cuesta Encantada"—the enchanted hill—and it is truly a fantasy come to life. Roam through the luxurious rooms filled with rich tapestries and artwork from Gothic castles. Tour the gardens, terraces, and pool areas outside—all of which have a view of the Pacific. You may even catch a glimpse of some of the zebras, left over from a zoo that closed down there in 1937.

▼ HOTEL DEL CORONADO (CORONADO, CA) Railroad tycoon Elisha Babcock created this resort hotel in 1888. Featuring sweeping views of the Pacific Ocean, "The Del" was one of the biggest wooden structures of its time and the largest electrically lit building outside New York City. Thomas Edison is said to have personally supervised installation of the lamps.

MONTICELLO (CHARLOTTESVILLE, VA) Besides being a statesman Thomas Jefferson was a very good architect. He designed his beautiful home, Monticello, and spent a good 40 years fixing it up. There are many clever gadgets, including a new kind of plow and a "wheel cipher," for putting messages in code. The staircases are mostly hidden, and a bed built in between two different rooms allowed him to roll out on either side.

Parthenon ▶

WORLD CITIES

ATHENS Towering above this ancient city is the mighty **Acropolis,** a 500-foot-high sandstone hill. On top of it are the ruins of the **Parthenon** and the **Temple of Athena Nike.** Both of these temples were built almost 2,500 years ago in honor of the goddess Athena. The first modern Summer Olympics were held here in 1896, and the city will again host this event 2004.

Big Ben & Houses of Parliament

BEIJING China's capital is one of the world's most populated cities. Two of its biggest attractions are **"The Forbidden City"** and the nearby **Great Wall.** For over 500 years, the only people allowed in The Forbidden City were emperors of the Ming and Qing dynasties. It's now called the **Palace Museum,** and anyone can visit. The year 2008 would be a good time to go to Beijing. That's when this city will host the Summer Olympics.

LONDON Ride the **double-decker buses**—on the left side of the street!—from the ancient **Tower of London** to the sleek new Ferris wheel called the **London Eye.** Or go underground to the secret rooms where British government officials hid out in World War II.

Eiffel Tower

NEW YORK Take the elevator to the top of the **Empire State Building** for a bird's-eye view of this huge city. Get a look at the past when you walk through **South Street Seaport.** See the dinosaurs at the **American Museum of Natural History.** Pet the real live zoo animals in **Central Park** and ride on the carousel. And don't forget the ferry to the **Statue of Liberty.**

PARIS A short walk from the cathedral of **Notre Dame** are the lively cafés of the **Left Bank.** After climbing the steps of Sacre Coeur in hilly **Montmartre,** enjoy a boat ride along the **Seine,** or visit the **Eiffel Tower** and look down below at where you've been.

PRAGUE This capital of the Czech Republic is one of the prettiest in all of Europe, and was spared from destruction in World War II. On both sides of the Vltava River that divides the city are many large buildings, towers, and cathedrals. In fact, the city's nickname is the **"City of 100 Spires,"** though there really more than that. You won't want to miss **Prague Castle**—it's been around since the 9th century. At 1,870 ft. long and 420 ft. wide, it's one of the largest ancient castles in the world.

ROME Pretend you're a gladiator at the **Colosseum** or explore the underground **Catacombs** or the ruins of the ancient **Forum.** Back on the street, watch out for those motorbikes!

TORONTO One thing you can't miss in this Canadian city is the **CN Tower** (see page 48). At 1,815 ft., it's the tallest freestanding structure in the world. Hockey fans won't want to miss the **Hockey Hall of Fame.** Toronto is a popular place to film movies and TV shows. Many movies that are set in U.S. cities have actually been filmed here. For example, the box office smash *My Big Fat Greek Wedding* was set in Chicago, but was mostly filmed in Toronto.

AMUSEMENT PARKS: THEN & NOW

Today's parks feature bright lights, food, fun, and lots of thrilling rides. But the first amusement parks, which appeared in Europe over 400 years ago, were very different. Attractions included flower gardens, bowling, music, and a few simple rides.

The first real roller coaster in the U.S. was the Switchback Gravity Pleasure Railway. It opened in Brooklyn's Coney Island in 1884 and went all of 6 miles per hour! In 1893, the **George Ferris Great Wheel** was introduced in Chicago. The "Ferris" Wheel weighed over 4 million pounds and stood 264 feet high. A year later, Chutes Park opened in Chicago—the first park to charge admission.

In the 1920s, some of the best **roller coasters** of all time were built—reaching speeds of 60 mph. Some large cities had as many as six amusement parks. But the stock market crash and Great Depression in the 1930s caused many to close.

In 1955, **Disneyland** opened in Anaheim, California. Sections of the park, such as Tomorrowland and the Magic Kingdom, had their own themes, making it the country's first theme park.

These days amusement parks—and rides—are more popular than ever.

WORLD'S FASTEST ROLLER COASTERS*

1. **Top Thrill Dragster:** 120 mph, Sandusky, Ohio
2. **Dodonpa:** 107 mph, FujiYoshida-shi, Japan
3. **Superman: The Escape:** 100 mph, Valencia, California
   Tower of Terror: 100 mph, Gold Coast, Australia
5. **Steel Dragon 2000:** 95 mph, Mie, Japan
6. **Millennium Force:** 92 mph, Sandusky, Ohio

WORLD'S TALLEST ROLLER COASTERS*

1. **Top Thrill Dragster:** 420 ft, Sandusky, Ohio
2. **Superman: The Escape:** 415 ft, Valencia, California
3. **Tower of Terror:** 377 ft, Gold Coast, Australia
4. **Steel Dragon 2000:** 318 ft, Mie, Japan
5. **Millennium Force:** 310 ft, Sandusky, Ohio

WORLD'S LONGEST ROLLER COASTERS*

1. **Steel Dragon 2000:** 8,133 ft, Mie, Japan
2. **The Ultimate:** 7,450 ft, North Yorkshire, Englar
3. **The Beast:** 7,400 ft, Cincinnati, Ohio
4. **Son of Beast:** 7,032 ft, Cincinnati, Ohio
5. **Millennium Force:** 6,595 ft, Sandusky, Ohio

*Rankings as of mid-2003. For more information check out www.ultimaterollercoaster.com

Top Thrill Dragster

FABULOUS FACTS

Biggest park: Walt Disney World, Lake Buena Vista, Florida, 28,000 acres

Most rides: 58 (41 major rides, 17 family "kiddie" rides), Blackpool Pleasure Beach, Blackpool, England

Most roller coasters: 16, Cedar Point, Sandusky, Ohio, and Six Flags Magic Mountain, Valencia, California

Oldest Ferris wheel: Wonderland, Gaultier, Mississippi (It opened at Palace Amusements in New Jersey in 1895 and moved to Wonderland in 1990.)

Tallest Ferris wheel: 443 feet, London Eye (also known as the Millennium Wheel), London, England

United States

Who was the first woman elected to the Senate?
•••
page 252

FACTS & FIGURES

AREA	LAND	WATER	TOTAL
50 states and Washington, D.C.	3,537,440 square miles	256,648 square miles	3,794,085 square miles

POPULATION (mid-2003): 290,342,554   **CAPITAL:** Washington, D.C.

LARGEST, HIGHEST, AND OTHER STATISTICS

Sears Tower

Largest state: Alaska (663,267 square miles)
Smallest state: Rhode Island (1,545 square miles)
Northernmost city: Barrow, Alaska (71°17′ north latitude)
Southernmost city: Hilo, Hawaii (19°44′ north latitude)
Easternmost city: Eastport, Maine (66°59′05″ west longitude)
Westernmost city: Atka, Alaska (174°12′ west longitude)
Highest settlement: Climax, Colorado (11,360 feet)
Lowest settlement: Calipatria, California (184 feet below sea level)
Oldest national park: Yellowstone National Park (Idaho, Montana, Wyoming), 2,219,791 acres, established 1872
Largest national park: Wrangell-St. Elias, Alaska (8,323,148 acres)
Longest river system: Mississippi-Missouri-Red Rock (3,710 miles)
Deepest lake: Crater Lake, Oregon (1,932 feet)
Highest mountain: Mount McKinley, Alaska (20,320 feet)
Lowest point: Death Valley, California (282 feet below sea level)
Tallest building: Sears Tower, Chicago, Illinois (1,450 feet)
Tallest structure: TV tower, Blanchard, North Dakota (2,063 feet)
Longest bridge span: Verrazano-Narrows Bridge, New York (4,260 feet)
Highest bridge: Royal Gorge, Colorado (1,053 feet above water)

···INTERNATIONAL BOUNDARY LINES OF THE U.S.···

U.S.-Canadian border . . . . 3,987 miles
(excluding Alaska)
Alaska-Canadian border . . . . . 1,538 miles
U.S.-Mexican border . . . . 1,933 miles
(Gulf of Mexico to Pacific Ocean)

Atlantic coast . . . . 2,069 miles
Gulf of Mexico coast . . . . 1,631 miles
Pacific coast . . . . 7,623 miles
Arctic coast, Alaska . . . . 1,060 miles

Did You Know?

THE BIGGEST BUILDING *by volume in the U.S. (and the world) is the Boeing Factory in Everett, WA. It's only 11 stories high, but it has the most room inside—472 million cubic feet, to be exact. They build Boeing's big passenger jets there. You could fit 74 football fields, 900 basketball courts, or even Disneyland inside. That's bigger than the five-story Pentagon in Arlington, VA, which at 77 million cubic feet is the world's biggest office building.*

THE U.S. CONSTITUTION
THE FOUNDATION OF AMERICAN GOVERNMENT

The Constitution is the document that created the present government of the United States. It was written in 1787 and went into effect in 1789. It establishes the three branches of the U.S. government, which are the executive (headed by the president), the legislative (the Congress), and the judicial (the Supreme Court and other federal courts). The first 10 amendments to the Constitution (the Bill of Rights) explain the basic rights of all American citizens.

You can find the constitution on-line at:

WEB SITE http://www.house.gov/Constitution/Constitution.htm

THE PREAMBLE TO THE CONSTITUTION

The Constitution begins with a short statement called the Preamble. The Preamble states that the government of the United States was established by the people.

> "We, the people of the United States, in order to form a more perfect Union, establish justice, insure domestic tranquility, provide for the common defense, promote the general welfare, and secure the blessings of liberty to ourselves and our posterity do ordain and establish this Constitution for the United States of America."

THE ARTICLES

The original Constitution contained seven articles. The first three articles of the Constitution establish the three branches of the U.S. government.

Article 1, Legislative Branch Creates the Senate and House of Representatives and describes their functions and powers.

Article 2, Executive Branch Creates the office of the President and the Electoral College and lists their powers and responsibilities.

Article 3, Judicial Branch Creates the Supreme Court and gives Congress the power to create lower courts. The powers of the courts and certain crimes are defined.

Article 4, The States Discusses the relationship of the states to one another and to the citizens. Defines the states' powers.

Article 5, Amending the Constitution Describes how the Constitution can be amended (changed).

Article 6, Federal Law Makes the Constitution the supreme law of the land over state laws and constitutions.

Article 7, Ratifying the Constitution Establishes how to ratify (approve) the Constitution.

AMENDMENTS TO THE CONSTITUTION

The writers of the Constitution understood that it might need to be amended, or changed, in the future, but they wanted to be careful and made it hard to change. Article 5 describes how the Constitution can be amended.

In order to take effect, an amendment must be approved by a two-thirds majority in both the House of Representatives and the Senate. It must then be approved (ratified) by three-fourths of the states (38 states). So far, there have been 27 Amendments. One of them, (the 18th, ratified in 1919) banned the manufacture or sale of liquor. It was cancelled by the 21st Amendment, in 1933.

The Bill of Rights: The First Ten Amendments

The first ten amendments were adopted in 1791 and contain the basic freedoms Americans enjoy as a people. These amendments are known as the Bill of Rights.

1 Guarantees freedom of religion, speech, and the press.

2 Guarantees the right to have firearms.

3 Guarantees that soldiers cannot be lodged in private homes unless the owner agrees.

4 Protects people from being searched or having property searched or taken away by the government without reason.

5 Protects rights of people on trial for crimes.

6 Guarantees people accused of crimes the right to a speedy public trial by jury.

7 Guarantees the right to a trial by jury for other kinds of cases.

8 Prohibits "cruel and unusual punishments."

9 Says specific rights listed in the Constitution do not take away rights that may not be listed.

10 Establishes that any powers not given specifically to the federal government belong to states or the people.

Other Important Amendments

13 (1865): Ends slavery in the United States.

14 (1868): Bars states from denying rights to citizens; guarantees equal protection under the law for all citizens.

15 (1870): Guarantees that a person cannot be denied the right to vote because of race or color.

19 (1920): Gives women the right to vote.

22 (1951): Limits the president to two four-year terms of office.

24 (1964): Outlaws the poll tax (a tax people had to pay before they could vote) in federal elections. (The poll tax had been used to keep African Americans in the South from voting.)

25 (1967): Gives the president the power to appoint a new vice president, if one dies or leaves office in the middle of a term.

26 (1971): Lowers the voting age to 18 from 21.

SYMBOLS of the United States

THE GREAT SEAL

The Great Seal of the United States shows an American bald eagle with a ribbon in its mouth bearing the Latin words "e pluribus unum" (out of many, one). In its talons are the arrows of war and an olive branch of peace. On the back of the Great Seal is an unfinished pyramid with an eye (the eye of Providence) above it. The seal was approved by Congress on June 20, 1782.

THE FLAG

The flag of the United States has 50 stars (one for each state) and 13 stripes (one for each of the original 13 states). It is called unofficially the "Stars and Stripes."

The first U.S. flag was commissioned by the Second Continental Congress in 1777 but did not exist until 1783, after the American Revolution. Historians are not certain who designed the Stars and Stripes. Many different flags are believed to have been used during the American Revolution.

The flag of 1777 was used until 1795. In that year Congress passed an act ordering that a new flag have 15 stripes, alternate red and white, and 15 stars on a blue field. In 1818, Congress directed that the flag have 13 stripes and that a new star be added for each new state of the Union. The last star was added in 1960 for the state of Hawaii.

1777   **1795**   **1818**

There are many customs for flying the flag and treating it with respect. For example, it should not touch the floor and no other flag should be flown above it, except for the UN flag at UN headquarters. When the flag is raised or lowered, or passes in a parade, or during the Pledge of Allegiance, people should face it and stand at attention. Those in military uniform should salute. Others should put their right hand over their heart. The flag is flown at half staff as a sign of mourning.

PLEDGE OF ALLEGIANCE TO THE FLAG

"I pledge allegiance to the flag of the United States of America and to the republic for which it stands, one nation under God, indivisible, with liberty and justice for all."

THE NATIONAL ANTHEM

"The Star-Spangled Banner" was a poem written in 1814 by Francis Scott Key as he watched British ships bombard Fort McHenry, Maryland, during the War of 1812. It became the National Anthem by an act of Congress in 1931. The music to "The Star-Spangled Banner" was originally a tune called "Anacreon in Heaven."

The Executive Branch:

The **executive branch** of the federal government is headed by the president, who enforces the laws passed by Congress and is commander in chief of U.S. armed forces. It also includes the vice president, people who work for the president or vice president, the major departments of the government, and special agencies. The **cabinet** is made up of the vice president, heads of major departments, and other officials. It meets when the president chooses. The chart at right shows cabinet departments in the order in which they were created. The Department of Homeland Security was created by a law signed in November 2002.

PRESIDENT
VICE PRESIDENT
CABINET DEPARTMENTS

1. State
2. Treasury
3. Defense
4. Justice
5. Interior
6. Agriculture
7. Commerce
8. Labor
9. Housing and Urban Development
10. Transportation
11. Energy
12. Education
13. Health and Human Services
14. Veterans Affairs
15. Homeland Security

HOW LONG DOES THE PRESIDENT SERVE?
The president serves a four-year term, starting on January 20. No president can be elected more than twice.

WHAT HAPPENS IF THE PRESIDENT DIES?
If the president dies in office or cannot complete the term, the vice president becomes president. If the president is disabled, the vice president can become acting president. The next person to become president after the vice president would be the Speaker of the House of Representatives.

The White House has an address on the World Wide Web especially for kids. It is:
WEB SITE *http://www.whitehousekids.gov*

You can send e-mail to the president at:
EMAIL *president@whitehouse.gov*

The White House, home of the U.S. president

DID YOU KNOW?
To make room for his large family and staff, President Theodore Roosevelt moved his offices to a temporary one-story building that he had built just west of the White House in 1902. One hundred years later, that building, which houses the Oval Office, is known as the West Wing of the White House.

ELECTIONS
Electing a President

Every four years on the first Tuesday after the first Monday in November, American voters go to the polls and elect a president and vice president. Right? Well, sort of. The president and vice president are are not actually elected by a direct vote of the people. They are really elected by the 538 members of the Electoral College.

The Electoral College is not really a college, but a group of people chosen in each state. The writers of the Constitution did not agree on how a president should be selected. Some did not trust ordinary people to make a good choice. So they compromised and agreed to have the Electoral College do it.

In the early days electors voted for whomever they wanted. In modern times the political parties hold primary elections and conventions to choose candidates for president and vice president. When voters choose the candidates of a particular party, they are actually choosing electors from that party. But these electors have agreed to vote for their party's candidate, and except in very rare cases this is what they do.

In the map below, the numbers not in parentheses show how many electoral votes each state had in the 2000 election. In parentheses are the electoral votes states will have in the 2004 and 2008 elections.

THE ELECTORAL COLLEGE STATE BY STATE

The number of electors for each state is equal to the total number of senators (2), plus U.S. House members each has in Congress. In addition the District of Columbia has 3 electoral votes. The numbers of representatives for some states changed in 2002, because of 2000 Census results. So the numbers of electoral votes for the 2004 presidential elections will also change (new numbers are shown in parentheses). The electors chosen in November meet in state capitals in December. In almost all states, the party that gets the most votes in November wins all the electoral votes for the state. This happens even if the results of the election in the state are very close.

In January the electors' votes are officially opened during a special session of Congress. If no presidential candidate wins a majority of these votes, the House of Representatives chooses the president. This happened in 1800, 1824, and 1877.

Can a candidate who didn't win the most popular votes still win a majority of electoral votes? Yes. That's what happened in 1876, 1888, and again in 2000.

PRESIDENTS AND VICE PRESIDENTS OF THE UNITED STATES

PRESIDENT VICE PRESIDENT	YEARS IN OFFICE
❶ George Washington	1789–1797
John Adams	1789–1797
2 John Adams	1797–1801
Thomas Jefferson	1797–1801
❸ Thomas Jefferson	1801–1809
Aaron Burr	1801–1805
George Clinton	1805–1809
4 James Madison	1809–1817
George Clinton	1809–1812
Elbridge Gerry	1813–1814
❺ James Monroe	1817–1825
Daniel D. Tompkins	1817–1825
6 John Quincy Adams	1825–1829
John C. Calhoun	1825–1829
❼ Andrew Jackson	1829–1837
John C. Calhoun	1829–1832
Martin Van Buren	1833–1837
8 Martin Van Buren	1837–1841
Richard M. Johnson	1837–1841
❾ William H. Harrison	1841
John Tyler	1841
10 John Tyler	1841–1845
No Vice President	
⑪ James Knox Polk	1845–1849
George M. Dallas	1845–1849
12 Zachary Taylor	1849–1850
Millard Fillmore	1849–1850
⑬ Millard Fillmore	1850–1853
No Vice President	
14 Franklin Pierce	1853–1857
William R. King	1853
⑮ James Buchanan	1857–1861
John C. Breckinridge	1857–1861
16 Abraham Lincoln	1861–1865
Hannibal Hamlin	1861–1865
Andrew Johnson	1865
⑰ Andrew Johnson	1865–1869
No Vice President	
18 Ulysses S. Grant	1869–1877
Schuyler Colfax	1869–1873
Henry Wilson	1873–1875
⑲ Rutherford B. Hayes	1877–1881
William A. Wheeler	1877–1881
20 James A. Garfield	1881
Chester A. Arthur	1881
㉑ Chester A. Arthur	1881–1885
No Vice President	

PRESIDENT VICE PRESIDENT	YEARS IN OFFICE
22 Grover Cleveland	1885–1889
Thomas A. Hendricks	1885
㉓ Benjamin Harrison	1889–1893
Levi P. Morton	1889–1893
24 Grover Cleveland	1893–1897
Adlai E. Stevenson	1893–1897
㉕ William McKinley	1897–1901
Garret A. Hobart	1897–1899
Theodore Roosevelt	1901
26 Theodore Roosevelt	1901–1909
Charles W. Fairbanks	1905–1909
㉗ William Howard Taft	1909–1913
James S. Sherman	1909–1912
28 Woodrow Wilson	1913–1921
Thomas R. Marshall	1913–1921
㉙ Warren G. Harding	1921–1923
Calvin Coolidge	1921–1923
30 Calvin Coolidge	1923–1929
Charles G. Dawes	1925–1929
㉛ Herbert Hoover	1929–1933
Charles Curtis	1929–1933
32 Franklin D. Roosevelt	1933–1945
John Nance Garner	1933–1941
Henry A. Wallace	1941–1945
Harry S. Truman	1945
㉝ Harry S. Truman	1945–1953
Alben W. Barkley	1949–1953
34 Dwight D. Eisenhower	1953–1961
Richard M. Nixon	1953–1961
㉟ John F. Kennedy	1961–1963
Lyndon B. Johnson	1961–1963
36 Lyndon B. Johnson	1963–1969
Hubert H. Humphrey	1965–1969
㊲ Richard M. Nixon	1969–1974
Spiro T. Agnew	1969–1973
Gerald R. Ford	1973–1974
38 Gerald R. Ford	1974–1977
Nelson A. Rockefeller	1974–1977
㊴ Jimmy Carter	1977–1981
Walter F. Mondale	1977–1981
40 Ronald Reagan	1981–1989
George Bush	1981–1989
㊶ George Bush	1989–1993
Dan Quayle	1989–1993
42 Bill Clinton	1993–2001
Al Gore	1993–2001
㊸ George W. Bush	2001–
Richard B. Cheney	2001–

PRESIDENTS
of the United States

GEORGE WASHINGTON Federalist Party   **1789-1797**
Born: Feb. 22, 1732, at Wakefield, Westmoreland County, Virginia
Married: Martha Dandridge Custis (1731-1802); no children
Died: Dec. 14, 1799; buried at Mount Vernon, Fairfax County, Virginia
Early Career: Soldier; head of the Virginia militia; commander of the
    Continental Army; chairman of Constitutional Convention (1787)

JOHN ADAMS Federalist Party   **1797-1801**
Born: Oct. 30, 1735, in Braintree (now Quincy), Massachusetts
Married: Abigail Smith (1744-1818); 3 sons, 2 daughters
Died: July 4, 1826; buried in Quincy, Massachusetts
Early Career: Lawyer; delegate to Continental Congress; signer of the
    Declaration of Independence; first vice president

THOMAS JEFFERSON Democratic-Republican Party   **1801-1809**
Born: Apr. 13, 1743, at Shadwell, Albemarle County, Virginia
Married: Martha Wayles Skelton (1748-1782); 1 son, 5 daughters
Died: July 4, 1826; buried at Monticello, Albemarle County, Virginia
Early Career: Lawyer; member of the Continental Congress; author of the
    Declaration of Independence; governor of Virginia; first secretary of
    state; author of the Virginia Statute on Religious Freedom

JAMES MADISON Democratic-Republican Party   **1809-1817**
Born: Mar. 16, 1751, at Port Conway, King George County, Virginia
Married: Dolley Payne Todd (1768-1849); no children
Died: June 28, 1836; buried at Montpelier Station, Virginia
Early Career: Member of the Virginia Constitutional Convention (1776);
    member of the Continental Congress; major contributor to the U.S.
    Constitution; writer of the *Federalist Papers*; secretary of state

JAMES MONROE Democratic-Republican Party   **1817-1825**
Born: Apr. 28, 1758, in Westmoreland County, Virginia
Married: Elizabeth Kortright (1768-1830); 2 daughters
Died: July 4, 1831; buried in Richmond, Virginia
Early Career: Soldier; lawyer; U.S. senator; governor of Virginia;
    secretary of state

JOHN QUINCY ADAMS Democratic-Republican Party   **1825-1829**
Born: July 11, 1767, in Braintree (now Quincy), Massachusetts
Married: Louisa Catherine Johnson (1775-1852); 3 sons, 1 daughter
Died: Feb. 23, 1848; buried in Quincy, Massachusetts
Early Career: Diplomat; U.S. senator; secretary of state

ANDREW JACKSON Democratic Party **1829-1837**
Born: Mar. 15, 1767, in Waxhaw, South Carolina
Married: Rachel Donelson Robards (1767-1828); 1 son
Died: June 8, 1845; buried in Nashville, Tennessee
Early Career: Lawyer; U.S. representative and senator; soldier in the
    U.S. Army

MARTIN VAN BUREN Democratic Party **1837-1841**
Born: Dec. 5, 1782, at Kinderhook, New York
Married: Hannah Hoes (1783-1819); 4 sons
Died: July 24, 1862; buried at Kinderhook, New York
Early Career: Governor of New York; secretary of state; vice president

WILLIAM HENRY HARRISON Whig Party **1841**
Born: Feb. 9, 1773, at Berkeley, Charles City County, Virginia
Married: Anna Symmes (1775-1864); 6 sons, 4 daughters
Died: Apr. 4, 1841; buried in North Bend, Ohio
Early Career: First governor of Indiana Territory; superintendent of
    Indian affairs; U.S. representative and senator

JOHN TYLER Whig Party **1841-1845**
Born: Mar. 29, 1790, in Greenway, Charles City County, Virginia
Married: Letitia Christian (1790-1842); 3 sons, 5 daughters
    Julia Gardiner (1820-1889); 5 sons, 2 daughters
Died: Jan. 18, 1862; buried in Richmond, Virginia
Early Career: U.S. representative and senator; vice president

JAMES KNOX POLK Democratic Party **1845-1849**
Born: Nov. 2, 1795, in Mecklenburg County, North Carolina
Married: Sarah Childress (1803-1891); no children
Died: June 15, 1849; buried in Nashville, Tennessee
Early Career: U.S. representative; Speaker of the House; governor
    of Tennessee

ZACHARY TAYLOR Whig Party **1849-1850**
Born: Nov. 24, 1784, in Orange County, Virginia
Married: Margaret Smith (1788-1852); 1 son, 5 daughters
Died: July 9, 1850; buried in Louisville, Kentucky
Early Career: Indian fighter; general in the U.S. Army

MILLARD FILLMORE Whig Party **1850-1853**
Born: Jan. 7, 1800, in Cayuga County, New York
Married: Abigail Powers (1798-1853); 1 son, 1 daughter
    Caroline Carmichael McIntosh (1813-1881); no children
Died: Mar. 8, 1874; buried in Buffalo, New York
Early Career: Farmer; lawyer; U.S. representative; vice president

FRANKLIN PIERCE Democratic Party   1853-1857
Born: Nov. 23, 1804, in Hillsboro, New Hampshire
Married: Jane Means Appleton (1806-1863); 3 sons
Died: Oct. 8, 1869; buried in Concord, New Hampshire
Early Career: U.S. representative, senator

JAMES BUCHANAN Democratic Party   1857-1861
Born: Apr. 23, 1791, Cove Gap, near Mercersburg, Pennsylvania
Married: Never
Died: June 1, 1868, buried in Lancaster, Pennsylvania
Early Career: U.S. representative; secretary of state

ABRAHAM LINCOLN Republican Party   1861-1865
Born: Feb. 12, 1809, in Hardin County, Kentucky
Married: Mary Todd (1818-1882); 4 sons
Died: Apr. 15, 1865; buried in Springfield, Illinois
Early Career: Lawyer; U.S. representative

ANDREW JOHNSON Democratic Party   1865-1869
Born: Dec. 29, 1808, in Raleigh, North Carolina
Married: Eliza McCardle (1810-1876); 3 sons, 2 daughters
Died: July 31, 1875; buried in Greeneville, Tennessee
Early Career: Tailor; member of state legislature; U.S. representative;
    governor of Tennessee; U.S. senator; vice president

ULYSSES S. GRANT Republican Party   1869-1877
Born: Apr. 27, 1822, in Point Pleasant, Ohio
Married: Julia Dent (1826-1902); 3 sons, 1 daughter
Died: July 23, 1885; buried in New York City
Early Career: Army officer; commander of Union forces during Civil War

RUTHERFORD B. HAYES Republican Party   1877-1881
Born: Oct. 4, 1822, in Delaware, Ohio
Married: Lucy Ware Webb (1831-1889); 5 sons, 2 daughters
Died: Jan. 17, 1893; buried in Fremont, Ohio
Early Career: Lawyer; general in Union Army; U.S. representative;
    governor of Ohio

JAMES A. GARFIELD Republican Party   1881
Born: Nov. 19, 1831, in Orange, Cuyahoga County, Ohio
Married: Lucretia Rudolph (1832-1918); 5 sons, 2 daughters
Died: Sept. 19, 1881; buried in Cleveland, Ohio
Early Career: Teacher; Ohio state senator; general in Union Army;
    U.S. representative

CHESTER A. ARTHUR Republican Party   **1881-1885**
Born: Oct. 5, 1829, in Fairfield, Vermont
Married: Ellen Lewis Herndon (1837-1880); 2 sons, 1 daughter
Died: Nov. 18, 1886; buried in Albany, New York
Early Career: Teacher; lawyer; vice president

GROVER CLEVELAND Democratic Party   **1885-1889**
Born: Mar. 18, 1837, in Caldwell, New Jersey
Married: Frances Folsom (1864-1947); 2 sons, 3 daughters
Died: June 24, 1908; buried in Princeton, New Jersey
Early Career: Lawyer; mayor of Buffalo; governor of New York

BENJAMIN HARRISON Republican Party   **1889-1893**
Born: Aug. 20, 1833, in North Bend, Ohio
Married: Caroline Lavinia Scott (1832-1892); 1 son, 1 daughter
         Mary Scott Lord Dimmick (1858-1948); 1 daughter
Died: Mar. 13, 1901; buried in Indianapolis, Indiana
Early Career: Lawyer; general in Union Army; U.S. senator

GROVER CLEVELAND   **1893-1897**
See 22, above

WILLIAM MCKINLEY Republican Party   **1897-1901**
Born: Jan. 29, 1843, in Niles, Ohio
Married: Ida Saxton (1847-1907); 2 daughters
Died: Sept. 14, 1901; buried in Canton, Ohio
Early Career: Lawyer; U.S. representative; governor of Ohio

THEODORE ROOSEVELT Republican Party   **1901-1909**
Born: Oct. 27, 1858, in New York City
Married: Alice Hathaway Lee (1861-1884); 1 daughter
         Edith Kermit Carow (1861-1948); 4 sons, 1 daughter
Died: Jan. 6, 1919; buried in Oyster Bay, New York
Early Career: Assistant secretary of the Navy; cavalry leader in
         Spanish-American War; governor of New York; vice president

WILLIAM HOWARD TAFT Republican Party   **1909-1913**
Born: Sept. 15, 1857, in Cincinnati, Ohio
Married: Helen Herron (1861-1943); 2 sons, 1 daughter
Died: Mar. 8, 1930; buried in Arlington National Cemetery, Virginia
Early Career: Reporter; lawyer; judge; secretary of war

WOODROW WILSON Democratic Party   **1913-1921**
Born: Dec. 28, 1856, in Staunton, Virginia
Married: Ellen Louise Axson (1860-1914); 3 daughters
         Edith Bolling Galt (1872-1961); no children
Died: Feb. 3, 1924; buried in Washington, D.C.
Early Career: College professor and president; governor of New Jersey

WARREN G. HARDING Republican Party   1921-1923
Born: Nov. 2, 1865, near Corsica (now Blooming Grove), Ohio
Married: Florence Kling De Wolfe (1860-1924); 1 daughter
Died: Aug. 2, 1923; buried in Marion, Ohio
Early Career: Ohio state senator; U.S. senator

CALVIN COOLIDGE Republican Party   1923-1929
Born: July 4, 1872, in Plymouth, Vermont
Married: Grace Anna Goodhue (1879-1957); 2 sons
Died: Jan. 5, 1933; buried in Plymouth, Vermont
Early Career: Massachusetts state legislator; lieutenant governor and governor; vice president

HERBERT HOOVER Republican Party   1929-1933
Born: Aug. 10, 1874, in West Branch, Iowa
Married: Lou Henry (1875-1944); 2 sons
Died: Oct. 20, 1964; buried in West Branch, Iowa
Early Career: Mining engineer; secretary of commerce

FRANKLIN DELANO ROOSEVELT Democratic Party   1933-1945
Born: Jan. 30, 1882, in Hyde Park, New York
Married: Anna Eleanor Roosevelt (1884-1962); 4 sons, 1 daughter
Died: Apr. 12, 1945; buried in Hyde Park, New York
Early Career: Lawyer; New York state senator; assistant secretary of the Navy; governor of New York

HARRY S. TRUMAN Democratic Party   1945-1953
Born: May 8, 1884, in Lamar, Missouri
Married: Elizabeth Virginia "Bess" Wallace (1885-1982); 1 daughter
Died: Dec. 26, 1972; buried in Independence, Missouri
Early Career: Farmer; haberdasher (ran men's clothing store); judge; U.S. senator; vice president

DWIGHT D. EISENHOWER Republican Party   1953-1961
Born: Oct. 14, 1890, in Denison, Texas
Married: Mary "Mamie" Geneva Doud (1896-1979); 2 sons
Died: Mar. 28, 1969; buried in Abilene, Kansas
Early Career: Commander, Allied landing in North Africa and later Supreme Allied Commander in Europe during World War II; president of Columbia University

JOHN FITZGERALD KENNEDY Democratic Party   1961-1963
Born: May 29, 1917, in Brookline, Massachusetts
Married: Jacqueline Lee Bouvier (1929-1994); 2 sons, 1 daughter
Died: Nov. 22, 1963; buried in Arlington National Cemetery, Virginia
Early Career: U.S. naval commander; U.S. representative and senator

36 **LYNDON BAINES JOHNSON** Democratic Party   **1963-1969**
Born: Aug. 27, 1908, near Stonewall, Texas
Married: Claudia "Lady Bird" Alta Taylor (b. 1912); 2 daughters
Died: Jan. 22, 1973; buried in Johnson City, Texas
Early Career: U.S. representative and senator; vice president

37 **RICHARD MILHOUS NIXON** Republican Party   **1969-1974**
Born: Jan. 9, 1913, in Yorba Linda, California
Married: Thelma "Pat" Ryan (1912-1993); 2 daughters
Died: Apr. 22, 1994; buried in Yorba Linda, California
Early Career: Lawyer; U.S. representative and senator; vice president

38 **GERALD R. FORD** Republican Party   **1974-1977**
Born: July 14, 1913, in Omaha, Nebraska
Married: Elizabeth "Betty" Bloomer (b. 1918); 3 sons, 1 daughter
Early Career: Lawyer; U.S. representative; vice president

39 **JIMMY (JAMES EARL) CARTER** Democratic Party   **1977-1981**
Born: Oct. 1, 1924, in Plains, Georgia
Married: Rosalynn Smith (b. 1927); 3 sons, 1 daughter
Early Career: Peanut farmer; Georgia state senator; governor
   of Georgia

40 **RONALD REAGAN** Republican Party   **1981-1989**
Born: Feb. 6, 1911, in Tampico, Illinois
Married: Jane Wyman (b. 1914); 1 son, 1 daughter
   Nancy Davis (b. 1923); 1 son, 1 daughter
Early Career: Film and television actor; governor of California

41 **GEORGE BUSH** Republican Party   **1989-1993**
Born: June 12, 1924, in Milton, Massachusetts
Married: Barbara Pierce (b. 1925); 4 sons, 2 daughters
Early Career: U.S. Navy pilot; businessman; U.S. representative; U.S.
   ambassador to the UN; CIA director, vice president

42 **BILL (WILLIAM JEFFERSON) CLINTON** Democratic Party **1993-2001**
Born: Aug. 19, 1946, in Hope, Arkansas
Married: Hillary Rodham (b. 1947); 1 daughter
Early Career: College professor; Arkansas state attorney general;
   governor of Arkansas

43 **GEORGE W. BUSH** Republican Party   **2001-**
Born: July 6, 1946, in New Haven, Connecticut
Married: Laura Welch (b. 1946); 2 daughters
Early Career: Political adviser; businessman; governor of Texas

PRESIDENTIAL FACTS

First president to throw out the ball on Major League Baseball's Opening Day: William Howard Taft, on April 14, 1910.

Most first pitches thrown by a president: Eight, by Franklin D. Roosevelt

Presidents to win the Nobel Peace Prize while in office: Theodore Roosevelt (1906), Woodrow Wilson (1919)

Only ex-president to win the Nobel Peace Prize: Jimmy Carter (2002)

Only president to win a Pulitzer Prize: John F. Kennedy, 1960, for his book *Profiles in Courage*

First president to live in the White House: John Adams

First president to leave the U.S. while in office: Theodore Roosevelt, who visited the Panama Canal in 1906

First president to fly in an airplane while in office: Franklin D. Roosevelt, in 1944; his plane was called "the Sacred Cow"

First president to speak from the White House on TV: Harry Truman, in 1947.

Meet the First Ladies

MARTHA WASHINGTON was the first First Lady. A wealthy widow when she married George Washington, she helped his position as a Virginia planter.

ELEANOR ROOSEVELT, wife of Franklin D. Roosevelt, was an important public figure. She urged her husband to support civil rights and the rights of workers. After his death she served as a delegate to the UN.

ABIGAIL ADAMS, wife of John Adams, didn't have much formal education. But the hundreds of letters she wrote to her husband provide a history of life during the Revolutionary era.

HILLARY RODHAM CLINTON, wife of Bill Clinton, was a successful lawyer and defender of women's and children's rights. In 2000, she became the first first lady to be elected to public office, as a U.S. senator from New York.

DOLLEY MADISON, James Madison's wife, was famous as a hostess and for saving a portrait of George Washington during the War of 1812, when the British were about to burn the White House.

LAURA BUSH, wife of George W. Bush, was a librarian and teacher. She is interested in books, history, art, and the well-being of children. She and her husband have twin daughters, both college students.

THE LEGISLATIVE BRANCH

CONGRESS

The Congress of the United States is the legislative branch of the federal government. Congress's major responsibility is to pass the laws that govern the country and determine how money collected in taxes is spent. It is the president's responsibility to enforce the laws. Congress consists of two parts—the Senate and the House of Representatives.

▲ *The Senate*

THE HOUSE OF REPRESENTATIVES

The number of members of the House of Representatives for each state depends on its population according to a recent census. But each state has at least one representative, no matter how small its population. A term lasts two years.

The first House of Representatives in 1789 had 65 members. As the country's population grew, the number of representatives increased. Since the 1910 census, however, the total membership has been kept at 435. After the results of Census 2000 were added up, 8 states gained seats and 10 states lost seats.

THE SENATE

The Senate has 100 members, two from each state. The Constitution says that the Senate will have equal representation (the same number of representatives) from each state. Thus, small states have the same number of senators as large states. Senators are elected for six-year terms. There is no limit on the number of terms a senator can serve.

▼ *The Capitol, where Congress meets*

The Senate also has the responsibility of approving people the president appoints for certain jobs: for example, cabinet members and Supreme Court justices. The Senate must approve all treaties by at least a two-thirds vote. It also has the responsibility under the Constitution of putting on trial high-ranking federal officials who have been impeached by the House of Representatives.

You can reach the Senate and the House on-line at:

WEB SITE

http://www.senate.gov
http://www.house.gov

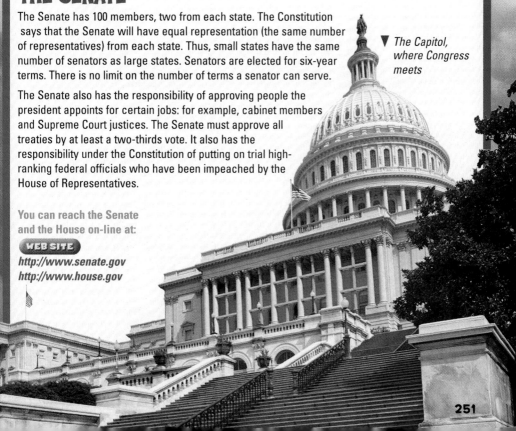

THE HOUSE OF REPRESENTATIVES, BY STATE

Here are the numbers of representatives each state will have by 2003, compared with 10 years earlier and 30 years earlier:

	2003	1993	1973		2003	1993	1973
Alabama	7	7	7	Montana	1	1	2
Alaska	1	1	1	Nebraska	3	3	3
Arizona	8	6	4	Nevada	3	2	1
Arkansas	4	4	4	New Hampshire	2	2	2
California	53	52	43	New Jersey	13	13	15
Colorado	7	6	5	New Mexico	3	3	2
Connecticut	5	6	6	New York	29	31	39
Delaware	1	1	1	North Carolina	13	12	11
Florida	25	23	15	North Dakota	1	1	1
Georgia	13	11	10	Ohio	18	19	23
Hawaii	2	2	2	Oklahoma	5	6	6
Idaho	2	2	2	Oregon	5	5	4
Illinois	19	20	24	Pennsylvania	19	21	25
Indiana	9	10	11	Rhode Island	2	2	2
Iowa	5	5	6	South Carolina	6	6	6
Kansas	4	4	5	South Dakota	1	1	2
Kentucky	6	6	7	Tennessee	9	9	9
Louisiana	7	7	8	Texas	32	30	24
Maine	2	2	2	Utah	3	3	2
Maryland	8	8	8	Vermont	1	1	1
Massachusetts	10	10	12	Virginia	11	11	10
Michigan	15	16	19	Washington	9	9	7
Minnesota	8	8	8	West Virginia	3	3	4
Mississippi	4	5	5	Wisconsin	8	9	9
Missouri	9	9	10	Wyoming	1	1	1

Washington, D.C., Puerto Rico, American Samoa, Guam, and the Virgin Islands each have one nonvoting member of the House of Representatives.

WOMEN IN CONGRESS

▶ As of January 2003, there were 62 women serving in the U.S. House of Representatives and 14 in the U.S. Senate. All together, 185 women have served in the House and 33 in the Senate.

▶ The first woman elected to the House was Jeannette Rankin (Montana) in 1916. In 1932, Hattie Caraway (Arkansas) was the first woman to be elected to the Senate.

▶ New York's Shirley Chisholm became the first African American woman in Congress after being elected to the House in 1968. Margaret Chase Smith, of Maine, was the first woman elected to both houses of Congress (House in 1940, Senate in 1948).

▶ California Representative Nancy Pelosi holds the highest position ever for a woman in the U.S. Congress. In November, 2002, her fellow Democrats selected her as their leader in the House of Representatives.

◀ Nancy Pelosi

HOW A BILL BECOMES A LAW

STEP 1 Senators and Representatives Propose Bill.

A proposed law is called a **bill**. Any member of Congress may propose (introduce) a bill. A bill is introduced in each house of Congress. The House of Representatives and the Senate consider a bill separately. A member of Congress who introduces a bill is known as the bill's **sponsor**. Bills to raise money always begin in the House of Representatives.

STEP 2 House and Senate Committees Consider the Bill.

The bill is then sent to appropriate committees for consideration. A bill relating to agriculture, for example, would be sent to the agriculture committees in the House and in the Senate. A committee is made up of a small number of members of the House or Senate. Whichever party has a majority in the House or Senate has a majority on each committee. When committees are considering a bill, they hold **hearings** at which people can speak for or against it.

STEP 3 Committees Vote on the Bill.

The committees can change the bill as they see fit. Then they vote on it.

STEP 4 The Bill is Debated in the House and Senate.

If the committees vote in favor of the bill, it goes to the full House and Senate, where it is debated and may be changed further. The House and Senate can then vote on it.

STEP 5 From the House and Senate to Conference Committee.

If the House and the Senate pass different versions of the same bill, the bill must go to a **conference committee**, where differences between the two versions must be worked out. A conference committee is a special committee made up of both Senate and House members.

STEP 6 Final Vote in the House and Senate.

The House and the Senate then vote on the conference committee version. In order for this version to become a law, it must be approved by a majority of members of both houses of Congress and signed by the president.

STEP 7 The President Signs the Bill into Law.

If the bill passes both houses of Congress, it goes to the president for his signature. Once the president signs a bill, it becomes law.

STEP 8 What if the President Doesn't Sign the Bill?

Sometimes the president does not approve of a bill and decides not to sign it. This is called **vetoing** it. A bill that has been vetoed goes back to Congress, where the members can vote again. If the House and the Senate pass the bill with a two-thirds majority vote, it becomes law. This is called **overriding** the veto.

◄ *President Lyndon B. Johnson, signing the Civil Rights Act, 1964.*

Above are the nine justices who were on the Supreme Court at the start of its 2002-2003 session.
Back row *(from left to right)*: Ruth Bader Ginsburg, David H. Souter, Clarence Thomas, Stephen Breyer.
Front row *(from left to right)*: Antonin Scalia, John Paul Stevens, Chief Justice William H. Rehnquist, Sandra Day O'Connor, Anthony M. Kennedy.

THE JUDICIAL BRANCH
The SUPREME COURT

The highest court in the United States is the Supreme Court. It has nine justices who are appointed for life by the president with the approval of the Senate. Eight of the nine members are called associate justices. The ninth is the chief justice, who presides over the Court's meetings.

What Does the Supreme Court Do?
The Supreme Court's major responsibilities are to judge cases that involve reviewing federal laws, actions of the president, treaties of the United States, and laws passed by state governments to be sure they do not conflict with the U.S. Constitution. If the Supreme Court finds that a law or action violates the Constitution, the law is struck down.

The Supreme Court's Decision Is Final.
Most cases must go through other state courts or federal courts before they reach the Supreme Court. The Supreme Court is the final court for a case, and the justices decide which cases they will review. After the Supreme Court hears a case, it may agree or disagree with the decision by a lower court. Each justice has one vote, and the majority rules. When the Supreme Court makes a ruling, its decision is final, so each of the justices has a very important job.

Not until its 146th year—1935—did the Supreme Court get its own building. Before that it met at different places, including the Capitol Building. In 1929, Chief Justice William Howard Taft (who had been the U.S. president from 1909 to 1913) persuaded Congress to authorize construction of a permanent home for the Court.

United States History TIME LINE

THE FIRST PEOPLE IN NORTH AMERICA: BEFORE 1492

14,000 B.C.–11,000 B.C.
Paleo-Indians use stone points attached to spears to hunt big mammoths in northern parts of North America.

11,000 B.C.
Big mammoths disappear and Paleo-Indians begin to gather plants for food.

AFTER A.D. 500
Anasazi peoples in the Southwestern United States live in homes on cliffs, called cliff dwellings. Anasazi pottery and dishes are well known for their beautiful patterns.

AFTER A.D. 700
Mississippian Indian people in the Southeastern United States develop farms and build burial mounds.

,000 B.C.

40,000 B.C.–11,000 B.C.
First people (called Paleo-Indians) cross from Siberia to Alaska and begin to move into North America.

9500 B.C.–1000 B.C.
North American Indians begin using stone to grind food and to hunt bison and smaller animals.

1000 B.C.–A.D. 500
Woodland Indians, who lived east of the Mississippi River, bury their dead under large mounds of earth (which can still be seen today).

700–1492
Many different Indian cultures develop throughout North America.

COLONIAL AMERICA AND THE AMERICAN REVOLUTION: 1492–1783

1492

1492
Christopher Columbus sails across the Atlantic Ocean and reaches an island in the Bahamas in the Caribbean Sea.

1513
Juan Ponce de León explores the Florida coast.

1524
Giovanni da Verrazano explores the coast from Carolina north to Nova Scotia, enters New York harbor.

1540
Francisco Vásquez de Coronado explores the Southwest.

1565
St. Augustine, Florida, the first town established by Europeans in the United States, is founded by the Spanish. Later burned by the English in 1586.

BENJAMIN FRANKLIN (1706-1790)

was a great American leader, printer, scientist, and writer. In 1732, he began publishing a magazine called *Poor Richard's Almanack*. Poor Richard was a make-believe person who gave advice about common sense and honesty. Many of Poor Richard's sayings are still known today. Among the most famous are "God helps them that help themselves" and "Early to bed, early to rise, makes a man healthy, wealthy, and wise."

1634

1634
Maryland is founded as a Catholic colony, with religious freedom for all granted in 1649.

1664
The English seize New Amsterdam from the Dutch. The city is renamed New York.

1699
French settlers move into Mississippi and Louisiana.

1732
Benjamin Franklin begins publishing *Poor Richard's Almanack*.

1754-1763
French and Indian War between England and France. The French are defeated and lose their lands in Canada and the American Midwest.

1764-1766
England places taxes on sugar that comes from their North American colonies. England also requires colonists to buy stamps to help pay for royal troops. Colonists protest, and the Stamp Act is repealed in 1766.

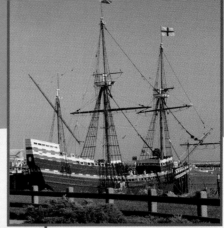

1607
Jamestown, Virginia, the first English settlement in North America, is founded by Captain John Smith.

1609
Henry Hudson sails into New York Harbor, explores the Hudson River. Spaniards settle Santa Fe, New Mexico.

1619
The first African slaves are brought to Jamestown. (Slavery is made legal in 1650.)

1620
Pilgrims from England arrive at Plymouth, Massachusetts on the *Mayflower*.

1626
Peter Minuit buys Manhattan island for the Dutch from Man-a-hat-a Indians for goods worth $24. The island is renamed New Amsterdam.

1630
Boston is founded by Massachusetts colonists led by John Winthrop.

FAMOUS WORDS FROM THE DECLARATION OF INDEPENDENCE, JULY 4, 1776

"We hold these truths to be self-evident, that all men are created equal, that they are endowed by their Creator with certain unalienable rights, that among these are life, liberty, and the pursuit of happiness."

1770
Boston Massacre: English troops fire on a group of people protesting English taxes.

1773
Boston Tea Party: English tea is thrown into the harbor to protest a tax on tea.

1775
Fighting at Lexington and Concord, Massachusetts, marks the beginning of the American Revolution.

1776
The Declaration of Independence is approved July 4 by the Continental Congress (made up of representatives from the American colonies).

1781
British General Cornwallis surrenders to the Americans at Yorktown, Virginia, ending the fighting in the Revolutionary War.

THE NEW NATION: 1783-1900

WHO ATTENDED THE CONVENTION?

The Constitutional Convention met in Philadelphia in the hot summer of 1787. Most of the great founders of America attended. Among those present were George Washington, James Madison, and John Adams. They met to form a new government that would be strong and, at the same time, protect the liberties that were fought for in the American Revolution. The Constitution they created is still the law of the United States.

THE LOUISIANA PURCHASE (1803)

1784

1784
The first successful daily newspaper, the *Pennsylvania Packet & General Advertiser*, is published.

1787
The Constitutional Convention meets to write a Constitution for the U.S.

1789
The new Constitution is approved by the states. George Washington is chosen as the first president.

1800
The federal government moves to a new capital, Washington, D.C.

1803
The U.S. makes the Louisiana Purchase from France. The Purchase doubles the area of the U.S.

The Trail of Tears

"THE TRAIL OF TEARS"

The Cherokee Indians living in Georgia were forced by the government to leave in 1838. They were sent to Oklahoma. On the long march, thousands died because of disease and the cold weather.

UNCLE TOM'S CABIN

Harriet Beecher Stowe's novel about the suffering of slaves was an instant bestseller in the North and banned in most of the South. When President Abraham Lincoln met Stowe, he called her "the little lady who started this war" (the Civil War).

1836

1836
Texans fighting for independence from Mexico are defeated at the Alamo.

1838
Cherokee Indians are forced to move to Oklahoma, along "The Trail of Tears."

1844
The first telegraph line connects Washington, D.C., and Baltimore.

1846–1848
U.S. war with Mexico: Mexico is defeated, and the United States takes control of the Republic of Texas and of Mexican territories in the West.

1848
The discovery of gold in California leads to a "rush" of 80,000 people to the West in search of gold.

1852
Uncle Tom's Cabin is published.

1804
Lewis and Clark, with their guide Sacagawea, explore what is now the northwestern United States.

1812–1814
War of 1812 with Great Britain: British forces burn the Capitol and White House. Francis Scott Key writes the words to "The Star-Spangled Banner."

1820
The Missouri Compromise bans slavery west of the Mississippi River and north of 36°30′ latitude, except in Missouri.

1823
The Monroe Doctrine warns European countries not to interfere in the Americas.

1825
The Erie Canal opens linking New York City with the Great Lakes.

1831
The Liberator, a newspaper opposing slavery, is published in Boston.

CIVIL WAR DEAD AND WOUNDED

The U.S. Civil War between the North and South lasted four years (1861-1865) and resulted in the death or wounding of more than 600,000 people. Little was known at the time about the spread of diseases. As a result, many casualties were also the result of illnesses such as influenza, measles, and infections from battle wounds.

1898
Spanish-American War: The U.S. defeats Spain, gains control of the Philippines, Puerto Rico, and Guam.

1858
Abraham Lincoln and Stephen Douglas debate about slavery during their Senate campaign in Illinois.

1860
Abraham Lincoln is elected president.

1861
The Civil War begins.

1863
President Lincoln issues the Emancipation Proclamation, freeing most slaves.

1865
The Civil War ends as the South surrenders. President Lincoln is assassinated.

1869
The first railroad connecting the East and West coasts is completed.

1890
Battle of Wounded Knee is fought in South Dakota—the last major battle between Indians and U.S. troops.

UNITED STATES SINCE 1900

WORLD WAR I

In World War I the United States fought with Great Britain, France, and Russia (the Allies) against Germany and Austria-Hungary. The Allies won the war in 1918.

1900

1903

The United States begins digging the Panama Canal. The canal opens in 1914, connecting the Atlantic and Pacific oceans.

1908

Henry Ford introduces the Model T car, priced at $850.

1916

Jeannette Rankin of Montana becomes the first woman elected to Congress.

1917-1918

The United States joins World War I on the side of the Allies against Germany.

1927

Charles A. Lindbergh becomes the first person to fly alone nonstop across the Atlantic Ocean.

SCHOOL SEGREGATION

The U.S. Supreme Court ruled that separate schools for black students and white students were not equal. The Court said such schools were against the U.S. Constitution. The ruling also applied to other forms of segregation—separation of the races supported by some states.

1954

1954

The U.S. Supreme Court forbids racial segregation in public schools.

1963

President John Kennedy is assassinated.

1964

Congress passes the Civil Rights Act, which outlaws discrimination in voting and jobs.

1965

The United States sends large numbers of soldiers to fight in the Vietnam War.

1968

Civil rights leader Martin Luther King Jr. is assassinated in Memphis. Senator Robert F. Kennedy is assassinated in Los Angeles.

1969

U.S. Astronaut Neil Armstrong becomes the first person to walk on the moon.

1973

U.S. participation in the Vietnam War ends.

THE GREAT DEPRESSION

The stock market crash of October 1929 led to a period of severe hardship for the American people—the Great Depression. As many as 25 percent of all workers could not find jobs. The Depression lasted until the early 1940s. The Depression also led to a great change in politics. In 1932, Franklin D. Roosevelt, a Democrat, was elected president. He served as president for 12 years, longer than any other president.

1929
A stock market crash marks the beginning of the Great Depression.

1933
President Franklin D. Roosevelt's New Deal increases government help to people hurt by the Depression.

1941
Japan attacks Pearl Harbor, Hawaii. The United States enters World War II.

1945
Germany and Japan surrender, ending World War II. Japan surrenders after the U.S. drops atomic bombs on Hiroshima and Nagasaki.

1947
Jackie Robinson becomes the first black baseball player in the major leagues when he joins the Brooklyn Dodgers.

1950-1953
U.S. armed forces fight in the Korean War.

WATERGATE

In June 1972, five men were arrested in the Watergate building in Washington, D.C., for trying to bug telephones in the offices of the Democratic National Committee. Some of those arrested worked for the committee to reelect President Richard Nixon. Later it was discovered that Nixon was helping to hide information about the break-in.

1985
U.S. President Ronald Reagan and Soviet leader Mikhail Gorbachev begin working together to improve relations between their countries.

1991
The Persian Gulf War: The United States and its allies defeat Iraq.

2000
George W. Bush narrowly defeats Al Gore in a hotly fought battle for the presidency.

1974
President Richard Nixon resigns because of the Watergate scandal.

1979
U.S. hostages are taken in Iran, beginning a 444-day crisis that ends with their release in 1981.

1981
Sandra Day O'Connor becomes the first woman on the U.S. Supreme Court.

1999
After an impeachment trial, the Senate finds President Bill Clinton not guilty.

2001
Hijacked jets crashed into the World Trade Center and the Pentagon, September 11, killing about 3,000 people.

2003
U.S.-led forces invade Iraq and remove its government.

African Americans Work for Change

Would you like to learn more about the history of African Americans from the era of slavery to the present? These events and personalities can be a starting point. Can you add some more?

Rev. Martin Luther King Jr. ▶

1619	First Africans are brought to Virginia as slaves.
1831	Nat Turner starts a slave revolt in Virginia that is promptly put down.
1856-57	Dred Scott, a slave, sues to be freed because he had left slave territory, but the Supreme Court denies his claim.
1861-65	The North defeats the South in the brutal Civil War; the 13th Amendment ends nearly 250 years of slavery. The Ku Klux Klan is founded.
1865-77	Southern blacks play leadership roles in government under Reconstruction; 15th Amendment (1870) gives black men the right to vote.
1896	Supreme Court rules in a case called *Plessy versus Ferguson* that segregation is legal when facilities are "separate but equal." Discrimination and violence against blacks are increasing.
1910	W. E. B. Du Bois (1868–1963) founds National Association for the Advancement of Colored People (NAACP), fighting for equality for blacks.
1920s	African American culture (jazz music, dance, literature) flourishes during the "Harlem Renaissance."
1954	Supreme Court rules in a case called *Brown versus Board of Education of Topeka* that school segregation is unconstitutional.
1957	Black students, backed by federal troops, enter segregated Little Rock Central High School.
1955-65	Malcolm X (1925–65) emerges as key spokesman for black nationalism.
1963	Rev. Dr. Martin Luther King Jr. (1929–68) gives his "I Have a Dream" speech at a March that inspired more than 200,000 people in Washington, D.C.—and throughout the nation.
1964	Sweeping civil rights bill banning racial discrimination is signed by President Lyndon Johnson.
1965	King leads protest march in Selma, Alabama; blacks riot in Watts section of Los Angeles.
1967	Gary, Indiana, and Cleveland, Ohio, are first major U.S. cities to elect black mayors; Thurgood Marshall (1908–93) becomes first black on the Supreme Court.
1995	Hundreds of thousands of black men in take part in "Million Man March" rally in Washington, D.C., urging responsibility for families and communities.
2001	Retired Gen. Colin Powell becomes first African American secretary of state, filling the top foreign policy position in President George W. Bush's cabinet.

THEY MADE HISTORY

The people below fought racial barriers in order to achieve their goals.

MARIAN ANDERSON (1897-1993) was the first African-American singer to sing with New York's Metropolitan Opera. She also served as a UN delegate, and won many awards, including the Presidential Medal of Freedom.

Marian Anderson

GEORGE WASHINGTON CARVER (1864-1943) invented nearly 300 products made from peanuts (including types of milk, cheese, flour, ink, soap, and cosmetics) and over 100 products from sweet potatoes. In 1896, he joined the faculty of Alabama's Tuskegee Institute, where he gained an international reputation as an educator.

BILL COSBY (born 1937) is one of America's most beloved humorists. With his role on *I Spy* in the 1960s, he became the first African-American actor to star in a weekly TV drama series. But he is best known for the 1980s family sitcom *The Cosby Show*. He has won many awards for his acting, and is also a best-selling author.

LANGSTON HUGHES (1902-1967) a leading figure of the Harlem Renaissance, the African-American artistic movement of the 1920s, was a hotel busboy before becoming a writer. Through poetry, novels, plays, essays, and children's books, he promoted equality, condemned racial bias, and celebrated black music, humor, and culture.

Langston Hughes

ROBERT L. JOHNSON (born 1946) founded BET (Black Entertainment Television) in 1980, the leading African American-owned and operated media company in the U.S. In 2002, he became the first black owner of a major professional sports franchise—a new NBA team to play in Charlotte, North Carolina.

REV. MARTIN LUTHER KING JR. (1929–1968) used stirring words, strong leadership, and commitment to nonviolence to help change U.S. history. From the mid-1950s to his assassination in 1968, he was the most influential leader of the U.S. civil rights movement.

MALCOLM X (1925–1965) was a forceful Black Muslim leader who spoke against injustices toward blacks and called for blacks to keep separate from whites. He was assassinated by rivals in 1965. His life story, *The Autobiography of Malcolm X*, became a best-seller and helped make him a hero to many people.

THURGOOD MARSHALL (1908–1993) became the first African-American justice on the Supreme Court in 1967. In 1954, he had won an historic case, *Brown v. Board of Education of Topeka*, before the Court. The Court ruled that separate schools for black and white students were not equal or legal.

COLIN POWELL (born 1937) is the first African-American secretary of state. In 1991, as the first black chairman of the Joint Chiefs of Staff, he oversaw Operation Desert Storm in the Persian Gulf War. In 2003, as secretary of state, he supported further military action against Iraq.

CONDOLEEZZA RICE (born 1954) is the first African-American, and the first woman, to be national security advisor, giving the U.S. president advice on foreign and defense policy. She is an expert on Eastern Europe and was a professor and t op official at Stanford University in California.

JACKIE ROBINSON (1919–1972) was the first black player in the history of Major League Baseball. He joined the Dodgers, then in Brooklyn, in 1947. In 1949, he won the National League's MVP award and in 1962 was elected to the Baseball Hall of Fame.

SOJOURNER TRUTH (1797-1883) was raised as a slave on an estate in upstate New York. Escaping in 1826, she took the name Sojourner Truth. She campaigned against slavery and, later, for women's right to vote.

Jackie Robinson ▶

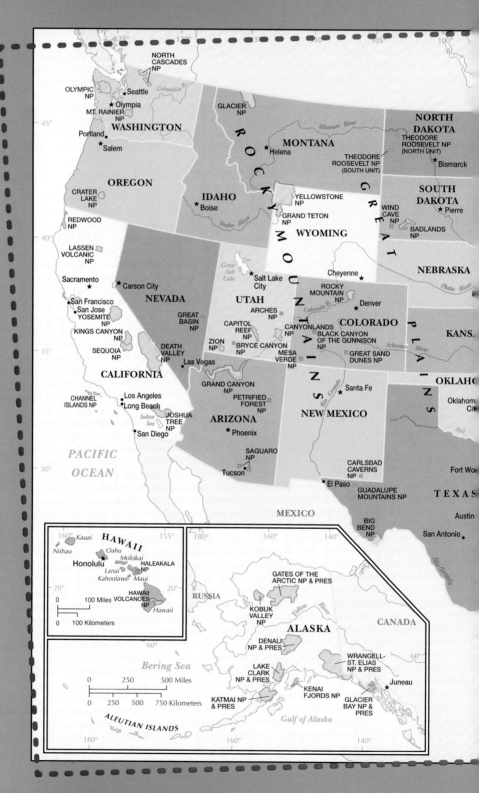

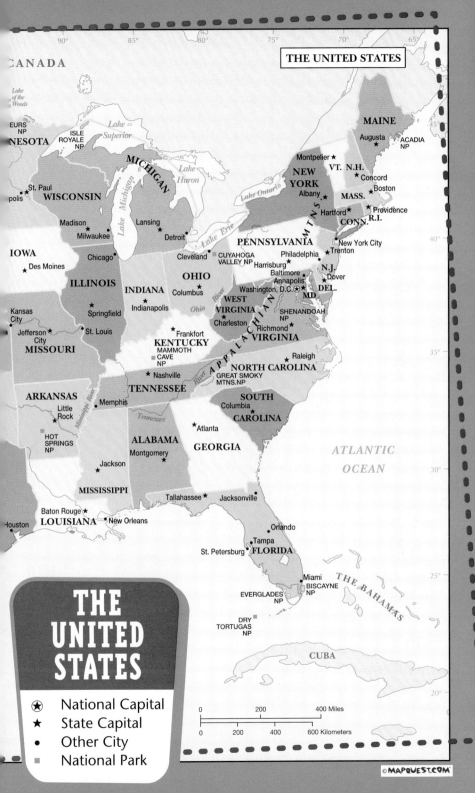

THE UNITED STATES

CANADA

Lake of the Woods

EURS NP
NESOTA

ISLE ROYALE NP
Lake Superior

MICHIGAN

Lake Huron

MAINE

Augusta ★

ACADIA NP

St. Paul
polis

WISCONSIN

Madison ★
Milwaukee

Lansing ★

Lake Michigan

Detroit

Lake Ontario

Montpelier ★

NEW YORK

Albany ★

Lake Erie

Cleveland

VT. N.H.
Concord ★
Boston ★

MASS.

Hartford ★
CONN.
R.I.
Providence ★

IOWA
Des Moines ★

Chicago

OHIO

Columbus ★

PENNSYLVANIA

Harrisburg ★

CUYAHOGA VALLEY NP

Philadelphia

New York City
Trenton ★

ILLINOIS

INDIANA

Springfield ★

Indianapolis ★

Ohio River

WEST VIRGINIA

Charleston ★

Baltimore
Annapolis
Washington, D.C. ⊛

N.J.
Dover ★
DEL.
MD.

Kansas City

Jefferson City ★
St. Louis

MISSOURI

Frankfort ★

KENTUCKY

MAMMOTH CAVE NP

Nashville ★

TENNESSEE

Tennessee River

SHENANDOAH NP

Richmond ★

VIRGINIA

Raleigh ★

NORTH CAROLINA

GREAT SMOKY MTNS.NP

ARKANSAS

Little Rock ★

Memphis

Mississippi River

Columbia ★

SOUTH CAROLINA

HOT SPRINGS NP

Atlanta ★

ALABAMA

Montgomery ★

GEORGIA

ATLANTIC OCEAN

Jackson ★

MISSISSIPPI

Tallahassee ★

Jacksonville

Baton Rouge ★
Houston

LOUISIANA

New Orleans

Orlando

Tampa

St. Petersburg

FLORIDA

Miami
BISCAYNE NP

THE BAHAMAS

EVERGLADES NP

DRY TORTUGAS NP

CUBA

THE UNITED STATES

⊛ National Capital
★ State Capital
• Other City
■ National Park

APPALACHIAN MTNS

0   200   400 Miles
0   200   400   600 Kilometers

©MAPQUEST.COM

THE A-MAZE-iNG RACE ACROSS THE U.S.A.

You can travel by land, sea, and air on your cross-country trip through this maze. A special pass will allow you to go from START in Washington to FINISH in Maine—so long as you only spend up to $100.

Every time you pass a plane, ship, bus, or other means of transportation, subtract the cost of the ride you take from your $100 total. If you run out of money before you get to Maine, you'd better go back and try another route. Hint: there is more than one way to go.

ANSWERS ON PAGES 314-317. FOR MORE PUZZLES GO TO WWW.WORLDALMANACFORKIDS.COM

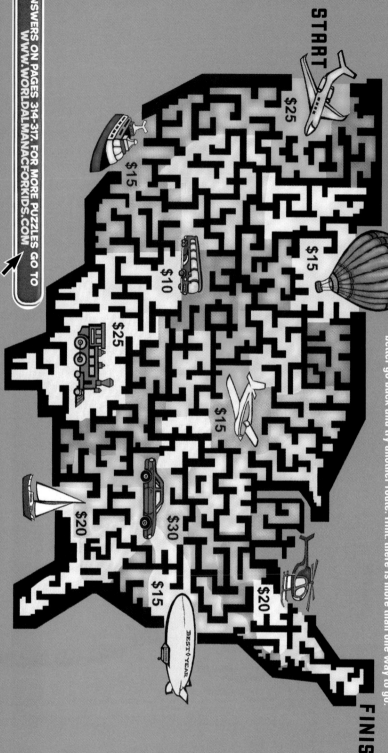

START

$25

$15

$15

$10

$25

$15

$20

$30

$15

$20

FINISH

ON THE JOB

Police Officer

Detective Sgt. Bruce Holloway has been a police officer in Boston, Massachusetts, for about 24 years. He started as a cop on the beat and went on to hold many other posts. He now oversees detectives who work in the fraud and fugitive units.

Q: Did you always want to go into police work?
Yes. It was either that or be a fireman.

Q: How old were you when you started? What did you do first?
I was 21. My first job was as a uniformed patrolman—assisting the public, responding to radio calls, and so on. The patrol officer's job is really about the most important in the department—they're the ones on the front line. They deal with crime, but they also do a lot to contribute to the quality of life—if a streetlight goes out, it's the patrol officer who reports it.

Q: And after that?
I worked undercover for a while. It was exciting. We handled drug cases, robberies, so on.

Q: Were you ever scared?
Once I was at home, off duty, and I heard a cry outside. I found a neighbor in the street. She was OK, but she had been robbed. I went in the direction her attacker had fled. But he had turned around and was coming back towards me, and he shot at me from a few feet away. I heard the bullet go by. I didn't return fire, because there were bystanders. After a chase I was able to tackle him and make the arrest. When it happened, I was too pumped up to be scared; later on, I realized I had had a close call.

Q: What do you like best about the job?
Like most things, it's what you make of it. It's satisfying to solve a crime when you have no good leads at the start. It's really good to know you've helped people. Also, not everyone who does something bad is bad himself: sometimes you can turn someone around.

Q: Any advice for kids who are thinking of becoming police officers?
I think all police departments have community relations offices—programs where you can get to know police officers, see what they do, maybe ride around with them. That's where you start: see what it's like and how you like it.

Q: Cop movies, TV shows—do you watch them? What's your opinion?
I do watch them. What I don't like is that a lot of them give a false impression of cops—that most cops lie or cheat. That's just not the way it is. I do like *Law and Order*.

FACTS ABOUT THE STATES

After every state name is the postal abbreviation. The Area includes both land and water; it is given in square miles (sq. mi.) and square kilometers (sq. km.). Numbers in parentheses after Population, Area, and Entered Union show the state's rank compared with other states. City populations come from the 2000 census.

ALABAMA (AL) *Heart of Dixie, Camellia State*

POPULATION (2002): 4,486,508 (23rd) **AREA:** 52,237 sq. mi. (30th) (135,294 sq. km.) **ENTERED UNION:** December 14, 1819 (22nd) **FLOWER:** Camellia **BIRD:** Yellowhammer **TREE:** Southern longleaf pine **SONG:** "Alabama" **CAPITAL:** Montgomery **LARGEST CITIES (WITH POP.):** Birmingham, 242,820; Montgomery, 201,568; Mobile, 198,915; Huntsville, 158,216 **IMPORTANT PRODUCTS:** clothing and textiles, metal products, transportation equipment, paper, industrial machinery, food products, lumber, coal, oil, natural gas, livestock, peanuts, cotton **PLACES TO VISIT:** Alabama Space and Rocket Center, Huntsville; Carver Museum, Tuskegee

WEB SITE http://alabama.gov • http://www.alabamatravel.org/tourism.html

DID YOU KNOW? *Alabama was the scene of major events in the Civil Rights Movement, starting with the black boycott of buses in Montgomery (1955) to protest segregation.*

ALASKA (AK) *The Last Frontier*

POPULATION (2002): 643,786 (47th) **AREA:** 615,230 sq. mi. (1st) (1,593,444 sq. km.) **ENTERED UNION:** January 3, 1959 (49th) **FLOWER:** Forget-me-not **BIRD:** Willow ptarmigan **TREE:** Sitka spruce **SONG:** "Alaska's Flag" **CAPITAL:** Juneau (population, 30,711) **LARGEST CITIES (WITH POP.):** Anchorage, 260,283; Fairbanks, 30,224 **IMPORTANT PRODUCTS:** oil, natural gas, fish, food products, lumber and wood products, fur **PLACES TO VISIT:** Glacier Bay and Denali national parks, Mendenhall Glacier, Mount McKinley

WEB SITE http://www.state.ak.us • http://www.dced.state.ak.us/tourism

DID YOU KNOW? *Three types of bears live in Alaska: black, grizzly, and polar. Seventeen of the 20 highest U.S. mountains are here, including Mt. McKinley, highest peak in North America.*

ARIZONA (AZ) *Grand Canyon State*

POPULATION (2002): 5,456,453 (20th) **AREA:** 114,006 sq. mi. (6th) (295,276 sq. km.) **ENTERED UNION:** February 14, 1912 (48th) **FLOWER:** Blossom of the Saguaro cactus **BIRD:** Cactus wren **TREE:** Paloverde **SONG:** "Arizona" **CAPITAL AND LARGEST CITY:** Phoenix (population, 1,321,045) **OTHER LARGE CITIES (WITH POP.):** Tucson, 486,699; Mesa, 396,375; Glendale, 218,812; Scottsdale, 202,705; Chandler, 176,581 **IMPORTANT PRODUCTS:** electronic equipment, transportation and industrial equipment, instruments, printing and publishing, copper and other metals **PLACES TO VISIT:** Grand Canyon, Painted Desert, Petrified Forest, Navajo National Monument

WEB SITE http://www.az.gov • http://www.arizonaguide.com

DID YOU KNOW? *Every year huge numbers of tourists travel on foot or by mule to the bottom of the Grand Canyon—the world's largest gorge.*

ARKANSAS (AR) *Natural State, Razorback State*

POPULATION (2002): 2,710,079 (33rd)
AREA: 53,182 sq. mi. (28th) (137,741 sq. km.)
FLOWER: Apple blossom **BIRD:** Mockingbird **TREE:** Pine
SONG: "Arkansas" **ENTERED UNION:** June 15, 1836 (25th)
CAPITAL AND LARGEST CITY: Little Rock (population, 183,133)
OTHER LARGE CITIES (WITH POP.): Fort Smith, 80,268, North Little
Rock, 60,433; **IMPORTANT PRODUCTS:** food products, paper,
electronic equipment, industrial machinery, metal products,
lumber and wood products, livestock, soybeans, rice, cotton, natural gas
PLACES TO VISIT: Hot Springs National Park; Arkansas House of Reptiles;
Band Museum in Pine Bluff; Ozark Folk Center, near Mountain View.

Little Rock ★

WEB SITE *http://www.state.ar.us • http://www.arkansas.com*

DID YOU KNOW? *Almost 1 million gallons of water flow out of the springs at Hot Springs every day. When Bill Clinton became governor in 1979 at the age of 32, he was the youngest in the nation.*

CALIFORNIA (CA) *Golden State*

POPULATION (2002): 35,116,033 (1st) **AREA:** 158,869
sq. mi. (3rd) (411,471 sq. km.) **FLOWER:** Golden poppy
BIRD: California valley quail **TREE:** California redwood **SONG:** "I Love You,
California" **ENTERED UNION:** September 9, 1850 (31st)
CAPITAL: Sacramento (population, 407,018)
LARGEST CITIES (WITH POP.): Los Angeles, 3,694,820; San Diego, 1,223,400;
San Jose, 894,943; San Francisco, 776,733
IMPORTANT PRODUCTS: transportation and industrial equipment,
electronic equipment, oil, natural gas, motion pictures, milk, cattle,
fruit, vegetables **PLACES TO VISIT:** Yosemite Valley, Lake Tahoe, Palomar
Observatory, Disneyland, San Diego Zoo, Hollywood, Sequoia National Park

Sacramento ★
San Francisco
Los Angeles
San Diego

WEB SITE *http://www.ca.gov • http://www.gocalif.ca.gov*

DID YOU KNOW? *In Death Valley, the hottest and driest place in the U.S., summer temperatures soar above 115° F. The oldest known living tree on Earth is a bristlecone pine tree called "Methuselah." It has stood in California's White Mountains for nearly 5,000 years!*

COLORADO (CO) *Centennial State*

POPULATION (2002): 4,506,542 (22nd) **AREA:** 104,100 sq. mi.
(8th) (269,619 sq. km.) **FLOWER:** Rocky Mountain
columbine **BIRD:** Lark bunting **TREE:** Colorado blue spruce
SONG: "Where the Columbines Grow" **ENTERED UNION:** August 1, 1876
(38th) **CAPITAL AND LARGEST CITY:** Denver (population, 554,636)
OTHER LARGE CITIES (WITH POP.): Colorado Springs, 360,890; Aurora,
276,393; Lakewood, 144,126 **IMPORTANT PRODUCTS:** instruments and
industrial machinery, food products, printing and publishing, metal
products, electronic equipment, oil, coal, cattle **PLACES TO VISIT:** Rocky Mountain
National Park, Mesa Verde National Park, Dinosaur National Monument, old mining towns

Denver ★
Colorado Springs

WEB SITE *http://www.colorado.gov • http://www.colorado.com*

DID YOU KNOW? *Denver is known as the Mile High City because of its altitude. Zebulon Pike discovered (1806), but never climbed, the famous mountain that bears his name, Pikes Peak.*

CONNECTICUT (CT) *Constitution State, Nutmeg State*

★ Hartford

POPULATION (2002): 3,460,503 (29th) **AREA:** 5,544 sq. mi. (48th) (14,359 sq. km.) **FLOWER:** Mountain laurel **BIRD:** American robin **TREE:** White oak **SONG:** "Yankee Doodle" **ENTERED UNION:** January 9, 1788 (5th) **CAPITAL:** Hartford **LARGEST CITIES (WITH POP.):** Bridgeport, 139,529; New Haven, 123,626; Hartford, 121,578; Stamford, 117,083; Waterbury, 107,271 **IMPORTANT PRODUCTS:** aircraft parts, helicopters, industrial machinery, metals and metal products, electronic equipment, printing and publishing, medical instruments, chemicals, dairy products, stone

PLACES TO VISIT: Mystic Seaport and Marine Life Aquarium, in Mystic; P. T. Barnum Circus Museum, Bridgeport; Peabody Museum, New Haven

WEB SITE http://www.ct.gov • http://www.tourism.state.ct.us

DID YOU KNOW? *The Hartford Courant is the country's oldest newspaper in continuous publication. It started as a weekly in 1764. George Washington placed an ad in the paper to rent out some of his land in Mount Vernon.*

DELAWARE (DE) *First State, Diamond State*

★ Dover

POPULATION (2002): 807,385 (45th) **AREA:** 2,396 sq. mi. (49th) (6,206 sq. km.) **FLOWER:** Peach blossom **BIRD:** Blue hen chicken **TREE:** American holly **SONG:** "Our Delaware" **ENTERED UNION:** December 7, 1787 (1st) **CAPITAL:** Dover **LARGEST CITIES (WITH POP.):** Wilmington, 72,664; Dover, 32,135; Newark, 28,547 **IMPORTANT PRODUCTS:** chemicals, transportation equipment, food products, chickens

PLACES TO VISIT: Rehoboth Beach, Henry Francis du Pont Winterthur Museum near Wilmington

WEB SITE http://www.delaware.gov • http://www.visitdelaware.net

DID YOU KNOW? *People from Sweden settled in Delaware, at Fort Christina (present-day Wilmington) in 1638.*

FLORIDA (FL) *Sunshine State*

Tallahassee
Jacksonville
Miami

POPULATION (2002): 16,713,149 (4th) **AREA:** 59,928 sq. mi. (23rd) (155,213 sq. km.) **FLOWER:** Orange blossom **BIRD:** Mockingbird **TREE:** Sabal palmetto palm **SONG:** "Old Folks at Home" **ENTERED UNION:** March 3, 1845 (27th) **CAPITAL:** Tallahassee (population, 150,624) **LARGEST CITIES (WITH POP.):** Jacksonville, 735,617; Miami, 362,470; Tampa, 303,447; St. Petersburg, 248,232 **IMPORTANT PRODUCTS:** electronic and transportation equipment, industrial machinery, printing and publishing, food products, citrus fruits, vegetables, livestock, phosphates, fish

PLACES TO VISIT: Walt Disney World and Universal Studios, near Orlando; Sea World, Orlando; Busch Gardens, Tampa; Spaceport USA, at Kennedy Space Center, Cape Canaveral; Everglades National Park

WEB SITE http://www.myflorida.com • http://www.flausa.com

DID YOU KNOW? *On his search for the legendary "Fountain of Youth," Ponce de León landed near the site of present-day Saint Augustine in spring 1513. He named the region Florida in honor of the Spanish name for Easter, Pascua Florida ("feast of the flowers").*

GEORGIA (GA) *Empire State of the South, Peach State*

POPULATION (2002): 8,560,310 (10th) **AREA:** 58,977 sq. mi. (24th) (152,750 sq. km.) **FLOWER:** Cherokee rose **BIRD:** Brown thrasher **TREE:** Live oak **SONG:** "Georgia on My Mind" **ENTERED UNION:** January 2, 1788 (4th) **CAPITAL AND LARGEST CITY:** Atlanta (population, 416,474) **OTHER LARGE CITIES (WITH POP.):** Augusta, 199,775, Columbus, 186,291; Savannah, 131,510 **IMPORTANT PRODUCTS:** clothing and textiles, transportation equipment, food products, paper, chickens, peanuts, peaches, clay **PLACES TO VISIT:** Stone Mountain Park; Six Flags Over Georgia; Martin Luther King Jr., National Historic Site, Atlanta

WEB SITE *http://www.georgia.gov • http://www.georgia.org/tourism/index.asp*

DID YOU KNOW? *Civil rights leader Martin Luther King Jr. (1929-1968) was born in Georgia. So was former President (and Georgia Governor) Jimmy Carter, who won the 2002 Nobel Peace Prize. Grits, made out of ground corn (or hominy), is the state's official food.*

HAWAII (HI) *Aloha State*

POPULATION (2002): 1,244,898 (42nd) **AREA:** 6,459 sq. mi. (47th) (16,728 sq. km.) **FLOWER:** Yellow hibiscus **BIRD:** Hawaiian goose **TREE:** Kukui **SONG:** "Hawaii Ponoi" **ENTERED UNION:** August 21, 1959 (50th) **CAPITAL AND LARGEST CITY:** Honolulu (population, 371,657) **OTHER LARGE CITIES (WITH POP.):** Hilo, 40,759; Kailua, 36,513; Kaneohe, 34,970 **IMPORTANT PRODUCTS:** food products, pineapples, sugar, printing and publishing, fish, flowers **PLACES TO VISIT:** Hawaii Volcanoes National Park; Haleakala National Park, Maui; U.S.S. Arizona Memorial, Pearl Harbor; Polynesian Cultural Center, Laie

WEB SITE *http://www.state.hi.us • http://www.gohawaii.com*

DID YOU KNOW? *Hawaii has eight main islands: Hawaii, Maui, Oahu, Kauai, Molokai, Lanai, Niihau, and Kahoolawe. Kilauea, a volcano on "the Big Island" of Hawaii, has been erupting continuously since 1983.*

IDAHO (ID) *Gem State*

POPULATION (2002): 1,341,131 (39th) **AREA:** 83,574 sq. mi. (14th) (216,456 sq. km.) **FLOWER:** Syringa **BIRD:** Mountain bluebird **TREE:** White pine **SONG:** "Here We Have Idaho" **ENTERED UNION:** July 3, 1890 (43rd) **CAPITAL AND LARGEST CITY:** Boise (population, 185,787) **OTHER LARGE CITIES (WITH POP.):** Nampa, 51,867; Pocatello, 51,466 **IMPORTANT PRODUCTS:** potatoes, hay, wheat, cattle, milk, lumber and wood products, food products **PLACES TO VISIT:** Sun Valley; Hells Canyon; Craters of the Moon, near Arco; World Center for Birds of Prey, Boise; ghost towns

WEB SITE *http://www.state.id.us • http://www.state.id.us*

DID YOU KNOW? *The famous ski resort at Sun Valley was opened in 1936 by the Union Pacific Railroad to attract more passengers to the West. The "Hokey Pokey" song was written in Sun Valley in the 1940s. Idaho grows two-thirds of all U.S. potatoes.*

ILLINOIS (IL) *Prairie State*

POPULATION (2002): 12,600,620 (5th) **AREA:** 57,918 sq. mi. (25th) (150,007 sq. km.) **FLOWER:** Native violet
BIRD: Cardinal **TREE:** White oak **SONG:** "Illinois"
ENTERED UNION: December 3, 1818 (21st) **CAPITAL:** Springfield (population, 111,454) **LARGEST CITIES (WITH POP.):** Chicago, 2,896,016; Rockford, 150,115; Aurora, 142,990; Naperville, 128,358; Peoria, 112,936;
IMPORTANT PRODUCTS: industrial machinery, metals and metal products, printing and publishing, electronic equipment, food products, corn, soybeans, hogs **PLACES TO VISIT:** Lincoln Park Zoo, Adler Planetarium, Field Museum of Natural History, and Museum of Science and Industry, all in Chicago; Abraham Lincoln's home and burial site, Springfield; New Salem Village

WEB SITE *http://www.illinois.gov • http://www.enjoyillinois.com*

DID YOU KNOW? *Abraham Lincoln moved from Indiana to Illinois in 1831. He served in the state legislature, and later represented Illinois in Congress. Illinois was his home until he became president in 1861. No wonder the state adopted the slogan, "Land of Lincoln."*

INDIANA (IN) *Hoosier State*

POPULATION (2002): 6,159,068 (14th) **AREA:** 36,420 sq. mi. (38th) (94,328 sq. km.) **FLOWER:** Peony **BIRD:** Cardinal
TREE: Tulip poplar **SONG:** "On the Banks of the Wabash, Far Away"
ENTERED UNION: December 11, 1816 (19th)
CAPITAL AND LARGEST CITY: Indianapolis (population, 791,926)
OTHER LARGE CITIES (WITH POP.): Fort Wayne, 205,727; Evansville, 121,582; South Bend, 107,789; Gary, 102,746; **IMPORTANT PRODUCTS:** transportation equipment, electronic equipment, industrial machinery, iron and steel, metal products, corn, soybeans, livestock, coal **PLACES TO VISIT:** Children's Museum, Indianapolis; Conner Prairie Pioneer Settlement, Noblesville; Lincoln Boyhood Memorial, Lincoln City; Wyandotte Cave

WEB SITE *http://www.state.in.us • http://www.in.gov/enjoyindiana*

DID YOU KNOW? *True to its motto, "Crossroads of America," Indiana has more miles of interstate highway per square mile than any other state.*

IOWA (IA) *Hawkeye State*

POPULATION (2002): 2,936,760 (30th) **AREA:** 56,276 sq. mi. (26th) (145,754 sq. km.) **FLOWER:** Wild rose
BIRD: Eastern goldfinch **TREE:** Oak **SONG:** "The Song of Iowa"
ENTERED UNION: December 28, 1846 (29th)
CAPITAL AND LARGEST CITY: Des Moines (population, 198,682)
OTHER LARGE CITIES (WITH POP.): Cedar Rapids, 120,758; Davenport, 98,359; Sioux City, 85,013 **IMPORTANT PRODUCTS:** corn, soybeans, hogs, cattle, industrial machinery, food products **PLACES TO VISIT:** Effigy Mounds National Monument, Marquette; Herbert Hoover Birthplace, West Branch; Living History Farms, Des Moines; Adventureland; the Amana Colonies; Fort Dodge Historical Museum

WEB SITE *http://www.state.ia.us • http://www.traveliowa.com*

DID YOU KNOW? *Iowa produces the most soybeans, corn, and hogs of any state. The 31st U.S. president, Iowa native Herbert Hoover, was the first president born west of the Mississippi.*

KANSAS (KS) *Sunflower State*

POPULATION (2002): 2,715,884 (32nd) **AREA:** 82,282 sq. mi. (15th) (213,110 sq. km.) **FLOWER:** Native sunflower
BIRD: Western meadowlark **TREE:** Cottonwood **SONG:** "Home on the Range" **ENTERED UNION:** January 29, 1861 (34th) **CAPITAL:** Topeka
LARGEST CITIES (WITH POP.): Wichita, 344,284; Overland Park, 149,080; Kansas City, 146,866; Topeka, 122,377 **IMPORTANT PRODUCTS:** cattle, aircraft and other transportation equipment, industrial machinery, food products, wheat, corn, hay, oil, natural gas **PLACES TO VISIT:** Dodge City; Fort Scott and Fort Larned national historical sites; Eisenhower Center, Abilene; Kansas Cosmosphere and Space Discovery Center, Hutchinson

WEB SITE http:// www.accesskansas.org • http://www.travelks.com

DID YOU KNOW? *The Chisholm Trail, used by cowboys to drive cattle from Texas through Indian Territory (now Oklahoma), ended in Abilene. Wyatt Earp, marshall of Dodge City, was among the legendary lawmen who kept the peace in rowdy frontier towns along the way.*

KENTUCKY (KY) *Bluegrass State*

POPULATION (2002): 4,092,891 (26th) **AREA:** 40,411 sq. mi. (37th) (104,665 sq. km.) **FLOWER:** Goldenrod
BIRD: Cardinal **TREE:** Tulip poplar **SONG:** "My Old Kentucky Home"
ENTERED UNION: June 1, 1792 (15th) **CAPITAL:** Frankfort (population, 27,741) **LARGEST CITIES (WITH POP.):** Lexington 260,512; Louisville, 256,231 **IMPORTANT PRODUCTS:** coal, industrial machinery, electronic equipment, transportation equipment, metals, tobacco, cattle **PLACES TO VISIT:** Mammoth Cave National Park; Lincoln's Birthplace, Hodgenville; Cumberland Gap National Historical Park, Middlesboro

WEB SITE http:// www.kentucky.gov • http://www.kentuckytourism.com

DID YOU KNOW? *Both Abraham Lincoln and Jefferson Davis, president of the Confederacy, were born here, less than 100 miles and one year apart. Most of the gold reserve of the U.S. government is stored at Fort Knox, in brick-size bars weighing about 28 pounds each.*

LOUISIANA (LA) *Pelican State*

POPULATION (2002): 4,482,646 (24th) **AREA:** 49,651 sq. mi. (31st) (128,596 sq. km.) **FLOWER:** Magnolia
BIRD: Eastern brown pelican **TREE:** Cypress **SONG:** "Give Me Louisiana"
ENTERED UNION: April 30, 1812 (18th) **CAPITAL:** Baton Rouge
LARGEST CITIES (WITH POP.): New Orleans, 484,674; Baton Rouge, 227,818; Shreveport, 200,145 **IMPORTANT PRODUCTS:** natural gas, oil, chemicals, transportation equipment, paper, food products, cotton, fish **PLACES TO VISIT:** Aquarium of the Americas, Audubon Zoo and Gardens, both New Orleans

WEB SITE http://www.state.la.us • http://www.louisianatravel.com

DID YOU KNOW? *In 1803 the U.S. paid France $15 million for the Louisiana Territory, which included most of present-day Louisiana and 12 more states. The purchase nearly doubled the size of the country. Thousands visit the world-famous Mardi Gras festival in New Orleans each year.*

MAINE (ME) *Pine Tree State*

POPULATION (2002): 1,294,464 (40th) **AREA:** 33,741 sq. mi. (39th) (87,389 sq. km.) **FLOWER:** White pine cone and tassel **BIRD:** Chickadee **TREE:** Eastern white pine **SONG:** "State of Maine Song" **ENTERED UNION:** March 15, 1820 (23rd) **CAPITAL:** Augusta (population, 18,560) **LARGEST CITIES (WITH POP.):** Portland, 64,249; Lewiston, 35,690; Bangor, 31,473 **IMPORTANT PRODUCTS:** paper, transportation equipment, wood and wood products, electronic equipment, footwear, clothing, potatoes, milk, eggs, fish, and seafood **PLACES TO VISIT:** Acadia National Park, Bar Harbor; Booth Bay Railway Museum; Portland Headlight Lighthouse, near Portland

WEB SITE *http://www.state.me.us • http://www.visitmaine.com*

DID YOU KNOW? *Maine is nearly as big as the other 5 New England states (Connecticut, Massachusetts, New Hampshire, Rhode Island, Vermont) combined. Maine harvests about 90% of all U.S. lobsters and blueberries.*

MARYLAND (MD) *Old Line State, Free State*

POPULATION (2002): 5,458,137 (18th) **AREA:** 12,297 sq. mi. (42nd) (31,849 sq. km.) **FLOWER:** Black-eyed susan **BIRD:** Baltimore oriole **TREE:** White oak **SONG:** "Maryland, My Maryland" **ENTERED UNION:** April 28, 1788 (7th) **CAPITAL:** Annapolis (population, 35,838) **LARGEST CITIES (WITH POP.):** Baltimore, 651,154; Frederick, 52,767; Gaithersburg, 52,613; Bowie, 50,269 **IMPORTANT PRODUCTS:** printing and publishing, food products, transportation equipment, electronic equipment, chickens, soybeans, corn, stone **PLACES TO VISIT:** Antietam National Battlefield; Fort McHenry National Monument, in Baltimore Harbor; U.S. Naval Academy in Annapolis

WEB SITE *http://www.state.md.us • http://www.mdisfun.org*

DID YOU KNOW? *Francis Scott Key wrote "The Star-Spangled Banner," inspired by the flag flying during the bombardment of Baltimore's Fort McHenry in the War of 1812. Annapolis was the nation's capital in 1783-84. The U.S. Naval Academy was founded there in 1845.*

MASSACHUSETTS (MA) *Bay State, Old Colony*

POPULATION (2002): 6,427,801 (13th) **AREA:** 9,241 sq. mi. (45th) (23,934 sq. km.) **FLOWER:** Mayflower **BIRD:** Chickadee **TREE:** American elm **SONG:** "All Hail to Massachusetts" **ENTERED UNION:** February 6, 1788 (6th) **CAPITAL AND LARGEST CITY:** Boston (population: 589,141) **OTHER LARGE CITIES (WITH POP.):** Worcester, 172,648; Springfield, 152,082; Lowell, 105,167 **IMPORTANT PRODUCTS:** industrial machinery, electronic equipment, instruments, printing and publishing, metal products, fish, flowers and shrubs, cranberries **PLACES TO VISIT:** Plymouth Rock; Minute Man National Historical Park; Children's Museum, Boston; Basketball Hall of Fame, Springfield; Old Sturbridge Village; Salem Witch Museum; Paul Revere's House, other sites on Boston's Freedom Trail

WEB SITE *http://www.mass.gov • http://www.massvacation.com*

DID YOU KNOW? *Four U.S. presidents were born here: John Adams and his son John Quincy Adams, John F. Kennedy, and George H. W. Bush. In 1891 James Naismith created the game of basketball in Springfield. A few years later, William G. Morgan developed volleyball in Holyoke.*

MICHIGAN (MI) *Great Lakes State, Wolverine State*

POPULATION (2002): 10,050,446 (8th) **FLOWER:** Apple blossom **BIRD:** Robin **TREE:** White pine **SONG:** "Michigan, My Michigan" **ENTERED UNION:** January 26, 1837 (26th) **CAPITAL:** Lansing (population, 127,825) **LARGEST CITIES (WITH POP.):** Detroit, 951,270; Grand Rapids, 197,800; Warren, 138,247; Flint, 124,943 **IMPORTANT PRODUCTS:** automobiles, industrial machinery, metal products, office furniture, plastic products, chemicals, food products, milk, corn, natural gas, iron ore, blueberries **PLACES TO VISIT:** Greenfield Village and Henry Ford Museum, Dearborn; Mackinac Island; Kalamazoo Aviation History Museum; Motown Historical Museum, Detroit

WEB SITE *http://www.michigan.gov • http://www.travel.michigan.com*

DID YOU KNOW? *Battle Creek, the headquarters for Kellogg's, Ralston Foods, and the Post cereal division of Kraft Foods, is known as the Cereal Capital of the World. The Mackinac Bridge, which connects Michigan's Lower and Upper Peninsulas, is one of the world's longest suspension bridges (main span, 3,800 feet).*

MINNESOTA (MN) *North Star State, Gopher State*

POPULATION (2002): 5,019,720 (21st) **AREA:** 86,943 sq. mi. (12th) (225,182 sq. km.) **FLOWER:** Pink and white lady's-slipper **BIRD:** Common loon **TREE:** Red pine **SONG:** "Hail! Minnesota" **ENTERED UNION:** May 11, 1858 (32nd) **CAPITAL:** St. Paul **LARGEST CITIES (WITH POP.):** Minneapolis, 382,618; St. Paul, 287,151 **IMPORTANT PRODUCTS:** industrial machinery, printing and publishing, computers, food products, scientific and medical instruments, milk, hogs, cattle, corn, soybeans, iron ore **PLACES TO VISIT:** Voyageurs National Park; Minnesota State Fair, Fort Snelling; U.S. Hockey Hall of Fame, Eveleth; Walker Art Center, Minneapolis

WEB SITE *http://www.state.mn.us • http://www.exploreminnesota.com*

DID YOU KNOW? *Minnesota's 11,000 lakes make boating a popular activity. The first TONKA truck was made near Lake Minnetonka, which it was named after. The Mall of America in Bloomington is the largest U.S. shopping mall, big enough to hold 32 Boeing 747 airplanes.*

MISSISSIPPI (MS) *Magnolia State*

POPULATION (2002): 2,871,782 (31st) **AREA:** 48,286 sq. mi. (32nd) (125,061 sq. km.) **FLOWER:** Magnolia **BIRD:** Mockingbird **TREE:** Magnolia **SONG:** "Go, Mississippi!" **ENTERED UNION:** December 10, 1817 (20th) **CAPITAL AND LARGEST CITY:** Jackson (population, 184,256) **OTHER LARGE CITIES (WITH POP.):** Gulfport, 71,127; Biloxi, 50,644; **IMPORTANT PRODUCTS:** transportation equipment, furniture, electrical machinery, lumber and wood products, cotton, rice, chickens, cattle **PLACES TO VISIT:** Vicksburg National Military Park; Natchez Trace Parkway; Old Capitol, Jackson; Old Spanish Fort and Museum, Pascagoula

WEB SITE *http://www.mississippi.gov • http://www.visitmississippi.org*

DID YOU KNOW? *Although very little snow falls in Mississippi, Flexible Flyer sleds are actually made there, in West Point. Elvis Presley, the "King" of rock and roll, was born in Tupelo.*

MISSOURI (MO) *Show Me State*

POPULATION (2002): 5,672,579 (17th) **AREA:** 69,709 sq. mi. (21st) (180,546 sq. km.) **FLOWER:** Hawthorn **BIRD:** Bluebird **TREE:** Dogwood **SONG:** "Missouri Waltz" **ENTERED UNION:** August 10, 1821 (24th) **CAPITAL:** Jefferson City (population, 39,636) **LARGEST CITIES (WITH POP.):** Kansas City, 441,545; St. Louis, 348,189; Springfield, 151,580; Independence, 113,288 **IMPORTANT PRODUCTS:** transportation equipment, electrical and electronic equipment, printing and publishing, food products, cattle, hogs, milk, soybeans, corn, hay, lead **PLACES TO VISIT:** Gateway Arch, St. Louis; Mark Twain Area, Hannibal; Harry S. Truman Museum, Independence; George Washington Carver Birthplace, Diamond; Pony Express Museum, St. Joseph

WEB SITE http://www.state.mo.us • http://www.missouritourism.org

DID YOU KNOW? *Gateway Arch in St. Louis, which honors the spirit of the western pioneers, is the tallest monument (630 feet high) in the U.S. In 1811-12, New Madrid was struck by three of the most powerful earthquakes in U.S. history, one of which was felt 1,000 miles away.*

MONTANA (MT) *Treasure State*

POPULATION (2002): 909,453 (44th) **AREA:** 147,046 sq. mi. (4th) (380,850 sq. km.) **FLOWER:** Bitterroot **BIRD:** Western meadowlark **TREE:** Ponderosa pine **SONG:** "Montana" **ENTERED UNION:** November 8, 1889 (41st) **CAPITAL:** Helena (population, 25,780) **LARGEST CITIES (WITH POP.):** Billings, 89,847; Missoula, 57,053; Great Falls, 56,690; Butte, 34,606 **IMPORTANT PRODUCTS:** cattle, copper, gold, wheat, barley, wood and paper products **PLACES TO VISIT:** Yellowstone and Glacier national parks; Little Bighorn Battlefield National Monument; Museum of the Rockies (in Bozeman); Museum of the Plains Indian, Blackfeet Reservation (near Browning)

WEB SITE http://www.state.mt.us • http://visitmt.com

DID YOU KNOW? *Grasshopper Glacier, in Custer National Forest, gets its name from the millions of grasshoppers trapped in its ice. Glacier National Park's 50-mile "Going-to-the-Sun Road" is considered one of the world's most scenic drives.*

NEBRASKA (NE) *Cornhusker State*

POPULATION (2002): 1,729,180 (38th) **AREA:** 77,358 sq. mi. (16th) (200,358 sq. km.) **FLOWER:** Goldenrod **BIRD:** Western meadowlark **TREE:** Cottonwood **SONG:** "Beautiful Nebraska" **ENTERED UNION:** March 1, 1867 (37th) **CAPITAL:** Lincoln **LARGEST CITIES (WITH POP.):** Omaha, 390,007; Lincoln, 225,581 **IMPORTANT PRODUCTS:** cattle, hogs, milk, corn, soybeans, hay, wheat, sorghum, food products, industrial machinery **PLACES TO VISIT:** Oregon Trail landmarks; Stuhr Museum of the Prairie Pioneer, Grand Island; Agate Fossil Beds National Monument; Boys Town, near Omaha

WEB SITE http://www.state.ne.us • http://www.visitnebraska.org

DID YOU KNOW? *Nebraska is the only state with a unicameral (one-house) legislature. Nebraska's Chimney Rock (a 500-foot-high natural rock formation) was the most famous landmark for travelers on the Oregon Trail.*

NEVADA (NV) *Sagebrush State, Battle Born State, Silver State*

POPULATION (2002): 2,173,491 (35th) **AREA:** 110,567 sq. mi. (7th) (286,368 sq. km.) **FLOWER:** Sagebrush **BIRD:** Mountain bluebird **TREES:** Single-leaf piñon, bristlecone pine **SONG:** "Home Means Nevada" **ENTERED UNION:** October 31, 1864 (36th) **CAPITAL:** Carson City (population, 52,457) **LARGEST CITIES (WITH POP.):** Las Vegas, 478,434; Reno, 180,480; Henderson, 175,381 **IMPORTANT PRODUCTS:** gold, silver, cattle, hay, food products, plastics, chemicals **PLACES TO VISIT:** Great Basin National Park, including Lehman Caves; Nevada State Museum, Carson City; Hoover Dam, Lake Tahoe, Pony Express Territory.

WEB SITE *http://www.nv.gov • http://www.travelnevada.com*

DID YOU KNOW? *The state's name is taken from the Sierra Nevada mountain range* (nevada *is Spanish for "snow covered"). Nevada produces 40% of all the silver mined in the United States.*

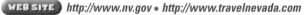

NEW HAMPSHIRE (NH) *Granite State*

POPULATION (2002): 1,275,056 (41st) **AREA:** 9,283 sq. mi. (44th) (24,043 sq. km.) **FLOWER:** Purple lilac **BIRD:** Purple finch **TREE:** White birch **SONG:** "Old New Hampshire" **ENTERED UNION:** June 21, 1788 (9th) **CAPITAL:** Concord **LARGEST CITIES (WITH POP.):** Manchester, 107,006; Nashua, 86,605; Concord, 40,687 **IMPORTANT PRODUCTS:** industrial machinery, electric and electronic equipment, metal products, plastic products, dairy products, maple syrup and maple sugar **PLACES TO VISIT:** White Mountain National Forest; Mount Washington; Old Man in the Mountain, Franconia Notch; Canterbury Shaker Village; Flume gorge and aerial tramway

WEB SITE *http://www.state.nh.us • http://www.visitnh.gov*

DID YOU KNOW? *New Hampshire was the first colony to declare its independence from England and start its own government—six months before the Declaration of Independence. Christa McAuliffe, who died in the 1986 explosion of the space shuttle* Challenger, *was a schoolteacher from Concord.*

NEW JERSEY (NJ) *Garden State*

POPULATION (2002): 8,590,300 (9th) **AREA:** 8,215 sq. mi. (46th) (21,277 sq. km.) **FLOWER:** Purple violet **BIRD:** Eastern goldfinch **TREE:** Red oak **SONG:** none **ENTERED UNION:** December 18, 1787 (3rd) **CAPITAL:** Trenton (population, 85,403) **LARGEST CITIES (WITH POP.):** Newark, 273,546; Jersey City, 240,055; Paterson, 149,222; Elizabeth, 120,568 **IMPORTANT PRODUCTS:** chemicals, pharmaceuticals/drugs, electronic equipment, nursery and greenhouse products, food products, tomatoes, blueberries, and peaches **PLACES TO VISIT:** ocean beaches; Edison National Historical Site, West Orange; Liberty State Park; Pine Barrens wilderness area; Revolutionary War sites

WEB SITE *http://www.state.nj.us • http://www.state.nj.us/travel*

DID YOU KNOW? *Inventor John P. Holland took the first practical submarine for its test dive in New Jersey's Passaic River. In the game Monopoly, the street names come from real streets in Atlantic City.*

NEW MEXICO (NM) *Land of Enchantment*

POPULATION (2002): 1,855,059 (36th) **AREA:** 121,598 sq. mi. (5th) (314,939 sq. km.) **FLOWER:** Yucca **BIRD:** Roadrunner **TREE:** Piñon **SONG:** "O, Fair New Mexico" **ENTERED UNION:** January 6, 1912 (47th) **CAPITAL:** Santa Fe **LARGEST CITIES (WITH POP.):** Albuquerque, 448,607; Las Cruces, 74,267; Santa Fe, 62,203
IMPORTANT PRODUCTS: electronic equipment, foods, machinery, clothing, lumber, transportation equipment, hay, onions, chiles
PLACES TO VISIT: Carlsbad Caverns National Park; Palace of the Governors and Mission of San Miguel, Santa Fe; Chaco Culture Natl. Historical Park; cliff dwellings

WEB SITE *http://www.state.nm.us • http://www.newmexico.org*

DID YOU KNOW? *The leaves of the yucca, New Mexico's state flower, can be used to make rope, baskets, and sandals. Hundreds of thousands of bats swarm out of New Mexico's Carlsbad Caverns every night to feed on insects.*

NEW YORK (NY) *Empire State*

POPULATION (2002): 19,157,532 (3rd) **AREA:** 53,989 sq. mi. (27th) (139,831 sq. km.) **FLOWER:** Rose **BIRD:** Bluebird **TREE:** Sugar maple **SONG:** "I Love New York" **ENTERED UNION:** July 26, 1788 (11th) **CAPITAL:** Albany (population, 95,658)
LARGEST CITIES (WITH POP.): New York, 8,008,278; Buffalo, 292,648; Rochester, 219,773; Yonkers, 196,086 **IMPORTANT PRODUCTS:** books and magazines, automobile and aircraft parts, toys and sporting goods, electronic equipment, machinery, clothing and textiles, metal products, milk, cattle, hay, apples **PLACES TO VISIT:** In New York City: American Museum of Natural History, Central Park, Empire State Building, United Nations, Bronx Zoo, Statue of Liberty, and Ellis Island. Niagara Falls; National Baseball Hall of Fame, Cooperstown; Fort Ticonderoga; Franklin D. Roosevelt National Historical Site, Hyde Park

WEB SITE *http://www.state.ny.us • http://www.iloveny.state.com*

DID YOU KNOW? *President George Washington was sworn in at Federal Hall in New York City, the first U.S. capital, in April 1789.*

NORTH CAROLINA (NC) *Tar Heel State, Old North State*

POPULATION (2002): 8,320,146 (11th) **AREA:** 52,672 sq. mi. (29th) (136,420 sq. km.) **FLOWER:** Dogwood **BIRD:** Cardinal **TREE:** Pine **SONG:** "The Old North State" **ENTERED UNION:** November 21, 1789 (12th) **CAPITAL:** Raleigh **LARGEST CITIES (WITH POP.):** Charlotte, 540,828; Raleigh, 276,093; Greensboro, 223,891; Durham, 187,035; Winston-Salem, 185,776; **IMPORTANT PRODUCTS:** clothing and textiles, tobacco and tobacco products, industrial machinery, electronic equipment, furniture, cotton, soybeans, peanuts
PLACES TO VISIT: Great Smoky Mountains National Park; Cape Hatteras National Seashore; Wright Brothers National Memorial, Kitty Hawk

WEB SITE *http://www.ncgov.com • http://www.visitnc.com*

DID YOU KNOW? *In 1903 the Wright Brothers made the first successful flight in a powered airplane near Kitty Hawk.*

NORTH DAKOTA (ND) *Peace Garden State*

POPULATION (2002): 634,110 (48th) **AREA:** 70,704 sq. mi. (18th) (183,123 sq. km.) **FLOWER:** Wild prairie rose **BIRD:** Western meadowlark **TREE:** American elm **SONG:** "North Dakota Hymn" **ENTERED UNION:** November 2, 1889 (39th) **CAPITAL:** Bismarck **LARGEST CITIES (WITH POP.):** Fargo, 90,599; Bismarck, 55,532; Grand Forks, 49,321; Minot, 36,567 **IMPORTANT PRODUCTS:** wheat, barley, hay, sunflowers, sugar beets, cattle, sand and gravel, food products, farm equipment, high-tech electronics **PLACES TO VISIT:** Theodore Roosevelt National Park; Bonanzaville, near Fargo; Dakota Dinosaur Museum, Dickinson; International Peace Garden

WEB SITE *hhttp://www.discovernd.com • http://www.ndtourism.com/frames.html*

DID YOU KNOW? *The state's nickname is taken from the International Peace Garden, which straddles the boundary between North Dakota and Manitoba in Canada.*

OHIO (OH) *Buckeye State*

POPULATION (2002): 11,421,267 (7th) **AREA:** 44,828 sq. mi. (34th) (116,103 sq. km.) **FLOWER:** Scarlet carnation **BIRD:** Cardinal **TREE:** Buckeye **SONG:** "Beautiful Ohio" **ENTERED UNION:** March 1, 1803 (17th) **CAPITAL AND LARGEST CITY:** Columbus (population, 711,470) **OTHER LARGE CITIES (WITH POP.):** Cleveland, 478,403; Cincinnati, 331,285; Toledo, 313,619; Akron, 217,074; Dayton, 166,179 **IMPORTANT PRODUCTS:** metal and metal products, transportation equipment, industrial machinery, rubber and plastic products, electronic equipment, printing and publishing, chemicals, food products, corn, soybeans, livestock, milk **PLACES TO VISIT:** Mound City Group, Indian burial mounds; Neil Armstrong Air and Space Museum; homes of and memorials to 8 U.S. presidents who lived here

WEB SITE *http://www.state.oh.us • http://www.ohiotourism.com/default_f.asp*

DID YOU KNOW? *The Rock and Roll Hall of Fame is in Cleveland, and the Pro Football Hall of Fame is in Canton. Ohio Senator John Glenn, in 1962 the first American to orbit Earth, returned to space in 1998 at the age of 77, the oldest person to fly in space.*

OKLAHOMA (OK) *Sooner State*

POPULATION (2002): 3,493,714 (28th) **AREA:** 69,903 sq. mi. (20th) (181,049 sq. km.) **FLOWER:** Mistletoe **BIRD:** Scissor-tailed flycatcher **TREE:** Redbud **SONG:** "Oklahoma!" **ENTERED UNION:** November 16, 1907 (46th) **CAPITAL AND LARGEST CITY:** Oklahoma City (population, 506,132) **OTHER LARGE CITIES (WITH POP.):** Tulsa, 393,049; Norman, 95,694; Lawton, 92,757 **IMPORTANT PRODUCTS:** natural gas, oil, cattle, nonelectrical machinery, transportation equipment, metal products, wheat, hay **PLACES TO VISIT:** Indian City U.S.A., near Anadarko; Fort Gibson Stockade; National Cowboy Hall of Fame; White Water Bay and Frontier City theme parks; Cherokee Heritage Center

WEB SITE *http://www.state.ok.us • http://www.travelok.com*

DID YOU KNOW? *Oklahoma has the largest Native American population of any state in the United States and is tribal headquarters for 39 tribes. Oklahoma City lies above an oil field, and derricks pump oil right on the Capitol grounds.*

OREGON (OR) *Beaver State*

POPULATION (2002): 3,521,515 (27th) **AREA:** 97,132 sq. mi. (10th) (251,572 sq. km.) **FLOWER:** Oregon grape **BIRD:** Western meadowlark **TREE:** Douglas fir **SONG:** "Oregon, My Oregon" **ENTERED UNION:** February 14, 1859 (33rd) **CAPITAL:** Salem **LARGEST CITIES (WITH POP.):** Portland, 529,121; Eugene, 137,893; Salem, 136,924 **IMPORTANT PRODUCTS:** lumber and wood products, electronics and semiconductors, food products, paper, cattle, hay, vegetables, Christmas trees **PLACES TO VISIT:** Crater Lake National Park; Oregon Caves National Monument; Fort Clatsop National Memorial; Oregon Museum of Science and Industry, Portland

WEB SITE *http://www.oregon.gov • http://www.traveloregon.com*

DID YOU KNOW? *The caves in Oregon Caves National Monument, discovered in 1874, are carved out of solid marble. Oregon has the only state flag with different pictures on each side—it has the state seal on the front and a beaver, the state animal, on the back.*

PENNSYLVANIA (PA) *Keystone State*

POPULATION (2002): 12,335,091 (6th) **AREA:** 46,058 sq. mi. (33rd) (119,290 sq. km.) **FLOWER:** Mountain laurel **BIRD:** Ruffed grouse **TREE:** Hemlock **SONG:** "Pennsylvania" **ENTERED UNION:** December 12, 1787 (2nd) **CAPITAL:** Harrisburg (population, 48,950) **LARGEST CITIES (WITH POP.):** Philadelphia, 1,517,550; Pittsburgh, 334,563; Allentown, 106,632; Erie, 103,717 **IMPORTANT PRODUCTS:** iron and steel, coal, industrial machinery, printing and publishing, food products, electronic equipment, transportation equipment, stone, clay and glass products **PLACES TO VISIT:** Independence Hall and other historic sites in Philadelphia; Franklin Institute Science Museum, Philadelphia; Valley Forge; Gettysburg; Hershey; Pennsylvania Dutch country, Lancaster County

WEB SITE *http://www.state.pa.us • http://www.experiencepa.com*

DID YOU KNOW? *A Civil War turning point, the battle at Gettysburg stopped the second, and last, major Confederate invasion of the North. Philadelphia opened the first U.S. public zoo in 1874. Williamsport is home to the Little League Baseball World Series.*

RHODE ISLAND (RI) *Little Rhody, Ocean State*

POPULATION (2002): 1,069,725 (43rd) **AREA:** 1,231 sq. mi. (50th) (3,188 sq. km.) **FLOWER:** Violet **BIRD:** Rhode Island red **TREE:** Red maple **SONG:** "Rhode Island" **ENTERED UNION:** May 29, 1790 (13th) **CAPITAL AND LARGEST CITY:** Providence (population, 173,618) **OTHER LARGE CITIES (WITH POP.):** Warwick, 85,808; Cranston, 79,269; Pawtucket, 72,958 **IMPORTANT PRODUCTS:** costume jewelry, toys, textiles, machinery, electronic equipment, fish **PLACES TO VISIT:** Block Island; International Tennis Hall of Fame, Newport; Newport Harbor; Green Animals Topiary Garden, Portsmouth

WEB SITE *http://www.state.ri.us • http://www.visitrhodeisland.com*

DID YOU KNOW? *The portrait of George Washington found on the $1 bill was painted by Rhode Islander Gilbert Stuart. Newport hosted the first circus in America, in 1774. Newport was also home to the first National Lawn Tennis Championship, in 1881.*

SOUTH CAROLINA (SC) *Palmetto State*

POPULATION (2002): 4,107,183 (25th) **AREA:** 31,189 sq. mi.
(40th) (80,779 sq. km.) **FLOWER:** Yellow jessamine
BIRD: Carolina wren **TREE:** Palmetto **SONG:** "Carolina"
ENTERED UNION: May 23, 1788 (8th) **CAPITAL AND LARGEST CITY:**
Columbia (population, 116,278) **OTHER LARGE CITIES (WITH POP.):**
Charleston, 96,650; North Charleston, 79,641; Greenville, 56,002
IMPORTANT PRODUCTS: clothing and textiles, chemicals, industrial
machinery, metal products, livestock, tobacco, Portland cement
PLACES TO VISIT: Grand Strand and Hilton Head Island beaches;
Revolutionary War battlefields; historic sites in Charleston; Fort Sumter.

Columbia

WEB SITE *http://www.myscgov.com • http://www.discoversouthcarolina.com*

DID YOU KNOW? *The Civil War began in Charleston harbor with the first shots fired on Fort Sumter in 1861.*

SOUTH DAKOTA (SD) *Mt. Rushmore State, Coyote State*

POPULATION (2002): 761,063 (46th) **AREA:** 77,121 sq. mi. (17th)
(199,743 sq. km.) **FLOWER:** Pasqueflower **BIRD:** Chinese
ring-necked pheasant **TREE:** Black Hills spruce **SONG:** "Hail, South
Dakota" **ENTERED UNION:** November 2, 1889 (40th) **CAPITAL:** Pierre
(population, 13,876) **LARGEST CITIES (WITH POP.):** Sioux Falls, 123,975;
Rapid City, 59,607 **IMPORTANT PRODUCTS:** food and food products,
machinery, electric and electronic equipment, corn, soybeans
PLACES TO VISIT: Mount Rushmore National Memorial; Crazy Horse
Memorial; Jewel Cave; Badlands and Wind Caves national parks; Wounded
Knee battlefield; Homestake Gold Mine

★ Pierre

WEB SITE *http://www.state.sd.us • http://www.travelsd.com*

DID YOU KNOW? *Massive sculptures in the Black Hills include the presidents' faces on Mt. Rushmore and the still-unfinished Crazy Horse Memorial, a mountain carved into the image of the Oglala Sioux chief seated on his horse.*

TENNESSEE (TN) *Volunteer State*

POPULATION (2002): 5,797,289 (16th) **AREA:** 42,146 sq. mi.
(36th) (109,158 sq. km.) **FLOWER:** Iris **BIRD:** Mockingbird
TREE: Tulip poplar **SONGS:** "My Homeland, Tennessee"; "When It's Iris
Time in Tennessee"; "My Tennessee"; "Tennessee Waltz"; "Rocky Top"
ENTERED UNION: June 1, 1796 (16th) **CAPITAL:** Nashville
LARGEST CITIES (WITH POP.): Memphis, 650,100; Nashville, 569,891;
Knoxville, 173,890; Chattanooga, 155,554 **IMPORTANT PRODUCTS:**
chemicals, machinery, vehicles, food products, metal products, publishing,
electronic equipment, paper products, rubber and plastic products, tobacco
PLACES TO VISIT: Great Smoky Mountains National Park; the Hermitage, home of President
Andrew Jackson, near Nashville; Civil War battle sites; Grand Old Opry, Nashville; Graceland,
home of Elvis Presley, in Memphis

★ Nashville
Memphis

WEB SITE *http://www.tn.gov • http://www.tennesseeanytime.org/main/travel*

DID YOU KNOW? *The Grand Ole Opry, the world's longest-running live radio program, is broadcast from Nashville, the world's country-music capital.*

TEXAS (TX) *Lone Star State*

POPULATION (2002): 21,779,893 (2nd) **AREA:** 267,277 sq. mi. (2nd) (692,247 sq. km.) **FLOWER:** Bluebonnet **BIRD:** Mockingbird **TREE:** Pecan **SONG:** "Texas, Our Texas" **ENTERED UNION:** December 29, 1845 (28th) **CAPITAL:** Austin **LARGEST CITIES (WITH POP.):** Houston, 1,953,631; Dallas, 1,188,580; San Antonio, 1,144,646; Austin, 656,562; El Paso, 563,662; Fort Worth, 534,694 **IMPORTANT PRODUCTS:** oil, natural gas, cattle, milk, eggs, transportation equipment, chemicals, clothing, industrial machinery, electrical and electronic equipment, cotton, grains **PLACES TO VISIT:** Guadalupe Mountains and Big Bend national parks; the Alamo, in San Antonio; Lyndon Johnson National Historic Site, near Johnson City; George Bush Presidential Library, College Station

WEB SITE *http://www.texasonline.com • http://www.traveltex.com*

DID YOU KNOW? *The Alamo, where in 1836 Texans fought against Mexico for independence, is considered the cradle of Texas liberty. The state was an independent nation from 1836 to 1845. Texas produces more oil and more cotton than any other state.*

UTAH (UT) *Beehive State*

POPULATION (2002): 2,316,256 (34th) **AREA:** 84,904 sq. mi. (13th) (219,902 sq. km.) **FLOWER:** Sego lily **BIRD:** Seagull **Tree:** Blue spruce **SONG:** "Utah, We Love Thee" **ENTERED UNION:** January 4, 1896 (45th) **CAPITAL AND LARGEST CITY:** Salt Lake City (population, 181,743) **OTHER LARGE CITIES (WITH POP.):** West Valley City, 108,896; Provo, 105,166 **IMPORTANT PRODUCTS:** transportation equipment, medical instruments, electronic parts, food products, steel, copper, cattle, corn, hay, wheat, barley **PLACES TO VISIT:** Arches, Canyonlands, Bryce Canyon, Zion, and Capitol Reef national parks; Great Salt Lake; Temple Square (Mormon Church headquarters) in Salt Lake City; Indian cliff dwellings

WEB SITE *http://www.utah.gov • http://www.utah.com*

DID YOU KNOW? *The last rails of the transcontinental railroad, connecting the tracks laid by the Union Pacific and Central Pacific railroad companies, were laid at Promontory Summit, Utah, in 1869. Utah's Great Salt Lake covers about 2,100 square miles, with an average depth of 13 feet.*

VERMONT (VT) *Green Mountain State*

POPULATION (2002): 616,592 (49th) **AREA:** 9,615 sq. mi. (43rd) (24,903 sq. km.) **FLOWER:** Red clover **BIRD:** Hermit thrush **TREE:** Sugar maple **SONG:** "These Green Mountains" **ENTERED UNION:** March 4, 1791 (14th) **CAPITAL:** Montpelier (population, 8,035) **LARGEST CITIES (WITH POP.):** Burlington, 38,889; Essex, 18,626 **IMPORTANT PRODUCTS:** machine tools, furniture, scales, books, computer parts, foods, dairy products, apples, maple syrup **PLACES TO VISIT:** Green Mountain National Forest; Teddy Bear Factory, Shelburne; Ben and Jerry's Ice Cream Factory, Waterbury; Montshire Museum of Science, Norwich

WEB SITE *http://www.vermont.gov • http://www.vermontvacation.com*

DID YOU KNOW? *With a population of about 8,000, Montpelier is the nation's smallest state capital. Vermont leads the U.S. in maple syrup production. Vermont has highest ratio of cows to people in the country.*

VIRGINIA (VA) *Old Dominion*

POPULATION (2002): 7,293,542 (12th) **AREA:** 42,326 sq. mi. (35th) (109,391 sq. km.) **FLOWER:** Dogwood
BIRD: Cardinal **TREE:** Dogwood **SONG:** "Carry Me Back to Old Virginia"
ENTERED UNION: June 25, 1788 (10th) **CAPITAL:** Richmond
LARGEST CITIES (WITH POP.): Virginia Beach, 425,257; Norfolk, 234,403; Chesapeake, 199,184; Richmond, 197,790; Newport News, 180,150 **IMPORTANT PRODUCTS:** transportation equipment, textiles, chemicals, printing, machinery, electronic equipment, food products, coal, livestock, tobacco, wood products, furniture **PLACES TO VISIT:** Colonial Williamsburg; Arlington National Cemetery; Mount Vernon (George Washington's home); Monticello (Thomas Jefferson's home); Shenandoah National Park

WEB SITE http://www.vipnet.org • http://www.virginia.org

DID YOU KNOW? *Founded in 1607, Jamestown was the first permanent English settlement in America and Virginia's first capital. Richmond, the capital today, was also capital of the Confederacy. The Pentagon in Arlington is one of the world's largest office buildings. It has 284 restrooms and 4,200 clocks.*

WASHINGTON (WA) *Evergreen State*

POPULATION (2002): 6,068,996 (15th) **AREA:** 70,637 sq. mi. (19th) (182,950 sq. km.) **FLOWER:** Western rhododendron
BIRD: Willow goldfinch **TREE:** Western hemlock **SONG:** "Washington, My Home" **ENTERED UNION:** November 11, 1889 (42nd) **CAPITAL:** Olympia (population, 42,514) **LARGEST CITIES (WITH POP.):** Seattle, 563,374; Spokane, 195,629; Tacoma, 193,556 **IMPORTANT PRODUCTS:** aircraft, lumber and plywood, pulp and paper, machinery, electronics, computer software, aluminum, processed fruits and vegetables **PLACES TO VISIT:** Mount Rainier, Olympic, and North Cascades national parks; Mount St. Helens; Seattle Center, with Space Needle and monorail

WEB SITE http://www.access.wa.gov • http://www.tourism.wa.gov

DID YOU KNOW? *Washington is the only state to be named after a U.S. president. It is no surprise that the apple is the state fruit, since Washington is the nation's top apple-producing state.*

WEST VIRGINIA (WV) *Mountain State*

POPULATION (2002): 1,801,873 (37th) **AREA:** 24,231 sq. mi. (41st) (62,759 sq. km.) **FLOWER:** Big rhododendron
BIRD: Cardinal **TREE:** Sugar maple **SONGS:** "The West Virginia Hills"; "This Is My West Virginia"; "West Virginia, My Home Sweet Home"
ENTERED UNION: June 20, 1863 (35th) **CAPITAL AND LARGEST CITY:** Charleston (population, 53,421) **OTHER LARGE CITIES (WITH POP.):** Huntington, 51,475; Wheeling, 33,099 **IMPORTANT PRODUCTS:** coal, natural gas, fabricated metal products, chemicals, automobile parts, aluminum, steel, machinery, cattle, hay, apples, peaches, tobacco **PLACES TO VISIT:** Harpers Ferry National Historic Park; Exhibition Coal Mine, Beckley; Monongahela National Forest

WEB SITE http://www.state.wv.us • http://www.callwva.com

DID YOU KNOW? *The New River Gorge Bridge near Fayetteville is the longest steel arch bridge (1,700 feet) in the world.*

WISCONSIN (WI) Badger State

POPULATION (2002): 5,441,196 (20th) **AREA:** 65,499 sq. mi. (22nd) (169,642 sq. km.) **FLOWER:** Wood violet **BIRD:** Robin **TREE:** Sugar maple **SONG:** "On, Wisconsin!" **ENTERED UNION:** May 29, 1848 (30th) **CAPITAL:** Madison **LARGEST CITIES (WITH POP.):** Milwaukee, 596,974; Madison, 208,054; Green Bay, 102,313; Kenosha, 90,352; Racine, 81,855 **IMPORTANT PRODUCTS:** paper products, printing, milk, butter, cheese, foods, food products, motor vehicles and equipment, medical instruments and supplies, plastics, corn, hay, vegetables **PLACES TO VISIT:** Wisconsin Dells; Cave of the Mounds, near Blue Mounds; Milwaukee Public Museum; Circus World Museum, Baraboo; National Railroad Museum, Green Bay

WEB SITE *http://www.wisconsin.gov • http://www.travelwisconsin.com*

DID YOU KNOW? *Wisconsin, the dairy capital of the U.S., produces more milk than any other state. One of the world's largest air shows takes place every year at the end of July in Oshkosh.*

WYOMING (WY) Cowboy State

POPULATION (2002): 498,703 (50th) **AREA:** 97,818 sq. mi. (9th) (253,349 sq. km.) **FLOWER:** Indian paintbrush **BIRD:** Western meadowlark **TREE:** Plains cottonwood **SONG:** "Wyoming" **ENTERED UNION:** July 10, 1890 (44th) **CAPITAL AND LARGEST CITY:** Cheyenne (population, 53,011) **OTHER LARGE CITIES (WITH POP.):** Casper, 49,644; Laramie, 27,204 **IMPORTANT PRODUCTS:** oil, natural gas, petroleum (oil) products, cattle, wheat, beans **PLACES TO VISIT:** Yellowstone and Grand Teton national parks; Fort Laramie; Buffalo Bill Historical Center, Cody; pioneer trails

WEB SITE *http://www.state.wy.us • http://www.wyomingtourism.org*

DID YOU KNOW? *Wyoming boasts the first official national park, Yellowstone, the first national forest, Shoshone, and the first national monument, Devils Tower.*

COMMONWEALTH OF PUERTO RICO (PR)

HISTORY: Christopher Columbus landed in Puerto Rico in 1493. Puerto Rico was a Spanish colony for centuries, then was ceded (given) to the United States in 1898 after the Spanish-American War. In 1952, still associated with the United States, Puerto Rico became a commonwealth with its own constitution. **POPULATION (2002):** 3,858,806 **AREA:** 3,508 sq. mi. (9,086 sq. km.) **FLOWER:** Maga **BIRD:** Reinita **TREE:** Ceiba **NATIONAL ANTHEM:** "La Borinqueña" **CAPITAL AND LARGEST CITY:** San Juan (population, 421,958) **OTHER LARGE CITIES (WITH POP.):** Bayamón, 224,431; Carolina, 186,935; Ponce, 186,286 **IMPORTANT PRODUCTS:** chemicals, food products, electronic equipment, clothing and textiles, industrial machinery, coffee, sugarcane, fruit, hogs **PLACES TO VISIT:** San Juan National Historic Site; beaches and resorts

WEB SITE *http://welcome.topuertorico.org/government.shtml*

DID YOU KNOW? *Puerto Rico is one of the world's most densely populated islands. La Fortaleza, dating from 1533, is the official residence of the governor, the oldest executive mansion in continuous use in the New World.*

WASHINGTON, D.C.

The Capital of the United States

Land Area: 61 square miles
Population (2002): 570,898
Flower: American beauty rose
Bird: Wood thrush

WEB SITE *http://www.washingtondc.gov*
http://www.washington.org

UNITED STATES

HISTORY

Washington, D.C., became the capital of the United States in 1800, when the federal government moved there from Philadelphia. The city of Washington was designed and built to be the capital. It was named after George Washington. Many of its major sights are on the Mall, an open grassy area that runs from the Capitol to the Potomac River.

Capitol, which houses the U.S. Congress, is at the east end of the Mall, on Capitol Hill. Its dome can be seen from far away.

Franklin Delano Roosevelt Memorial, honoring the 32nd president of the United States, and his wife, Eleanor, was dedicated in 1997. It is outdoors in a parklike setting.

Jefferson Memorial, a circular marble building located near the Potomac River. Its design is partly based on one by Thomas Jefferson for the University of Virginia.

Korean War Veterans Memorial, dedicated in 1995, is at the west end of the Mall. It shows troops ready for combat.

Lincoln Memorial, at the west end of the Mall, is built of white marble and styled like a Greek temple. Inside is a large, seated statue of Abraham Lincoln. His Gettysburg Address is carved on a nearby wall.

National Archives, on Constitution Avenue, holds the Declaration of Independence, Constitution, and Bill of Rights.

National Gallery of Art, on the Mall, is one of the world's great art museums.

National World War II Memorial, to be located between the Lincoln Memorial and the Washington Monument at the Mall, will honor all 16 million Americans who served during the war. Ground was broken in November 2000.

Smithsonian Institution has 14 museums, including the National Air and Space Museum and the Museum of Natural History. The National Zoo is part of the Smithsonian.

U.S. Holocaust Memorial Museum presents the history of the Nazis' murder of more than six million Jews and millions of other people from 1933 to 1945. The exhibit *Daniel's Story* tells the story of the Holocaust from a child's point of view.

Vietnam Veterans Memorial has a black-granite wall shaped like a V. Names of the Americans killed or missing in the Vietnam War are inscribed on the wall.

Washington Monument, a white marble pillar, or obelisk, standing on the Mall and rising to over 555 feet. From the top, there are wonderful views of the city.

White House, at 1600 Pennsylvania Avenue, has been the home of every U.S. president except George Washington.

Women in Military Service for America Memorial, near the entrance to Arlington National Cemetery. It honors the 1.8 million women who have served in the U.S. armed forces.

◀ *Jefferson Memorial*

285

HOW THE STATES

ALABAMA comes from an Indian word for "tribal town."

ALASKA comes from *alakshak*, the Aleutian (Eskimo) word meaning "peninsula" or "land that is not an island."

ARIZONA comes from a Pima Indian word meaning "little spring place," or the Aztec word *arizuma*, meaning "silver-bearing."

ARKANSAS is a variation of *Quapaw*, the name of an Indian tribe. *Quapaw* means "south wind."

CALIFORNIA is the name of an imaginary island in a Spanish story. It was named by Spanish explorers of Baja California, a part of Mexico.

COLORADO comes from a Spanish word meaning "red." It was first given to the Colorado River because of its reddish color.

CONNECTICUT comes from an Algonquin Indian word meaning "long river place."

Colorado

DELAWARE is named after Lord De La Warr, the English governor of Virginia in colonial times.

FLORIDA, which means "flowery" in Spanish, was named by the explorer Ponce de León, who landed there during Easter.

GEORGIA was named after King George II of England, who granted the right to create a colony there in 1732.

HAWAII probably comes from *Hawaiki*, or *Owhyhee*, the native Polynesian word for "homeland."

IDAHO's name is of uncertain origin, but it may come from a Kiowa Apache name for the Comanche Indians.

ILLINOIS is the French version of *Illini*, an Algonquin Indian word meaning "men" or "warriors."

INDIANA means "land of the Indians."

IOWA comes from the name of an American Indian tribe that lived on the land that is now the state.

KANSAS comes from a Sioux Indian word that possibly meant "people of the south wind."

KENTUCKY comes from an Iroquois Indian word, possibly meaning "meadowland."

LOUISIANA, which was first settled by French explorers, was named after King Louis XIV of France.

MAINE means "the mainland." English explorers called it that to distinguish it from islands nearby.

MARYLAND was named after Queen Henrietta Maria, wife of King Charles I of England, who granted the right to establish an English colony there.

MASSACHUSETTS comes from an Indian word meaning "large hill place."

MICHIGAN comes from the Chippewa Indian words *mici gama*, meaning "great water" (referring to Lake Michigan).

Michigan

MINNESOTA got its name from a Dakota Sioux Indian word meaning "cloudy water" or "sky-tinted water."

MISSISSIPPI is probably from Chippewa Indian words meaning "great river" or "gathering of all the waters," or from an Algonquin word, *messipi*.

MISSOURI comes from an Algonquin Indian term meaning "river of the big canoes."

Idaho

GOT THEIR NAMES

MONTANA comes from a Latin or Spanish word meaning "mountainous."

Nebraska

NEBRASKA comes from "flat river" or "broad water," an Omaha or Otos Indian name for the Platte River.

NEVADA means "snow-clad" in Spanish. Spanish explorers gave the name to the Sierra Nevada Mountains.

NEW HAMPSHIRE was named by an early settler after his home county of Hampshire, in England.

NEW JERSEY was named for the English Channel island of Jersey.

NEW MEXICO was given its name by 16th-century Spaniards in Mexico.

NEW YORK, first called New Netherland, was renamed for the Duke of York and Albany after the English took it from Dutch settlers.

NORTH CAROLINA, the northern part of the English colony of Carolana, was named for King Charles I.

NORTH DAKOTA comes from a Sioux Indian word meaning "friend" or "ally."

OHIO is the Iroquois Indian word for "fine or good river."

OKLAHOMA comes from a Choctaw Indian word meaning "red man."

OREGON may have come from *Ouaricon-sint,* a name on an old French map that was once given to what is now called the Columbia River. That river runs between Oregon and Washington.

PENNSYLVANIA meaning "Penn's woods," was the name given to the colony founded by William Penn.

RHODE ISLAND may have come from the Dutch "Roode Eylandt" (red island) or may have been named after the Greek island of Rhodes.

SOUTH CAROLINA, the southern part of the English colony of Carolana, was named for King Charles I.

South Dakota

SOUTH DAKOTA comes from a Sioux Indian word meaning "friend" or "ally."

TENNESSEE comes from "Tanasi," the name of Cherokee Indian villages on what is now the Little Tennessee River.

TEXAS comes from a word meaning "friends" or "allies," used by the Spanish to describe some of the American Indians living there.

UTAH comes from a Navajo word meaning "upper" or "higher up."

Utah

VERMONT comes from two French words, *vert* meaning "green" and *mont* "mountain."

VIRGINIA was named in honor of Queen Elizabeth I of England, who was known as the Virgin Queen because she was never married.

WASHINGTON was named after George Washington, the first president of the United States. It is the only state named after a president.

WEST VIRGINIA got its name from the people of western Virginia, who formed their own government during the Civil War.

WISCONSIN comes from a Chippewa name that is believed to mean "grassy place." It was once spelled *Ouisconsin* and *Mesconsing.*

Wyoming

WYOMING comes from Algonquin Indian words that are said to mean "at the big plains," "large prairie place," or "on the great plain."

NATIONAL PARKS
—AND THE LIKE

The world's first national park was Yellowstone, established in 1872. Today, there are 55 national parks, including one in the Virgin Islands and one in American Samoa. The National Park Service oversees 384 areas in all, also including national monuments, battlefields, military parks, historical parks, historic sites, lakeshores, seashores, recreation areas, scenic rivers and trails, and the White House—84.2 million acres all told! For more information, you can write the National Park Service, Department of the Interior, 1849 C Street NW, Washington, D.C. 20240.

For information on-line, go to **WEB SITE** *http://www.nps.gov/parks.html*

ALCATRAZ ISLAND NATIONAL HISTORIC LANDMARK

The island of Alcatraz is part of the Golden Gate National Recreation Area in San Francisco. The area, established in 1972, is the largest urban national park (75,000 acres) in the world. While the island is noted for its beautiful view, it's more famous for its prison, which housed such gangsters as Al Capone and George "Machine Gun" Kelly. It was a military prison from 1868 to 1933. It was a maximum-security penitentiary from then until it closed in 1963. The cold water and rough currents of San Francisco Bay made Alcatraz hard to escape from. More than 100 prisoners tried to get away over the years; only a handful made it.

ARCHES NATIONAL PARK

Located in southeastern Utah, this park (established in 1971) is famous for its beautiful natural rock formations. The eroding reddish sandstone has formed into amazing sculptures—peaks, pedestals, windows, and the largest gathering of natural arches in the world. The arches range in size from small ones about 3 feet wide to Landscape Arch, which is 306 feet wide and 105 feet high. The park, in a "high desert" more than 4,000 feet above sea level, has hot summers, cold winters, and very little rainfall. Temperatures can vary 50 degrees in one day. The desert may seem quiet and lifeless, but many kinds of birds, lizards, and rodents live there. Many of the plant and animal species are found nowhere else in the world.

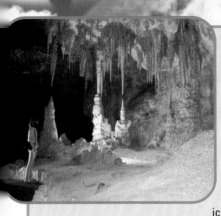

CARLSBAD CAVERNS NATIONAL PARK

This park, established in 1930, includes the 100 caves of Carlsbad Cavern and 33,125 acres of rugged wilderness in southeastern New Mexico. The caverns, a series of connecting halls and chambers, started forming 60 million years ago by the dissolving of water on limestone. The Big Room is the world's largest underground chamber. It's 4,000 feet long, 625 feet wide, and 285 feet high—enough for six football fields. In the caverns' chambers, icicle-shaped mineral formations hang from the ceiling *(stalactites)* and grow upward from the floor *(stalagmites);* these come in all different colors and sizes. There are 750 plant species, 331 types of birds, 64 species of mammals, and 44 species of reptiles and amphibians in the park. The caves are the summer home for a colony of a million Mexican free-tailed bats, which migrate there in search of insects.

STEAMTOWN NATIONAL HISTORIC SITE

Founded in 1986, this is the only place in the National Park System where the story of steam railroading is told. It's in Scranton, Pennsylvania, and was once part of the Delaware, Lackawanna, and Western Railroad Yard. Steamtown has steam, diesel, and electric locomotives and passenger and freight cars. It has history and technology museums and a working locomotive repair shop. Visitors can also ride 26 miles to Moscow, Pennsylvania, and back on restored 1920s Pullman passenger cars, pulled by a real steam engine.

YELLOWSTONE NATIONAL PARK

Located mostly in northwestern Wyoming, partly in eastern Idaho and southwestern Montana, Yellowstone is known for its 10,000 hot springs and geysers—more than anyplace else in the world. Old Faithful, the most famous geyser, erupts for about 4 minutes every 1-2 hours, shooting 3,700-8,400 gallons of hot water as high as 185 feet. Other geysers include the Giant, which shoots a column of hot water 200 feet high, and the Giantess, which erupts for over 4 hours at a time, but only about twice a year. There are grizzly bears, wolves, elk, moose, buffalo, deer, beavers, coyotes, antelopes, and 300 species of birds. In 1995, the endangered North American gray wolf—not seen in the area for 60 years—was reintroduced into the park.

Weather

Which is colder, –40°C or –40°F? ••• page 292

WEATHER WORDS

Barometer

BAROMETER An instrument that measures atmospheric pressure. Falling pressure means stormy weather, while rising pressure means calm weather.

BLIZZARD A heavy snowstorm with strong winds that, with blowing snow, make it hard to see.

DEW POINT The temperature the air needs to cool down to before precipitation can come.

FREEZING RAIN Water that freezes as it hits the ground.

FOG Tiny water droplets that float in the air. Fog is essentially a cloud formed at ground level.

FRONT Boundary between two air masses.

FROST Ice crystals that form on the ground or other surfaces.

HAIL Frozen water droplets that keep getting coated with ice until heavy enough to fall to the ground as hailstones.

HUMIDITY Amount of water vapor (water in the form of a gas) in the air.

PRECIPITATION Water that falls from clouds as rain, snow, hail, or sleet.

SLEET Water that reaches the ground as ice pellets or a mixture of snow and rain.

TORNADO A violently rotating column of air (wind) that forms a funnel. A tornado can suck up and destroy anything in its path, and also cause severe damage from flying debris.

Tornado

TYPHOON A hurricane (see page 291) that forms in the northern Pacific Ocean, west of the International Date Line.

WIND CHILL A measure of how cold it feels when there is a wind. When it is 35°F and the wind is 15 miles an hour, it will feel like 25°F.

WHAT IS EL NIÑO?

El Niño

EL NIÑO describes a change in the normal pattern of warm currents in the tropical Pacific Ocean that happens every 2 to 7 years. It is called "El Niño"—a Spanish phrase referring to the Christ child—because fishermen from Peru noticed that the warm waters in their area, indicating the current change, usually came around Christmas. In a normal year, warm water collects in the western Pacific and cold water rises near South America. But during El Niño, a large zone of warm water— 2 to 10 degrees warmer than the the the ocean around it—collects off the coast of South America (see orange on map). A change in wind patterns is one of the reasons this happens, but scientists still aren't sure of the exact causes. Other possible causes include changes in air pressure, global warming, and even undersea earthquakes.

Scientists use satellites as well as a network of buoys in the ocean to measure temperature, currents, and winds in the tropical Pacific Ocean. It is important to study El Niño because it leads to big changes in weather around the world. During El Niño, Australia often has droughts and terrible brushfires. The eastern U.S. gets colder (it snowed in Miami, Florida, in 1977). And in California, coastal storms cause a lot of damage.

WHAT IS A HURRICANE?

Hurricanes are the largest storms. They form over warm, usually tropical, oceans. As the warm seawater evaporates into the air, the pressure drops and winds begin to circulate, creating a huge wall of clouds and rain, wrapped around a calm center. As warm, moist air continues to feed the storm, it gets stronger and can spread out to an area 300 miles wide. Winds up to 250 miles an hour can rip trees out by their roots and tear roofs off buildings. Torrential rains and giant waves caused by the fierce wind can cause flooding and massive damage before the storm finally moves out over land and dies down.

HURRICANE NAMES IN THE NORTH ATLANTIC

Until the 20th century, people named storms after saints. In 1953, the U.S. government began to use women's names for hurricanes. Men's names were added in 1978.

2003: Ana, Bill, Claudette, Danny, Erika, Fabian, Grace, Henri, Isabel, Juan, Kate, Larry, Mindy, Nicholas, Odette, Peter, Rose, Sam, Teresa, Victor, Wanda

2004: Alex, Bonnie, Charley, Danielle, Earl, Frances, Gaston, Hermine, Ivan, Jeanne, Karl, Lisa, Matthew, Nicole, Otto, Paula, Richard, Shary, Tomas, Virginie, Walter

All About... LIGHTNING

The key to lightning is found in the ice particles that form in cumulonimbus (storm) clouds. Gravity and air currents cause these particles to rise and fall. As they bump into each other, they become positively or negatively charged. Negatively charged particles drop lower in the cloud and attract positive particles on the ground—in lightning rods, trees, and anything else nearby. When the negative and positive charges connect—zap!—there is a huge transfer of electricity (as much as 200 million volts), which we call lightning.

Lightning coming from the top of a cloud is called positive lightning and can be especially dangerous. It can strike as far as 5-10 miles away from the storm. It usually has a very strong electrical current and lasts longer than other lightning, making it more likely to start a fire.

Most lightning strikes (about 80%) are from cloud to cloud. Lightning can heat the air to over 50,000°F. The air expands and contracts rapidly as it heats and cools. This makes the shockwaves you hear as thunder. Because light travels more quickly than sound, the thunder usually takes much longer to reach your ears than the lightning does to reach your eyes.

According to the National Weather Service, lightning strikes the ground in the U.S. an estimated 25 million times a year. Even though 90% of lightning victims survive, there are an average of about 70 reported deaths and 300 injuries in the U.S. each year. For safety, follow the "30-30 Rule": Go indoors if you hear thunder 30 seconds or less after you see lightning, and don't go back out until 30 minutes after the last thunderclap. For more information, visit :

WEB SITE http://www.lightningsafety.noaa.gov

DID YOU KNOW? In 1753 Benjamin Franklin proved that lightning was electricity and not a supernatural force. He also invented the lightning rod, which provides an easier path for the electrical current to follow—away from a building or a house.

Taking Temperatures

Two systems for measuring temperature are used in weather forecasting. One is **Fahrenheit** (abbreviated F). The other is **Celsius** (abbreviated C). Another word for Celsius is Centigrade. Zero degrees (0°) Celsius is equal to 32 degrees (32°) Fahrenheit.

TO CONVERT FROM CELSIUS TO FAHRENHEIT:
Multiply by 1.8 and add 32. (°F = 1.8 x °C + 32)
Example: 20° C x 1.8 = 36; 36 + 32 = 68° F

TO CONVERT FROM FAHRENHEIT TO CELSIUS, REVERSE THE PROCESS:
Subtract 32 and divide by 1.8.
Example: 68° F – 32 = 36; 36/1.8= 20° C

DID YOU KNOW? –40° is –40°, whether you measure it in Celsius or Fahrenheit. It's the one point where the two scales meet. In really cold places, a thermometer containing colored alcohol (freezing point –202°) is better than one that uses mercury—which freezes at about –40°!

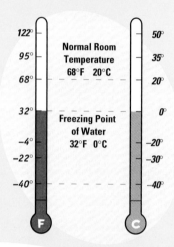

THE HOTTEST AND COLDEST PLACES IN THE WORLD

CONTINENT	HIGHEST TEMPERATURE	LOWEST TEMPERATURE
Africa	El Azizia, Libya, 136°F (58°C)	Ifrane, Morocco, –11°F (–24°C)
Antarctica	Vanda Station, 59°F (15°C)	Vostok, –129°F (–89°C)
Asia	Tirat Tsvi, Israel, 129°F (54°C)	Verkhoyansk, Russia, and Oimekon, Russia, –90°F (–68°C)
Australia	Cloncurry, Queensland, 128°F (53°C)	Charlotte Pass, New South Wales, –9°F (–23°C)
Europe	Seville, Spain, 122°F (50°C)	Ust'Shchugor, Russia, –67°F (–55°C)
North America	Death Valley, California, 134°F (57°C)	Snag, Yukon Territory, –81°F (–63°C)
South America	Rivadavia, Argentina, 120°F (49°C)	Sarmiento, Argentina, –27°F (–33°C)

HOTTEST PLACES IN THE U.S.

State	Temperature	Year
California	134°F	1913
Arizona	128°F	1994*
Nevada	125°F	1994*

* Tied with a record set earlier

COLDEST PLACES IN THE U.S.

State	Temperature	Year
Alaska	–80°F	1971
Montana	–70°F	1954
Utah	–69°F	1985

CLOUDS

Clouds come from moisture in the atmosphere that cools and forms into tiny water droplets or ice crystals. The science of clouds is called **nephology**. The names we still use for clouds come from a lecture given in December 1802 by the English meteorologist Luke Howard. Here are some of the cloud types that he named using Latin words. They fall into three main categories:

HIGH CLOUDS Cirrus clouds and other clouds that start with the prefix "cirro-" are generally found above 20,000 feet. (*Cirrus* in Latin means "lock of hair.")

❶ **Cirrus clouds** are thin, wispy high-altitude clouds made of ice crystals. They often appear in nice weather.

❷ **Cirrocumulus clouds** are small rounded white puffs that sometimes form in long rows. Sunlight can make them look like fish scales, which makes for a "mackerel sky."

Other clouds at this level are cirrostratus and contrails. Contrails (**con**densation **trails**) are man-made clouds formed when the hot humid jet exhaust hits very cold high altitude air.

MID-LEVEL CLOUDS Clouds that begin with the prefix "alto-" ("high") are usually found between 6,500 and 23,000 feet. They are high, though not the highest.

Altostratus clouds form a smooth gray or bluish sheet high up in the sky. The sun or moon can usually be seen faintly. (*Stratus* in Latin means "spread out.")

Altocumulus clouds are puffy gray blobs that appear in rows or waves. Part of the cloud is usually a little darker, distinguishing it from cirrocumulus.

LOW CLOUDS These clouds have no prefix and are generally found below 6,500 feet.

❸ **Cumulus clouds** are puffy white vertical clouds that get biggest during mid-afternoon. They form in many different shapes. (*Cumulus* means heap "heap" or "pile.")

❹ **Cumulonimbus clouds**, also known as storm clouds, are darkish and ominous-looking. They can bring heavy storms, often with thunder and lightning. (*Nimbus* means "storm cloud.")

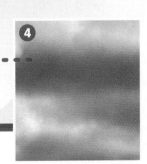

Nimbostratus clouds form a shapeless dark layer across the sky blocking out the sun and moon. They often bring a long period of snow or rain.

To read more about the weather try the Weather Channel at *http://www.weather.com* or try the government's National Oceanic and Atmospheric Administration at *http://www.noaa.gov*

Weights & Measures

How many cups are there in a quart?
•••
page 295

THE EARLIEST MEASUREMENTS

We use weights and measures all the time—you can measure how tall you are, or how much gasoline a car needs. People who lived in ancient times—more than 1,000 years ago—developed measurements to describe the amounts or sizes of things. The first measurements were based on the human body and on everyday activities.

Ancient measure

| **1 foot =** | **1 yard =** | **1 acre =** |
| length of a person's foot | from nose to fingertip | land an ox could plow in a day |

Modern measure

| 12 inches | 3 feet or 36 inches | 43,560 square feet or 4,840 square yards |

MEASUREMENTS WE USE TODAY

The system of measurement used in the United States is called the U.S. customary system. Most other countries use the metric system. A few metric measurements are also used in the United States, such as for soda, which comes in 1-liter and 2-liter bottles. In the following tables, abbreviations are given in parentheses the first time they are used.

LENGTH, HEIGHT, and DISTANCE

The basic unit of length in the U.S. system is the inch. Length, width, depth, and thickness all use the inch or larger related units.

1 foot (ft.) = 12 inches (in.)
1 yard (yd.) = 3 feet or 36 inches
1 rod (rd.) = 5½ yards
1 furlong (fur.) = 40 rods or 220 yards
    or 660 feet
1 mile (mi.) (also called statute mile) =
    8 furlongs or 1,760 yards or 5,280 feet

1 nautical mile = 6,076.1 feet or 1.15 statute miles
1 league = 3 miles

AREA

Area is used to measure a section of a flat surface like the floor or the ground. Most area measurements are given in square units. Land is measured in acres.

1 square foot (sq. ft.) = 144 square inches
    (sq. in.)
1 square yard (sq. yd.) = 9 square feet or
    1,296 square inches
1 square rod (sq. rd.) = 30¼ square yards
1 acre = 160 square rods or 4,840 square
    yards or 43,560 square feet
1 square mile (sq. mi.) = 640 acres

CAPACITY

Units of **capacity** are used to measure how much of something will fit into a container. **Liquid measure** is used to measure liquids, such as water or gasoline. **Dry measure** is used with large amounts of solid materials, like grain or fruit.

Dry Measure Although both liquid and dry measures use the terms "pint" and "quart," they mean different amounts and should not be confused. Look at the lists below for examples.

1 quart (qt.) = 2 pints (pt.)

1 peck (pk.) = 8 quarts

1 bushel (bu.) = 4 pecks

Liquid Measure Although the basic unit in liquid measure is the **gill** (4 fluid ounces), you are more likely to find liquids measured in pints or larger units.

1 gill = 4 fluid ounces

1 pint (pt.) = 4 gills or 16 ounces

1 quart (qt.) = 2 pints or 32 ounces

1 gallon (gal.) = 4 quarts = 128 ounces

For measuring most U.S. liquids,
 1 barrel (bbl.) = 31½ gallons

For measuring oil,
 1 barrel (bbl.) = 42 gallons

Cooking Measurements Cooking measure is used to measure amounts of solid and liquid foods used in cooking. The measurements used in cooking are based on the **fluid ounce**.

1 teaspoon (tsp.) = ⅙ fluid ounce (fl. oz.)

1 tablespoon (tbsp.) = 3 teaspoons or ½ fluid ounce

1 cup = 16 tablespoons or 8 fluid ounces

1 pint = 2 cups

1 quart = 2 pints

1 gallon = 4 quarts

VOLUME

The amount of space taken up by an object (or the amount of space available within an object) is measured in **volume**. Volume is usually expressed in **cubic units**. If you wanted to buy a room air conditioner and needed to know how much space there was to be cooled, you could measure the room in cubic feet.

1 cubic foot (cu. ft.) = 1,728 cubic inches (cu. in.)

1 cubic yard (cu. yd.) = 27 cubic feet

DEPTH

Some measurements of length are used to measure ocean depth and distance.

1 fathom = 6 feet

1 cable = 120 fathoms or 720 feet

WEIGHT

Although 1 cubic foot of popcorn and 1 cubic foot of rock take up the same amount of space, they wouldn't feel the same if you tried to lift them. We measure heaviness as **weight**. Most objects are measured in **avoirdupois weight** (pronounced a-ver-de-POIZ), although precious metals and medicines use different systems.

1 dram (dr.) = 27.344 grains (gr.)

1 ounce (oz.) = 16 drams or 437.5 grains

1 pound (lb.) = 16 ounces

1 hundredweight (cwt.) = 100 pounds

1 ton = 2,000 pounds
 (also called short ton)

Did You Know?

The letters we use to symbolize a pound (lb.) are actually an abbreviation for libra, the Latin word for a Roman unit that was about 12 oz. The letters oz., which stand for ounces, are an abbreviation of an Italian word for ounce, onza, which is no longer used, The word ounce comes from the Latin uncia, which means twelfth part.

THE METRIC SYSTEM

The metric system started in France in 1795. It is now used in many countries. In the metric system, the basic unit for length is the **meter**. The **liter** is a basic unit of volume or capacity, and the **gram** is a basic unit of mass. Related units are made by adding a prefix to the basic unit. The prefixes and their meanings are:

MILLI- = 1/1,000   **DECI- = 1/10**   **HECTO- = 100**
CENTI- = 1/100   **DEKA- = 10**   **KILO- = 1,000**

FOR EXAMPLE:

millimeter (mm)	= $\frac{1}{1,000}$ of a meter	milligram (mg)	= $\frac{1}{1,000}$ of a gram
kilometer (km)	= 1,000 meters	kilogram (kg)	= 1,000 grams

To get a rough idea of measurements in the metric system, it helps to know that a liter is a little more than a quart. A meter is a little over a yard. A kilogram is a little over 2 pounds. And a kilometer is just over half a mile.

An African elephant gets to be about 7,000 kilograms. That's about 15,400 pounds. ▶

Homework Help Converting Measurements

From:	Multiply by:	To get:	From:	Multiply by:	To get:
inches	2.5400	centimeters	centimeters	.3937	inches
inches	.0254	meters	centimeters	.0328	feet
feet	30.4800	centimeters	meters	39.3701	inches
feet	.3048	meters	meters	3.2808	feet
yards	.9144	meters	meters	1.0936	yards
miles	1.6093	kilometers	kilometers	.621	miles
square inches	6.4516	square centimeters	square centimeters	.1550	square inches
square feet	.0929	square meters	square meters	10.7639	square feet
square yards	.8361	square meters	square meters	1.1960	square yards
acres	.4047	hectares	hectares	2.4710	acres
cubic inches	16.3871	cubic centimeters	cubic centimeters	.0610	cubic inches
cubic feet	.0283	cubic meters	cubic meters	35.3147	cubic feet
cubic yards	.7646	cubic meters	cubic meters	1.3080	cubic yards
quarts (liquid)	.9464	liters	liters	1.0567	quarts (liquid)
ounces	28.3495	grams	grams	.0353	ounces
pounds	.4536	kilograms	kilograms	2.2046	pounds

World History

Who was the first woman in space?
•••
page 311

HIGHLIGHTS

Each of the five sections within this chapter covers a major region of the world: the Middle East, Africa, Asia, Europe, and the Americas. Major events from ancient times to the present are described under the headings for each region.

THE ANCIENT MIDDLE EAST 4000 B.C.–1 B.C.

4000–3000 B.C.
- ► The world's first cities are built by the Sumerian peoples in Mesopotamia, now southern Iraq.
- ► Sumerians develop a kind of writing called cuneiform.
- ► Egyptians develop a kind of writing called hieroglyphics.

2700 B.C. Egyptians begin building the great pyramids in the desert. The pharaohs' (kings') bodies are buried in them.

1792 B.C. Some of the first written laws are created in Babylonia. They are called the Code of Hammurabi.

ACHIEVEMENTS OF THE ANCIENT MIDDLE EAST

Early peoples of the Middle East:
1. Studied the stars (astronomy).
2. Invented the wheel.
3. Created written language from picture drawings (hieroglyphics and cuneiform).
4. Established the 24-hour day.
5. Studied medicine and mathematics.

eroglyphics

1200 B.C. Hebrew people settle in Canaan in Palestine after escaping from slavery in Egypt. They are led by the prophet Moses.

THE TEN COMMANDMENTS

Unlike most early peoples in the Middle East, the Hebrews believed in only one God (monotheism). They believed that God gave Moses the Ten Commandments on Mount Sinai when they fled Egypt.

1000 B.C. King David unites the Hebrews in one strong kingdom.

ANCIENT PALESTINE Palestine was invaded by many different peoples after 1000 B.C., including the Babylonians, the Egyptians, the Persians, and the Romans. It came under Arab Muslim control in the 600s and remained mainly under Muslim control until the 1900s.

336 B.C. Alexander the Great, King of Macedonia, builds an empire from Egypt to India.

63 B.C. Romans conquer Palestine and make it part of their empire.

AROUND 4 B.C. Jesus Christ, the founder of the Christian religion, is born in Bethlehem. He is crucified about A.D. 29.

◄ *The pyramids and sphinx at Giza*

ISLAM: A RELIGION GROWS IN THE MIDDLE EAST 570–632

Muhammad is born in Mecca in Arabia. Around 610, as a prophet, he starts to proclaim and teach Islam, a religion which spreads from Arabia to all the neighboring regions in the Middle East and North Africa. His followers are called Muslims.

THE KORAN

The holy book of Islam is the Koran. It was related by Muhammad beginning in 611. The Koran gives Muslims a program they must follow. For example, it gives rules about how one should treat one's parents and neighbors.

▲ *Muhammad*

632 Muhammad dies. By now, Islam is accepted in Arabia as a religion.

641 Arab Muslims conquer the Persians.

LATE 600s Islam begins to spread to the west into Africa and Spain.

711–732 Umayyads invade Europe but are defeated by Frankish leader Charles Martel in France. This defeat halts the spread of Islam into Western Europe.

1071 Muslim Turks conquer Jerusalem.

1095–1291 Europeans try to take back Jerusalem and other parts of the Middle East for Christians during the Crusades.

THE SPREAD OF ISLAM

The Arab armies that went across North Africa brought great change:
❶ The people who lived there were converted to Islam.
❷ The Arabic language replaced many local languages as an official language. North Africa is still an Arabic-speaking region today, and Islam is the major faith.

Dome of the Rock and the Western Wall, Jerusalem ▼

ACHIEVEMENTS OF THE UMAYYAD AND ABBASID DYNASTIES

The Umayyads (661–750) and the Abbasids (750–1256) were the first two Muslim-led dynasties. Both empires stretched across northern Africa across the Middle East and into Asia. Both were known for great achievements. They:
❶ Studied math and medicine.
❷ Translated the works of other peoples, including Greeks and Persians.
❸ Spread news of Chinese inventions like paper and gunpowder.
❹ Wrote great works on religion and philosophy.

1300–1900s The Ottoman Turks, who are Muslims, create a huge empire, covering the Middle East, North Africa, and part of Eastern Europe. The Ottoman Empire falls apart gradually, and European countries take over portions of it beginning in the 1800s.

1914–1918 World War I begins in 1914. The Ottoman Empire has now broken apart. Most of the Middle East falls under British or French control.

1921 Two new Arab kingdoms are created: Transjordan and Iraq. The French take control of Syria and Lebanon.

1922 Egypt becomes independent from Britain.

JEWS MIGRATE TO PALESTINE

Jewish settlers from Europe began migrating to Palestine in the 1880s. They wanted to return to the historic homeland of the Hebrew people. In 1945, after World War II, many Jews who survived the Holocaust migrated to Palestine. Arabs living in the region opposed the Jewish immigration. In 1948, after the British left, war broke out between the Jews and the Arabs.

THE MIDDLE EAST 1940s-2000s

1948 The state of Israel is created.

THE ARAB-ISRAELI WARS Arab countries near Israel (Egypt, Iraq, Jordan, Lebanon, and Syria) attack the new country in 1948 but fail to destroy it. Israel and its neighbors fight wars again in 1956, 1967, and 1973. Israel wins each war. In the 1967 war, Israel captures the Sinai Desert from Egypt, the Golan Heights from Syria, and the area known as the West Bank from Jordan.

1979 Egypt and Israel sign a peace treaty, providing for Israel to return the Sinai to Egypt.

THE MIDDLE EAST AND OIL
Much of the oil we use to drive our cars, heat our homes, and run our machines comes from the Arabian peninsula in the Middle East. For a brief time in 1973-1974, Arab nations would not let their oil be sold to the United States because of its support of Israel. The United States still relies heavily on oil imports from the region.

THE 1990s AND 2000s
▶ In 1991, the U.S. and its allies go to war with Iraq after Iraq invades Kuwait. Iraq is defeated and signs a peace agreement but is accused of violating it. In 2003, the U.S. and Britain invade Iraq and remove the regime.
▶ Tensions between Israel and the Palestinians increase, fueled by suicide bombings by Palestinians, and Israeli military actions in the occupied territories.

Oil fire in Kuwait during the 1991 Persian Gulf War

ANCIENT AFRICA 3500 B.C.-A.D. 900

ANCIENT AFRICA In ancient times, northern Africa was dominated, for the most part, by the Egyptians, Greeks, and Romans. However, we know very little about the lives of ancient people in Africa south of the Sahara Desert (sub-Saharan Africa).
The people of Africa south of the Sahara did not have written languages in ancient times. What we learn about them comes from such things as weapons, tools, and other items from their civilization that have been found in the earth.

2000 B.C. The Kingdom of Kush arises just south of Egypt. It becomes a major center of art, learning, and trade. Kush dies out around A.D. 350.

500 B.C. The Nok culture becomes strong in Nigeria, in West Africa. The Nok use iron for tools and weapons. They are also known for their fine terra-cotta sculptures of heads. ▶

AROUND A.D. 1 Bantu-speaking peoples in West Africa begin to move into eastern and southern Africa.

50 The Kingdom of Axum in northern Ethiopia, founded by traders from Arabia, becomes a wealthy trading center for ivory.

300s Ghana, the first known African state south of the Sahara Desert, takes power in the upper Senegal and Niger river region. It controls the trade in gold that is being sent from the southern parts of Africa north to the Mediterranean Sea.

660s-900 The Islamic religion spreads across North Africa and into Spain.

Niger River, Mali

AFRICA 900s-2000s

900 Arab Muslims begin to settle along the coast of East Africa. Their contact with Bantu people produces the Swahili language, which is still spoken today.

1050 The Almoravid Kingdom in Morocco, North Africa, is powerful from Ghana to as far north as Spain.

1230 The Mali Kingdom begins in North Africa. Timbuktu, a center for trade and learning, is its main city.

1464 The Songhay Empire becomes strong in West Africa. By around 1500, it has destroyed Mali. The Songhay are remembered for their bronze sculptures.

1505–1575 Portuguese settlement begins in Africa. Portuguese people settle in Angola, Mozambique, and other areas.

THE AFRICAN SLAVE TRADE

Once Europeans began settling in the New World, they needed people to harvest their sugar. The first African slaves were taken to the Caribbean. Later, slaves were taken to South America and the United States. The slaves were crowded onto ships and many died during the long journey. Shipping of African slaves to the United States lasted until the early 1800s.

1652–1835

1. Dutch settlers arrive in southern Africa. They are known as the Boers.
2. Shaka the Great forms a Zulu Empire in eastern Africa. The Zulus are warriors.
3. The "Great Trek" (march) of the Boers north takes place. They defeat the Zulus at the Battle of Bloody River.

1899: BOER WAR The South African War between Great Britain and the Boers begins. It is also called the Boer War. The Boers accept British rule but are allowed a role in government.

1948 The white South African government creates the policy of apartheid, the total separation of blacks and whites. Blacks are banned from restaurants, theaters, schools, and jobs considered "white." Apartheid sparked protests, many of which ended in bloodshed.

1983 Droughts (water shortages) lead to starvation over much of Africa.

THE 1990s AND 2000s

Apartheid ends in South Africa. Nelson Mandela becomes South Africa's first black president in 1994. Also in 1994, civil war in Rwanda leads to the massacre of 500,000 civilians. Meanwhile, the disease AIDS kills thousands each year. Africa accounts for 70 percent of AIDS cases worldwide. In Zimbabwe, for example, one out of every four adults has HIV/AIDS.

▲ Nelson Mandela

COLONIES WIN THEIR FREEDOM

Most of the countries on the African continent and nearby islands were once colonies of a European nation such as Britain, France, or Portugal, but later became independent. Here are some major African countries that achieved independence in the 1900s.

Country	Became Independent	From
Egypt	1952	Britain
Morocco	1956	France
Sudan	1956	Britain
Ghana	1957	Britain
Burkina Faso	1960	France
Cameroon	1960	France
Congo, Dem. Rep. of	1960	Belgium
Côte d'Ivoire	1960	France
Mali	1960	France
Niger	1960	France
Nigeria	1960	Britain
Zimbabwe	1960	Britain
South Africa	1961	Britain
Tanzania	1961	Britain
Algeria	1962	France
Uganda	1962	Britain
Kenya	1963	Britain
Malawi	1964	Britain
Angola	1975	Portugal
Mozambique	1975	Portugal

ANCIENT ASIA 3500 B.C.-1 B.C.

3500 B.C. Communities of people settle in the Indus River Valley of India and Pakistan and the Yellow River Valley of China.

2500 B.C. Cities of Mohenjo-Daro and Harappa in Pakistan become centers of trade and farming.

AROUND 1523 B.C. Shang peoples in China build walled towns and use a kind of writing based on pictures. This writing develops into the writing Chinese people use today.

1500 B.C. The Hindu religion (Hinduism) begins to spread throughout India.

AROUND 1050 B.C. Chou peoples in China overthrow the Shang and control large territories.

700 B.C. In China, a 500-year period begins in which many warring states fight one another.

563 B.C. Siddhartha Gautama is born in India. He becomes known as the Buddha—which means the "Enlightened One"—and is the founder of the Buddhist religion (Buddhism).

551 B.C. The Chinese philosopher Confucius is born. His teachings—especially the rules about how people should treat each other—spread throughout China and are still followed today. ▶

TWO IMPORTANT ASIAN RELIGIONS
Many of the world's religions began in Asia. Two of the most important were:
1. **Hinduism.** Hinduism began in India and has spread to other parts of southern Asia and to parts of the Pacific region.
2. **Buddhism.** Buddhism also began in India and spread to China, Japan, and Southeast Asia. Today, both religions have millions of followers all over the world.

320-232 B.C.: INDIA
1. Northern India is united under the emperor Chandragupta Maurya.
2. Asoka, emperor of India, sends Buddhist missionaries throughout southern Asia to spread the Buddhist religion.

221 B.C. The Chinese ruler Shih Huang Ti makes the Chinese language the same throughout the country. Around the same time, the Chinese begin building the Great Wall of China. Its main section is more than 2,000 miles long and is meant to keep invading peoples from the north out of China.

202 B.C. The Han people of China win control of all of China.

ACHIEVEMENTS OF THE ANCIENT CHINESE
1. Invented paper.
2. Invented gunpowder.
3. Studied astronomy.
4. Studied engineering.
5. Invented acupuncture to treat illnesses.

The Great Wall of China

320 The Gupta Empire controls northern India. The Guptas are Hindus. They drive the Buddhist religion out of India. The Guptas are well known for their many advances in the study of mathematics and medicine.

618 The Tang dynasty begins in China. The Tang dynasty is well known for music, poetry, and painting. They export silk and porcelains as far away as Africa.

THE SILK ROAD ▶

Around 100 B.C., only the Chinese knew how to make silk. Europeans were willing to pay high prices for the light, comfortable material. To get it, they sent fortunes in glass, gold, jade, and other items to China. The exchanges between Europeans and Chinese created one of the greatest trading routes in history—the Silk Road. Chinese inventions such as paper and gunpowder were also spread over the Silk Road. Europeans found out how to make silk around A.D. 500, but trade continued until about 1400.

960 The Northern Sung dynasty in China makes advances in banking and paper money. China's population of 50 million doubles over 200 years, thanks to improved ways of farming that lead to greater food production.

▼ *Statues from Angkor Wat temple, Cambodia*

1000 The Samurai, a warrior people, become powerful in Japan. They live by a code of honor known as Bushido. ▶

1180 The Khmer Empire based in Angkor is powerful in Cambodia. The empire became widely known for its beautiful temples.

1206 The Mongol people of Asia are united under the ruler Genghis Khan. He builds a huge army and creates an empire that stretches all the way from China to India, Russia, and Eastern Europe.

1264 Kublai Khan, the grandson of Genghis Khan, rules China as emperor from his new capital at Beijing.

1368 The Ming dynasty comes to power in China. The Ming drive the Mongols out of the country.

1467–1603 WAR AND PEACE IN JAPAN

❶ Civil war breaks out in Japan. The conflicts last more than 100 years.

❷ Peace comes to Japan under the military leader Hideyoshi.

❸ The Shogun period reaches its peak in Japan (it lasts until 1868). Europeans are driven out of the country and Christians are persecuted.

1526 THE MUGHALS IN INDIA

❶ The Mughal Empire in India begins under Babur. The Mughals are Muslims who invade and conquer India.

❷ Akbar, the grandson of Babur, becomes Mughal emperor of India. He attempts to unite Hindus and Muslims but does not succeed.

1644 The Ming dynasty in China is overthrown by the Manchu peoples. They allow more Europeans to trade in China.

1739 Nadir Shah, a Persian warrior, conquers parts of western India and captures the city of Delhi.

MODERN ASIA 1800s-2000s

1839 The Opium War takes place in China between the Chinese and the British. The British and other Western powers want to control trade in Asia. The Chinese want the British to stop selling opium to the Chinese. Britain wins the war in 1842.

1858 The French begin to take control of Indochina (Southeast Asia).

1868 The Shogunate dynasty ends in Japan. The new ruler is Emperor Meiji. Western ideas begin to influence the Japanese.

THE JAPANESE IN ASIA Japan became a powerful country during the early 20th century. It was a small country with few raw materials of its own. For example, Japan had to buy oil from other countries. The Japanese army and navy took control of the government during the 1930s. Japan soon began to invade some of its neighbors. In 1941, the United States and Japan went to war after Japan attacked the U.S. Navy at Pearl Harbor, Hawaii.

1945 Japan is defeated in World War II after the U.S. drops atomic bombs on the Japanese cities of Hiroshima and Nagasaki.

1947 India and Pakistan become independent from Great Britain, which had ruled them as colonies since the mid-1800s.

1949 China comes under the rule of the Communists led by Mao Zedong. ▶

CHINA UNDER THE COMMUNISTS The Communists brought many changes to China. Private property was abolished, and the government took over all businesses and farms. Religions were persecuted. Many people were put in jail or executed.

1950-1953 THE KOREAN WAR
North Korea, a Communist country, invades South Korea. The U.S. and other nations join to fight the invasion. China joins North Korea. The Korean War ends in 1953. Neither side wins.

1954-1975 THE VIETNAM WAR
The French are defeated in Indochina in 1954 by Vietnamese Communists. The U.S. sends troops in 1965 to fight on the side of South Vietnam against the Communists in the North. The U.S. withdraws in 1973. In 1975, South Vietnam is taken over by North Vietnam.

1972 President Richard Nixon visits China to improve relations.

1989 Chinese students protest for democracy, but the protests are crushed by the army in Beijing's Tiananmen Square.

THE 1990s Japan, South Korea, Taiwan, and some other countries show great strength in the early 1990s, but then have serious financial trouble. Iraq invades Kuwait but is driven back (1991) in a war with the U.S. and its allies. Britain returns Hong Kong to China (1997). China builds its economy, but is accused of widespread human rights abuses.

THE 2000s U.S.-led military action overthrows the Taliban regime in Afghanistan (2001) and seeks to root out terrorists there. North Korea admits it has been developing nuclear weapons. The U.S. and Britain (2003) go to war against Iraq and drive out the regime of Saddam Hussein.

Tokyo, Japan ▶

ANCIENT EUROPE 4000 B.C.–300s B.C.

4000 B.C. People in many parts of Europe start building monuments out of large stones called megaliths. Examples can still be seen today, including Stonehenge in England.

2500 B.C.–1200 B.C.
THE MINOANS AND THE MYCENAEANS

❶ People on the island of Crete (Minoans) in the Mediterranean Sea built great palaces and became sailors and traders.

❷ People in the city of Mycenae in Greece built stone walls and a great palace.

Treasury of Atreus at Mycenae

❸ Mycenaean people invaded Crete and destroyed the power of the Minoans.

THE TROJAN WAR The Trojan War was a conflict between invading Greeks and the people of Troas (Troy) in Southwestern Turkey around 1200 B.C. Although little is known today about the real war, it has become a part of Greek poetry and mythology. According to a famous legend, a group of Greek soldiers hid inside a huge wooden horse. The horse was pulled into the city of Troy. Then the soldiers jumped out of the horse and conquered Troy.

900-600 B.C. Celtic peoples in Northern Europe settle on farms and in villages and learn to mine for iron ore.

600 B.C. Etruscan peoples take over most of Italy. They build many cities and become traders.

SOME ACHIEVEMENTS OF THE GREEKS The early Greeks were responsible for:

❶ The first governments that were elected by people. Greeks invented democratic government.

❷ Great poets such as Homer, who composed the *Iliad*, a long poem about the Trojan War, and the *Odyssey*, an epic poem about the travels of Odysseus.

❸ Great thinkers such as Socrates, Plato, and Aristotle.

❹ Great architecture, like the Parthenon and the Temple of Athena Nike on the Acropolis in Athens (*see below*).

431 B.C. The Peloponnesian Wars begin between the Greek cities of Athens and Sparta. The wars end in 404 B.C. when Sparta wins.

338 B.C. King Philip II of Macedonia in northern Greece conquers all the cities of Greece.

336 B.C. Philip's son Alexander becomes king. He conquers lands and makes an empire from the Mediterranean Sea to India. He is known as Alexander the Great. For the next 300 years, Greek culture dominates this vast area.

Temple of Athena Nike ▼

The Parthenon

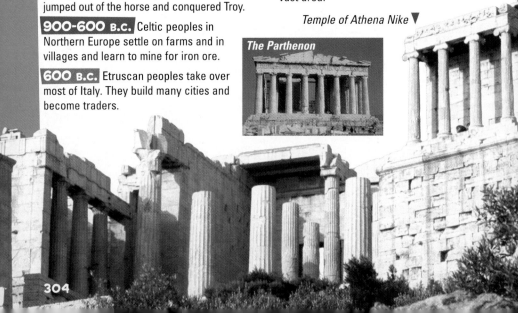

EUROPE 300 B.C.–A.D. 800s

264 B.C.–A.D. 476
ROMAN EMPIRE The city of Rome in Italy begins to expand and captures surrounding lands. The Romans gradually build a great empire and control all of the Mediterranean region. At its height, the Roman Empire includes Western Europe, Greece, Egypt, and much of the Middle East. The Roman Empire lasts until A.D. 476.

ROMAN ACHIEVEMENTS
1. Roman law. Many of our laws are based on Roman law.
2. Great roads to connect their huge empire. The Appian Way, south of Rome, is a Roman road that is still in use today.
3. Aqueducts to bring water to the people in large cities.
4. Great sculpture. Roman statues can still be seen in Europe.
5. Great architecture. The Colosseum, which still stands in Rome today, is an example of great Roman architecture.
6. Great writers, such as the poet Vergil, who wrote the Aeneid.

49 B.C. A civil war breaks out that destroys Rome's republican form of government.

45 B.C. Julius Caesar becomes the sole ruler of Rome but is murdered one year later by rivals in the Roman army. ▶

27 B.C. Octavian becomes the first emperor of Rome. He takes the name Augustus. A peaceful period of almost 200 years begins.

THE CHRISTIAN FAITH Christians believe that Jesus Christ is the Son of God. The history and beliefs of Christianity are found in the New Testament of the Bible. Christianity spread slowly throughout the Roman Empire. The Romans tried to stop the new religion and persecuted the Christians. They were forced to hold their services in hiding, and some were crucified. Eventually, more and more Romans became Christian.

337 The Roman Emperor Constantine becomes a Christian. He is the first Roman emperor to be a Christian.

410 The Visigoths and other barbarian tribes from northern Europe invade the Roman Empire and begin to take over its lands.

476 The last Roman emperor is overthrown.

THE BYZANTINE EMPIRE, centered in modern-day Turkey, was made up of the eastern half of the old Roman Empire. Byzantine rulers extended their power into western Europe. The great Byzantine Emperor Justinian ruled parts of Spain, North Africa, and Italy. The city of Constantinople (now Istanbul, Turkey) became the capital of the Byzantine Empire in 330.

768 Charlemagne becomes king of the Franks in northern Europe. He rules a kingdom that includes parts of France, Germany and northern Italy.

800 Feudalism becomes important in Europe. Feudalism means that poor farmers are allowed to farm a lord's land in return for certain services to the lord.

▼ *The Colosseum, Rome*

The Temple of Saturn, Rome

896 Magyar peoples from lands east of Russia found Hungary.

800s–900s Viking warriors and traders *Viking helmet* ▼ from Scandinavia begin to move into the British Isles, France, and parts of the Mediterranean.

989 The Russian state of Kiev becomes Christian.

1066 William of Normandy, a Frenchman, successfully invades England and makes himself king. He is known as William the Conqueror.

1096–1291 THE CRUSADES In 1096, Christian European kings and nobles sent a series of armies to the Middle East to try to capture the city of Jerusalem from the Muslims. Between 1096 and 1291 there were about ten Crusades. During the Crusades the Europeans briefly captured Jerusalem. But in the end, the Crusades did not succeed in their aim.

One of the most important results of the Crusades had nothing to do with religion: trade increased greatly between the Middle East and Europe.

1215 THE MAGNA CARTA The Magna Carta was a document agreed to by King John of England and the English nobility. The English king agreed that he did not have absolute power and had to obey the laws of the land. The Magna Carta was an important step toward democracy.

1290 The Ottoman Empire begins. It is controlled by Turkish Muslims who conquer lands in the eastern Mediterranean and the Middle East.

1337–1453 WAR AND PLAGUE IN EUROPE

❶ The Hundred Years' War (1337) begins in Europe between France and England. The war lasts until 1453 when France wins.

❷ The bubonic plague begins in Europe (1348). The plague, also called the Black Death, is a deadly disease caused by the bite of infected fleas. Perhaps as much as one third of the whole population of Europe dies from the plague.

1453 The Ottoman Turks capture the city of Constantinople and rename it Istanbul.

1517 THE REFORMATION The Reformation led to the breakup of the Christian church into Protestant and Roman Catholic branches in Europe. It started when the German priest Martin Luther opposed some teachings of the Church. He broke away from the pope (the leader of the Catholic church) and had many followers.

1534 King Henry VIII of England breaks away from the Roman Catholic church. He names himself head of the English (Anglican) church.

▲ *Queen Elizabeth I*

1558 The reign of King Henry's daughter Elizabeth I begins in England. During her long rule, England's power grows.

1588 The Spanish Armada (fleet of warships) is defeated by the English navy as Spain tries to invade England.

Ottoman Palace of Ciragan, Istanbul ▶

MODERN EUROPE 1600s-2000s

1600s The Ottoman Turks expand their empire through most of eastern and central Europe.

1618 The Thirty Years' War begins in Europe. The war is fought over religious issues. Much of Europe is destroyed in the conflict, which ends in 1648.

1642 The English civil war begins. King Charles I fights against the forces of the Parliament (legislature). The king's forces are defeated, and he is executed in 1649. But his son, Charles II, eventually returns as king in 1660.

1762 Catherine the Great becomes the Empress of Russia. She allows some religious freedom and extends the Russian Empire.

1789 THE FRENCH REVOLUTION
The French Revolution ended the rule of kings in France and led to democracy there. At first, however, there were wars, much bloodshed, and times when dictators took control. Many people were executed. King Louis XVI and Queen Marie Antoinette were overthrown in the Revolution, and both were executed in 1793.

1799 Napoleon Bonaparte, an army officer, becomes dictator of France. Under his rule, France conquers most of Europe by 1812.

1815 Napoleon's forces are defeated by the British and German armies at Waterloo (in Belgium). Napoleon is exiled to a remote island and dies there in 1821.

1848 Revolutions break out in countries of Europe. People force their rulers to make more democratic changes.

1914–1918 WORLD WAR I IN EUROPE At the start of World War I in Europe, Germany, Austria-Hungary and the Ottoman Empire opposed England, France, Russia, and, later, the U.S. (the Allies). The Allies won in 1918.

1917 The czar is overthrown in the Russian Revolution. The Bolsheviks (Communists) under Vladimir Lenin take control. Millions are starved, sent to labor camps, or executed under Joseph Stalin (1929-1953).

Vladimir Lenin

THE RISE OF HITLER Adolf Hitler became dictator of Germany in 1933. He joined forces with rulers in Italy and Japan to form the Axis powers. In World War II, the Axis powers were defeated by the Allies— Great Britain, the Soviet Union, and the U.S. During his rule, Hitler killed millions of Jews (the Holocaust) and others.

1945 The Cold War begins. It is a long period of tension between the United States and the Soviet Union. Both countries build up their armies and make nuclear weapons but do not go to war against each other.

THE 1990s Communist governments in Eastern Europe are replaced by democratic ones. Divided Germany becomes one nation. The Soviet Union breaks up. The European Union (EU) takes steps toward European unity. The North Atlantic Treaty Organization (NATO) bombs Yugoslavia in an effort to protect Albanians driven out of the Kosovo region.

2002 The euro becomes the single currency in 12 European Union nations.

2003 Yugoslavia ends as its last 2 republics, Serbia and Montenegro, join in a loose union.

Napoleon Bonaparte ▶

10,000–8000 B.C. People in North and South America gather plants for food and hunt animals using stone-pointed spears.

AROUND 3000 B.C. People in Central America begin farming, growing corn and beans for food.

▲ *The landing of Columbus*

1500 B.C. Mayan people in Central America begin to live in small villages.

500 B.C. People in North America begin to hunt buffalo to use for meat and for clothing.

100 B.C. The city of Teotihuacán is founded in Mexico. It becomes the center of a huge empire extending from central Mexico to Guatemala. Teotihuacán contains many large pyramids and temples.

A.D. 150 Mayan people in Guatemala build many centers for religious ceremonies. They create a calendar and learn mathematics and astronomy.

900 Toltec warriors in Mexico begin to invade lands of Mayan people. Mayans leave their old cities and move to the Yucatan Peninsula of Mexico.

1000 Native Americans in the southwestern United States begin to live in settlements called pueblos. They learn to farm.

1325 Mexican Indians known as Aztecs create huge city of Tenochtitlán and rule a large empire in Mexico. They are warriors who practice human sacrifice.

Mayan pyramid, Yucatan Peninsula, Mexico ▶

1492 Christopher Columbus sails from Europe across the Atlantic Ocean and lands in the Bahamas, in the Caribbean Sea. This marked the first step toward the founding of European settlements in the Americas.

1500 Portuguese explorers reach Brazil and claim it for Portugal.

1519 Spanish conqueror Hernán Cortés travels into the Aztec Empire in search of gold. The Aztecs are defeated in 1521 by Cortés. The Spanish take control of Mexico.

WHY DID THE SPANISH WIN? How did the Spanish defeat the powerful Aztec Empire in such a short time? One reason is that the Spanish had better weapons. Another is that the Aztecs became sick and died from diseases brought to the New World by the Spanish. The Aztecs had never had these illnesses before and, as a result, did not have immunity to them. Also, many neighboring Indians hated the Aztecs as conquerors. Those Indians helped the Spanish to defeat them.

1534 Jacques Cartier of France explores Canada.

1583 The first English colony in Canada is set up in Newfoundland.

1607 English colonists led by Captain John Smith settle in Jamestown, Virginia. Virginia was the oldest of the Thirteen Colonies that turned into the United States.

1619 First African slaves arrive in English-controlled America.

1682 The French explorer Robert Cavelier, sieur de la Salle, sails down the Mississippi River. The area is named Louisiana after the French King Louis XIV.

THE AMERICAS 1700s–2000s

EUROPEAN COLONIES By 1700, most of the Americas are under the control of Europeans:

Spain: Florida, southwestern United States, Mexico, Central America, western South America.

Portugal: eastern South America.

France: central United States, parts of Canada.

England: eastern U.S., parts of Canada.

Holland: eastern U.S., West Indies, eastern South America.

1700 European colonies in North and South America begin to grow in population and wealth.

1775–1783 AMERICAN REVOLUTION

The American Revolution begins in 1775 when the first shot is fired in Lexington, Massachusetts. The thirteen original British colonies in North America become independent under the Treaty of Paris, signed in 1783.

SIMÓN BOLÍVAR: LIBERATOR OF SOUTH AMERICA

In 1810, Simón Bolívar began a revolt against Spain. He fought for more than 10 years against the Spanish and became president of the independent country of Greater Colombia in 1824. As a result of his leadership, ten South American countries had become independent from Spain by 1830. However, Bolívar himself was criticized as being a dictator. ▶

1810–1910 MEXICO'S REVOLUTION

In 1846, Mexico and the United States go to war. Mexico loses parts of the Southwest and California to the U.S. A revolution in 1910 overthrows Porfirio Díaz.

BECOMING INDEPENDENT

Most countries of Latin America became independent of Spain in the early 1800s. Some took longer.

COUNTRY	YEAR OF INDEPENDENCE
Argentina	1816
Bolivia	1825
Brazil	1822[1]
Chile	1818
Colombia	1819
Ecuador	1822
Guyana	1966[2]
Mexico	1821
Paraguay	1811
Peru	1824
Suriname	1975[3]
Uruguay	1825
Venezuela	1821

[1]From Portugal.
[2]From Britain.
[3]From the Netherlands.

1867 The Canadian provinces are united as the Dominion of Canada.

1898 THE SPANISH-AMERICAN WAR Spain and the U.S. fight a brief war in 1898. Spain loses its colonies Cuba, Puerto Rico, and the Philippines.

U.S. POWER IN THE 1900s During the 1900s the U.S. strongly influenced affairs in the Americas. The U.S. sent troops to various countries, including Mexico (1914; 1916–1917), Nicaragua (1912–1933), Haiti (1915–1934; 1994–1995), and Panama (1989). In 1962, the U.S. went on alert when the Soviet Union put missiles on Cuba.

1994 The North American Free Trade Agreement (NAFTA) is signed to increase trade between the U.S., Canada, and Mexico.

2001 Terrorists crash planes into U.S. targets, killing about 3,000 people; the U.S. launches a "war on terrorism."

WOMEN IN HISTORY

Down through the ages, women have made many different kinds of contributions to history and culture and have sometimes played big roles in shaping events.

JOAN OF ARC (1412-1431), French heroine and patron saint of France, known as the Maid of Orléans. She led French troops to a big victory over the English in the battle of Orléans (1429), a turning point in the Hundred Years' War. Joan believed she was guided by voices, and dressed like a male warrior. In 1431 the French burned her at the stake as a heretic. The Catholic Church later declared her innocent, and she was made a saint in 1920.

ELIZABETH I (1533-1603), queen of England and Ireland (1558-1603). Known for her colorful personality and shrewd policies, Elizabeth worked to end war with France, put the economy in good shape, and promote the growth of England as a world power. She fostered national pride and creativity during her long period on the throne, which came to be known as the Elizabethan Age.

Elizabeth I

CATHERINE THE GREAT (1729-1796), empress of Russia (1762-1796). Catherine made Russia a European power and greatly expanded the territory of the Russian Empire. She raised the status of the nobles by granting them privileges such as freedom from military service and legal control over their serfs. She promoted culture as well as the education of women and religious tolerance.

ABIGAIL SMITH ADAMS (1744-1818), wife of John Adams, the second president of the United States, and mother of John Quincy Adams, the sixth president. During long absences from her husband, she ran the family farm and raised her five children. Abigail was very well-read and well-informed, and often discussed political issues with her husband. Her many letters to him reveal a lot about early American history.

ELIZABETH CADY STANTON (1815-1902), social reformer and leader of the women's rights movement. Along with Lucretia Mott, she organized the first women's rights convention (1848), and won passage of a resolution demanding voting rights for women. She was president of the National Woman Suffrage Association, which she and Susan B. Anthony founded in 1869.

Elizabeth Cady Stanton & Susan B. Anthony

SUSAN B. ANTHONY (1820-1906), radical reformer who, with Elizabeth Cady Stanton, led the struggle for women's rights. She was a lifelong campaigner for woman suffrage, but died 14 years before the adoption of the 19th Amendment, which allowed women to vote. She opposed the use of liquor and worked to free slaves. In 1979, the U.S. Mint issued the Susan B. Anthony dollar coin in her honor.

JULIETTE GORDON LOW (1860-1927), founder of the Girl Scouts of the USA. In 1912, a year after meeting Boy Scouts founder Sir Robert Baden-Powell in England, she organized the first Girl Guides troop in the U.S. It had 18 members. The name of the group was changed to Girl Scouts in 1913. She devoted the rest of her life to working with the Girl Scouts. Today there are nearly 4 million Girl Scouts in the United States.

Juliette Gordon Low ▶

MOTHER TERESA (1910-1997), Albanian-born Roman Catholic nun who devoted her life to helping the poor. She became a missionary nun at the age of 18. While serving as principal of a high school in Calcutta, India, she was greatly moved by the sick and dying on the city's streets. She founded her own religious order, the Missionaries of Charity, in Calcutta, and extended their work with the sick and dying worldwide. She received the Nobel Peace Prize in 1979.

ELLA FITZGERALD

(1917-1996), American jazz singer known for the technique called *scat* (singing with nonsense sounds). She was first discovered at age 16 at an amateur-night show in New York's Apollo Theater. Over the next 50 years, she toured the world, performing with Louis Armstrong and other jazz greats. She won 13 Grammys and a National Medal of Arts award

Ella Fitzgerald

(1987).

BETTY FRIEDAN (born 1921), American feminist leader whose book *The Feminine Mystique* (1963) challenged the idea that women could be happy only as wives and mothers. She was a co-founder (1966) and the first president (1966-1970) of the National Organization for Women (NOW), which seeks equal rights for women.

SANDRA DAY O'CONNOR (born 1930), the first woman Supreme Court justice. She grew up on a ranch in Arizona and became a lawyer. In 1972, while serving in the Arizona state senate, she became the first female statehouse majority leader in the United States. She later served as a judge. President Reagan named her to the Supreme Court in 1981.

TONI MORRISON (born 1931), American writer whose novels often deal with the struggles and experiences of black people. She received the National Book Critics Circle Award in 1977 for *Song of Solomon* and a Pulitzer Prize for fiction for the novel *Beloved* in 1988. In 1993 she became the first African American to win a Nobel Prize in literature.

◄ VALENTINA TERESHKOVA

(born 1937), Russian cosmonaut and the first woman in space. During her 3-day spaceflight in June 1963 aboard the *Vostok 6,* she orbited Earth 48 times. Five months later, she married cosmonaut Andrian Nikolayev. In 1964, she gave birth to a daughter, the first child born to parents who had both flown in space.

BILLIE JEAN KING ►

(born 1943), American tennis player who fought for women's equality in tennis. King won 12 Grand Slam singles titles. But her most famous victory may have been in the 1973 "Battle of the Sexes" match, when she beat male player Bobby Riggs in 3 straight sets. King helped start the first successful women's pro tennis tour in 1970. In 1971 she became the first woman athlete to win more than $100,000 in one season.

MAYA LIN (born 1959), Chinese-American architect and sculptor, who designed the Vietnam Veterans Memorial in Washington, D.C., when she was a 21-year-old college student. Her design beat out 1,400 other entries in a nationwide competition. Dedicated in 1982, the wall became one of the most visited sites in Washington.

Maya Lin ►

LOOKING BACK

FROM 2003

50 YEARS AGO—1953

▶ The death of Joseph Stalin, one of the cruelest dictators in history, ended his reign of terror in the Soviet Union.

▶ Edmund Hillary and Tenzing Norgay became the first humans to climb to the top of Mount Everest, the world's highest mountain.

▶ Francis Crick and James Watson figured out the structure of DNA, opening up a new era in biology. ▶

▶ The first mass-produced American sports car, the Corvette, rolled off the Chevrolet assembly line in Flint, Michigan.

▶ Reaching a speed of more than 760 mph as she flew her Sabre jet, Jacqueline Cochran became the first woman to fly a plane faster than the speed of sound.

▶ Based on the adventures of the "Man of Steel" in DC Comics, *The Adventures of Superman* (starring George Reeves) made its debut as a TV series.

100 YEARS AGO—1903

▶ The first Crayola crayons hit the market. Since then, more than 100 billion have been sold.

▶ In the first World Series, the Boston Pilgrims upset the Pittsburgh Pirates, five games to three.

▶ Orville Wright took off on a 12-second, 120-foot flight at Kitty Hawk, North Carolina, the first successful airplane flight in history. ▶

▶ The first cross-country automobile trip began in New York City and ended 52 days later in San Francisco.

▶ William Harley, 21, and Arthur Davidson, 20, sold the first Harley-Davidson motorcycle. Harleys came to be known as "hogs" after the racing team's mascot, a pig.

▶ The silent film *The Great Train Robbery* became the first major American movie. It was also the first movie with a realistic plot.

FROM 2004

50 YEARS AGO—1954

▶ Sir Roger Bannister, a British doctor, broke the 4-minute barrier for the mile when he ran the mile in a world-record 3 minutes, 59.4 seconds.

▶ *The Fellowship of the Ring,* the first book in *The Lord of the Rings* trilogy by J.R.R. Tolkien, was published. The 2002 movie based on the book won four Academy Awards.

▶ In a landmark decision, the U.S. Supreme Court ruled that segregating white and black students into different schools violated the U.S. Constitution.

▶ The first nuclear-powered submarine, the USS *Nautilus,* was launched in Groton, Connecticut.

▶ A vaccine against polio, developed by Dr. Jonas Salk, came into use and nearly wiped out this crippling disease in most of the world.

▶ Ellis Island closed its doors. Some 100 million Americans are descended from someone who entered the U.S. through this immigration station in New York Harbor.

100 YEARS AGO—1904

▶ The first thermos bottles were made for home use. The word *thermos* comes from a Greek word meaning "hot."

▶ The New York City subway system opened. It grew to become the biggest in the U.S., and one of the biggest in the world.

▶ Denton True "Cy" Young became the first player in major league history to pitch a perfect game, allowing no batter to reach first base. ▶

▶ The first Olympic Games in the U.S. were held in the summer in St. Louis, Missouri. They were part of the World Exposition celebrating the 100th anniversary of the Louisiana Purchase.

▶ Helen Keller, who was both blind and deaf, graduated from Radcliffe College; she had already written a famous book, *The Story of My Life* (1902).

HISTORY SEARCH

Find all the words in the Word Box. They go across, up, down, backward, and diagonally. Some letters are used for more than one word, and a few are not used at all.

```
P  P  J  A  K  O  S  A  X  M  E  O
E  Z  S  I  D  D  H  A  R  T  H  A
A  A  P  A  R  T  H  E  I  D  I  Z
R  L  N  H  A  H  S  G  H  V  M  N
L  M  E  S  O  P  O  T  A  M  I  A
H  S  T  A  N  T  O  N  A  E  D  P
A  I  R  Y  S  K  U  L  G  G  D  A
R  R  I  R  A  Q  I  Y  Y  C  L  J
B  X  A  M  A  O  P  B  V  A  E  C
O  V  C  B  N  T  A  T  D  N  E  Q
R  G  N  I  M  X  K  O  R  E  A  Y
J  O  A  N  O  F  A  R  C  Q  S  L
R  Q  W  L  E  A  R  S  I  Q  T  U
```

WORD BOX

Japan	Egypt	Shah	Joan of Arc
Mao	Israel	Mali	Oil
Ming	Arab	Stanton	Middle East
Korea	Pearl	Asoka	
Syria	Harbor	Siddhartha	
Iraq	Mesopotamia	Apartheid	

ANSWERS ON PAGES 314-317. FOR MORE PUZZLES GO TO WWW.WORLDALMANACFORKIDS.COM

PUZZLE ANSWERS

ANIMALS, Page 33: EAGLE MAZE

BOOKS, Page 42: ARE YOU A MUGGLE OR A MAGICIAN?

MATCH THE CHARM WITH ITS NAME:

1. (c) Rictusenpra; 2. (a) Tarantallegra; 3. (d) Finite Incantatem; 4. (b) Wingardium Leviosa

PICK THE ANSWER:

5. (c) The Shrieking Shack; 6. (d) Albus Dumbledore; 7. (a) Hagrid; 8. (d) Tom Riddle; 9. (b) Mr. Weasley; 10. (c) The Death Eaters

COMPUTERS, Page 56: COMPUTER CROSSWORD

¹E	N	²C	R	Y	P	T	I	O	³N
		P							E
	⁴B	U	⁵G		⁶I	N	⁷P	U	T
	R		B		C		O		W
⁸R	O	M			O		R		O
	W				N		T		R
	S			⁹C			A		K
¹⁰P	E	N		¹¹H	T	M	L		
	R			I					
			¹²S	P	A	M			

ENERGY, Page 64: POWER MATCHUP

Bus: *gasoline* (can also run on ethanol, natural gas, electricity, or diesel); **Electric Car:** *electricity* (can also be powered by gasoline, ethanol, diesel, natural gas, or hydrogen); **Sailboat:** *wind* (can also have diesel or electric engines); **Bullet Train:** *electricity;* **Lawn Mower:** *gasoline;* **Fan:** *electricity;* **Steam Train:** *coal* (can also be powered by diesel or electric); **Race Car:** *gasoline;* **Stove:** *natural gas* (can also be electric); **Aircraft Carrier:** *nuclear* (can also be powered by diesel); **Windmill:** *wind;* **Waterwheel:** *water*

FOR MORE PUZZLES GO TO WWW.WORLDALMANACFORKIDS.COM

HEALTH, Page 93: OPTICAL ILLUSIONS

Here are the actual letters behind the blue bar. Based on the shape of the letter tops you can see and their relationship to each other, your brain fills in the rest to try to make sense of it.

WQBID AIMANAG EQP KJDS

The black and white squares are known as **Hermann's Grid**. You probably see ghostly gray dots. They appear because of an effect called "lateral inhibition." This means that when light-receiving cells on your retina are activated, others next to them don't work as well. The place where the spots appear is an area that is surrounded by other receptor cells on your retina receiving white light. Where the cells don't work so well, the dots appear. This effect is greater in your side vision. If you look right at the dots, they disappear.

The blue circles are exactly the same size. This is an example of the **Titchner Illusion**. Your brain generally wants to increase the differences between things to make it easier to tell them apart. Inside the larger circles, your brain makes the blue circle look smaller than it really is. Inside the smaller circles, the blue circle looks bigger than it is.

INVENTIONS, Page 104: FAST FORWARD

1780: (C) bifocal glasses; **1879:** (E) practical lightbulb; **1903:** (D) propeller airplane; **1958:** (A) laser; **1977:** (B) space shuttle

1447: (B) moveable type; **1608:** (J) telescope; **1714:** (F) mercury thermometer; **1752:** (D) lightning rod; **1837:** (I) telegraph; **1867:** (A) typewriter; **1923:** (E) television; **1969:** (H) videotape cassette; **1980:** (C) rollerblades; **2001:** (G) Segway Human Transport

MONEY, Page 119: COIN CHALLENGES

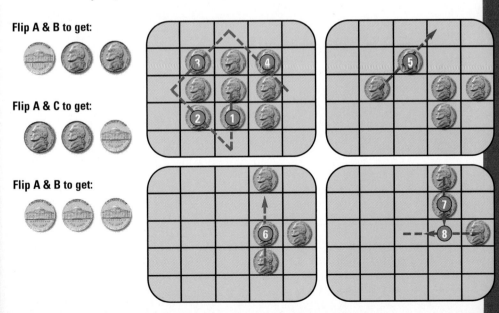

Flip A & B to get:

Flip A & C to get:

Flip A & B to get:

FOR MORE PUZZLES GO TO
WWW.WORLDALMANACFORKIDS.COM

MUSIC & DANCE, Page 130: A MUSICAL REVOLUTION?

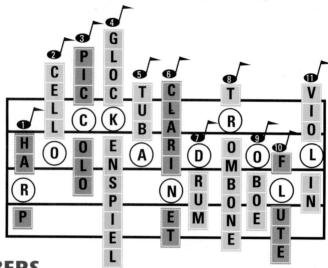

NUMBERS,

Page 172: ROMAN NUMERALS   DCCLIII

Page 177: OPERATION: GIANT SQUID   The length of the squid was 59 feet.

POPULATION, Page 182: A CITIZENSHIP TEST

1. To escape religious persecution; **2.** *Mayflower;* **3.** Great Britain; **4.** Abraham Lincoln; **5.** Republican and Democratic; **6.** November; **7.** January; **8.** 100; **9.** Six years; **10.** Patrick Henry

SPACE, Page 211: PLANETARY CROSS-SEARCH PUZZLE

Names of nine planets: Mercury; Venus; Earth; Mars; Jupiter; Saturn; Uranus; Neptune; Pluto

SUN
MOON
STARS
MILKYWAY
SATELLITE

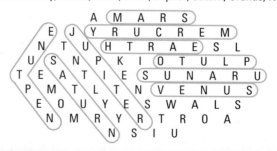

FOR MORE PUZZLES GO TO
WWW.WORLDALMANACFORKIDS.COM

UNITED STATES, Page 266:
THE AMAZING RACE ACROSS THE U.S.A.

WORLD HISTORY, Page 313: HISTORY SEARCH

P	P	J	A	K	O	S	A	X	M	E	O
E	Z	S	I	D	D	H	A	R	T	H	A
A	A	P	A	R	T	H	E	I	D	I	Z
R	L	N	H	A	H	S	G	H	V	M	N
L	M	E	S	O	P	O	T	A	M	I	A
H	S	T	A	N	T	O	N	A	E	D	P
A	I	R	Y	S	K	U	L	G	G	D	A
R	R	I	R	A	Q	I	Y	Y	C	L	J
B	X	A	M	A	O	P	B	V	A	E	C
O	V	C	B	N	T	A	T	D	N	E	Q
R	G	N	I	M	X	K	O	R	E	A	Y
J	O	A	N	O	F	A	R	C	Q	S	L
R	Q	W	L	E	A	R	S	I	Q	T	U

CONTEST WINNERS, Page 334: AUTO EVOLUTIONS

1. (C) Steam; 2. (A) Henry Ford; 3. (C) Quadricycle; 4. (B) Oxygen

FOR MORE PUZZLES GO TO
WWW.WORLDALMANACFORKIDS.COM

INDEX

D

E

THE WORLD ALMANAC FOR KIDS
"YOU BE THE EDITORS"
CLASSROOM CONTEST WINNERS

The World Almanac For Kids is happy to announce the two winning classes in the 2003 You Be the Editors classroom contest for grades 3 to 8. For the lower grades the winners were the third grade class at East School in New Canaan, Connecticut. For the upper grades the winners were a group of seventh grade students at Helen Keller Middle School in Royal Oaks, Michigan.

The winning classes received:
► A *World Almanac For Kids* Deluxe 25-book classroom kit
► A year's subscription to *Weekly Reader*

Each member of the winning class or group received:
► A copy of *The World Almanac For Kids 2004*

► A limited edition World Almanac For Kids T-shirt
► A gift certificate for a CD or cassette of their choice

Runner-up classes received limited-edition World Almanac For Kids T-shirts.

◄ *Upper-Grade Contest Winners for 2003—Seventh Grade Group at Helen Keller Middle School. Left to right: Brittany Voshol, Kala Groscurth, Daniel Brown, Sean English, teacher Donna Mitchell.*

Lower-Grade Contest Winners for 2003—Third Grade Class at East School. Shown with teacher Thomas Dempsey (in white shirt and tie), Titanic explorer Dr. Robert Ballard (in plaid shirt), and adult helpers, at a visit to Mystic Aquarium in Mystic, Connecticut. ►

The winning layouts, on the *Titanic* Disaster and Auto Evolutions, appear on the next three pages.

TITANIC DISASTER

The R.M.S. (Royal Mail Ship) *Titanic* was considered the safest ship in the world, but it did not survive its first voyage across the Atlantic Ocean. The *Titanic* got its name because "titanic" means huge and immense. It was as long as three football fields and as tall as an 11-story building. It had room for more than 3,500 people. At 11:40 P.M. on Sunday, April 14, 1912—the fourth night of its journey—the *Titanic* hit an iceberg. It sank 2 hours and 40 minutes later.

THAT FATEFUL NIGHT
April 14-15, 1912
In Memory of 1,523 Souls
April 15, 1912
02:20 A.M.
41.46 N 50.14 W

▲ *Captain Edward Smith*

KEY TERMS

Hypothermia—lower than normal body temperature, especially one low enough to cause very harmful changes to the body

Iceberg—large mass of ice, detached from a glacier and floating in the sea. About 90 percent of its mass is under the water.

Bow—the forward part of a ship or boat.

Stern—the rear part of a ship or boat.

HOW DID THE PEOPLE DIE?

A few of the crew members died from the flood in the boiler room. Some of the first-class passengers didn't want to go out in the cold, so they didn't leave their rooms while the ship was sinking. Of the 1,523 people who died, many of them drowned. But many others who fell or jumped into the water died of hypothermia because the water was so cold.

REASONS WHY THE *TITANIC* HIT THE ICEBERG

1. There was no moonlight in the sky. If there had been moonlight that night, the lookouts might have been able to see the iceberg by reflection.

2. The lookouts had no binoculars. They were either lost or removed for some reason before the ship left Southampton, England.

3. There were no waves. The waves would have hit the iceberg and bounced back, causing a rippling effect on the water, which would have made it easier to see the iceberg.

4. Captain Edward Smith retired for the evening. First Officer William Murdoch oversaw the controls. A lookout warned him about the iceberg and he turned the ship, but still hit it sideways at high speed.

5. Not listening to other ships warnings about the ice. The *Titanic*'s wireless room received several warnings about the thick ice in the North Atlantic. The warnings were disregarded.

SHIP AND ROOM COSTS

	Then (1912)	Now
To build the *Titanic*	$7,500,000	over $400,000,000
First Class Suite	$4,350.00	$69,000
Second Class Rooms	about $60.00	about $960.00

On September 1, 1985, Dr. Robert Ballard discovered the *Titanic* wreck, using his submersible sub named *Argo*.

DID YOU KNOW THESE IMPORTANT FACTS?

1. The series of gashes in the ship's bow totaled 12 square feet. That was all it took to sink the Titanic!
2. The *Titanic* carried people, mail, food, coal, clothing, animal skins, wine, books, and even several grandfather clocks.
3. It took two years to build the *Titanic*.
4. Skilled ship builders for the *Titanic* were paid $10 a week!
5. Only one, or maybe two, lifeboats looked for more survivors at the wreck site.

Auto Evolutions

First Cars

No one really knows what the first car was or who invented it. Henry Ford is often credited with inventing it, but that's not true. Many other cars came before Ford's Quadricycle in 1896. Leonardo da Vinci designed a car, but he never built it. People also say Father Ferdinand Verbiest built a car for a Chinese emperor, but no one knows for sure. Almost all the earliest cars were powered by steam. Can you believe that the average speed of the first steam car race was 6 miles per hour?

Early Evolutions

In the late 1800s "horseless carriages" made their debut. As more autos were produced, engines became more powerful. Gas was now stored in the same compartment as it was burned. The car could actually get up to 1000 rpm! Cars, which were once viewed as only for the rich, gained in popularity as people began to realize their advantages.

Henry Ford in his Quadricycle ▶

The Assembly Line

Henry Ford was born in Michigan and lived on a farm, but he didn't like farming. Instead, he wanted to be a mechanic. He started the Ford Motor Company, but they could only produce two cars per day, so in 1913 Ford invented the moving assembly line. This made it possible to make more cars per day. The first moving assembly line was located in Highland Park, a suburb of Detroit, and was 250 feet long. Ford's assembly line helped to make cars more affordable.

QUIZ

1. Most of the earliest cars were powered by _____?
A. Gasoline
B. Pedal power
C. Steam
D. Electricity

2. Who invented the moving assembly line?
A. Henry Ford
B. Walter P. Chrysler
C. Leonardo da Vinci
D. Nobody knows

3. Henry Ford's first car, in 1896, was the _____?
A. Model A
B. Model T
C. Quadricycle
D. Mustang

4. Fuel cells produce their own power by combining hydrogen and _____?
A. Carbon
B. Oxygen
C. Sulfur
D. Lead

ANSWERS ON PAGES 314-317.

Future Vehicles

As gas prices go up, and the ozone deteriorates, fuel cells are becoming more important. Fuel cells produce their own electricity by combining hydrogen and oxygen to create water vapor.

Another type of futuristic car is the electric or hybrid vehicle. There is only one problem... designing a lightweight battery that can hold a long charge. Many people think these cars are the way of the future. I guess we will have to wait and see!

Electric car ▶

ILLUSTRATION AND PHOTO CREDITS

This product/publication includes images from Artville, Comstock, Corbis, Corel, Map Art, PhotoDisc, and the ArtToday web site, which are protected by the copyright laws of the U.S., Canada, and elsewhere. Used under license.

ILLUSTRATION: Kerria Seabrooke: **33, 176, 266.**

PHOTOGRAPHY: 9: *Holes,* Disney Enterprises; others, AP/Wide World Photos. **10:** AP/Wide World Photos. **11:** Timberlake, AP/Wide World Photos; Pink, AFP Photo/Don Emmert. **12:** *Harry Potter,* HARRY POTTER AND THE CHAMBER OF SECRETS © 2002 MIRACLE Productions GmbH & Co. KG. All rights Reserved; *Holes,* Disney Enterprises. **13:** *X2,* AP/Wide World Photos; *Bend It Like Beckham,* BEND IT LIKE BECKHAM © 2003 Twentieth Century Fox. All rights reserved. **14:** DCI/Discovery Virtual Library. **15:** Cannon, Courtesy of Nickelodeon; "Zoom," WGBH Educational Foundation/Mark Ostow for WGBH © 2003. **16-19:** AP/Wide World Photos. **20:** Shuttle, crew, NASA; children, AP/Wide World Photos **21:** Rowling, William De La Hey; WTC site plans, Lower Manhattan Development Corp. **22:** Kids, Shi'a, AP/Wide World Photos; marines, U.S. Marine Corps photo by Lance Cpl. Brian L. Wickliffe. **23:** Rumsfeld, Dept. of Defense photo by Helene C. Stikkel; Lynch, Dept. of Defense; protesters, AP/Wide World Photos. **29:** Goodall, Michael Neugebauer. **34:** Mural, Jack Ramsdale. **35:** *Three Musicians,* Digital image © The Museum of Modern Art, NY/Licensed by Scala/Art Resource, NY © 2003 Estate of Pablo Picasso/Artist Rights Society (ARS), New York; Watts Tower, Library of Congress (LOC), Prints & Photographs Division, Historic American Buildings Survey or Historic American Engineering Record, (HABS,CAL,19-OSAN,73-4)/Walter Smalling, Jr. **36:** Kerria Seabrooke. **37:** *December,* John Lamka; Longo, Garrick Imatani. **38:** Lucid, NASA; Irwin, DCI/Discovery Virtual Library; Earhart, LOC Prints & Photographs Div. [LC-USZ62-20901]. **39:** Wright, LOC Prints & Photographs Div. [LC-DIG-ppprs-00683]; Hawk, Prince William, AP/Wide World Photos. **40:** Bush, Eric Draper—The White House; Armstrong, NASA; Lavigne, AP/Wide World Photos. **41:** Roosevelt, LOC Prints & Photographs Div. [LC-USZ62-25812]; Rice, The White House; Woods, AP/Wide World Photos. **42:** *Harry Potter and the Order of the Phoenix,* HARRY POTTER, characters, names, and related indicia are trademarks of and © Warner Bros. Harry Potter Publishing Rights © J.K. Rowling; Rowling, William De La Hey. **43:** *Crispin: The Cross of Lead,* From CRISPIN: THE CROSS OF LEAD by Avi. Copyright © 2002 Avi. Reprinted by permission of Hyperion Books For Children. **44:** *A Corner of the Universe* by Ann M. Martin, Scholastic Inc. **47:** Handler, HarperCollins; Twain, LOC Prints & Photographs Div. [LC-USZ62-5513]. **48:** Petronas, AP/Wide World Photos. **49:** Home Insurance, Courtesy of the Frances Loeb Library, Graduate School of Design, Harvard Univ. **50:** Burj al Arab, Courtesy of Jumeirah International; Guggenheim, Allan Jaworski. **55:** Eightythree, Tiqit Computers; Digi Pen, Logitech; *Backyard Baseball,* Atari, Inc. **56:** Earth Simulator, AP/Wide World Photos. **57:** Microraptor, Portia Sloan for IVPP. **64:** Solar car, Schenck & Schenck 2001. **69:** Rob Domenech. **79:** Mattel, Inc. **100:** Kristyn Romaine. **101:** Transporter, Courtesy of Segway LLC. **103:** Microchain, Courtesy Sandia National Laboratories, SUMMiT™ Technologies, www.mems.sandia.gov. **113:** U.S. Dept. of Defense. **114:** B-2A, U.S. Air Force; RQ-1, U.S. Dept. of Defense; F-117A, U.S. Air Force photo by Staff Sgt. Derrick C. Goode. **115:** Aircraft carrier, U.S. Navy photo by Photographer's Mate 1st Class Michael W. Pendergrass; Abrams tank, Stryker, U.S. Army. **118:** U.S. Mint. **119:** $20 bill, © 2003 Dept. of the Treasury Bureau of Engraving and Printing. **120:** *Lord of the Rings,* © 2002 New Line Productions, Inc. **121:** Disney Enterprises. **122:** SpongeBob, "SpongeBob SquarePants" created by Stephen Hillenburg, © 2003 Viacom International Inc. All rights reserved. Nickelodeon, SpongeBob SquarePants and all related titles, logos and characters are trademarks of Viacom International Inc. **123:** Duff, AP/Wide World Photos; LaBeouf, Ute Ville. **124:** Keith Stanley, www.kestan.com. **125:** St. Johns County VCB/www.byways.org. **126:** Museum, San Francisco Maritime National Historical Park. **128:** AP/Wide World Photos. **132-133:** Egypt, Guatemala, Japan, UN/DPI Photo. **181:** LOC, Prints & Photographs Div. [LC-B201-5202-13). **183:** Carter, Rick Diamond/The Carter Center; Annan, UN/DPI PHOTO. **184:** Morrison, Timothy Greenfield-Sanders; Angelou, Ms. Nancy Robinson. **185:** Clay Patrick McBride, Jr. **187:** Car, Babette Romaine; Anaya, Angel Fire Resort. **195:** Texas A&M Univ. College of Veterinary Medicine. **197:** Ontario Science Centre. **200:** Lori P. Wiesenfeld. **205-206:** NASA. **209:** Lucid, NASA. **212:** Zito, AP/Wide World Photos. **213:** Bonds, AP/Wide World Photos; Mays & Campanella, Courtesy of LOC, NY World-Telegram & the Sun Newspaper Photograph Collection (LC-USZ62-112029); plaque, © Jay Jaffe. **214:** Hall, Russell, Naismith Memorial Basketball Hall of Fame. **215-217:** AP/Wide World Photos. **219:** Palmer, AP/Wide World Photos. **220:** Wie, AP/Wide World Photos. **223-224:** AP/Wide World Photos. **225:** Special Olympics, AP/Wide World Photos. **226:** Williams, AP/Wide World Photos. **227:** Hawk, AP/Wide World Photos. **234:** Fallingwater, LOC, Prints & Photographs Div., Historic American Buildings Survey or Historic American Engineering Record, (HABS,PA,26-OHPY-V,1-87); Coronado, Courtesy of the Hotel del Coronado. **236:** © 2003 Cedar Fair, L.P. **244:** © 1967 by Dover Publications. **245:** Jackson, Harrison, Tyler, © 1967 by Dover Publications; Van Buren, Polk, Taylor, Fillmore, LOC Prints & Photographs Div. **246:** Pierce, Buchanan, Johnson, Hayes, © 1967 by Dover Publications; Lincoln, Grant, Garfield, LOC Prints & Photographs Div. **247:** Arthur, Harrison, McKinley, Roosevelt, Wilson, © 1967 by Dover Publications; Cleveland, Taft, LOC Prints & Photographs Div. **248:** Harding, Hoover, Roosevelt, Eisenhower, © 1967 by Dover Publications; Coolidge, Truman, Kennedy, LOC Prints & Photographs Div. **249:** Johnson, Lyndon B. Johnson Library; Nixon, LOC Prints & Photographs Div.; Ford, Courtesy of Gerald R. Ford Museum; Carter, Courtesy of Jimmy Carter Library; Reagan, Courtesy of Ronald Reagan Library; G. Bush, Official White House Photo/LOC Prints & Photographs Div.; Clinton, Courtesy of the White House; G. W. Bush, Eric Draper—The White House. **250:** Washington, LOC Prints & Photographs Div. [LC-USZC2-3273]; Adams, LOC Prints & Photographs Div. [LC-USZ62-10016]; Madison, Roosevelt, Clinton, LOC, Prints & Photographs Div.; Bush, Eric Draper—The White House. **252:** U.S. Senate. **253:** Lyndon B. Johnson Library. **254:** Courtesy of the Supreme Court Historical Society. **260:** Model T, Courtesy of the Center for American History, Univ. of Texas at Austin. **261:** Bush, Eric Draper—The White House. **262:** Lyndon B. Johnson Library. **263:** Anderson, LOC Prints & Photographs Div. [LC-USZ62-42524]; Hughes, LOC Prints & Photographs Div. [LC-USZ62-42503]; Robinson, Courtesy of LOC, Look Magazine Photograph Collection (LC-L9-54-3566-0,#7). **267:** Provided by Bruce Holloway. **288:** Arches, Allan Jaworski. **289:** Carlsbad, National Park Service; Steamtown, Photo by Alan M. Miller, courtesy SteamCentral.com. **290:** El Niño, NOAA. **294:** 1 yard, Timothy Bryk. **297:** Hieroglyphics, © Edward A. Thomas. **310:** Stanton & Anthony, LOC Prints & Photographs Div. [LCPP003A-02558]; Low, Girl Scouts of the USA. **311:** Fitzgerald, King, Lin, AP/Wide World Photos; Tereshkova, AP/Wide World Photos/Tass. **331:** Lower grade, Greg Raymond. **332:** From *Sinking of the Titanic and Great Sea Disasters,* ed. Logan Marshall, 1912. **333:** LOC Prints & Photographs Div. (LC-USZ62-90833). **334:** Quadricycle, From the Collections of Henry Ford Museum & Greenfield Village; electric car, Electric Vehicles of Texas.

FRONT COVER: Toshiba Tablet PC, Courtesy of Toshiba Computer Systems Group; sunflower, PhotoSpin; test tube, PhotoDisc; satellite, Getty Images Royalty Free; Marshall Pletcher, Ken Karp Photography; ship, Corel; dinosaur, Corbis Royalty Free; guitar, Artville; soccer girl, Brand X Pictures/Getty Images; flag, PhotoDisc; motocross, EyeWire; elephant, Corel; hand, Ken Karp Photography.

BACK COVER: London Eye, British Airways - London Eye; horse, Corel; space, PhotoDisc; yo-yo, PhotoSpin.

The World Almanac For Kids 2004
"KIDS SPEAK OUT!" Contest

You Can Get Your Picture in The World Almanac For Kids, and Win an All-Expense-Paid Trip for Four to Washington, D.C.!

The *World Almanac For Kids 2004* is proud to present its annual "Kids Speak Out!" Contest. One Grand Prize Winner and 750 Runners-Up will be chosen from among the entries received.

► The **Grand Prize Winner** will receive an all-expense-paid trip for four to Washington, D.C.

► **750 Runners-Up** will receive a limited edition *World Almanac For Kids* T-shirt.

The Grand Prize includes transportation to Washington, D.C., lodging for four nights, and three meals per day for four days. The winner will receive the opportunity to meet with a member of Congress, plus the chance to visit such noted national landmarks as the White House, the Capitol, the Washington Monument, the Lincoln Memorial, the Air & Space Museum, and Arlington National Cemetery.

To enter, kids must write and explain:

> Who do you think are the three most important people in the world today—and why?

Entry is limited to kids aged 7-13, and all entries must be received by February 29, 2004. All entries must include the respondent's name, complete address, age, and daytime phone number. Entries should be sent via our Web site www.worldalmanacforkids.com or via mail, fax, or e-mail to:

World Almanac Books
World Almanac For Kids
"Kids Speak Out!" Contest
512 Seventh Avenue, 22nd Floor
New York, NY 10018
Fax: (646) 312-6839
E-mail: sdevos@waegroup.com

Kaia Marie Lunde, winner of The World Almanac For Kids 2003 "Kids Speak Out!" Contest. For her entry, go to **www.worldalmanacforkids.com.**

The World Almanac For Kids 2004 "Kids Speak Out!" Contest Rules: No purchase necessary to enter or win. Purchasing does not improve chances of winning. The Competition is open to legal residents of the United States who are between the ages of 7-13 at the time of entry. Enter by explaining who you think are the three most important people in the world today and why. Entry should be sent by mail or e-mail together with your printed name, address, ZIP code, and daytime phone number with area code to: World Almanac For Kids "Kids Speak Out!" Contest, 512 Seventh Avenue, 22nd Floor, New York, NY, 10018. Entries must be received before 11:59 P.M. EST on February 29, 2004. You may enter the Competition either on-line or by mail, but each entry must be made separately. No other methods of entry are accepted. All entries become the property of World Almanac Education Group and will not be acknowledged or returned. Entries will be judged for originality of content and description. One Grand Prize winner will receive an all-expense-paid trip for four to Washington, D.C., including transportation, lodging for four nights, and three meals per day for four days; seven hundred fifty (750) runners-up will receive a specially designed World Almanac For Kids T-shirt. All taxes on prizes are the responsibility of the winners. Winners will be notified on or about March 15, 2004. Submission of entry constitutes entrant's consent (or that of their parent/legal guardian) to irrevocably assign to World Almanac Books any and all rights to entry, including, but not limited to, intellectual property rights. Acceptance of prize constitutes winners' permission to use their names, likenesses, cities and states, and to be photographed for advertising and publicity purposes without additional compensation except where prohibited by law. Void where prohibited or restricted by law. All federal, state and local laws and regulations apply. All entries are bound by the Full Rules. To obtain Full Rules, send a self addressed, stamped envelope to the address above.